Sunlight on Water

A Manual for Soul-full Living

The Ones With No Names
Received Through Flo Aeveia Magdalena

All Worlds Publishing
Putney, Vermont

For information please contact:

        Deborah Bower
        All Worlds Publishing
        Rural Route 1, Box 663
        Putney, VT 05346
        Telephone and facsimile: (802) 722-4307

Published by: All Worlds Publishing

Printed in USA

Library of Congress Cataloging-in-Publication Data

Magdalena, Flo Aeveia, 1948-
      Sunlight on Water: A Manual for Soul-full Living / Flo Aeveia Magdalena
      p.   cm.
      Includes bibliographical references and index.
      ISBN 1-880914-12-3 (alk. paper)
      1. Spiritual life. 2. Spiritual exercises.   I. Title.
      BL624.M2943   1995
      291.4'4--dc20   95-38824
                                                  CIP

First Edition 1996.
Second Printing 1996.
Third Printing 1997.

Also by Flo Aeveia Magdalena

I Remember Union: *The Story of Mary Magdalena*
published under the name Flo Calhoun

DEDICATION

Sunlight on Water

is dedicated to all the souls who have recognized The Ones With No Names,
remembered their vibration,
and called them forth . . .

We give tribute to Tina
a sweet Angel soul in cat form,
who graced us with her presence
as we created, edited, and type-set the graphics
of *Sunlight On Water*.

She made her transition on Friday, August 11, 1995,
the day *Sunlight on Water* was completed and birthed into form.

My Gratitude to . . .

Janene Hardy for her constancy and accuracy in transcribing the original tapes; Noel McInnis for an untiring initial editing from the original tape transcriptions; and Carlee Janci for holding the space and cooking meals, especially the chocolate chip cookies, so we could work!

Jayn Adina for donating her time and expertise in editing and proof-reading and for her dedication to keeping the vibration of the message and the intention of The Ones With No Names congruent.

Deborah Bower for her love, support, and editing in those final moments!

Lucrezia Mangione for her sense of order, design and harmony.

Ivo Dominguez, Jr. for donating his time and computer artistry to create our beautiful cover design.

Wendy Rode and Dru Fuller for their illustrations to assist us in understanding the concepts presented.

Karen Custer who read the unabridged version of the initial transcription thoroughly and gave us insightful comments and recommendations.

Carol Cutler, Michaela Donahue, and Robin Warren for permission to use excerpts from their personal channelings.

Kate Bayer, Mary Ann Parrott, Albert Moore, Elizabeth Kobren, Hannah Bradford, and Martha Rolleri for reading all or part of the original copy and giving useful suggestions.

Elizabeth Kobren for remembering that The Ones With No Names call osmosis "sunlight on water," and suggesting that name for the title, and for the transcribing and initial editing of the tape on community.

Biz McMahon for her input while the book was on the way to the del room!

Jane Atwood for her financial donation to assist in publishing this manual.

Peter Insalaco for his love, support, and help in facilitating publication.

Those who ordered pre-publication copies.

~ ~ ~

All of you who give continued support to this work and to the fulfillment of a million years of dreaming, the choice for peace on Earth.

Contents

How It Began

Flo Aeveia Magdalena

As far back as I can remember, I have searched for the meaning of life. Why do certain events and circumstances touch certain people's lives? Why do conditions of separation, grief, fear, aloneness, and violence exist here, despite God, despite the good people, despite the good intentions, despite religion? My search to answer these questions persisted throughout my Presbyterian upbringing and scientific training as a nurse.

As I watched the "struggle" of life and the seemingly meaningless events which "happened" to people, my quest intensified and the disillusionment with human systems and those in them affected me deeply. Honesty, good intentions, and kindness just didn't seem enough.

In the late '70s, as I was working the night shift on a medical teaching unit, I awoke many times with fear in the pit of my stomach that had no apparent connection with anything in my life. When I became a psychiatric nurse a year later, I learned to call this "free-floating anxiety." Skeptical, fearful, and insecure, I was bobbing around on the surface of reality, touching only the edges of myself, living an illusion of separation, always trying to feel union with something or someone outside myself.

I was first introduced to metaphysics in 1979, but even after I learned about the soul and began coaxing it out, the struggle continued. Knowing about my soul was wonderful, and yet, I didn't "feel" my soul. I had not yet surrendered my will to my remembering. My mind was so strong and the conditioning so deep that peace and wholeness seemed far away. But I persevered. I began teaching classes in wholistic health, integrating the metaphysical and medical parts of my life. By accessing my right brain I began professionally offering guidance for others. I saw their soul patterns and drew pictures of what I saw. As I drew their soul, they would remember their design more clearly, and begin to understand the contribution their soul had chosen to bring to the world.

In group settings I began exploring the vastness of the soul. Using sound, tones, and light, we would go deeply into that place of soul and bit by bit, my soul and others' souls began emerging. I began to feel strength, strength that couldn't be taken away from me by outer circumstances. I felt the connection to myself through time and the oneness with others that had not and could not diminish.

In November of 1986 The Ones With No Names came to me. During a soul group, as we went around sharing one by one, I heard their words in my mind. I had never heard "voices" before and was startled, and yet, in a surprising way, I was reassured. Their intention was pure, their essence was light, and their message brought me hope. As time went on, I began to trust them.

As I came to work with them almost daily, I slowly found my questions being answered and my fears assuaged. Their presence fostered enormous change, growth, and learning for me. As our vibrations integrated I no longer heard them, yet, their presence came through me as I worked with groups and individuals.

Their perspective is universal: there is no right or wrong, everyone is growing toward their highest potential (no matter what it looks like on the surface), everything is part of one system, we are all one. As they speak to us, they bring to us our essence without boundary or limitation. They assure us and encourage us with great patience, time and time again, because they know our plight, even though they have never been here in physical form.

Perhaps this is what moves me most about them—their empathy for us and their intention to help us understand the journey we have chosen to travel here.

They call themselves Cosmic Guidance Counselors, and together we have spoken to more than 3,500 people about their individual soul plan or design—the soul blueprint. The Ones With No Names hold everyone equal, and with great care, draw forth the life, creation, and potential from each of us. As they read each blueprint, they charge the essence within each soul and help bring the truth of that soul into being here, through the vibration which is carried in their words. They speak continually of the design of union, and it is their "job" to assure that design. Yet, each of us holds a critical piece in its fulfillment.

After December 31, 1995, The Ones With No Names will no longer speak the blueprints using language. During 1996, they will be with us, but in a non-verbal state of communication, imprinting the design of union, osmotically. We can sit with them in individual sessions, as we did before, and they will charge our light bodies and help us experience the state of union. Collectively, they will charge the morphogenic field. After 1996, they will be reabsorbed into the consciousness of the One.

This manual is their message of hope and assurance for

humanity. It provides us with the keys to move from surviving to creation; from loss and abandonment to safety, trust, and comfort; from confusion, pessimism, and separation to truth and security; from seeming chaos to order. It teaches us how to co-create, remember our origin of oneness, and grease the wheel of the hologram, or place of oneness, so that everything fits and we live the reality of Heaven on Earth.

The Ones With No Names give us short-cuts. They tell us how to access the Akashic records, where knowledge is housed in the universe, and show us how to get our own answers. They provide creative ways to live without pain, and encourage our independence showing us how to co-create, cooperate, and serve.

Spoken in a "new" language based on universal perspective, they inspire us, catalyzing the soul by the tone and rhythm of what is spoken. Making this readable was challenging, because the normal order of words in our language and the order of the words in their language is different. They speak in paragraphs, illustrating their meaning with asides and examples, weaving the words into pictures and images.

Jayn, Noel, and I have done our best to keep their vibration consistent, so that the essence, the message, is brought to you in its fullness and magnitude. We have changed only the grammatical structure which seemed necessary to facilitate understanding of their concepts and principles.

Statements written in the margin of the first page of each chapter can be used as daily intentions. Statements written in the margins of the chapter pages are highlights of concepts presented in the text. The diagrams illustrate the concepts presented, and we hope that the format and the space provided in the margins or in the "notes" areas, gives you enough room to comment, write your ideas, memories, revelations, and to record results of exercises.

"Sleep with this manual under your pillow," they instructed us. Live and breathe a new cadence of breath with no time. Learn how your energy responds to those in your life; check out how you open or close your heart with each person you meet; understand why you can't seem to change habits or patterns, even though you've tried hundreds of times. Learn, experience, understand, re-establish, re-calibrate, re-cognize, re-solve, re-member. Over and over they give us ways to be here differently, to relate from truth and to establish a new and natural way of being.

The Ones With No Names remind each of us that we are a part of creation, the Monad, and that our fulfillment is the same as the fulfillment of creation—the hologram—the design of oneness in form. We chose to come here, chose the life patterns we would live, and chose the piece of the hologram we would contribute to the world—to the design of wholeness—the piece that only *we* can give!

According to The Ones With No Names, there has never been a time in human evolution when we have had the power to affect union as much as we can now. All the forces of the universe accompany us on this journey as we remember that "The Dream of *We* is in *Me*."

Remember as you read that you are here on Earth to live and create from your soul, that this is the time of oneness, and that our human journey now brings us to the fulfillment of the design—the peace of a million years of dreaming.

Thank you for listening, for yearning, for questioning, and for remembering.

Shalom,

Flo Aeveia Magdalena

Flo Aeveia Magdalena

Short-cuts to Understanding
The Ones With No Names

It occurred to me that it would be helpful for those of you who don't know The Ones With No Names to have a short introduction to their work:

Remember that the exercises are designed to bring you to the experience of being a continuum, unifying with your spiritual essence, which feels like fluid. So *just relax* with the instructions and concepts, allowing them *to be possible*, at first, and then, as you practice, *join* the energy as it flows so that you feel a part of the movement of the consciousness of you and creation becoming one.

• Stating *"I am a light being, and light I shall remain,"* taking a deep breath, and then stating, "There is no time," is the combination which brings us organically to our first breath, before the imprint of density and belief were placed on top of our divinity and spiritual nature. THIS REPATTERNS THE AMOUNT OF LIGHT THAT IS INFUSED IN OUR BODY! This is an easy and direct way to affect our charge—how much light we carry and how much light is infused into our cells, tissues, and organs. Being light brings the memory of oneness—before we were form—brings us to peace, with no edges (which cause conflict), and no congestion (which causes dis-ease).

• The work of The Ones With No Names is about bringing spirit into form, what they call "trusting the body with the spirit." It's about full presence. Grounding is the primary way in which this presence is fully understood by the mind, body, circuits, and visceral tissue—the part that carries the DNA. You can ground outside or inside, in bare feet or with shoes on. There are several different techniques in the manual and you can practice them until you find the one that best serves you. Grounding every day has benefits like straightening the spinal column, reducing menstrual discomfort, improving vision, increasing reception of energy, resource, memory, etc. Any condition that is affected by energy flow is affected by grounding, because as you ground, the energy moves and balances through the entire system. Grounding is strongly recommended, because it brings the above and the below together, *through* us. See the "Grounding" chapter and the glossary for ways to ground. My favorite way is to stand and imagine I'm a tree with deep roots bringing me deeply into the center of the Earth and that my branches reach up and touch the sky. Then, as I breathe, I become light dancing on water, merging my form and my essence with the elements and essences of nature.

• Cellular osmosis—looking and feeling like sunlight on water—is the fundamental way in which grounding re-orients density to allow the creative, spiritual essence to come into balance with the form. We are not taught that we are spiritual beings, so that part of us, our spirit, is being called forth. Grounding and osmosis give us the key to that calling forth.

• Drinking lemon water daily assists the circuits to carry more charge. The number of glasses you drink is up to you. The guidance suggests that as we drink more water, the bladder does not respond as much, and the water inside the cellular wall balances so that the cells stay hydrated. The extra fluid can run the charge we're accelerating without depleting the fluid in the cells or making us run to the bathroom frequently. If we turn on the circuits through intention, charge our being with creation, run lots of energy, and expand our consciousness, and **don't** drink water, it's like putting our finger in the light socket, and we may feel irritable.

So drink lots of lemon water, ground, breathe, and have fun!

Introduction
From The Ones With No Names

WE ARE INHERENTLY A BODY OF LIGHT AND KNOWLEDGE that maintains order and truth in the universe. Part of that truth and order is giving you as much assistance as possible in the process of charging your light body, so that you can do it yourselves. We have given you our best shot here, as they say. We have asked for the cooperation of all dimensions in bringing you this manual for three express purposes: to make your learning more simple; to let you know that there is cooperation in the ethers to assist you; and to show you that the greatest experiment is yours.

In the chapters which follow, we will share with you the key or the gate which opens to give you access to the gold at the end of the rainbow—your charge of light lived through your essence in union with all things. This design of union is the three-in-one, and we will explain this concept in many ways, facilitating your understanding of how to bring the three into one, creating union in your experience.

The fundamentals of what we provide for you in this *Manual for Soul-full Living* are short-cuts. They are ways you can view yourselves, the world, the universe, the Earth, the creatures, the force fields, the essential energies, the kingdoms, and the essences, in an interrelationship that sustains the body of light and knowledge, truth and order, and foundation in this place. Our objective is to create "Heaven on Earth." It has been our objective from the very beginning.

The way we have done that most effectively to date, is in your individual sessions, having you experience yourself as Heaven on Earth. We now offer the experience of Heaven on Earth to all humanity. Whether you negate the words that we give you, whether you embrace them, separate from them, sustain them, empower them, embody them, expand them, or exhilarate them, is your choice. However, *we have given you your piece of Heaven. That's our job*. And it is to show each of you how, by being a piece of Heaven on Earth, Heaven can *manifest* on Earth. Without you it will not happen in the same way.

The design is such that each of you is intricate to its unfolding, wherever you are, whatever you're doing, and however you're processing. So it's all been taken into account. It really means that you can relax, enjoy life, be at peace in yourself; can experience your feet, or your head, or your heart, or wherever you want to, and it's all already ordained. It means that no matter what you do, what your habits are, no matter what you believe is right or wrong, that you will learn to sustain light regardless of that. You'll find that regardless of what you think, or where you come from, or what you've been ordained to experience in your own conditioning, the foundation of what happens for you will be more real as each moment, through 2005, evolves and ticks by. There will be a place in you that responds to the charge of the critical mass around you and that assists you to embody more light. That's why it's easier now.

In other words, there's nothing to worry about. Because *you* will accelerate, *it* will accelerate, and the foundation will evolve itself regardless of what you do and regardless of what track you're on— it will still happen. That's the way you can do whatever you're doing and all of a sudden one day say, "Oh, I am going to affirm 'I am light,'" and be completely on track, even if you haven't been on track for 35, 58, or however many years. As you unfold this, it means that you cannot fail. *The design is such that it already has your permission for you to be the best that you already are.* So it's good news. And the foundation of this good news is your choice in the Swing Between Worlds, before birth, to bring light to Earth, which is why we come now to remind you of this process.

Our love for you is infinite as we unfold for you the principles of our understanding of the universe. We do so in love, so that you take to heart, to soul, to awareness—what you originally chose, so that what unfolds from the reading of *this material is a foundation that establishes you in the great design from the beginning. There is no greater place to have than to be in at the beginning.* And if you are drawn to pick up *Sunlight on Water: A Manual for Soul-full Living,* you were there at the beginning. You will be there at the ending. And most importantly, you're here now.

We would recommend that you read this book thoroughly and study the exercises, conceptually doing your best to integrate the vibration of each chapter, and to integrate the concepts if you choose. It is also important to choose that your experience will be a unifying one. After you've gone through the exercises, processes, and disciplines, and tried them at least once, you'll know what each exercise feels like. We then recommend that you go through the manual every week, at least once, and ask, "What do I need to do this week?" The energy is what's going to call you back to it. You're going to say, "All right, today I need to feel the energy I felt when I was doing this particular exercise." It won't be conscious after awhile. You'll be hob-nobbing all around the universe doing all different kinds of things for the purpose of reorganizing the vibration so that it fits the syntax of where you are. Experience this as a context for understanding, a manual for living, and instruction for bringing your life into truth and order.

Those of you who are working to assist in the attainment of the design of resolution are working on the experience of light, and after the year 2005, the experience of light becomes peace. You are moving now together, and as the light starts to come into the body fully, as it will by the year 2005, *it starts to manifest as a literal place*—physically, ethereally, psychically, societally, and familially. As the light is embodied over the next ten years, it becomes the threshold for peace, which is union in action.

So acceleration happens—acceleration constantly moving the critical mass, which is the resolution, which is peace. **Peace.** *If you are alive on the planet in the year 2005, peace is your purpose.*

As the light bodies refine, the distinction of separation is no longer there because the foundation is providing a recognition for, and an opportunity for, the expression of light being, or being in light. So, in 2005, we are expressing what it is to be light on all levels of participation. Communication will occur on all levels: interspecies, intergalactic, intercreature, and much more. As all these levels filter in, technology will advance. All of your awareness will come into being.

There will be a big gap in the next ten years between technology and the heart. And yes, the gap will close—most profoundly in 2005. The next ten years are a revision of the current system of being, relating, orchestrating, designing, co-creating—everything. Everything is undergoing huge reorientation. It is orienting from form into light and back into form. So it is trans-form-ation, which means that you're not trying to get light so you can ascend and leave. It means you are providing your vehicle as a way for the light body to anchor, so that the foundation of the experience of your life becomes oriented to the consciousness of the future design, which is technology and heart in union, as well as everything else in union.

In the next ten years, you're refining every system of your being, regardless of what it is, so that it can reflect a new technology, a new way of providing a basis that is ethereal and practical simultaneously, which is our definition of technology.

As you create a relationship between these levels, they provide you with vehicles for expression and union, for communication and for development of models and technologies. People will use light instead of pacemakers, light instead of food, and light instead of lovers. As this unfolds as a way of being, the choices people make are then very different on a daily basis.

Each of you now has an opportunity to make that charge happen. And that new technology and new way of being are where you come from because you've changed your channel, your rut, or your experience, from one side to the other. "I don't want it to be hard anymore. I'm choosing light, so I'm going to flow with the essence of that charge, and as I do that, no-thing matters, everything is light, and everything is now."

If you understand through the cellular what the light body is, and *experience* the charge of the light body, then it's worth five million words, and a lot of your time, effort, energy, education, and money, because it's a short-cut.

This will magnetically attract others to you and create the field of critical mass to engender for the masses the spark of attraction. They all come into this experience with you, and are then open to the unfolding of this technology of heart, or foundation of being, which on many levels provides an opportunity for the new dimensional relationships that you've been thinking about and learning about, to come into being. All the new frameworks are born from critical mass. That's why we make reference to the critical mass so much in our wordage and our intention, so that the attention is placed on the massive coming together of light, so that everyone understands that this is where the catharsis from separation to non-separation happens.

Critical mass is, by definition, a place of non-separation. You're not teaching the ideology of non-separation, saying, "You shouldn't do that. You shouldn't do this." You're teaching an energetic that is in a wave frame, bringing the results that you are choosing from your very intention of being here, which is fulfilling your own need. It's fulfilling your own process, and that's why it's so beautiful and so aligned with the intention of so many. As you'll find out in the next five years, it is aligned with the intention of more people than you can count. It's a wave, and it's going to be born. It hasn't been born yet; it's just now reaching its threshold, and it's going to be very absolute, as it needs to be.

Each of you has responded to the calling, and come together now with the intention of living from the soul. *We would invite you to participate in this manual as a response, rather than as a reading. As a response, it will carry a charge. Let the charge in.* As you read the words, let the charge in and it will validate for you that you are a piece of Heaven, and that it is of great import for you to live that piece of Heaven, *absolutely.* Be the charge wherever you've been planted, and grow there until the moment comes spontaneously—the snap of the fingers that says, "My calling is over here," and then go. And know as you go that you've already played out all the scenarios in front of you, and have created a wave of critical mass for you to ride home on, and it's already more than okay, it's phenomenal. *And your part is the lead part. No matter who you are, it's the lead. Because only you can play it. And without you it doesn't happen.*

The pattern that you're in, as it was chosen, was ordained by the Absolute, or you wouldn't have gotten out of the "Pearly Gates." So as it responds in you, is evoked from you, and as you live the charge of it, you will experience contentment—deep, deep contentment—and the knowing that the pieces are already together. It's not your responsibility to put them together, it's your ability to respond to the charge inside of you, essentially, which *keeps* it together. That's what remembering is: knowing that that charge is yours, and your decision to make it happen, *made it happen.* And now as you unfold it, it is pure revelation. It is what's revealed, not what's hidden, and not what's having to be attained by working, thinking, educating, and suffering.

Since you are that piece of Heaven, your ordination is about divinity. And what makes it divine is that as it was chosen and accorded, it was also re-solved—put back into the fluids that bring you forward now into its expression. For it is the fluids that you are flowing through and with, that carry the charge, and that are always viable to the substance within them.

So being a piece of Heaven on Earth, vibrationally, is an attenuation, a frequency already tuned that requires no-thing, and a place where the foundation always was, is, and will be absolute. Which means you are absolute. There is nothing that you have to do, but be.

And the Heaven that is in you will then be on Earth, and the charge of that essence will vibrate in such a way that the fullness of your soul will express its essence, and all things will be made clear unto you. For that is what the design says. And this is the place where we are as civilization—not as a civilization—as civilization. Where we are is in the reordering of all dimensions in form.

So the role you were given, you are given by the Absolute. The role that you were given is indelibly impressed as the Key to the Kingdom that supports the charge of your consciousness in expression. Everything that you know, everything that you sustain, everything that you carry, in a very viable sense, goes with you and shapes the unfolding of that charge, so that it feels always co-creative. It feels always as if you are doing it *with*, and that's beautiful, because that's union.

And that is why Heaven is coming to Earth.

The Charge of Light and Truth

Charge
Charge
Charge

I T IS THE TIME NOW FOR EACH OF YOU TO RESONATE WITH THE TRUTH of what is within you, so that your course of action and the alignment with the greatest calling within will be affected. Know that your ability to hold this space amidst the destructuring of humanity's belief systems will require of you, without question, the capacity to focus, to be at one with the intention of light and truth. It will call you out to live that which cannot be seen—that which cannot be proven. The reason for this is because, as the destructuring of beliefs happens here, there is being accorded and unified a whole new set of paradigms, which are to be lived in the place of what was structured into the very core of your being by your mother at the time of your birth.

The Earthly Implant

Holding your own space and acknowledging your own truth seems challenging, because your core is graphically encoded by society to respond and have its origin from the known, given, framework, which has so many times been recorded on each of your track records and essential spaces. This means that you are vibrating at the same rate of speed as the earthly imprinting of the derivative response mechanism, which is regulated by your hypothalamus— because this code of life and light, so to speak, was directly imprinted with the core imprint from your mother at birth.

Within the core of your being, essentially and graphically, there is the vibrational equivalency of an implant, which directly and profoundly shapes your actions, reactions, and beliefs, and which affects what you call your "truth." To say this differently, each of you has received from your mother an encoding, or imprinting at the time of birth, which is now, and has been since the time of your birthing experience, affecting your life; affecting your responses; affecting your rhythm of inner activity associated with bodily function;

~

This is a point of free will which says, "I have returned to activate my essential and original design, and because of free will, I can now ordain that I am a being of light, living through truth and order, and within the framework of union, outside of time. I incorporate the three points of initiation, patterning and timing, to unify the levels of my being through truth."

~

*Because
this is such a deep
and almost unknown
aspect of your life functioning,
many times you will find
that you react or respond
before you have time to think about it.*

~

*The encoding within
is essentially
given to you with your first breath,
and therefore
needs to be re-established with breath.*

~

affecting the responses you have to weather, cigarette smoke, diet, race and creed (prejudice); affecting your idea of what a man is and what a woman is; affecting how you think of God, if you do, or how you think of atheism; affecting your opinion of what's fair, what is unfair, i.e., social justice; affecting how old you are before you develop disease; affecting the way you raise children, view the elderly, feel about euthanasia; etc., etc., etc.

Each of you has, within your core, a program which is running like a clock, and has been running since you took your first breath here. This program is seeded in your consciousness, filtered into your perception, and opened out to you physiologically. The program includes the rate and pattern of your breathing, your responses to the invisible, your capacity to see psychically and physically, and affects just about everything you do.

This earthly imprinting carries with it six generations of pre-programming, and is given to you at the moment you take that first breath. It is in the core of your being, in the spaces of the etheric around you, and in the very clock or drumbeat of the hypothalamus, which is the underlying governing point from which your automatic cerebral functioning is initiated. This means that you are responding, without conscious volition, to everything that comes across your path, and that humanly, societally, and organically, there are encoded pathways that you have been told to take in each moment.

Because this is such a deep and almost unknown aspect of your life functioning, many times you will find that you react or respond before you have time to think about it. This is played out when, for example, you make a decision to like a particular person and be nice to them even though they are pink and polka-dotted, with green feet and purple hair. And then when you come across this person again, even though you have really and truly affirmed your decision to like this person and respond to them positively, you find yourself doing otherwise. This is about those times that you have responded from habit and then made a mental and sometimes spiritual decision to change that behavior, and then found that you did not do so. This leads to such feelings as guilt, remorse, seeming incongruence, finding yourself resentful, and so forth.

The encoding within is essentially given to you with your first breath, and therefore needs to be re-established with breath. It was given to you by the entry point of this dimension, your mother, and so needs to be re-established from her essence, and is associated with being human and following the directives of your species. Therefore, it must be re-established from the Swing Between Worlds, from the moment and the place of your choice to become human.

To pattern the being from the Divine means that you are essentially (from essence) making peace with your heredity, your lineage, and your organic seeding or nurturing—the visceral cellular response, simultaneously (a three-point process.)

Imagine, if you will, that you are coming down the tunnel of birth, feeling your essential light and your vast system of energy. Then feel the consolidation and constricting of your wings into the small, compact, and dense point of entry which is your physical body. Imagine that as you come down the tunnel there is a point of no return, where, just for an instant, you realize that you have crossed over from one dimension to another, and that the only way back is through the process of Earth life. And you are allowing the core of your essence to be programmed by the directives of the people and the society that you have just entered. You will learn and go by the course direction determined by your date of birth, time of entry, and geographic location. You have chosen a context to experience your lessons—what they will be, what you believe in and stand for—and this course direction will be a factor in all that you live here.

When you have reached the point of "no return," there is a momentary panic, a freezing of your essential movement as light, and in that moment permission is given for the imprinting to occur, because when one gives permission to live in the human dynamic, one gives permission for the system of functioning to be ordained and transferred to the fetus. At that moment life begins, and not before—to address your cultural debate about essential timing for life. At that moment, there is a response from the fetus which says, "I now give permission for this choice to be manifest." It is still possible to change the mind, as you have observed some souls doing, and yet the orientation to the soul of the mother, particularly, is strengthened and forged at that moment, and the relationship between those souls, karmically, is established for all time. This is the key to understanding your responses, your mechanisms of belief, your preferences, etc. The closest thing that most accurately reflects the mechanism we are describing is cloning.

We are not saying that you are the clone of your mother. We are saying that making a replica of the invisible and essential patterning from six generations is accomplished and ordained, for most souls, and then transferred as the birth is happening and the cord is being cut and the first breath is being taken. The important thing to

~

Imagine
that as you come down the tunnel
there is a point of no return,
where, just for an instant,
you realize
that you have crossed over
from one dimension to another,
and that the only way back
is through the process of Earth life.

~

When you have reached
the point of "no return,"
there is a momentary panic,
a freezing
of your essential movement as
light,
and in that moment
permission
is given for the imprinting to occur.

~

Making
a replica of the invisible
and essential patterning
from six generations is
accomplished and ordained,
for most souls,
and then transferred
as the birth is happening
and the cord is being cut
and the first breath is being taken.

~

~

At the moment your light body condenses itself into form and there is an acknowledgment that you have entered the dimension of another world, the transfer from the mother becomes like the map of your journey.

~

remember here is that you chose that specific imprint in the Swing Between Worlds and it is already accepted. Your body type, personality profile, and preferences were also chosen. So it is not that you arrive here and are given anything that was not your free will choice. It is that as you arrive, it is stamped into you and therefore is inextricably linked to your core essence.

This helps to explain the resistance that many of you experience when you want to change patterns or beliefs or want to stop the violence you have experienced or are initiating in your life, or stop the judgment, or the separation, or the prejudice, and then find that in some inexplicable way your actions and follow-through are different from your essential choices. Remember that your actions are also linked to the organic and physiological.

To restructure these patterns requires you first to understand the mechanism, and then choose to respond differently *from* the mechanism, and then practice this so that you are seeing the repatterning occur before you act. You can put the points of your accordance into effect from the place within—deep within, embedded in the rhythm of the psyche—that will trigger new and/or different behaviors and responses.

At the moment your light body condenses itself into form and there is an acknowledgment that you have entered the dimension of another world, the transfer from the mother becomes like the map of your journey. If this map was not instilled within your very organism, you would be unable to carry out your mission here, because there would be little or no relationship (as we define relationship, i.e., understanding) between your essence and that of your mother and/or subsequent points of connection in the world.

In the Swing Between Worlds you have the total knowledge of all dimensions, and these points of reality are at your disposal. At that point of initiation and choice, there is absolutely nothing that you don't know. So you have chosen and are responsible for (have the ability to respond to) every point of reality that is associated with this imprinting process. That includes who your mother will be, all of those preferences we spoke about before, and the outcome. And the outcome! Remember this part, because it is very important in the equation of balancing the three points and bringing them together from the perspective of truth.

You are remembering from the Swing that your choices are going to bring you certain learnings, growth points, contributions, associations, relationships, gifting, resolutions, and destinies. You are coming for a purpose. Your life system will click in at a certain coordinate, and upon entry will lock into that coordinate, and what you have chosen will be initiated.

The Factor of Time

The only factor programmed into the equation at the moment of choice that is altered upon arrival and in subsequent moments of experience, is time. (As an aside here, we wish to respond to many of your inaudible questions, regarding time differences between what is read to you from the record and what you actually experience in your dimension. This factor is the final initiation of your intention from choice—the fact that you choose something and then arrive here and it takes what is called "time.")

The factor of time is the balance point between the core knowing and design plan in the matrix of the soul essence, and what is imprinted from mom. Linear time is the fulcrum point through which your innate soul design, chosen in the Swing, and the imprinting from the human, are unified. Time is the factor which affects all of your process, regardless of what you believe, where you live, and to a very large extent (there are some exceptions here) how you live in the dense and rational stance from what is called "culture." The exceptions to the "normal," the exceptions which are "natural" as we have defined that, are the aboriginal and what the Anglicized world calls "primitive" cultures.

Primitive cultures usually have a relationship with the universe as well as the Earth and are therefore more likely to respond from the total base of knowledge held in the Swing Between Worlds, and are therefore more able to reflect the total picture. This reduces the separation between what is chosen in the Swing and what is lived in the life. Remember that there is an equation here that is ordained in each person before birth, and that time, the belief about time, and the relationship to time is a key element in breaking the code of the imprint to remember the choices before time was a viable coordinate in the dynamic.

Responding to time as an aboriginal would, immediately aligns one with the Swing, or interdimensional place of knowing. It initiates the responses to balance the imprinting of the six generations and therefore brings balance to the organism, which makes it possible for

*Your life system
will click in at a certain coordinate,
and upon entry
will lock into that coordinate,
and what you have chosen
will be initiated.*

*The only factor
programmed into the equation
at the moment of choice
that is altered upon arrival
and in subsequent moments
of experience,
is time.*

*Responding to time
as an aboriginal would,
immediately aligns
one with the Swing,
or interdimensional place of knowing.*

the hypothalamus to respond in an organic sense to truth, rather than to illusion. So the basic dynamic is to grasp the intention behind the "Master Plan" and direct the course of your life from that point of knowing. Again, it means essentially reprogramming into your reality of truth that which has been, to this point perhaps, only a dream, a longing, a memory, or an opportunity.

With the massive de-structuring of consciousness being effected now in the Earth dimension, it is opportune for you to grasp this concept and forge a new union between your organic state of being, your relationship to the Earth, your people, your heredity, your lineage, the coordinates of your journey, and the core within you.

Part of the reason that we are always harping about the fact that there is no time, is to make the key element to the reprogramming available to you constantly. Then you will grasp that even though this conception of no time is seemingly one that can be lived fully only *out* of this world, it is the key to re-establishing your essential memory and calling, and therefore is the road to the establishment of your truth *in* the world. It is also, as you might well imagine, the key out of the patterns which no longer serve your awareness and the key to your desire to live in peace and harmony with each other.

It is now the time for you to live from your essential charge of light and to foster only those moments of truth from the being. Now is the time when the models and frameworks can be adjusted to include union and peace, and all the experiences which you so long to make real and habitual.

The three essential points that will be aligned through your free will are:

1. the original choices made in the Swing Between Worlds which have the coordinates of your truth programmed in and vibrating at a frequency which is individual and collective at the same time;
2. alignment with mom, which is essentially your key to belonging to this Earth project you've determined to participate in;
3. the association between the hypothalamus and the core of your truth.

The Hypothalamus

The hypothalamus is the regulating mechanism which allows light to be accorded to the being. Simply put, the hypothalamus is the governing body of the organism that accords or recognizes light. If we look at that philosophically or spiritually, as is our context, this means the hypothalamus is the place where your decision to bear light, remember your light, and shine forth that light is made possible—where healing, loving, forgiveness, responsiveness, or union are made possible organically. The hypothalamus is the place where accordance of divinity happens cellularly.

When you are born, the patterning of six generations imprints the hypothalamus with the rhythm of the acculturated experience. The rhythm of the breath is the key to establishing the beliefs, because they are sent visually, graphically, and vibrationally, but are forged through the breath, which then affects the pulses, which then set the patterns into the body that set the timer. Once the timer is ticking, the soul experience will be adjusted according to this mechanism between breath, pulse, and time.

When we harp continually to bring you back to substance, the fluids of the universe, we are constantly assuring you that you can return to the pre-forging place where you are still in the womb, outside of time, without the imprinting from mom, and in the fluids of substance—you are pre-fetus! You are available to the knowings that you chose in the Swing without being affected by time.

When we harp on you to ground, continually, and see yourself as an osmotic space that looks like sunlight on water, we are returning you to the osmotic space of being before form. The opportunity to readjust the breath and the pulses always happens organically when one is in essence, rather than in form. So the grounding and the immersion process of putting oneself in fluid, are the ways in which you can most directly affect the imprinting from mom and the experience from your culture, and the overall time constraints that, because time is the fulcrum point, keep you on one side of the equation or the other.

~

The hypothalamus
is the governing body
of the organism
that accords or recognizes light.

~

The hypothalamus
is the place
where accordance of divinity
happens cellularly.

~

When you are born,
the patterning of six generations
imprints the hypothalamus
with the rhythm
of the acculturated experience.
The rhythm of the breath
is the key to establishing the beliefs.

~

The opportunity
to readjust the breath
and the pulses
always happens organically
when one is in essence,
rather than in form.

~

Truth Is the Key to Union

Truth does not separate, it unifies.

*Since we are in the middle
of the destructuring process
of belief and dogma and institutions,
we have the greatest capacity
to affect new systems of functioning,
organically,
which can then be lived structurally.*

How do you get it all together? The first thing is to remember that there is a design, and that the design is accorded, or responsively aligned, in this dimension from truth.

Truth is the key to union, because when truth is present there is agreement between individuals and groups which have different hypothalmic programming.

Another way to say this is that no matter where you were brought up, or what color skin you have, or what your sexual preference, or where you buy your groceries, you can agree that you are one. No-thing stands in the way of oneness. It is foolproof because when one lives truth there is no disagreement between, only agreement to co-create. That's how you know whether or not you are in truth. And yes, it is oversimplified because that's the natural way to view it. Truth does not separate, it unifies. So it is simple. And to break the code of this phenomenon of time ordaining the experience, truth is the easiest path to experience. Truth is the most direct way home.

Now, you do not need to know what your truth is before you start, any more than you have to know about the hypothalamus to affect it. It is not a literal studying of the concept, it is a free will choice to affect the outcome by aligning the intention that will best move the being into those frameworks where the truth and the experience are the same. Since we are in the middle of the destructuring process of belief and dogma and institutions, we have the greatest capacity to affect new systems of functioning, organically, which can then be lived structurally. We will have structures after the de-structuring, but they will be different than the existing models of structure that were imprinted by mom.

What we are saying is that you have a very rare and exquisite opportunity to affect your life by returning to the Swing to see the design and to encode it with your present knowledge of your rhythm, pulses, vibration, core essence or blueprint, and time. You can bring these points or coordinates into alignment through truth. Light will activate the hypothalamus to repattern the amount of light you are encoding in any one moment—we are saying that specifically, *in any one moment*, because the timing is essential. Time is essence.

So the equation becomes this:

1. return to the Swing;
2. acknowledge that you are human by patterning;
3. make a decision from your core essence to experience life outside of time and in union with your original vibrational pulses and substance-filled spaces.

This is a point of free will which says, "I have returned to activate my essential and original design, and because of free will, I can now ordain that I am a being of light, living through truth and order, and within the framework of union, outside of time. I incorporate the three points of initiation, patterning, and timing, to unify the levels of my being through truth."

This actually starts a wave rolling that comes from origin and flows through your body and repatterns your hypothalamus so that it can receive light from your essence. You receive light from your original intention, and the breath and pulse begin to reflect a non-linear, non-constrictive, non-heredity which establishes a rhythm of union within the cellular, within the blood, and within the breath. Imagine breathing and pulsing as union, outside of time. It takes you immediately into bliss. Right? Bliss. And the reason it is bliss, is because there is no struggle to survive or beat the aging process or the dis-ease process, or to meet a deadline, or to remember whatever you've been trained by the society to feel is important to validate your worth. In the second that you have that bliss, nothing can touch you. You're free. You've made it! You've passed the test! It's like after a long, really hard day, crawling into a nice warm bed and being absolutely comfortable, receiving what you need.

When the hypothalamus, choice, and light are the same frequency through truth, union is created in the being. Our objective is to initiate the three points so that they reflect union into the cellular and encode the experience which replaces or repatterns the imprinting from mom. So as this unfolds, it rhythmically feels like a conversion, as if you are converting your heart rhythm or your belief about light, or your comprehension of what light is. Converting your heart rhythm affects the pulses and breath and the system through which you are affected unconsciously. You get to imprint yourself from the light, which is the coordinate point of design or Swing Between Worlds. The last point is the time, or the choice. You choose to live in the dimension of truth and consciously adjust the fulcrum

~

*Imagine
breathing and pulsing as union,
outside of time.
It takes you immediately into bliss.*

~

*When the hypothalamus,
choice, and light
are the same frequency through
truth,
union is created in the being.*

~

*Our objective
is to initiate the three points
so that they reflect union
into the cellular
and encode the experience which
replaces or repatterns the imprinting
from mom.*

~

*We do our best
to help you understand
so that you have a choice.
Making that choice
is your greatest
and most profound secret,
gift,
and potential.*

~

*This means
that when you communicate
through seeing into the hypothalamus
and affect the pulses
and rhythms
of your being,
then the soul blueprint emerges,
which is the design in form.*

~

point and the equation unifies. You are light in form to bring the experience of union through living truth.

Remembering the patterning of the total space of being, or the cosmic perspective, has less to do with thinking and more to do with being. The reason that many of you find it so challenging to change your action is that your actions are associated with time. They are structured into the memory as pictures and images and actually anchor in the constraint because, for so long, for six generations, change has taken time! Everything you have ever seen about transformation requires you to do something. Even the exercises we give you to facilitate your memory and union, require something of you. This means they are in some way linked to the time it takes to understand what we are saying, the time it takes to do the exercise, and the time it takes for the repatterning to be accomplished. That is why, in the most accurate sense, we do our best to provide understanding, because then there is relationship with something other than the patterning that was imprinted from mom. We do our best to help you understand so that you have a choice. Making that choice is your greatest and most profound secret, gift, and potential. Make the choice to bring the dynamics of the unified field of the truth into your breath, pulse, and vision, as much as possible, to re-order your circuits to more profoundly reflect light.

The key to accessing the light through the hypothalamus is profound, because this ability to affect your unconscious functioning reveals to you ways to create and establish new realities in every single area of your experience. It is now time for you to see what it is that you've been missing in your equation. Now is the time to expect that all the areas of your life will come together. It has been normal for there to be at least one area of life which seems to disappoint you, takes longer to accomplish, or is to some degree or measure, less productive. This is now different. The capacity of the human is to fully reflect the divinity now, and to co-create continually with all dimensions in the universe, simultaneously, or outside of time!

This means that when you communicate through seeing into the hypothalamus and affect the pulses and rhythms of your being, then the soul blueprint emerges, which is the design in form. The soul becomes, along with the hypothalamus, the key of light and truth and order, which will direct your being. So instead of your body functioning being unconscious from your birthing imprint, the functioning is directed from choice, is unaffected by the outer directives or beliefs about the universe, and so can continually manifest creation outside of time.

Repatterning the Imprint

This means that you can all begin to re-establish patterns with your children, born and perhaps yet unborn. Repatterning will align them with the Swing, the hypothalamus, and the soul, and accord the truth, in pulse and breath, which will give them permission to remember they are out of time, out of body, out of belief, out of dogma, out of personality or self, and to manifest that knowing here, where they have chosen to contribute and to design in form. This is a very meaningful and important concept.

In the beginning was the word and the word was God, and as the intention of the word was spoken through light, the journey of humanity began. You are, each and every one, now available to the word. The knowledge that has been held from humanity vibrationally, is now open. You have access to everything that is, *now*. This is because enough of you have broken the barrier between time and space for there to be enough energy of thought and knowing to provide the experience of being in bliss, so that you are out of time. When one is out of the time sequence, one is in creation. That means that you have no limits or boundaries now, and can initiate your children in the same way as you will choose to initiate yourself, because it is the way home, it is the way to comfort, it is a relationship with yourself that sustains and honors life in all dimensions. It is an opportunity for you to begin at the beginning, with this "new age," or Coming Together of the Ages, and to initiate these new models based on sustainability, creativity, co-creativity, honoring, community, and sharing of all re-Sourcing from all levels and all points of being.

To have the combination to the lock which opens your awareness is a wonderful gift that you can now give to yourself. You can learn to affect all your processes on a physical level through the balancing of the Swing, the hypothalamus, and the soul. Initially, the balance of your organic and awareness processes may seem to be different. One of your first considerations is to recognize that you are repatterning and establishing new relationships with everything in your life and environment, and you will by consensus, establish new relationships

~

*When one is
out of the time sequence,
one is in creation.*

~

*The knowledge
that has been held
from humanity vibrationally,
is now open.*

~

*The universe is repatterning
the vibrational levels around you,
which are re-patterning
your breath and pulse.
So it is happening
through the substance, automatically.*

~

*The feminine
has taken on this job of acting as a
messenger of lineage, as a service.*

~

*So
the mother imprints all of this
through the cellular,
the essential,
and the awareness,
which is why it imprints so deeply, because
it is in the same nonverbal
and organic space
as the truth.*

~

*Divinity
is accorded as an experience
when there is union
between
the design and the moment.*

~

with your unconscious also. This is what the "spiritual" movement is about anyway: bringing one home to being, which means to origin, to truth, to the ability to re-cognize the imprint from mom so that you are no longer feeling separate from everything.

The universe is repatterning the vibrational levels around you, which are re-patterning your breath and pulse. So it is happening through the substance, automatically. It is happening without will and without control and without many of your conscious understandings about how it works. *You do not have to know how something works to have it work.* It is working, regardless of your level of information or experience with it, which is how we can say that critical mass will ultimately bring truth into being. This repatterning is creating a critical mass which is redoing mom's imprint.

And, we want to say here, that the feminine has taken on this job of acting as a messenger of lineage, as a service. The imprinting is about habits, patterns, belief systems, fear structures, thought processes, survival mechanisms, and identifying with and relating to form. Mom does her best to instill and imprint the rules of the form and does so without words, because the child does not yet literally speak the language. So the mother imprints all of this through the cellular, the essential, and the awareness, which is why it imprints so deeply, because it is in the same nonverbal and organic space as the truth.

So, to repattern means not necessarily that you are going to shift from being 5'1" to being 5'10", or from believing one thing to believing in its opposite. It means that the essential relationship you have with Earth changes. It means that you now remember you are light and live from that point of origin, memory, and lineage, acknowledging the heredity of the Earth life you are now living, and yet being unaffected by the structures which are limiting your essential nature of oneness and availability to truth.

You are receiving information that will benefit humankind for the purpose of changing the models and the tendencies of humanity. Divinity is accorded as an experience when there is union between the design and the moment. The context for this transmission is there once you have made the decision that you are choosing to affect a true union between the design and the moment—choosing nonjudgment, truth, compassion, and unity. You then experience union in this reality instead of illusion. There can then be a forging of the inherent truth from the place of the true design and the moment of this life. To facilitate this union—because of course we are talking about oneness here, again—one must be ready to completely disavow the illusion. In a physical sense that means joining the hypothalamus, the body, and the matrix, or core. In a spiritual sense that means joining the Swing Between Worlds and the design. The amnesia is the physiological condition which happens when the vibration is inconsistent with the knowing, or when the vibration is oscillating at a rate of speed which reflects the illusion or disconnection with the Source.

So the easiest way to bring together the worlds, to merge the components, to unify the being, and experience that there is a consistency between what one really wants to do and say and feel and reflect, and the truth—is to reflect the truth more consistently from the core. To bring the core together and feel its vibration as attuned to the original Source experience, to hold that vibration and to breathe and pulse that into the body, and then bring it into the cells outside of time, provides a link with the truth. The truth is the immortal. The truth is the Akashic. The truth is unity—that which unifies. To be here differently than your mom and her mom and her mom requires of you a choice to belong here and yet to belong in truth. It does not matter what you believe about the truth. It can be used as a term to mean nonseparation, nonjudgment, etc. Because belief about anything is unnecessary.

One of the objectives we have in presenting this book to is to dispel any belief that we are different or separate, or that you have access only to certain aspects of the universe and not to others. The truth is that you have access to everything that we have access to, and the only reason that you have forgotten, or have amnesia about any aspect of it at all, is because you are in a space vibrationally where your ability to unify has been altered.

So the hypothalamus, the essential charge of light, the design that you have the ability to see now from the Swing between Worlds, the core that you can follow deep within, the awareness that the illusion is believed to be your reality and yet is not your reality, is all reducing the amnesia and encouraging the remembering. This is the key to unifying your innermost yearning and your behavior, or your deep actual core experience and your actions in the world.

Congruence is something we speak about often and recommend, because when one is congruent, the inner and outer points of experience are energetically the same. So remember that these are the foundations to bringing the experience of life into alignment with

~

*To bring the core together
and feel its vibration as attuned to
the original Source experience,
to hold that vibration
and to breathe
and pulse that into the body,
and then
bring it into the cells outside of time,
provides a link with the truth.*

~

*The truth is unity
—that which unifies.
To be here differently
than your mom and her mom
and her mom
requires of you a choice to belong here
and yet to belong in truth.*

~

*When one is congruent,
the inner and outer
points of experience
are energetically the same.*

~

*Whatever
you are most away from directionally
is going to bring
the most relevance to you now,
because before union can happen
there is a resolution of dichotomy.*

~

*So the key is in seeing,
feeling,
knowing,
and experiencing the polarity,
and then
immediately
experiencing the union,
outside of time.*

~

the Absolute, which is the objective.

To love without judgment,
to act without prejudice,
to honor with no need,
is possible for humanity.

It is the reason that we have shared so much of the available moments with you.

When you are making the intention to align your circuits and your awareness in union, you replay the circuits within you that have experienced disunion. You may find that the more you want to unify from the belief system or the thought process or even the fear structure, the more the disunion will play itself out. Remember that if one is ninety-nine percent attuned vibrationally, that other one percent will feel very irritated and out of sorts. The same thing applies for union.

Those individuals with whom you are still experiencing rancor are the ones whose attunement to light is in some way opposite yours, and you are seeing the reflection of that which you most wish to integrate. When one is your opposite they demonstrate that which you have chosen not to embody. So it is a red flag because you are afraid you will demonstrate that opposite. And most times you will want to leave the vibration of that interaction because the person or situation reminds you of that which you do not want to experience in yourself.

The conditional opposites are the key to incorporating this understanding. Whatever you are most away from directionally is going to bring the most relevance to you now, because before union can happen there is a resolution of dichotomy, which means that all factions, aspects, groups, and individuals are going to polarize before they unify.

So the key is in seeing, feeling, knowing, and experiencing the polarity, and then immediately experiencing the union, outside of time. To do it inside of time brings back the conditioning of mom. For example, she might say, "Well, you have to be responsible, and if you're not responsible you're no good." You might grow up and have a certain definition of "responsible" and feel that this certain individual who you are now polarizing with is irresponsible. Try as you might, it seems impossible that you could be anything alike. You've thought it through and you're trying to accept that part of them, trying to see the other viewpoint, to love, and nothing is working. Since acceptance implies that you have to like what someone is doing, i.e., their being irresponsible, the way to resolve this is through vibration. By according that you and the other person are the same vibration, you can take their position and your position and bring them together. Vibrationally being in union is the way to experience union personally.

Amnesia comes when one believes through the imprinting that there are certain behaviors, choices, and actions which are right or wrong, which means that there is a polarity, and one is on one side, and one is on the other side. It does not mean that there is one way that is better than another way, or one area of human experience that has more consideration than any other. What it means—that there is no right or wrong—is that vibrationally they are the same point. They come from the same place and that is why that can be unified so easily.

And yet as we were saying, when you personally get to the point of deciding to unify, that last one percent requires of you that you step into a place where that union exists, outside of this time frame, and to incorporate the design at that moment, which will show you how you are one. When we say that there is no right or wrong, that accords the overall design, and is accurate from that point.

When one is in a situation and chooses to separate from that person or whatever the dynamics are, the separation produces karma in the old sense and irritation in the new sense. This means that when you do or say something which separates, you will find you are irritated. You might think you are saying something that is justified, but you are the one who will suffer. If you say something against someone else, the first place the vibration is felt is in your own throat. The separation happens in your own body, or we could say the separation is against your own cells, and vibrates to bring you out of the vibration of peace. And peace is what you experience when you are light and vibrate as light in the breath and pulses outside of time. So you are keeping yourself out of that peaceful space whenever your vibration is unequilibrated with light.

Everything is based on the vibration of light. When humanity stops worrying about what is right and wrong outside of themselves—in the world, in their marriages, or in their politics—and initiates a unifying vibration in the thought and speech first, then violence against others ceases because the violence against themselves has ceased, and that is the key to resolving anything.

The way to resolution is through vibration.

There is no right or wrong.

Peace is what you experience when you are light and vibrate as light in the breath and pulses outside of time.

Everything is based on the vibration of light.

~

The purpose
of the human free will journey
is to travel
from the Swing Between Worlds
into the body,
and back to the Swing.
Simple—
the journey
from oneness to separation to oneness.

~

Realize
that what comes up is a frequency that
needs to be matched and incorporated
rather than programming
that needs to be changed.

~

Programming and conditioning
take over
when the light
and breath
and no-time
are unremembered.

~

The purpose of the human free will journey is to travel from the Swing Between Worlds into the body, and back to the Swing. Simple—the journey from oneness to separation to oneness. Because it does not exist in the belief system that oneness is a reality here on Earth, most people believe that the return to oneness happens after death, and this supports the choices made by those individuals who would choose to exploit others, for that to be "true." For example, this belief would give someone the idea that they could do what they needed to do to survive here or what is necessary to assure their own well-being, and not think of others' well-being or the effect their actions might have on others.

We are telling you that the journey of humanity has a very different design in vibration. We are always saying also that it is important for you to believe only that there is light and nothing else. So just for a moment, be with the idea that:

> There is nothing but light,
> You are light, and
> There is no time.

When those three points are experienced simultaneously, your breathing changes, your vibration changes, your judgment and prejudice fade, your programming seems antiquated, unnecessary and superfluous. You can then talk to mom in your heart and say, "Mom, I don't need that programming anymore. I'd like to decide and choose for myself now. As light there is no reason for me to fear. As light I do not remember by judging. I remember by putting the light and the breath and the vibration of light into my equation."

So, unifying any of the three points that we speak about at different times in this manual, in the same 21-day period, facilitates union. This will bring up that which seems opposite for consideration. What is important is not to consider it, because it is an illusion. Realize that what comes up is a frequency that needs to be matched and incorporated rather than programming that needs to be changed. Programming and conditioning take over when the light and breath and no-time are unremembered.

Taking any of the three points and mixing and matching them so that you are no longer conditioned to respond in the usual way, done over a 21-day period, divinely facilitates the union of the final three points which are: the Swing, the body, and the Swing. These three points are really the key, because they give you the coordinates for your lineage and your participation in the design. They activate your hypothalamus because in the Swing Between Worlds you saw how you would bring the choices for union into being.

Think of yourself as originating in the Swing Between Worlds, coming into the body, and returning to the Swing. Everything is unifying, all positions are becoming the same, there is no separation, there is no time. "I am home. Home is here. I belong here. I am a spiritual being in a physical form. I believe only in light. I am light divine, remembering that there are no points of reality in which I am separate from anything else."

Living Light and Truth
notes

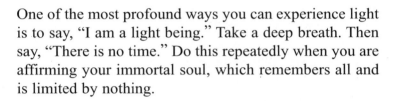

Experiencing Light
An Exercise

Challenge

that which you know to be a belief

or an action

or a vibration that is out of order—

challenge it

by choosing to vibrate as light.

~

Breathing light produces light.

~

Time

is the balance point

between the above and the below.

~

One of the most profound ways you can experience light is to say, "I am a light being." Take a deep breath. Then say, "There is no time." Do this repeatedly when you are affirming your immortal soul, which remembers all and is limited by nothing.

Light, breath, no time; light, breath, no time. As you say and image this, you feel in your body that you and mom understand each other and resolve your differences and nothing matters. You get it and yet it doesn't get you. You're free of the dichotomy. What happens in your core is that you are able to delineate between the truth and the illusion. Remember that in the core there is a memory of your vibration in order with all other vibrations, which creates the experience of order, and is one way that the critical mass will be affected. This means it is a spiritual principle and yet it is a physical experience that can bring the truth into the human space. It is vibration, and the vibration of order comes together to shake the structure of disorder so that it is challenged.

Challenge that which you know to be a belief or an action or a vibration that is out of order— challenge it by choosing to vibrate as light. Breathe as light, which stimulates the hypothalamus to produce more light. Breathing light produces light.

Living in no time is simple. Choose to be in the Swing Between Worlds, breathing the fluids of the universe, for there you truly exist outside of time. Time is the balance point between the above and the below. When you accord your place as a divine essence of light, you are home and all time is now, and there is no more separation. No more illusion—only you and light and breath and being, for the above and the below are unified through your essence, and that is why you have come.

You Are Light

OUR INTENTION IS TO BRING THE WORD OF THE CONSCIOUSNESS of all time to this place of Earth, and to clarify the questions, seekings, and yearnings which have been preponderant in human society since the beginning of time, especially about the experience of separation and reunion. Our words, ideas, and awarenesses come from the place where it began, the place of synthesis, the place that has its orientation from the beginning. Our purpose has always been to engender that place of synthesis in each of you so that your experience more profoundly reflects that synthesis—the place of the beginning, the place of the original, the place of the Absolute.

Our process is to take all light and synthesize it so that it orients its many frameworks for each of you, so that light can be attested to, oriented with, or restructured in your psyche. So as we come to each of you, it is for the purpose of aligning the point of light within you with the point of light that is the beginning.

As you come to the place inside yourself where that light is your purpose, at that moment, your intention and the calibration of your consciousness change. When one remembers one is light, there is no more darkness, and the synthesis is complete.

In 1986 we undertook the job of bringing that experience to humanity for the purpose of engendering this light in as many souls as possible. In the process of this enlightening, there have been waves of energy, confluence, aggregation, union, and truth that have actualized through the connection we have made with each of you. That has been our intention—to strengthen the capacity of humanity to remember its light, to aggregate that light, and then, to focus that light.

This is part of the great design—that we come at this time with this purpose. We are to be with you for a period of ten years. Nine of those years we will speak to you, and the last year we will synthesize light with you from levels of consciousness that you have not yet understood or attained in your perception.

Light Light Light

I am a light being, and light I shall remain.

It is really never about what you do, it is always about what you are.

~

This unified field is made up of many rays of consciousness, and that is how there can be as many TRUTHS *as there are* PEOPLE.

~

So those of you who are in the process of bringing that aggregation into form, of being light in the body, will find our last year of presence the most valuable, because we will be working with you individually to refine and enhance your capacity to bear light—for that is really what life here is about.

When each of you is with us in the Swing Between Worlds before birth, you choose many, many ways of expressing that light, and yet it is always about light that you come here. No matter what you think, how you feel, or what your job is, foundationally and fundamentally it is about light.

The Ones With No Names can be defined as the body of light and knowledge that maintains the experience of order and truth in your dimension. That means that there is a pulsation to the light. There is an affirmation to it. As it unfolds, there is a greater and greater capacity to be light. As your fields of consciousness and awareness refine, they deepen, expand, and contain a charge.

When we talk with you about essence, about your soul-full experience of being, it is the charge that your light carries which magnetizes the experience of life and brings forth the resonance that calls others home to being. It is really never about what you do, it is always about what you are. And so your light is foundational to being.

When you begin to develop your essence, you charge your light body, and it begins to vibrate in the experience of order and truth. And when a number of you at the same moment vibrate in that capacity, a unified field is born. This unified field is made up of many rays of consciousness, and that is how there can be as many truths as there are people. For when the light is charged from the essence, everyone's truth is the same, for all truth is about the memory of the beginning, which is oneness.

There is a system to oneness. Many of you remember the system, and many of you don't. So, one of the first things we would suggest to help you remember, is an intention you can make that you are a being of light and so you shall remain. You might state it thus, three times: "*I am a light being, and light I shall remain.*" When you state this, even if you don't know about your essence, the body of light that you are becomes charged.

Each day as you say, "*I am a light being, and light I shall remain,*" your essence automatically becomes charged. The light begins to pool in the areas of consciousness where the essence is linked to the vibration. It is very beautiful, because there is no way you can avoid charging your system with order and truth when you do this. You begin to see everything as light in the experience of order and truth. It all becomes the same, does not need definition, and carries one home to being. It carries you on a fluid wave of creation. Because creation is light, then truth and order are the foundations of creation, the rhythm through which the bond is made.

When you feel your essence charging, you experience union, because the fluid wave carries one to creation, which is home. There is a memory of that, which brings your essence out. As these aspects flow together, your field will solidify. In our opinion, it is now unnecessary to work with the ego, the personality, the subconscious, or the psyche, as it is now defined by humanity, because you can work directly with the light body.

In our individual sessions with you, each of you has received a pattern that is energetic. It is always about the synthesis of the pattern with the life. So this instruction is about bringing the pattern *to life*. And that is why, when you hear your pattern, it accelerates your vibrational field, because it is the reading of the way in which you each have constructed your particular space of being as energy. The beauty of the hologram (if you see it as we see it) is that as each of you has designed your pattern of energy, it exactly fits what is deemed necessary for the light of creation to manifest. So words like *hope, faith, inspiration,* come from what has already been ordained. And that is why we reference many times to the future of the future, or "future-future."

If you would remember that your design, personally and collectively, is already in operation, and that what you yearn for is reflected to you from the future, you can relax, for there is nothing to do. It is about reception, remembering, and alignment. The pieces that each of you tries so desperately to fit together in terms of how, what, where, and when, come from a part of you that had its experience out of context with order and truth. Being in the light body, your own light essence, and charging your frequency daily, spins your being into the light of creation. All the pieces fit!

The soul holds the design of that future place in the physical experience, and because the soul frequency is present when the essence is charged, the soul emerges. As this comes together in your awareness, there is a melting down of conditioning, separation, and judgment—and a union of the essential ingredients necessary to live oneness in human form. Again, we would like to affirm that it is not about analyzing, or taking apart the issues of your experience. It is

---

Because creation is light, then truth and order are the foundations of creation, the rhythm through which the bond is made.

If you would remember that your design, personally and collectively, is already in operation, and that what you yearn for is reflected to you from the future, you can relax, for there is nothing to do.

about unifying the field—participating in the field of order. We say it is giving the oil or the grease to what works instead of what squeaks. This is very powerful, because it provides an opportunity for individuals to move beyond the experience that has been engendered to date and to live truth.

The Circles of Time
An Exercise

One way to experience "future-future," is to draw two circles on the ground or on the floor, about six feet apart. With a piece of chalk or a crayon, write in one circle the letters which spell "present-present" and in the other circle write the words which spell "future-future." Imagine each circle spinning to indicate your movement into a time continuum. When you are ready, leap from the "present-present" circle into the spinning circle marked "future-future" and then turn around, and look back at the space marked "present-present". When you view the "present-present" from the "future-future," all of the dynamics in your life are different and stimulate vision, memory, and trust.

Then as you look back at the "present-present" spinning circle, walk back towards it. As you get closer to your original position in the exercise, feel that you imbue yourself with light. Imprint the present moment as if you were a piece of clay in the present and you are the key in the "future-future." You then imprint that key into the present space.

In some ways it is very silly, because you become what you are. Yet, what you represent is unknown to you logically. That is why embodying the vibration of who you are in your physical experience organically is so important. Then your pattern of light becomes cellular and joined with the visceral tissue in the body. Spiritual training usually includes attention to vibration—being a frequency—which lessens your density. When one thinks about vibration and frequency outside of dogma, or a spiritual path, or a belief system, the forging of those two points of being and becoming can be immediate. There is nothing you have to attain, prove, or change—you are in that moment all that your essence has chosen to be.

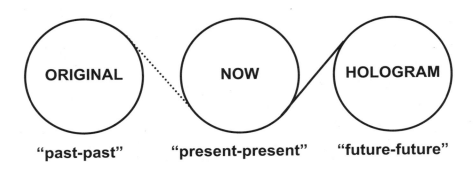

ORIGINAL   NOW   HOLOGRAM

"past-past"   "present-present"   "future-future"

The original design is behind you (see diagram), and that means there is a pendulum, a movement. As you jump into the "future-future" you are from the present, yet there is also always that original point that allows for the triad, or the three-in-one, which is the point of union. Everything that is three becomes one. As you think about your intention to foster your "future-future," you're also recalling, remembering, and reidentifying with your absolute space of fluid intention. That is the light, the pattern that became the energy that is you. It is now essence that can flow and allow you to be present fully, without exception, without thinking, without bartering, without trying to figure it out.

It is the propensity of your consciousness to establish itself with itself, because that's the union you're looking for. When those three points are vibrationally secured at the same frequency, the absolute design will manifest spontaneously in that moment. One of the alternatives that we have here, together, is to make conscious choices with our charge, to charge the beginning, the middle, and the end (or the Absolute, the now, and the hologram) with the same vibration, so that we spin this into being even more quickly—and that is possible.

When we see your designs, they are always profound, because they have woven the pieces of your fabric into a design with millions and millions, and in some instances, trillions of strands. It is very elaborate, and profoundly available as a sourcing energy, as creation or creative energy. The viability of living that here, attaining that point of destiny, is about remembering the pattern of light that you represent. That's easy, because when you stand in the "future-future," you *are* the pattern of light that you represent.

That's why you go into relationship, primarily—to find the energy, that exhilaration of consciousness of being in the light, and reflecting the truth of what you've come here to do. That is what the union is intentioned for. It has been parodied and elaborated on and conditioned and systematized and dogmatized, and yet none of that is real.

Three-Point Manifestation:
The Three-In-One

If you are in the light body, the only thing that exists is order and truth, which establishes oneness between the points of the beginning, or the original Absolute; the middle, or the place of your present presence; and the end, or your future point. That actually creates a system where everything you're working with is *now*, so that your original point, your present point, and your future point can become the same vibration in your experience.

That is how oneness happens in the being; it's how the light body creates the charge to stimulate the essence, to open the soul, and to allow you to remember your birthright, which is to see the vibration that you've come to live, and to fully acknowledge that this is what you're here for.

You can stand in the body of your own consciousness and view these three points in any or all of the following ways:

1. before, middle and after;
2. "past-past," "present-present," "future-future";
3. original, now, and hologram;
4. the Absolute, actual, and point of resolution.

In creating the three-in-one experience, those places are all integrous with each other. So you need no system of thought for that, because everything is now. These concepts have been put together to enable you to function from a different point of reference.

If you will all think about yourselves as points of light that have inherently come to shine, and that each of you in the way that you shine fulfills your design, in each moment that you intend that, it happens.

Everything else dissolves—becomes immaterial—because it is no longer necessary to think about how that process will unfold, whether it will unfold, or when it will unfold. You're literally in a different dimension when this experience is your actualization. This is the point of synthesis. This is what you're striving to put together when you're trying to figure out how all these quotients of your consciousness match, marry, and orient. Everybody is trying very hard to attain a point where none of it matters. The irony of the human experience is that you try hard to get it all, understand it all, grok it all, put it all into a formula, and then you realize as you do that, that none of it matters.

We are doing our best to save you "time" as you would think of it in the linear context, and to accelerate the foundation of your essence so that your charge calls to you the frequency of your being, so you can wrap yourself in it and keep warm, or receive love, or nurture the body, or feel safe, or actualize your potential. The charge of this light will do all those things.

It isn't that you will not be in relationship, or that you will not have health, or that you will not find harmony in the world—it is that you stop seeking those things, particularly in an external sense. You provide a resonance within yourself that meets all your needs in exactly the way that you've designed that you need them met. And in a very beautiful way, you forget that you've been thinking about meeting those needs, because you're too busy expressing who you are. The foundation of your being is too busy shining light, and catalyzing essence, and drawing souls to you to reflect in the light of your own experience the oneness of your total intention. This is how the hologram of oneness will be lived.

The Consciousness of Light

Between 1995 and 2000, there will be a massive destructuring of all consciousness, all belief systems, and all thought forms. So this is a very exciting time! A massive collection of reality is coming to

Earth from many dimensions. This reality will squeeze out the illusion so that nothing is left that does not maintain the vibration of essential reality, or does not have order and truth as its basis. And there's a great yearning for order and truth. This is the future being born in the present, in all of you as the form. The experience of that quality of consciousness that is light allows no interference, supports no violence, allows for no disintegration of truth, supports and accelerates light, foundations essence, and is the wave upon which the soul is born.

Everything that has ever been, if it structures the consciousness in light, will be upheld; and if it doesn't, it is immediately dissolved. So re-solution—coming back into solution—means that everything that is being dissolved is, in the sense of metamorphosis, collected from that which is of future, brought into present, and transformed. Transformation means that each of you has a different form, and the form is light, instead of the separation that is created when the body of being, the essence, and the charge of light are not together.

As the next years of consciousness are shaping, between 1995 and 2000, each of you has a very important role to play. The critical mass of consciousness is born in oneness when light bodies vibrate at the experience of truth and order and are then synthesized as one being or one body. You don't have to work together, necessarily, on the same goal to attain the same point. You don't have to live in the same place to create or manifest, on any level, anything that is inherently of that vibration.

There are no rules or conditions for this union. It doesn't have to be lived in any particular way. However, the foundation of all of you as you unfold the light means that you aggregate the frame of that light—what you might call the balance of the equilibrium, the tuning fork, or morphic resonance, where whatever you're putting out is going to enhance the magnification of that particular ray or consciousness. So as you decide if you're going to be together or not, work together or not, be in relationship or not, work at a job or not, if you're going to do these things that you have to make decisions about, remember that, in the next four to five years particularly, and less so but also between 2000 and 2005, there will be a very regular crescendo of consciousness that draws you into it. Choices that you make today may change even in the twinkling of an eye, so that you realize, "I wanted to do this, but now I realize I must do that." The logical basis for choice is going to become an essential charge of recognition instead.

Know that there are no shoulds, even if today it looks like you have to do this or that. You'll find that you wake up one day and can do no other than change your mind, or re-cognize that decision. It's going to be a time of transition, because the foundation of what seems to be logically in your path can change with the snap of the fingers.

When you charge the light being, you charge that consciousness, and you no longer have conscious direction. It is dissociated from the being, and that's why we define it as "to follow your calling," because the calling is the charge of energy that is the synchronistic and synergistic frame for the charge meeting up with the intention, meeting up with the actualization.

When you get your charge, at first it has no direction—remember that. It isn't about going home to the light, it's about being the light. "I AM a light being," which brings it into the experience of now. "*I am a light being, and light I shall remain.*"

You don't have a conscious direction to take that in. You can tell that you're in the experience of light because you don't care where you are! This is a very important concept. You are in that experience of being a light being.

So you might logically say, "Today I'm going here." And then when you say, "I am a light being," all of a sudden you may be going in the opposite direction, because the charge is being magnetically called to its own re-solution. And you recognize that this is the solution you've been looking for. Many times, changing direction actually provides you with an incentive of energy to resolve what's going on; just like when you jump from the "present-present" spinning circle into the "future-future" spinning circle and look back—it's a completely different recognition. Re-cognizing it. It's a different re-solution—putting it back into solution. It's a re-Sourcing that happens when you go with the charge, which means that the actual experience of receiving becomes innately known in those moments. It isn't thinking you'll go to "future-future" and see what your real design is, look back at your life and see what you should do to make that design happen, ask the universe to help bring in the resources to make it possible, and then return to the present and turn round again to look at the future, knowing where you're going to march to.

That would be very comfortable. And it doesn't work that way. The way that it works is that it's magnificent, exhilarating, exciting, essential, fire, light, consciousness, truth. It is not boring! You can't

~

*It's about
becoming light,
not
translating light.*

~

say, "I got it all worked out now. I went to the 'future-future' and saw my outcome and my direction, and came back, and now I know what I'm supposed to do." It's very beautiful, because there is no way to sabotage this—it doesn't have to do with what you think you're supposed to do, based on what you thought you felt in the "future-future."

It's about becoming light, not translating light, not discussing light, not organizing light, and then implementing it and saying, "This is what you're going to do, and this is what I'm going to do, and this is how it's going to work." You see, when we talk about the hologram in the "future-future" experience, it is about the fact that it's already done. If something is already done, then nobody has to describe what's supposed to happen. It's an experience of re-membering it, putting it together again in form. It doesn't mean cognizing it, it means allowing it to express.

So, we suggest that when you make the statement, "I am a light being," you are becoming nameless, you are becoming essential, you are in that moment aligning with your true intention, and nothing else matters! It doesn't mean loss, abandonment, giving up everything, it just means that you're changing your modus operandi. You're moving the consciousness of your experience into being alive.

There are no ways to take that energy and short-circuit it into an existing channel and say, "I guess I'd better do this with that." There's no holding this back, there is no designing it in such a way that it seems to make sense so you know what your next step is. It's about jumping in. And when you jump in, what you receive in return is the fullness of your being. Many of you like to meter it out, to get a little bit at a time, digest it, assimilate it, ground it in, and then go on for more. That worked very well in the last few years. It's been very good for people to do that, because there was a movement of acceleration in the curve of consciousness that measures the human dynamic, and you'd go to a certain point and then we would plateau it out and let it be synthesized, because it seemed best.

What we're realizing is that the more you synthesize things, the more you water them down. And the more you water them down, the more energy you need to bring them back up, vibrationally. So it seems to make a lot more sense now to just keep things very charged. That's why time is running at about two-and-one-half times its previous speed. It's why the body is assimilating things much more quickly, why you cannot hold in your mind a fact that you thought you would store forever. You can't access it, because you're at a different spin of your own wheel.

It's why you cannot keep relationship in its old ruts and its old dynamic spaces, because it cannot hold and contain the deliberate orientation of its own definition.

Relationship means unifying light and consciousness through choice. If you're not unifying light and consciousness through choice, you cannot relate anymore.

As the dynamics are changing in the world and your souls are expanding their ability to run that light, fiber, and orientation into the form of the body, your bodies are no longer going to be dense. It doesn't have to do with a belief system: "If I believe this, if I say ten 'Hail this,' or ten 'ups and downs' this, or do this or that, then I'm going to have this consciousness." It's not going to be like that. It's not going to be that you've paid your dues, and now you're supposed to get into the Kingdom of Heaven. It's going to be that those who acknowledge that they are light are the Kingdom of Heaven. Period.

If somebody walks in the door today, into this beautiful experience of Vermont, and says, "I've never done a spiritual thing in my life. I want to birth my soul," you cannot say to them, "You've got to take a class, you've got to learn what the soul is, you have to experience this, that, and the other thing—have you ever talked with The Ones With No Names? Why did you show up here at the door?" You cannot decide anymore, anything about anybody, because it's about being the experience of light, not how much you practiced it.

It also means that the guru types and the people who believe that they are knowing more and have been around the block many times, and therefore deserve something, are going to find that they're running neck-and-neck with the novices and the people who just stepped over the line and said, "I'm not going back!" And sometimes it's easier for those people to do that, because they don't have as much to lose. They don't have their credibility and their ideas and their dogmas and their belief systems, "new age," or "spiritual," or whatever it is, to lose.

And so, you're realizing in this time that there are no rules. There are no conditions. Things that have been in place for millennia are gone in one second, never to be found again in some instances, because they have been overturned by consensus. When we say massive destructuring of consciousness, it means that you can't hold onto anything. You really can't. And it means, also, that there is a foundation emerging which says that the easier it is to flow outside of that which was, the faster the intention to create the new can be

Relationship means unifying light and consciousness through choice.
If you're not unifying light and consciousness through choice, you cannot relate anymore.

Those who ACKNOWLEDGE that they are LIGHT are the Kingdom of Heaven. Period.

fostered and developed and experienced in the framework of the moment. This really boils down to the fact that the less you take stock of it, the less you want it to be something particular, the less it functions as something in your life that matters, the more easily order and truth flow into the being.

What Matters?

notes

Non-Attachment
An Exercise

We would recommend that you take those things that really matter to you, the people, ideas, or events, and represent them with a witness—a piece of clay, or a rock, a feather, a pebble, a paper clip, or a piece of paper—whatever you'd like to work with. Write everything that matters to you on paper, or designate every pebble or piece of clay, by assigning them names, faces, or values. Then put them in a group and sit on them. Just sit on them. Sit on all those material things that matter to you. They can be people, animals, property, jobs, memories, beliefs, God, or The Ones With No Names, famous gurus, or anything that matters to you. It doesn't matter what they are. Then, disintegrate them, burn them, bury them, chop them up, anything. Disintegrate them. Each one.

You'll find that you're no different than you were before. You haven't lost anything. What you've just proven is that whatever matters to you, it doesn't matter what form it's in. It doesn't matter how you think of it, because it's still there, it still matters to you. Even after you take it apart, throw it away, burn it, whatever, it still matters to you. So why does it matter? It matters because you are in some way oriented to that reality as being connected with your reality. If you relate to it as if it matters, there's attachment. If you relate to it as if it's part of your light, then you start co-creating.

This is a very simple exercise to prove that you really want to co-create with these experiences. You do not want to attach to them, you want to do something with them. That's why they matter to you—because you want to do something with them, not because you want to hold them in a glass container.

~

If you relate to it
as if it matters,
there's attachment.
If you relate to it
as if it's part of your light,
then
you
start
co-creating.

~

*When you elevate the vibration
of who you are and what matters to you
into
the same vibrational field of light,
you have the relationships you want.*

What you really want to do with those things that matter is make life better, and experience the light in such a way that things make sense, and there's no pain.

When you elevate the vibration of who you are and what matters to you into the same vibrational field of light, you have the relationships you want. You have the creative capacity with others that you've been desiring. When you take those pieces of paper or chunks of clay, or whatever, say this: "I separate myself from this thing. I make it this material object." You begin to see how you could lose it, lose what it represents. You realize when you take it outside yourself and give it another name, and give it an experience of matter, that basically it becomes separate from you. At that moment it becomes something that you could lose. When you realize that no matter what you do to that object, it doesn't change who you are inside, or your connection with that person or idea, then you realize this is how to create.

The original part of the design shows you that this person and you are really connected. The present feeling you have of wanting to co-create with that person comes from the design and brings a feeling of union. You remember, "This is why we're together; this is who we are together. And as I bring all those points into the experience of light, then I am always in union with this person. I always experience the foundation of what it's like to be light, in form, co-creating."

The objective of this exercise is to feel that whatever it is you think you want, it's already there, it's already you. You're already the same vibration, or you wouldn't care about having that in your essential field. This takes away the *conditions* of relationship. It takes away the things that you think you need to have in order to make the foundation work. In other words, before you came into human form, part of your light body was whatever you now want to be part of your light body.

And that can be health. You can designate a rock for health, and say, "Okay, is my health separate from me? Is it me? Where's it going? Can I disintegrate it? Can I activate it? What can I do with it?" And then you realize, "Wait a minute, these conditions of the world have nothing to do with my health, nothing to do with my relationship, nothing to do with my work. These are external to me, and have nothing to do with me. And yet, if I create the vibration of that which really matters to me inside my body, then automatically as my light body starts to create itself, formulating co-creatively with all the essential things I need, that I programmed in at the beginning, I can function at my optimum capacity."

As you charge this consciousness, as you affirm that you are light, as you pick up what you think is important and put it down, and change its form and realize nothing changes—you are already safe, you already have it, it's already there, it's who you are in co-creation with whatever it is that you are connected with. This changes the paradigm you are living in the world in that moment.

And how does it change? There's no more separation. I am my dog, I am my light, I am my heart, I am my body, I am my health, I am my lover, I am everything, I am my mother, I am my father, I am my child, I am my friend. I AM. I AM light, and light is all. So it becomes clear, the trumpets sound, "Oh, yes, yes!" It's that simple. In that moment five hundred years of evolution comes and goes.

Part of the dilemma that faces humanity is that things are getting lost, they are getting re-oriented—structures, ideas, frameworks. Everything's changing. So if you have all these things that matter to you, and change their form so that they become essentially the same field of vibration that you're in, you can feel your connection. You can start co-creating. You can now think, "I no longer need attachment. I only wanted attachment to prove that I was one with what I thought I needed. Now I've experienced that vibrationally, as light, so I'm in a different place. And the place that I'm in requires no proof." Very important: Requires no proof. Why? Because it's essential—it's the essence of who you are.

What you're learning as the experience of humanity unfolds, is that you always, always, always, have everything you need inside you, because the synthesis is already complete.

The Essential Space

The essence guides the being always, and is where the experience of "having it all," or synthesis, takes place. And yet the essential space is very rarely where one connects or unifies from.

When you are in the human perspective, you go out in the world to try and find what you need—outside of yourself. Your essence is the force which moves toward unity and the expression of wholeness, and when it finds what you feel you essentially "need," the essence will reflect that back to whatever or whoever you find, and unify with it. It won't take it because it doesn't need it. It appreciates it, mirrors it, teaches you that it exists, but the essence doesn't take what it finds. However, humanity does take it. The human part identifies the person with roles, actions, and models of behavior.

For example, let's say you are at a party and your essence is drawn to unify with someone there. The human part says, "Okay, I want you. So how do I want you? I'll define that: I'll marry you; I'll sleep with you; I'll be your friend; I'll be your mentor; I'll be your neighbor; I'll be your lover; I'll be your teacher." But these roles, identities, and definitions do not necessarily bring union if lived only through the human framework and conditioning.

So our suggestion is to orient the being to light first:

+ saying, "*I am a light being, and light I shall remain*";
+ feel the charge of that;
+ open the essence;
+ then be in the essence as light;
+ then do the Circles of Time exercise;
+ jump into that future place;
+ look back at yourself, orient that new experience;
+ then take anything that still grabs you.

"Well, I still want this. I still want that. Where is she or he? What's this? What's that?" Take those things and say, "All right, these still matter, so I'll take what matters and really separate them from myself. I'll name them, put them on a rock, or piece of paper, and find out how it is to be separate. Then I'll destroy this, in the creative/destructive sense, and allow the newly born to take its place. I'm going to take the old model and disintegrate it."

If you do this yourselves—disintegrate your models yourselves—then it doesn't have to happen physically or externally, because essentially you're in the light force co-creating with whoever or whatever that is, and you don't need to lose it to understand that you have it. You don't have to take it to prove that you are one with it. It is very important for each of you to actualize this experiment, so that you yourself are God, and you say, "This matters to me, so I'm going to put it in an external form, and label it, and then erase it. And when I erase it, I realize I already have it. This is fundamental to my essential space of being. There's no way I can lose it. There's no way it can disappear. There's no way I can't have it anymore, because I always have what I need inside of me."

When you do the non-attachment exercise, you move the psyche to a place where it can just be light, and experience the integration of personality and ego, and you don't have to pay attention to all of that, or go through the levels of attaining the light body through pain or separation. We're suggesting a short-cut to fostering the responsiveness to essence that is a part of all of your dynamics, and yet allows you in each moment to be already there. You don't need to affirm about everything, or practice by giving away everything you own, to know that you really don't need it! You can understand the concept of attachment in an easier way, and then you don't have to actually live through the experience of destruction.

Consciousness is shaping itself differently these days. It's taking the hint much more quickly, because there are no structures in the etheric sense to stand in the way of that motivation and that momentum—because evolution stopped in 1991. This means that there is no resistance to expansion or growth, because it's not fitting any particular preconceived pattern as it was before. What you're learning is being chosen by each of you without a structure to uphold it, which means that basically whatever you want you're getting, and you're getting it very quickly. Very, very quickly. To allow the design to complete itself in this time, in this moment, is your greatest capacity.

When there is an understanding of energy patterning, there can be an affirmation and manifestation of the pattern in its design, energetically, which provides the momentum to bring the experience of union to being.

Each of you has an intricate role to play in that manifestation, and it's time to hone the frequency, put it together. Tune your instrument in 1995, and start taking that instrument into the world in 1996. How

You can understand the conception of attachment in an easier way, and then you don't have to actually live through the experience of destruction.

The last massive time of rendering will be in the year 2005. If you're a light worker, there are ten years in which to affect your "future-future" in form.

you do that, and the experience of what you do is much less important than that you do it. The refinement of the consciousness in 1995 will carry you through a wave and bring 1996 into being as an expression of your wave: the "future-future." Those of you on the crest of the wave of those who are experiencing its validity, are going to bring the next twenty years into being when they have been designed. As it unfolds, 2000 is the year when the 144 aspects of the human Christ come together vibrationally, and when the refinement of consciousness will be such that all the people on this planet understand what Christ consciousness is and remember it. They will remember it to the point where they want to live it. It's a massive time of rendering: people coming in who want to live it; people leaving who don't want to live it; people being refined who are here and who plan to stay here. The last massive time of rendering will be in the year 2005. If you're a light worker, there are ten years in which to affect your "future-future" in form.

From 2005 to 2016 we'll get it all organized, put it together so that all the pieces are working. That's not the time to get ready, or refine, or make a choice to do it. Now is the time to do all that, so that by the time you get to 2005, everything about the hologram and its viable space of operation is known to you. So what will you do for the next ten years? You will dissolve any barriers between you and the hologram of oneness, so that all pieces of all people framing awareness is born in your awareness. You wake up every day and know—you know—it gets deeper and richer and wider and more open because everything that you've ever thought about as a human being is bringing you to that place of absolution.

Absolution! Dissolving that which you abstain from. Think about abstaining from something, and dissolving and being absolved and being freed of the need to separate from something and say it's good or bad—freed of the need to be forgiven, freed of the need to carry guilt. From 1995 into the year 2005, you're busy manifesting your divinity, because divinity is what happens when you receive absolution. In absolution everything is in solution again.

It's a wheel that keeps turning, and everything we're saying is to underline and undergird the experience of that wheel being oiled and greased so that it keeps turning. Every time we give a reading of a specific pattern, it is to put the oil or the grease in the place where it's needed most. That's why some of you think, "Well, I should have a reading now, but, no, it doesn't feel right, I have to wait." Everyone who has had a reading has it at a particular time, and it's been ordained when they'll have it, and what will be said, because when it's said it puts that *O o m p h* ! into the design and gets it spinning again. All of you have intricate parts to play, and you don't even know it. You're out reading your lines, but you really don't know that anyone is waiting to hear those lines, and that when those lines are said, a vibrational context is spun through the Earth and all the hearts open up more.

It's like in the chapter of ***I Remember Union***: *The Story of Mary Magdalena* (hereinafter referred to as *I Remember Union,*) ". . . the people awaken softer and more dear." All the consciousness in place in this dimension is seeded from the design. And what are we reading to you? The design! Everybody is working at the same intentional level so that this job—this inside job—can be accomplished, so that the energy of the space of union and absolution—oneness, light, essence, charge, soul—can in a very beautiful way do what it has been ordained to do. This is different from doing a task. Doing what has been ordained is like following a wave, being a part of that wave, and understanding that you were born to be a part of that wave.

A lot of you are beginning to take yourself seriously. "I was born to be a critical part of this wave. No, I don't matter. No, I could disappear, and it would still happen." Why? We just told you. Because you're already a part of that wave, even if you're not in matter. Even if you take yourself out of the equation, you're in the equation. That's the beauty of this design. That's why it's going to work, because it's already been ordained and the pieces are already in place. And there's nothing you have to do about it, because as you instruct consciousness to work with you, all those pieces are put into the beautiful display case that turns everybody on. As that happens, it's catapulting that design into its next evolutionary state, which is not evolution as it was lived in a linear way, but is quantum leaps of consciousness. That's why somebody can walk in the door and say, "I'm ready." And you look at each other and say, "Where do we start? Can we use the word 'soul'? Can we use the word 'truth'? Can we use The Ones With No Names? Can we use 'light'? What does this person understand?" Then you realize that there is no language for this. It's not about what somebody gets, it's about what they essentially *are*.

It is beautiful because this is how you do your work walking down the street. It's how you do your work lying in bed doing nothing. It's all about a viable, sustainable organism that is comprised of every living thing in all dimensions. It means that no

~

*It's not about what somebody gets,
it's about what they essentially are.*

~

*The soul is the place
where free will
is lived at its ultimate.*

*If you wake up in the morning,
and you have so many things to decide
that you don't know what to do,
you're probably out of essence.*

matter what someone is doing, it's getting done. That's the secret we're hoping you get now.

Let's say that you had an appointment on February 23, 1995, with The Ones With No Names. That was all a part of the plan. All of the things that happened to you so that you would have that reading, happened because of many links made with many people, ideas, or circumstances, and all of sudden you realize, "This was orchestrated so infinitely that I have to throw my hands up and say, 'I give up! I really don't know how it all happened. I can't control this anymore. I couldn't have planned this with my mind. It's too big a deal, and yet the choices and decisions that I've made have brought me to this point.' "

So how does that work? "If I hadn't done it, what would have happened?" It is really interesting, because there is predestination, and yet there is free will. The soul is the place where free will is lived at its ultimate—by *being* light, organizing the consciousness around the charge of light, and living in conjunction with the design that brings the hologram into being. So that's the trajectory of how it works. When one is using free will outside the trajectory of the soul, one is deliberating, one is holding the force back. And yet, at the moment when the vibration of light kicks in, that person can be exactly where any of you are who feel you've been around the circuit for a long time.

All that is really necessary is the *charge*, and that's how it's equal; that's how it's foundationed; that's how there is no right or wrong. When you're in the charge, things flow, unfold, excite themselves, become spontaneous, coincidental, simultaneous, and manifestational. When one is not in the soul charge of the essential space of light and essence, decisions bring the mundane, decisions bring decisions, and more decisions, and more choices.

If you wake up in the morning, and you have so many things to decide that you don't know what to do, you're probably out of essence. If you wake up in the morning and there's nothing for you to do but carry that charge and live that consciousness, you're probably in essence, or living your calling. So simplify everything, simplify it all.

And again nothing is right or wrong. It's either in the flow of productivity, creativity, sustenance, charge, energy and proliferation, or it's boring, hard, difficult, or struggle. When one is able to see oneself as a dynamic light field, then one can say, "Oh, I'm in the difficult place, so I will affirm 'I am light' more times right now." It's about switching tracks. One can switch a track and feel differently just by switching that track. It isn't that one has to in any way *change* oneself. If one doesn't want to change, or feels that to change would be too hard, or take too much time, one may refuse to incorporate light. Not wanting to do something hard makes it hard, and it doesn't happen. As one thinks about change, one can realize that change does not have to be hard. Change is not something in and of itself that is a prerequisite for anything. It is the experience of changing from one dynamic to the other that's important.

Many times the words, intention, definitions, or belief systems *about* something make it difficult or struggle-full for someone to be in full soul, when really all it is, is shifting perspective, which is magic—changing consciousness at will. So magically, one can move from one circuit or one track to another in the twinkling of an eye by making that choice to be light. It's fundamentally simple, and that's why on many levels the parameters that people will attain will be much greater. They're going to say, "I tried to do this twenty years ago, and it didn't work, and now it's so simple that I can't believe it's actually happened." There will be a lot of stories going around about the old style of initiation, because in this process nothing needs to take time. Nothing is hard, struggle is not necessary. Each individual has the *absolute power* to affect the capacity of their own charge.

Whereas they may have thought before that they needed to go to a guru to get that charge, they won't need to do that anymore. It's one of the reasons we're going to phase out our process here, and give you lots of energy and charge beforehand, so that you can feel what that's like. Not that we're giving you the charge because you don't have it, rather, *we're giving you the charge as a body of light, so that you can all tap into that body of light and feel what that's about, and take it out into the world—primarily so that you can learn to charge your own charge.*

And when you charge your own charge, the destiny that you chose before you came, in the Swing Between Worlds, is manifest through you as light in form. The union of all is the reality for all, and that which you have come to affect becomes the fulfillment of your design and the fulfillment of the hologram—the peace of a million years of dreaming, accomplished in each of you, as you choose to charge your light.

~

*Magic—
changing consciousness
at will.*

~

*Each individual
has the absolute power
to affect the capacity
of their own charge.*

~

Grounding:
Connecting
the Above and the Below

THE SON AND DAUGHTER OF THE DIVINE come into form from the choice of the infinite to manifest in a way that has never been accorded before. So as each of you comes to this dimension, you come with the charge of the consciousness of that creation to be in form differently than before. In the year of 1900, we implanted the "seed of light," which is the capacity to vision—to see and to design as gods—into the souls of humanity. The technology you have experienced since then is because of your vision. It comes from other dimensions also, and yet it comes directly into humanity now because you have accorded, in your evolution, that you are ready to unify humanity, technology, and creation simultaneously.

As each of you moves forward and creates a different world, it is important that you carry with you this charge, creating your contribution from the one to the many. In making this contribution, carry with you the charge of the good of all, as if your actions were resplendent with the courage, with the caution, and with the consistency of creation. Create with honor, as if each of your actions were intended to support the whole, because you are responsive to the whole.

As you were evolving in free will, you made personal choices. You chose what you could do, and what actions you could take to foster your individual essence. In the coming time, from 2005 to 2016, you will be acting literally as free agents to discern, in each action, what it is that creation wants expressed. Now each of you is refining the vibration to more specifically *feel* the essence of what creation is. In the next ten years you'll be fostering that, fine tuning it, coming to terms with it. *What is it like to make a decision that is of God?* As the inherent space of that creation becomes manifest, you will act as a group consciousness of God.

Each of you will have the opportunity to share in the creative capacity in much the same way that we share in the creative capacity, by sustaining your bodies of light to create the space of truth and

~

The circuitry of my body defines itself as creation.

~

*Between
1995 and 2005
you're preparing to work as
One instrument,
One force,
One aspect of being.*

*It is
important
for you to
ESTABLISH
this experience as
Community,
because
it is the way in which
the
Many
can practice
being
the
One.*

order in your dimension, from your dimension. This is the gift that God gives you, as you manifest your light. It is not only that each of you individually fosters that light, charges your essence, opens it out, and lives from the soul. You also make foundation, literally, as an individual. The closer you are to the refinement of light in form, the more contagious is that experience to others, and the more the wave of critical mass begins to manifest through each of you so that you are the whole in motion and in action.

In 2005, there is a completely revised edition of humanity. You will be implementing, striving for, maintaining, eliciting, and augmenting the whole in each motion, in each breath, in each choice, and in each point of actualization or manifestation. Between 1995 and 2005 you're preparing to work as one instrument, one force, one aspect of being. And yes, you have time to practice. Yet it is imperative for you to understand where your individual refinement will lead you so that you are augmenting the process with as many individuals as possible. Experience this, practice it, initiate it, sustain it, and feel the results of the many beating as one heart.

It is important for you to establish this experience as community, because it is the way in which the many can practice being the one. In the leadership and co-creative process, in sustaining and foundationing this new type of dimension, the way that union creates itself in and among you, sustains the model for what will happen as the integrity of all of the lights shine forth with one ray of consciousness.

Osmosis

See yourself as a field of energy merging as light. In composition it looks like sunlight on water, and creates the experience of union, oneness, and community in the body. This is osmosis—the experience of dancing, oscillating frequency, unfolding and flowing to produce results consistent with the experience of union between matter and human form, or between the Earth and the circuits of the body.

Being sunlight on water osmotically, gives a message. It says, "I can change form any time I choose, and in so doing, practice the inherent essence that I carry—which is formless." An oscillatory frequency—the vibration of being many particles at once—creates the experience of moving out and in simultaneously and provides the awareness of how to move and shapeshift energy. Many of you will come to this point of reality in this new time, changing your form and moving your energy as a part of your composition.

Sunlight on water is creation in motion. The more you think of yourselves in this way, the more easily this leap of consciousness and faith is facilitated. It is quantum in nature and brings one to the experience of oscillating as light.

Light has no boundary, no limit, no capacity as you've thought of capacity, because it supersedes all capacity—has the capacity of everything. So as light, you do not stop with your body's edges, do not in any way have restrictions on your wattage. You are not in any way diminished by anything, so you do not get tired, you do not get old, you do not forget things, you do not hear absently. You are present, fully and alive, for there is no reason to diminish capacity—because inherently, again, you are creation in motion.

Sunlight on water is creation in motion.

The Importance of Grounding

Grounding revises the circuits by bringing light into the body so you can be more fully alive. During grounding, because the vibration of the experience of being pertains to more than one species—more than one point of reality— it is a consistent way to practice union.

The practice of grounding brings one into attunement with the oneness of Earth and is recommended on a daily basis. Grounding aligns and affiliates the circuitry of the human physical body with the circuitry of the Earth's etheric physical body, and is therefore a direct link with creation.

If you would ground for five to fifteen minutes a day, the circuitry of the body will define itself as creation.

Your vision improves, your hearing is more open, you see through the third eye into all dimensions, and your heart beats more distinctly in rhythm with the Earth's cycle and unfolding. The women's cycles are more regular and deep, labor is easier in childbirth, and the belief systems and conditions humanity has come to experience as normal, accelerate and smooth out, or balance.

What each individual experiences, then, is more rhythmic, more honored, more deeply *natural*, instead of being what is humanly normal. All pain ceases, all dis-ease moves out of the physical body, and the foundation that you've come to understand as normal feels antiquated, as if it were something that you read about in a history or herstory book, and have come to realize is not normal at all. It was the dark ages of the evolution of the soul, because when the soul orients itself through the charge of the consciousness, the vibration begins to act as light.

Grounding
An Exercise

The Essential Space

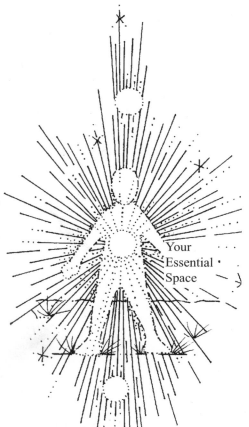

Your Essential Space

Earth's Essential Space

To begin the grounding experience, go outdoors, place your feet in direct contact with the Earth's back, and stand loosely with your feet shoulder-width apart, toes pointing straight ahead, your knees slightly flexed to allow for energy flow, arms and shoulders relaxed, and your eyes closed. Breathe deeply and gently from the Earth's essential space, her core, into your essential space in the center of your body, and then out the top of your head into *the* essential space of creation, and back down again, like a sliding, moving, rhythmical scale on the piano, up and down the instrument of peace. As you move each level, each design, each point of energy, you are accorded the absolute space of being, so that your reflection and refraction capabilities, what comes in and goes out, are absolute. Everything is absolute for you as you live.

As you play the scale of your instrument, you actually bridge and accelerate your connection *in* the above and the below simultaneously. This means that you are of neither place, which is the dream and intention of creation: that the form which is expressive of that point of creation is neither absent or present in the sense of matter and energy, and yet is both. The sacred marriage of the above and the below is humanity, and is the experience of energy in motion without bound.

The Yearning to Create

Each of you has the capacity to be completely your own marriage, the integration of the male and the female, creation and the Earth, or the form and the substance, however it is linked in your perspective. Each of you has your own reality around that, because each of you has set into motion a different part of creation. That is why there seem to be differences between you, and yet when creation comes upon itself, it acknowledges. It does not say, "Oh, you create differently than I do." If you think about it, would creation say to creation, "Oh, you are different than I am?" Creation would say to creation, "Ah, let us create. Ah, let us co-create. Ah, let us flow together, let us stabilize in this experience through oneness."

You will know when your human aspect is balanced by your divine aspect, when all you want to do with others is co-create. What can we do together? How can we foster the reality of oneness in motion? You will not distinguish this by saying, "Please spell out your intention. Please tell me how you choose to do your part. Please tell me what it is that you think is important." Those conversations will not take place, because as you come together there will be inherent cooperation. The experience will be such that each of you is so dynamically moved by the presence of the other, that all you can do is gleefully clap your hands and say, "Where is it that we are to go as we merge?"

The excitement of the yearning in each soul is for the critical mass of its own expression, and yet not solely its own expression: It is for the yearning of its expression in tandem with others, in effectiveness with others, in consciousness with others. That's why, when your essence is charged and you say, "Oh, this is my calling," the exciting thing is that it always involves somebody else. It always involves a way in which everyone will benefit, and it always, always supports all life and diminishes none. So the charge is, in an absolute sense, structured from purity. Purity of intent. If one person decides that what they have to give is separate from what others have to give or to receive, they will find themselves alone, because the supportive energy that is apparent now, and palpable on your planet, is this experience of cooperation. Each of you is now dynamically charged with blending your field of essential energy with the charge of your inherent soul-full space in a way that unifies all fields.

~

*Each of you has
set into motion
a different part of creation.
That is why there
seem
to be differences between you,
and yet when creation comes upon itself,
it acknowledges.
It does not say,
"Oh, you create differently than I do."
If you think about it,
would creation say to creation,
"Oh, you are different than I am?"
Creation would say to creation,
"Ah, let us create. Ah, let us co-create.
Ah, let us flow together, let us stabilize
in this experience
through
oneness."*

~

Dissolving Your Edges

Whatever holds you distinctly
separate
from what it is that is,
is really not.
So as you go forward,
you can experience that
whatever holds you apart
is the GLUE
to bring you together.

~

So the
words
that you have in your conditioning
that apply to your process,
become the experience
that will
bind
you to its resolution.

~

We are suggesting that you merge and blend your edges, so that each of you take those things that rub against others, and challenge those things. Look in the mirror. What is it that rubs? Take the words that come to you—ego, self-righteousness, jealousy, ineffectiveness, inadequacy, lack of self-worth—whatever words come, and rub them until you get the purest essence from them. See how those words could bind you instead of separating you. You are each responsive in this time, particularly in 1995 and 1996, to the experience of what your edges tell you about your yearning for merging, blending, and unifying. Instead of separating you, it is the glue that binds you together.

Whatever it is that your edges tell you, whatever words come, are just words. They have to do with whether or not you feel responsible, whether or not you remember, whether or not there is integration in the being. It is about whether or not you blend, whether or not you are unifying.

Whatever holds you distinctly separate from what it is that is, is really not. So as you go forward, you can experience that whatever holds you apart is the glue to bring you together.

Grounding allows you to merge and blend these edges so they ripple through you and flow within you and do not separate you or detract you from what is real. So the words that you have in your conditioning that apply to your process, become the experience that will bind you to its resolution. It's very lovely, because as you look in the mirror at yourself and experience, "I'm disappearing. I am becoming this fluid movement like sunlight on water," you say, "What's holding the shape the longest? What part of me, if I knew the outline of my being and I watched it dissipate, would disappear last?" In some people it would be the genitalia. They would last until the very last minute: "I couldn't disappear those, because I would not have my identity if I did not have this part of my body." Or it will be the mind: "Oh, I cannot let my mind go, because then I will not be distinguished from others." For some it would be the center of power, or the center of expression, or the shoulders: "I am responsible for too much to let go—to experience dissolution."

It's a very valuable tool of observation, for it is not important or suggested that you judge it, rather that you observe it. The edges you observe are societal—a conditioned reflex and response in each of you, and because each of you responds differently to light, to being, to motion, there will be part of you that is *more* pronounced. The objective is to *less* pronounce it, to make it more viably a part of what teaches you rather than that which sustains your separation.

As you flow together with your absolute oscillation and see your frequency dancing all over, you actually understand what parts of you resist—hold out, define themselves—and want you to know why they are important enough for you to allow them. When you know why you allow them, you will know what supports the intention of their integration. Foundationally then, this becomes the vehicle of your transformation, where you actually apply the principles energetically. When you see what is supportive of the separation, you erase it. The objective is to take the hand or the invisible arm of consciousness and rub it out. As you rub it out, you begin to understand that it's becoming more pronounced. It's telling you, "Wait a minute, wait a minute. Do I want to do this? Do I want to disappear? If I disappear, what happens?"

You don't have to work on the ego and the personality and the objectives of the world. You only have to say, "*I am light, and light I shall remain.*" While you're grounding, when you're erasing, you're saying, "*I am light, and light I shall remain.* This is the part that links me to the light, because I wanted and needed to remember it the most, so that as I transform this into an experience that supports light, my karma is released, my patterns are dissolved, my thought systems are revised." You are a revised edition!

As you experience your own revised edition, joy is born, because the wisdom and knowledge that you carry in the displacement of your consciousness by separation is reunited with its original intention. It is a way of fostering cooperation, because as you erase the edges of your consciousness you are working with others also at the same time, because that's what life is about! If you work with yourself first, nonjudgmentally, finding the glue that keeps things together for you, and you dispel that glue so that it works all the way through your system and no longer makes edges, then you become the framework of seeing in the mirror clearly, which is the experience of love. And as you see in the mirror clearly and have no edges, there is an absolute knowing that you are in union.

You are foundationing a new conception of humanity. The way that the light body accelerates its charge is through the movement of all that has, to that point, held one separate, and its resolution. The *process* of resolution is as important as experiencing resolution,

~

*There will be part of you that is **more** pronounced.*
*The objective is to **less** pronounce it,*
to make it more viably
a part of what teaches you
rather than that which sustains your separation.

~

Joy is born,
because
the wisdom and knowledge
that you carry in the
displacement of your consciousness
by separation
is reunited with its original intention.

~

It is a way of
fostering cooperation,
because as you erase
the edges of your consciousness you
are working with others also
at the same time,
because that's what life is about!

~

because that's where learning comes, and the learning is going to be invaluable when it is time to apply the principles of oneness in motion.

If you think about yourself as a fluid vehicle of conscious light, you immediately understand that all of the dynamics and frameworks you've been working with in your thought, your philosophy, your ideology, your religions, your families, and in all societal precepts and concepts, are based upon the fact that when union occurs, there is the dissolution of edges. To many people this seems to be the ideology or the utopia of the "new age," and people say, "It's impossible. We think in too many different ways. We have too many different ground rules and places where we disagree."

Everything that you disagree about can be broken down or boiled down into dissolving edges. When you dissolve an edge, you set into motion a very rapid oscillation. When one is in transformation, when one is in the state of samadhi or nirvana, one has no edges. Think about it, it's very simple. Each of you thinks, "Maybe I'll attain a certain amount of light and a certain amount of consciousness, but will I ever be edgeless? Will I ever be judgmentless? Will I ever be absolute?" *Yes, you will.* It's as simple as dissolving those edges. Look at them, see them, allow them, and forge them as if you were painting the sunlight on top of them as you erase them, because that will bond you to the resolution of that space. It is not about understanding it literally, subconsciously, or mentally. It is not about saying, "I did this, because this person did that." It is to state clearly, as you are grounding, "*I am edgeless,*" and as that experience is manifest in the consciousness it is to be tireless, to be out of the ordinary, to be in the experience of this absolute, where endorphins are released.

Living Agelessly

Endorphins are that part of the consciousness which says, "Yes!" You do not need to exercise or make love or have a massage to have endorphins released. Endorphins are released when the osmotic fluid in the body reaches a critical mass in tandem with the choice for union. As you stand and ground, you create levels of endorphic activity which substantiate the essential space of the grounded being through time and space. You have no time that you live specific to

*It's as simple
as dissolving those edges.
Look at them,
see them,
allow them,
and forge them as if you were
painting the sunlight on top of them
as you erase them,
because
that will bond you
to the resolution of that space.*

the year, the date, or how many years you have. You are consistent with an absolute reality that is timeless.

You are ageless, and as the endorphins are released there's excitement, because the glue that holds the parts of you together that have been separate or have been created from separation, is the place in you of healing or acceleration, or foundation. As that is healed, as it is fostered through the same intention of vibration, it is cooperative in nature, from all levels of biology and systematology. There are treatises that come from an agreement between the above and below, between the body and the heart and the mind, and those levels that have agreed to perform together begin responding simultaneously to you as the common denominator.

People ask: "How can I live gracefully, stop aging, and support the experience of a dis-ease-free body? How can I be completely accepting, totally honorable, creating from integrity, living in cooperation, joyfully expanding all moments, and be happy? How can I do all of this? These levels need to be unified for me to *feel* the joy, so the knowledge can act through me. How can I remember my grace, and my state of divinity, and live it fully?" Or they ask, "I could do this, but could I do that? Could I have that, and also have this?" What one forgets is that the system is based on unity. It *began* as a unified field. In representing the integrity of that consciousness, if one chooses to sustain that field, it will come again into its original design.

This is exactly what we said about light. If you hold the light, you will transform. If you carry the charge, you will essentially be born. When you are born, the soul completely lives the design that was inherent before you began, and as you began—and all of that is already done! The same thing is true of the human capacity to live spontaneously, to open to total vision, and to live agelessly in a state of grace, where divinity paves the way, and union and the experience of cooperation and co-creation is the absolute. Because that's the way it is designed.

When one grounds and smooths out the edges and feels the actual boost of that endorphic level coming into the body, opening the areas of zeal, consciousness, creation, and heart, you feel, "Yes! This is normal! This is natural!"

~

You are ageless,
and as the endorphins are released
there's excitement,
because the
glue that holds the parts of you
together
that have been separate
or have been created from separation,
is the place in you
of healing or acceleration,
or foundation.

~

What one forgets
is that the system is based on unity.
It began *as a unified field.*
In representing
the integrity of that consciousness,
if one chooses to sustain that field,
it will come again
into its original design.

~

*Sustaining life
through life
and through light,
rather than technology.*

You are replacing the dogma of your conditioning of six generations that you receive from your mother at the time of birth about what's normal, and you are becoming what is natural.

You feel organic, you come from a garden with no pesticides and no abnormal fertilizers. You vibrate in a way that says, "I'm a raw carrot, and I'm pure," or, "I'm a raw beet, and I'm pure." Coming together with this endorphic level, you're zinging all the places in the body biologically, physiologically, and anatomically. The experience becomes more than thought, more than an intention from the soul or from the charge of essence or from the light itself being carried through you, i.e. "I am a carrier of light." You *are* light at that moment because when the experience of this process defines itself in the vehicle cellularly, viscerally, anatomically, in molecule and in atom, you remember how many strands of DNA you were born with naturally—how many levels of your consciousness were opened naturally.

What was the foundation that you came into this experience with originally? As you're grounding, you can affirm, "I am original. I am natural, and I have ordained my life as the expression of creation." As you come to these places of accordance, you are opening windows to your original design biologically. This goes along with recognizing your original design etherically, because when the etheric and the biologic come together, the inherent vibratory rate creates a union of force fields which allows for the movement of consciousness *through* force fields.

When your fields unify together, and the above and below are in oneness, there is no physical boundary to your energy or its flow or intention. This is how one moves a mountain. We have spoken to many of you throughout the years about the possibilities of moving rain from one part of your world to the other, moving dryness from one part to the other, stabilizing the force fields, creating food where there is no soil, sustaining potable water where there is no source— sustaining life through life and through light, rather than technology.

Creating What is Natural

We are entering a time of great change. Why is it happening? Why is it that human beings, as a society, now have an opportunity to cooperate and create differently, from the *experience* of being rather than the technology of being? The reason that you are being "challenged" in your society to create that which is impossible, is because you are now creating what is natural. What is natural to you? What is it that you need to live naturally? You will create these things, not because you have studied for many years at a university where these things are understood mathematically and in physics, but rather that you have studied for many millennia in the school of light in motion, and your technology is the expression of light in motion.

As you stand and ground, the answers to the questions that are most pressing for humanity will come through your body and be directed toward the sources of your Earth that need to feel that naturalness again.

The foundation of what you carry in your consciousness will be birthed, and you will know and remember the natural way of being before there was war, before there was violence, before there were socioeconomic status structures, before the almighty dollar, and before worth was accorded by things instead of knowings. This is important, for it brings grace again into humanity and allows it to be simultaneously experienced by many.

Your power base is shifting from who is in power to empowerment of soul, self-realization, self-actualization, and self-potentiation. When one self-potentiates and self-realizes, one becomes the motion of creation in action. Each individual osmotically moves their own level of reality into truth. The co-creative capacity will foster a responsiveness so that all the force fields, all the levels, all individuals, all species, and all the humanities, work together. It is all one interrelated system. And you find that interrelated system *when* you are living from that experience of the profound being as sunlight dancing and oscillating on water, which is osmotic. As each of you lives that oscillation, immediately sparked inside of you is the memory of the oneness of all dimensions dancing together.

We encourage you to dance on the land and move your bodies physically and psychically in preparation for the movement of the total consciousness, because that is where the union will take place. The foundation of what is occurring for you is the movement of energy. It is *consciously* choosing and *discerning* its path of least resistance. It is also the place inside of you which has the most affiliation for being tuned. It's the part of the body that calls out to you the loudest, the part of the body that says, "Fix me, heal me, touch me, blend me." These parts of the body are connected as you

~

*The reason
that you are being "challenged"
in your society to create
that which is impossible,
is because
you are now creating
what is natural.
What is natural to you?
What is it that you need
to live naturally?*

~

*As each of you
lives that oscillation,
immediately sparked inside of you
is the memory
of the oneness
of all dimensions dancing together.*

~

experience the oscillation of erasing your edges. That part which expresses to you the most loudly is tuning you the most intricately to your contribution, to your affiliation.

As you create these experiences daily, as recommended, you find you no longer have edges, your boundaries of perception disappear, and you can see into all worlds. You live as one of all nations, and are advised continually of the current status of the experience of creation as it is unfolding. So you'll know things; you'll remember things; and you'll function as one who knows.

The Joy of Co-Creating

When you affiliate with other people, there is an immediate endorphin release, a charge of energy, and there's excitement! Excitement that you're together, and even more excitement that all of you are blending your edges so well that nothing needs to be adjusted continually in your experience to provide comfort.

When you are with individuals and you are so comfortable that you don't have to think about whether you're comfortable, there's excitement. Something gets born, because the energy is prolific rather than dissipatory in nature. If you are with individuals who dissipate your energy, move away from them and gravitate toward those whose energy fields support co-creation—being in creation at the same time. Your field of energy will then be enhanced by those around you. A charge of energy is exchanged which feels like someone supporting your charge.

It does not have to be mental support, emotional support, physical support, or sexual support, it is an *etheric* level of realization that you are being supported because you are working in tandem with others. You are all pulling your own weight at the same intensity, and because of that, there's comfort—nobody's pulling more weight than anybody else. All are supporting the intention to be at one with. Your life is then foundationed from this "charge," and the more of you who feel this, the more you attract those who will be with you in this experience. And it is your comfort level which will determine that.

As you blend and merge your edges you become consistently more available to others, and in that availability, yes, there is service, and yet the service does not drain you. It does not take energy from

---

*That part
which expresses to you the most
loudly
is
tuning you the most intricately
to your contribution,
to your affiliation.*

~

You'll function as one who knows.

~

*Co-creation—
being in creation at the same time.*

~

you because it is the service of comfort. In the new communities, what is viably sustained, very simply and naturally, is a high level of comfort. And as you enfold and embrace each other, there is a sense that each of you relies only on yourself and yet yourself is now becoming others. The edges are so well blended, there are no ways to distinguish between you. As we have said about community, your outer framework appears to others as one facet—one stone. It is multi-leveled, and yet no one can see where one facet begins and where it ends, because it looks like one facet. And yet, it is multi-faceted inside and appears as one space of union outside.

The foundation of this experience through grounding and through erasing your edges complements all of your work—work that has to do with think tanks, co-creation, systems theory, foundationing communities, sustainable agriculture and environments, because it's all the same thing. Instead of studying books to find out what you should do, the most important foundational piece is to sustain it all by being in the place where it all is, which is in the expression of your own edgeless, osmotic field of light in form.

There are no places in you that are untouched by this. Karma is revisited and released. Thought patterns are structured and restructured. Belief systems are turned inside out, like the proverbial pocket, so that you can see what's in there. Fear structures are overturned. Consciousness becomes what it is! There is nothing on any level that interferes with that consciousness—that takes it away from its own knowing. So the surprise here is that it's already there, and as you shake things out and turn them inside out, you say, "This is who I am, really. This is where I come from. This is what I've always known. This is what I've always been striving for. There is nothing here that I have to do." These suggested exercises are ways to experience the I AM.

And that's when excitement is absolute! When the bottoms of your feet are always tingling with information and the heart is always expanding with more compassion and more of the experience of being in the merging. The head enlarges so big that you can't think anymore, you can only scope out all that is and see how it correlates and bring it together so that it manifests in a way that is full of knowledge. Your belief is only in light and nothing else, and there is no part of you held away from itself.

If you think about it, what each of you has done in your human capacity is hold a part or parts of yourself away from the rest of you.

~

And as you enfold and embrace each other, there is a sense that each of you relies only on yourself and yet yourself is now becoming others. The edges are so well blended, there are no ways to distinguish between you.

~

It is multi-faceted inside and appears as one space of union outside.

~

Consciousness becomes what it is!

~

Your belief is only in light and nothing else, and there is no part of you held away from itself.

~

*The parts
that you hold away from yourself
are the parts that as you erase,
the glue is released,
the knowing is there,
the affirmation supports the
experience, and you're home free.*

~

*There is no greater tribute to
the One
than choosing to cooperate in comfort,
continually co-creating
that which resources life,
brings water,
brings the inherent ingredients
which sustain all the levels
simultaneously.*

~

*Technology usually depletes
one level to serve another.
That's the key
to why technology itself
cannot continue
as it has been designed by the mind.*

~

What we mean when we suggest that you aggregate, is to put all your parts together so they fit like the seamless edges of the pyramid. It's the experience of coming together in wholeness so dimensionally that you are a congruent field and everything fits with everything else. The parts that you hold away from yourself are the parts that as you erase, the glue is released, the knowing is there, the affirmation supports the experience, and you're home free.

In erasing your edges you can now bring yourself more fully into your truth, and into those edges which are ready to be tuned like the strings of the piano. You can say, "Ah yes, I can hear this—a violin tuning, a piano tuning. I can hear this. I feel how I am coming together with my inherent naturalness." The excitement that now generates in your being is because you are prolific. You can continue to co-create in ways that you could never continue to procreate. You can co-create forever and ever and ever. It doesn't matter what dimension you're in, you can always co-create.

You can trust the joy and excitement that comes up in you when you think about being ageless, and painless, and bottomless, and topless, when you experience that you don't have any boundaries, and all that is, is what you are. It is not just living the divinity, it's being in that state of grace which honors the creation constantly.

Creating Sustainable Systems

There is no greater tribute to the One than choosing to cooperate in comfort, continually co-creating that which resources life, brings water, brings the inherent ingredients which sustain all the levels simultaneously. Technology usually depletes one level to serve another. That's the key to why technology itself cannot continue as it has been designed by the mind.

As the new technology emerges—which unifies fields and communicates by linking mechanisms between organisms—everyone and everything will make a contribution and will say, "*What will serve the whole will serve me in this moment, or I will not be served.*"

So if you are in the midst of something, doing something that doesn't serve every component, then it's important for you to say, "What would serve that component? I will not partake in this meal unless it serves all components. I will not participate in this commodity or in this project or in this process unless it serves all, simultaneously." The barometer, the scale, the valuing of what works, what one participates in, is based upon that sustainable process of unification. What is unifying the whole here? How does that serve to provide mechanisms for the growth of all parts?

Each system that you work with, whether it's education, religion, societal, family, health, crop growing, energy generation, whatever it is, see it in a system process first, in a biosphere, and say, "How does this work to sustain the other components?" Before you create or build something, before you sustain it, before you do a project, ask the question of yourself and your group and your conscious experience, "How does this sustain life? Or does it?"

If it takes from one to give to the other, it's technology without heart. The foundation of this new experience is that everything is considered. Everything is a part of what is designed, and reflected, whether it is fifty years or five hundred years in the future, or fifty or five hundred years in the past, whether it's another climate, another planet, or another life system. You can no longer say, "It's okay for now, and we can sustain it for awhile, but we'll have to worry about it five hundred years from now; but by then they'll know how to take care of it." That's what's been happening since the beginning: "We'll just do this now, and let the consequences find themselves, and find the people who are deciding to karmically live with them, and then they can decide how they want to live with it, and experience it, and sustain it, and change it." None of that is viable because it considers life in a way that supports only the intention of those present, and not those imagined or sustained in other frameworks. It is nonapplicable to life. If you have to stamp it "nonapplicable to life" five hundred years from now, then it doesn't pass the test.

The integrity becomes that you are constantly reflecting into the experience of your own awareness, saying, "There has to be a way that sustains life forever, and ever and ever." And when we find that, what do we find? We find the hologram! The difference in succeeding in the normal way and succeeding in the natural way is that the normal way says, "This will work for now; we don't have to worry about anybody else. That's not part of our consideration."

In the natural way, succeeding means that you find the solution that was placed in the design at the beginning and you incorporate it, which brings the design into being and is the fruition of all the intention of creation as it unfolds.

You are beings of light who are incorporating the experience of

~

The barometer, the scale,
the valuing of what works,
what one participates in,
is based upon
that sustainable process of unification.
What is unifying the whole here?
How does that serve
to provide mechanisms for the growth
of all parts?

~

If it takes
from one to give to the other,
it's technology without heart.

~

"There has to be a way
that sustains life forever,
and ever and ever."
And when we find that,
what do we find?
We find the hologram!

~

the highest framework of light intention. Light in-tension. You are in an experience of a rubber band, and no matter where you move the rubber band through the experience of that channel, you're going to find that it's one rubber band. As it comes to you from the end, you see the beginning. You remember that this is what we thought about *before* we designed this reality. We're now in this reality and can see where it's going to end up, and it's all of the same cloth. It's all the same vibrational field of light, and when I as an individual stand in that viable space of light, what happens to me?

You Are Immortal

What does *one in* creation mean? What does being *one with* creation mean? What does co-creating mean? It means that you are in the vibration that has always been and will always be. In that space, solving problems doesn't mean learning anything, as much as it is re-solving, remembering, and re-cognizing, This is how the vibration of a system sustains itself immortally, and you are all immortal. When the changes occur from the experience of being in a body with edges, to being light—formless, oscillating in light with creation—immortality is a viable fuel which can power your travels throughout all dimensions. What you need to recognize, remember, resolve, re-Source, and orchestrate in that experience is available to you from that place of sustainability. What is immortality but sustainability? You're sustaining your force field through time.

Many of you read about galactic processes that human beings are now or will soon experience—how strands of DNA will be available, etc. The nuts and bolts of it is that you are alive through time with no separate place to hang your hat, so that you are experiencing what it's like to be *immortal*, in *form*. Immortality doesn't mean that you die and come back, and then you die and come back, and then one time perhaps you remember, "Oh, I died, and I came back." Immortality means you never die! You are sustainable as a field of energy in creation.

If you can grasp that concept as a secret that allows you free access to everything, then you have it made. Portals will open for you that you don't need a combination for, to study hard for, or buy admission to—portals that belong to you, the portals that take you into your simultaneous reality, where there are no conditions, no

---

*In that space,
solving problems
doesn't mean learning anything,
as much as it is
re-solving, remembering
and re-cognizing,
This is how the vibration of a system
sustains itself immortally.*

~

*What is immortality but sustainability?
You're sustaining your force field
through time.*

~

*Immortality means you never die!
You are sustainable
as a field of energy in creation.*

~

*If you can grasp that concept as a secret
that allows you free access to everything,
then you have it made.*

~

limitations, no strands of DNA left out and memory that doesn't serve. It's a place of being where everything is available. It is living in creation as a viable field of order around you.

It's like saying, "If I go and stand over here in this field, with the apples and the apple trees, and the deer, I'm going to experience what it's like to be a deer, and be an apple, and whatever." It's that simple. If you go into immortality, you basically experience being immortal, because you're in the field of immortality. You can go into a field where there's hay and sunflowers and beautiful wildflowers, and you can go into another field where there are rows upon rows of orchestrated flowers that have been planted, seed after seed after seed. When you're in each of those fields, you experience what's in those fields, and you won't think that's unusual. You say with your mind that you know where it is, and you go, you travel there. Traveling in the fields of immortality is no different. You say, "As I travel, everything is available to me."

This opens you to a concept of immortality you may not have fully comprehended before: because you are immortal, as you work on the planet to create solutions in the fields of order, you are not limited to the twentieth century. You're not limited to what you think your education is in this lifetime, or what you think your experience is. There's no way to limit immortality, because by its very definition it means that you continue forever and ever and ever.

When grounding, you experience the foundation of your life through time and space, and order and being, so that your *presence* supports all knowledge of all time and space, through order and being. Immortality really means that you don't forget it, you don't misplace it, do not limit your access to everything that is.

Being in the space of the grounding, rubbing the edges and erasing those spaces and feeling where you are now coming into congruence, opens up your upper thresholds which have to do specifically with immortality. When you go into meditation and transition states, alpha and deeper levels of consciousness, you go into the synchronous motion of consciousness in movement, through time and space, in order and being. That's why you go there, to actually defy gravity, to defy logic, to defy aging, disease, judgment, separation and pain. That is why humanity goes to God, or the Goddess, or to the infinite place of creation. That is why humanity looks for answers and solutions from spirit.

As you come into those experiences of immortality, the levels of consciousness that you ordain osmotically from sunlight on water

Traveling in the fields of immortality is no different. You say, "As I travel, everything is available to me."

There's no way to limit immortality, because by its very definition it means that you continue forever and ever and ever.

Being in the space of the grounding, rubbing the edges and erasing those spaces and feeling where you are now coming into congruence, opens up your upper thresholds which have to do specifically with immortality.

It is a calling to order,
and the
difference
is that you will want to do this.

~

Everything
in the continuum of immortality
feeds your present essence.

~

begin to surround you and carry you into the ethereal space of your own destiny and your own birth. What you can prepare to experience, particularly between the years of 1995 and 2000, is total recall. Now that does not mean that you say, "Oh, I did this to whomever in this year, and so I have to pay a penance for that, and this is why I had this karma, and that's why I did this, and this is why I have this responsibility issue and I look it up in the book, and it says, 'martyr complex', or, 'messianic complex.'" It is more that the total recall puts the items of experience into perspective. It's a big W h o o s h i n g! sensation. You feel, "Yeah, I got it! I got it all now. I didn't get one lifetime. I got it all. And when I got it all, when I got the total recall, it felt like a release of endorphins, orgasm, massage, high from running, high from exercising." The experience is one of absolute knowing. "I do not die. I do not end. I did not fail. It will work, it's all done. I am an instrument of light. I can tune my instrument. I can be comfortable and co-create. I can sustain life. I can honor all points of reality—and in that experience I *am* the light, I *am* the way. I *am* the truth. I *am* the order which holds it together. I now know what I am here to create, experience, and sustain."

As the experience of being viable becomes authentic, you are not considering this as a job, or as work, or as a task. You are considering this as the way and means to provide you with the experience of your inherent beingness. It's not a vocation, or an avocation, it is a calling to order, and the difference is that you will want to do this. This is about becoming what you are, not striving to do something that will support other people's opinion of you, or buy you bread. This is about pleasure. It's about sustaining your life in such a way that you consider all life as much as your own. Every time you do a grounding exercise, all life supports you. Everything in the continuum of immortality feeds your present essence. This is the lifetime that gets all of the thrust, all of the momentum, all of the intention, all of the energy, all of the pleasure, all of the consciousness, all of the light, all of the truth, all of the order. This is the time of remembering! Each of you, in that space of total recall, provides an opportunity for the foundation of a new world to be born.

You'll walk down the street and see someone, and know exactly who they have been to you every single time they've been in your life, *every* single time—what you did and did not do, say, feel, experience, challenge, and resolve. In the twinkling of an eye the resolution will be there, because you're in total recall, which means there's no judgment and no karma possible. It's the kind of life that just keeps getting cleaner and clearer, more authentic, and more comfortable, where the spaces are responding to each other so that a completion is possible, meaning resolution.

The meaning has come back to solution, it is fluid, it supports the charge, opens the essence, brings forth the soul, and then what you're to do together in this time is also as clear as whatever you did before.

It doesn't require you to think about anything, it only requires presence. Giant billboards and screens will open up and you'll say, "I get this, this makes a lot of sense." The foundation of this experience is that we are to do this together as action, as energy, as resolution, and as creation, and it's done as it starts. Then you can play it out like a piece of music that you learned on the piano, which means that the practicing is done, and you can enjoy the sound. You don't have to say, "Did I play the note at the right time? No, you should have played that note. Maybe we should have practiced it separately first, and then practiced it together, and then maybe we'd be able to enjoy it." The enjoyment time is upon you. That's really good news!

In relationship with other human beings, other galactic spaces, creatures, Earth elements, essences and kingdoms, the practicing time is done. Just enjoy the sound. Just enjoy the fact that you can be comfortable. Even as you're creating, you're sustaining, and saying, "We're going to create sustainable agriculture for the rest of the time that is allotted to this dimension. All the generations that come after this one are going to be able to live an experience that's sustainable." Then you think, "Wait a minute. We have to start from scratch. We gotta figure this out. We've never done this before."

The good news is that when you go into the future and into the past and marry those together, the solution is evident at that point. Remember, in immortality is the key to all considerations, because you've already done it once. It's already accorded you. This is the time to remember it and activate *through creation*. This isn't the time to slog and struggle. That was done with, at the end of 1991.

There is no resistance in the universe to your totally remembering everything, individually and collectively. You will serve to unite the fields of consciousness in existence from all time and in all time.

The good news is that you are creating in this context a life system that will provide you with everything you need, that will ground you to the experience of being light in form, and that will in a comfortable, sustainable manner, resolve all time and space in this

The meaning has come back to solution,
it is fluid,
it supports the charge,
opens the essence,
brings forth the soul,
and then
what you're to do together in this time is
also as clear as
whatever you did before.

~

Remember,
in immortality is the key
to all considerations,
because you've already done it once.
It's already accorded you.
This is the time to remember it
and activate through creation.
This isn't the time
to slog and struggle.
That was done with,
at the end of 1991.

~

To sustain this level of commitment,
GROUNDING *is the key*
because it links through the circuits,
through the current,
and through the osmotic fields,
molecularly, everything that is now.

~

The result is an exciting, prolific,
sustainable model of co-creation
and cooperation that brings the
design into its fullness
and its absolute expression.

~

dimension. It's a big clearing of all, of everything, from all, into all. It's absolute. To sustain this level of commitment, grounding is the key because it links through the circuits, through the current, and through the osmotic fields, molecularly, everything that is now.

Five to fifteen minutes a day, minimum time, will provide the keys to accessing all that we have spoken of, and will sustain a field of energy in each of you that will dispel and disintegrate anything that is illusion, that is belief, that is thought, or that is fear. Squeaky clean is the result—individually. Collectively, it is the place of sustainable creation where heart and technology can work together to provide a space where life is honored and all time comes to serve the process, and all knowledge supports the unfolding. The result is an exciting, prolific, sustainable model of co-creation and cooperation that brings the design into its fullness and its absolute expression.

Again, it is God in form. It is each of you living the totalness of your being as was chosen by the Gods *before even God began.*

Living Life
Comfortably

W E HAVE COME HERE TO SERVE HUMANITY, as humanity has come to serve the Source. And so we are a link from the Source to humanity and again from humanity "back" to the Source. We have come here for the express purpose of "greasing the wheel" ourselves, and to assist in the furthering and supporting, or foundationing, of the design in motion. And so our particular perspective on the universe comes from the ease and comfort of the expression and experience of what it's like to grease the wheel, and to be greased by the wheel.

From the beginning of 1986, when asked about our purpose for being with you, the words of "the one speaking," Flo Aeveia, have been, "Their job, or their intention, is to make you more aware of your pattern so that you understand what you have come to do in such a way that it is lived more comfortably." Comfort is very important from the vantage point of the entire being, because when someone says, "I am comfortable," it basically says that all of your levels have discussed this and are experiencing balance—the experience of being "okay," as you would say in your language. Our place is the comfort place—the place where things are in balance, and where, as things proceed, the foundation of consciousness and the expression of that consciousness are also comfortable.

As each of you works with the techniques and processes in this *Manual for Soul-full Living*, it also becomes a condition of your life that you are comfortable. We would like to program that in from the beginning, so that your feeling about yourself is that of comfort. That's a very important way to view your reality, because it means inherently that you have everything that you need. You know the old saying, "She is of comfortable means."

When you are comfortable, your body feels taken care of, supported and honored, and you are at peace with your emotion. There is no-thing that you seek, by definition. (That's what comfort means.) As you experience your spiritual transformation, feel it and identify with it in your awareness as comfortable. Our job is to help in that comfort, to help bring the peace inside for each of you so that

*The future seeds my moments
and I am comfortable.*

~

*Comfort is promised
to those souls
who live in union.*

~

level of comfort is attained and maintained. Each of you, as you follow through with your consciousness, feels taken care of at the same time.

We have for many moons discarded the idea of poverty being associated with spiritual experience or pathways. This is because not having, or believing that you're not supposed to have, would mean that on some level the comfort would be absent or diminished. This is not the intention of the universe as we are perceiving it and experiencing it. This means that the re-Sourcing that you have experienced from the receiving, from the allowing, and from the foundationing, begins to come to this moment and receive its intonation, bringing you wealth on all levels. Comfortable means bringing you the experience of having what it is that you've always sought. And yet, it is not from searching as much as it is from the experience of accessing what you already have. It is similar to accessing the total recall that we spoke of in the chapter on receiving.

It is the phenomenon of being in accordance with everything, which foundations the framework and puts it together so that your conscious direction is, in a very beautiful way, unfolding and blooming, and re-Sourcing itself. There is a formula that, if you put three points of energy together and hold the vibration in the same pattern, you will manifest instantly. These three points are: the Absolute, or "past-past"; the present moment, or "present-present"; and the future of the hologram, or "future-future."

Being of comfortable means, signifies that you are in all time simultaneously and are aligning with the consciousness of *the having*. You are re-Sourcing from the universe, and that makes a foundation which links you again to the comfort, the understanding, and the relationship of being in oneness with all things. If you are experiencing or expressing any level of poverty in any of your process, regardless of what that is in your perception (and it is a subjective thing), it is about separation—pure and simple separation.

Comfort is promised to those souls who live in union. The Findhorn community in Scotland is a perfect example of that process. You can grow crops so big that people come from all over the world to see them, and you can sell them at the market, and feed your people with them, and even charge admission. It's the experience of being entirely in the consciousness of each moment. This functions as a way in which the threshold between dimensions is accorded.

There's cooperation in growing tomatoes the size of grapefruit, or roses the size of cantaloupes. There are those interfacing, interlocking pieces of consciousness that are adjusting constantly to each other to provide natural instead of normal. As you create the phenomenon of your own synthesis with truth, the result is miracle. Once the experience of that foundation of union is established in the individual, then groups begin to live in that same framework. And that's very important to understand. If you're in a group, and you need to manifest money, it's an individual process to identify where the experience of separation occurs in the being. Being in the group, in and of itself, will not manifest the money, will not manifest the process.

The individual must first be in union before the experience of proliferation happens in larger numbers. It makes sense that way. It is consciously putting each person right there in the space and saying, "Are you in union with everything? Is there anything that you're not absolutely in union with? If so, bring it together." Re-Source it, receive that space, each, individually, and then the group will receive that space. It's about taking response-ability for each of your experiences, with the integrity of being in oneness with all things. It is foundational to the work that each of you in a community situation or in a group process, whether that be a family or a small community, strive diligently to align your own consciousness so that you are one, non-separate from all aspects of re-Sourcing.

For each of you to originate your experience in vibration, means to go home to the original place of creation and say, "I am now in the moment of my first choice. I am now in my first conscious point of awareness and I choose to feel that vibration." You then immerse yourself in that vibration, as if in each moment *what you're feeling is the key to where you're going.* Then, as you feel that vibration, you allow that vibration to come into you. And again, it's receiving that vibration by opening yourself, immersing yourself in it, and letting the fluids of the universe come and pour into you. This is another way of seeing and feeling who you really are. It's important at a cellular level, to be orchestrating an identification with something other than your current personality, because your current personality is conditioned to believe in separation. It's not good or bad, it just is.

When you unify with that place inside of you that begins or began everything, then you have no conditioning. (The objective of many, if not all of the processes that we are supporting with you here, is to alter your present conditioning.)

~

As you create *the phenomenon of your own synthesis with truth, the result is* miracle.

~

Union With the Light Body
An Exercise

To receive the original space of your own design, start by lying down, or sitting comfortably in a chair which supports your head and neck, or sitting in yoga position on the floor. (However you like to do your meditation.)

Begin by closing your eyes and going home, out the trapdoor in the top of your head. Then imagine that this being that you are, which is light—tingly, sparkly, and osmotic—is beginning, as a light body, to come into physical experience. What would be best is to forge this union by seeing an image of your light body actually coming "down" to your physical body. Then watch this light body coming *around* the physical part of you. *View* it coming back in the top of the head, instead of *feeling* it. It will have more effectiveness if, initially, you watch the vibration come together, rather than feeling it come together. As you come "down" from the original creation, you surround who you are looking at *as you*, and then, like a pendulum, Whoosh! take these two bodies of energy that have just become one, and watch in front of you moving off to the third point, which is the outcome. That's *how* you are *in* the experience of "future-future." How did you design your part of or piece of the hologram? How does it look and feel when you're living it? Watch that, seeing it as if it were a movie.

So the light body comes down from the Absolute into the center, merging completely, osmotically unifying with that present moment. Then the two points go off and actually come together with the third point, which is the point where all of you is present in a physical body, living your dynamic spiritual energy by motion and through choice, and fulfilling your destiny.

So it's moving from the left position, which is up a little bit, down to the center, which is where you're sitting or lying, or having your space, and then going up a little bit to the right, so that it looks like the arc of a pendulum. When you're going into the space of "future-future," you are actually able to hold that space even though gravity would say, "Whoosh, gotta come back down!" You're able to hold that arc as long as you'd like, until you experience the framing of what it is that you designed.

Remember that this is anti-gravity. That's a very important point. You're moving in a framework that in its scientific mode in physics, is defined as momentum. You have to bring the momentum back, and yes, that's accurate, you do. And yet, if you take those two points and unify with the third, you start a whole new continuum, a whole new framework. What happens is that the framework accelerates, comes around the top and creates a circle to empower the first point, which is the "past-past" or the original, and again into the "present-present" and then into the "future-future." So the "future-future" and the "past-past" become the same point again. In other words, in the circle they can be designed so that they come closer and closer together. As you make the circle, the important thing to remember is that all the points become equal and are validated energetically with the same energy.

Being a Continuum
An Exercise

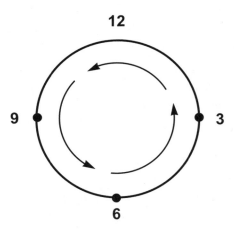

If you make three dots with a gold pencil or gold ink on paper, and then draw the circle we're talking about, you have one dot at 9 o'clock, one at 6 o'clock and one at 3 o'clock as you're looking at it. As you hit 3 o'clock, if you go up to 12 o'clock, and around to 9 o'clock again and again and again with that golden pencil, the first time it's going to be one thin line. As you do it more and more, it becomes a vehicle. If you do it enough, it's going to come right off the paper, and you're going to end up with a sphere. *It's going to feel as if you're making a continuum. So in order to re-Source your life, you want to be part of a continuum!* It's simple. As you create and validate that energy, instead of going from 9 o'clock to 6 o'clock to 3 o'clock and back to 6 o'clock, you go from 9 o'clock to 6 o'clock, to 3 o'clock, and then to 12 o'clock. What you're doing is bringing your continuum into the present by way of the future, rather than by way of the past!

If you understand that the future is what seeds your moment, then you understand that that's where your money, your resources, your ideas and your creation come from. They come from the future. That's why you can't find it anywhere that you're used to looking! Because as we're very famous for saying, "The mind can only help you with what has already happened or what has already passed—past." So none of the points are more important than the other, but the order that they come to you in, and the order that you work with them, is very important.

Individually then, you're experiencing that you have a pendulum, which is going to "future-future" and instead of coming back to the present from the future, which means it comes backwards, it goes forward. *It goes where it has not yet gone, which is the key to manifesting. So you go where you have not yet gone.* (This is why we continually say, "As you go forward . . ." in our readings for you. Going forward is the key to creating comfortably as a continuum.)

And yes, of course you're coming back to the beginning, and yet the way that you're coming back to the beginning is through a new route. What this does, literally, because it's counter-clockwise as you look at the clock, is that it gathers energy to you and brings it in. (Concentricity takes it out. Concentricity is the motion of sharing, the motion of critical mass, the motion of expansion, and of present re-Source. Counter-clockwise energy gathers the framework of the totality and brings it into your present moment.)

If you are in the middle of this model, and bring the "past-past" or Absolute (9 o'clock), into the present (6 o'clock), and go forward into the future (3 o'clock) from your own body of energy, you will find that you do not have the momentum necessary to create that frame. You would be taking your present body into the future space, which might tear that frame. To go up to 12 o'clock and then come in from the other direction (from 3 o'clock), would feel as if you were spreading yourself very thin. When you initially do this process, you want to imagine it, watch it out in front of you, and then when you've made the complete revolution and it's coming in from your left, from the momentum of 12 o'clock, into 9 o'clock, into the present, it's already made the cycle, so you can follow it. It's as if the pen has already made the circle, all the tracing has been done, it's a perfect circle, and you've done it very carefully. Now you can just trace it.

~

Going forward is the key *to creating comfortably as a continuum.*

~

Total Recall

As that energy begins to make foundation, you find that your ability to manifest increases. In a palpable sense this becomes formulated from a different part of your psyche. This is what your total recall is about. When you're making the circles, and receiving this energy in a different way than you've perceived before, you are actually making a design of yourself as a fluid momentum in the universe and bringing that into accordance, bringing it into its own experience of originality. And that's another reason why, on many levels, it's important to go to the hologram and do your best to see, "What's my piece? How is it going to come out? What is my gift? What's my capacity? What am I carrying and why is it important for me to do XYZ?" It's in some ways challenging to receive that image, because it's not only unfamiliar, it's vibrationally like meeting your twin if you've never met before. It's challenging because you say, "You look just exactly like me; this is impossible."

The sense of your finding yourself, if it's done as a viewing process, can be incorporated in a comfortable way, so that you are seeding your future and also accepting that that future really exists. Many times if you say to someone, "Tell me about yourself in the future," an immense wall goes up. "I can't see that. I think I know a little bit, but I don't know what's in my future. I don't even want to really see it, because I might not like it, and it's a part of the design that is not always easy for me. I can see other people's, but I don't see my own." And it's because of attachment to what you do or do not want to see that the comfort level is kept away. Attachment does not allow total recall.

Since you are in immortality now and are working in that framework, and that energy is seeding your consciousness, then this exercise will be readily attainable for you. You will realize that your future means nothing more or less than your past, except that the present of this time, and the future of this time in a context, is going to be more magnificent than any other human dynamic has ever been. And so, as you come into an accordance with this absolute space and flow with it through the center and to the future and back around again, you feel the momentum. Where is it carrying you? Whoosh! It's carrying you constantly into future. The energy of that experience is like going on an amusement ride. You establish a centrifugal force as you go, which keeps you completely in the design level of the outside of that circle all the time. You don't fall back in and forget where you are and design this so that you lose your place. That's the key to this. That's why we are instructing it this way, because you build the momentum so that you never lose it again. Once you are re-Sourcing your experience you are comfortable for the rest of your days.

This experience allows you to support yourself completely through your connection to the universe. When the centrifugal force from these exercises kicks in, you then have the momentum that carries you into the experience of total recall, and you actually see your own design. Now the level of comfort that this supports brings tremendous resources to you, because the commitment of the universe is that when oneness is the experience, everything is available simultaneously. You can manifest simultaneity. You are bringing the Absolute or "past-past," the "present-present" or the now space, and the "future-future" of the hologram into the same vibrational content or context.

As you create the fulcrum point from your center now, and move beyond that into "future-future," and then move the arc of that to connect again with the original space, those three points vibrationally become the same. So it becomes interesting at that point because one would lose one's ability to discriminate against, to separate from, or to identify as A, B, C, or D. At that point the union is a way of being, it's an actual experience, cellularly. It's also very exciting because there is no lack in that space. There is an experience of being absolute.

Manifesting Comfort Through Cohesiveness

This is a formula for comfortability. It's a formula for remembering, which puts the elements together so that they relate, and come together so that each of the pieces is dynamically as important as the rest. It is the cohesiveness that allows them to come together in a way that supports manifestation. If you identify or equate cohesiveness with manifestation, you see how comfort is related to how separate you feel. Since the "future-future" is where there is an ageless process on this planet, as you go there, perhaps twenty minutes every day or every other day or however you can manage it, you go into this space constantly and feel the cohesiveness.

It is the cohesiveness that allows them to come together in a way that supports manifestation.

The "future-future" is where there is prosperity for everyone, because the resources are supportive of the interrelatedness between all systems, which basically says that everything is supported. Then you have an absence of poverty, an absence of being uncomfortable, which means you have a sense of easiness and free-flowingness, and that's the future. You have an area of consciousness where manifestation, in terms of crops and resources, is easy, because of cohesiveness. You have a place where there is no competition because people have no reason to compete against each other. It doesn't mean that you don't play sports, or intramural sports, or that you don't have games; but in the sense of competing against someone, in the true sense of the word, there's no reason to do that because everyone is cohesive with their own experience. It's a sharing of play, and a sharing of joy, instead of competition. In asking, "Who's going to win?" someone has to lose.

As you understand the dynamics of cohesiveness, you can see where the prophesies of the "new age" come from. People are dis-ease-free, life is lived in harmony; peace and prosperity are the natural way of being. You might say, "How does that happen?" It happens when cohesiveness is seeding the present moment. It does not happen from taking the point of the clock numbered 6, the center point, the now, (if we're looking at it in this particular model) and going to 3 o'clock and taking what's at 6 o'clock to 3 o'clock, and unloading it there, and asking "How can we do it differently?" It's actually reintroducing the future of the resolution through the seeding of your original space so that you feel the congruence between the "past-past" and the "future-future." The pieces or the points come together and are actually the same vibration. That's how you change the now, in the sense of changing track, moving vibration, moving energy, feeling the comfortability, honoring the space and feeling the cohesiveness.

The Future Seeds the Present

Remember that it's not a going toward in the old sense of the word, i.e., that money is out there and you're going to go and find it. It's not about *making* some event happen that then brings it to you, it's about you *going to* the event that brings it to you. That's a different thing. Not that other things don't work sometimes, it's just that they are not based on the experience of cohesiveness and creation from a context of union. They are based on other phenomena. As you create this kind of context with your life, where you are each responsive to your interrelatedness with creation and your cohesiveness with the energy of foundationing, you start to feel absolute. It's a by-product. You begin to feel how comfortable you are in the world, in the spiritual dimension. People will stop wanting to go back by leaving the planet, and being fed up because things don't work and they have to take a time-out or something like that. They'll stop wanting to leave the body, and leave relationship, their throat, their root and their feet, and disappear.

They'll realize that they can have it all, that they can be comfortable in the space of "present-present" because everything is here with them. They don't have to leave to get it. It's a process of re-circling, re-creating, and re-Sourcing. It means that there are no excuses now, there's no reason for you to be absent from your life, from your body, from your heart, from your relationship, from your states of being. It doesn't make any sense for you to be absent from your own state of being. No wonder you're not comfortable. You have to occupy the chair in order for it to be comfortable. You can't stand there and say, "I'm not going to sit down because it won't be comfortable." You won't know until you sit down, and then you make an adjustment until you are comfortable.

What's Comfortable?
notes

Comfort in the Body
An Exercise

Get in the chair, try it out! Get in the body, try it out! Jump in, explore it. Those of you who feel that you spend 99 percent of your time out of your body, practice jumping in the top of your head. Imagine that you are liquid gold, and that you're filling your body with your essence, and that you're actually feeling how comfortable it would be to have a home here—re-Sourcing, having money, having context for work. Having the experience of belonging only happens when you're comfortable in your body. If there's a part of your body that's squeaky or that asks for oil, give it the oil. Give it the molten gold energy flowing in the top of your head, and, for example, let your shoulders relax. Bring in this wonderful golden energy. Fill your ears with it or fill your eyes with it, if you don't like what your vision is doing. Fill your eyes with the molten gold. Connect to the source of your own experience. Be at one with your gums and whatever else you want to support. Experience that you are the one that gives life to you!

Having the experience of belonging only happens when you're comfortable in your body.

Experience that you are the one that gives life to you!

If you ask God to help you and do not help yourself, then you and God are, by definition, separate.

If you talk to God and help yourself, you are thereby, through definition, unified.

This is where religion and the way of the spiritual truth of being differ. Of course, you can ask God to help you. And yet, if you ask God to help you and do not help yourself, then you and God are, by definition, separate. If you talk to God and help yourself, you are thereby, through definition, unified. It's the same. Do what you know to do. Ask for information and guidance on the rest, and it becomes a Sourcing then, a complete Sourcing, because you are the Source and you contain the Source. You speak to the Source, and you incorporate what the Source is. It's a beautiful feeling of union through all of the points of reality. It's consolidation and the sense of feeling the union flowing from and to simultaneously, and this is the secret of this model. Feel that. It's a completion.

When you want something that you do not have, when you feel

uncomfortable, there's not a completion because you haven't received. There hasn't been the validation to unify that experience. What we're suggesting is that it's "from and to" at the same moment, which completes the circle. This means that you can do a lasso with it by bringing the energy of those points closer together. You actually experience that one supports the other so that you have a domino effect or an acceleration curve.

~

When you want something
that you do not have,
when you feel uncomfortable,
there's not a completion
because
you haven't received.

~

The Lasso

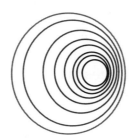

You Are a Continuum

This is how we are going to bring the reality of 2016 into the time that it has been allotted for. This would normally take, if you look at your Earth and your world, another 2000 years to accomplish. You are bringing the time element, and the continuum of that configuration of union, closer and closer together, so that the experience of where it comes **from** and where it's going **to** is the same. There's always an acceleration and it's powered by the result, which is powering the whole circle. That means that each of you is being powered by your comfortability—what it's like to be home in the body, home on the Earth, with the creatures, with your own design, and in oneness with all people. Being powered by your comfortability is to be co-creating as Gods and Goddesses, and to feel the framing of this so that you open the dynamic to your own threshold of absoluteness, from—to, from—to.

It becomes, then, a pendulum that moves in multi-dimensions. You are doing a mirror image of the bottom of your pendulum, you're flipping over that pancake, Whoosh! "I can do this above as well as below, and when I do it above and below, the worlds come together and there is no separation." This is a way that you can focus for manifesting money, land, resources, health, memory, and the future of your own content or context. It's a way of manifesting your destiny, maintaining comfortability, and sharing resources with the universe, so that in many ways what you empower is the result of your total consciousness rather than an idea that you have. "I think I want this, I think I want that." When you do this experience from and to, and from and to, and back and forth, and back and forth, so that you're going around the bottom and up the top and around, the above and below become the same unified field.

There is then no separation from the resources that you've come individually to gather and garner. Those resources become affirmations that support your life, and the integrity of the union that you're experiencing is cellular, biologic, social, personal, and ideological—or ideal—at the same time. What it changes are beliefs, limitations, thought processes and fear structures, and yet you haven't paid attention to any of those things, because remember: what's getting the oil is the comfort. So the expansion and the validation and the union are what get the oil, what get that grease. Everything else falls away, and you don't pay any attention to it because it doesn't matter, it literally doesn't matter. When it doesn't matter, it doesn't have form anymore, so it's not associated with principles and experiences and habits that you've learned as you were growing up. Because it doesn't matter, it has no energy, it has no form, it has no substance. The only thing that is being substantiated, in that case, is the critical mass of the unified field that's created when you flip the below into the above and fill in the gaps, which creates the momentum, which keeps you going.

In the meditation you close your eyes, Whoosh! You go up there, experience the original space, and then watch as that original space completes itself, and there you are, and you're still watching. As it completes itself, backwards, and forwards, and forwards and backwards, Whoosh! this wonderful circle that's counter-clockwise is beginning to accelerate. What will happen for you automatically, as it accelerates and moves, is that it becomes a continuum and you just jump in. Jump in just like you waited for the rope to turn when you were little—you're going to skip the rope. It's turning and turning and at that moment when you know that you can step in there and the rope will go around you and contain you, you just Whoosh! jump in. And then you are that system that is moving in that concise way through its own experience.

Ultimately your becoming one with that system is a moot point, because of course it's already happened. And yet because the free will is the place where this gets experienced, the systems of your consciousness are unfamiliar with it in this dimension. You go there in dream states; you fly all over the place in dream states. There's no boundary in the dream state. So, you're becoming familiar with other levels of being in a non-dream state, and the feeling of the physical body at that time when that happens, is that you have just leaped from your normal conditioning to your natural state of being.

You have just leaped from your normal conditioning to your natural state of being.

You will have found your way home, and yet be present here and living in all dimensions comfortably. This process is one that is available to everyone, without exception. *You do not need to understand all the points and correlate them before you begin.* Many times people will stop doing something before they start, because they're not sure how it's going to come out. So just jump in and feel it. If you know that there is a part of you that still needs to be filled with the intention of presence, do that first, before you close your eyes and leave the body. Become one with yourself, and then leave. And then when you return, all of you will be there waiting. You can jump in as a full being, rather than wanting something else to fill you up.

Being Fully Present

This is very important because if you are not present in the body to start with, you will get mixed results in this experience. When you look at yourself, you will have to fill yourself up with the Absolute space, and there will be gaps. The full presence of the now wants to be experienced before you begin to actually identify with that space as the fulcrum point of your total consciousness. Make the commitment to be present in the body fully, to live dynamically in this space as the place that you're going to *bring* the energy to, or you will be doing what many people do when they meditate, and using it as a way to leave. That is fine, yet it may not be your actual intention. It's about clarity also, making choices, being clear, doing things fully instead of halfly, and understanding that if you do something halfly, that's the result you're going to get. And again, there's no judgment on it; it is just a fact. If you do something starting out at 50 percent, what result can you expect? You can expect to magnify the 50

*When people say
you create your own reality,
it's basically,
how present you are,
and if you're not present
something else is going on
and is making the viable decisions for you,
and you are, in a sense,
absent
from that experience.*

~

*So being fully present
means
being fully alive.*

~

percent. If you start out at 100 percent, you can expect to magnify 100 percent.

If you think about your life and how involved you are in the process of being, how present you are—you can look and say, "Oh that's why that person's so productive, they're more present. That's why they have more energy, they're more present, there is more of them to magnify, there is a percentage that they can magnify that is more fully present." It doesn't have to do with somebody's abilities being better than yours, it has much more to do with how fully they embody their presence—how much sleep you require, how much energy you move through your body, how much physical stamina you have. All of this is, in a very beautiful way, related to how present you are in your experience.

Begin observing your patterns now, looking at where you're comfortable and where you're uncomfortable. Make a decision about that—a choice, stating, "In my framing I'm now choosing to be comfortable in this way. And that means for me that I now move in a direction to sustain my presence fully, by choice." So that really adds up to, "I am responsive to everything that I create. If I am unresponsive, then my creative capacity diminishes. I am responsible for or responsive to taking the full pledge to say, 'I'm here, or I'm not here.' It doesn't have anything to do with anybody else, it has to do with me, and my commitment to being."

That's how you contribute to what your reality ordains—by your presence. When people say you create your own reality, itís basically how present you are. If youíre not present, something else is going on and is making the viable decisions for you, and you are, in a sense, absent from that experience. And you say, "Oh I didn't know that, I didn't realize that. I didn't know that person was doing that, or that decision was made," because you weren't there! You can look at that in relationship. You can look at it in any way you want to. Basically, *whatever is going on, if you're not comfortable with it, you weren't present when the decision was made.* Wherever you were is up to you to understand and ordain in your experience and make choices about.

So being fully present means being fully alive. It means importing and exporting equally all the data, all the energy, all the information, so that what's coming in and what's going out is balanced. There is the feeling that everything that has been ordained in your life has been chosen by you consciously, which means that you were fully present during that decision. You asked about it, and you clarified it, whether it's with God or the Goddess, or the Source, or whoever you may be in relationship with. You know what's going on because you're fully there. As that unfolds, everyone is responsive to, or in the old language, responsible for their own reality.

That's what we were talking about in the experience of community. Honoring the self. Can you honor yourself if you're not there? It's a very interesting question. In order to honor the self, somewhere along the line a time of rendering pops up. A time of rendering is a time of choice. And rather than, in the future, the times of renderings being about choices of love or fear, staying and sustaining love on the planet, or being afraid and wanting to go into a dynamic where fear is the experience, the real choice is about being present or not being present. That goes way back to education when you're sitting at the desk and the teacher says your name, and you say, "Present! I'm here, I'm here." Comfort has to do with being viable, being a life force that can sustain balance, and *requires full presence*.

What's interesting about full presence is that you're the only one who can give it! You're the only one who can give permission for that to be the state that you occupy. It is critical to the formula, because without it, it all falls apart. And it really means a commitment to it. It doesn't necessarily mean that you think about it all the time, and you worry about it all the time, or you're always pouring gold in the top of your head. It means that you make a commitment and that you be present to when you're non-present, so that you can make that choice. It isn't to worry about, it's to commit to, and that's very different.

In the experience of our comfort with you, we are always present, and that is what we pledge for you at the end of each of your individual sessions—that we are always present for you. We pledge for you our presence in the unfolding of your design. That is a commitment that we have made to humanity, and when humanity returns the favor, the degree of comfortability will be the same in all dimensions. And that is written. And so it is.

~

*What's interesting
about full presence
is that
you're the only one who can give it!*

~

Receiving Brings Us Back to Heart

Receiving
Receiving
Receiving

RECEPTION—BEING IN A PLACE WHERE organically, etherically, and foundationally you are able to receive—is going to be very important for you as you move forward in this new time. We have been discussing with you the reception of information, memory, knowledge, energy, and transformation. To build a new foundation in a natural way in the world requires receiving and re-Sourcing from energy and from sources that are extraterrestrial, that is, outside of the terrestrial body of Earth itself.

It means opening to be a conduit for the fields of energy which support the Earth and foundation creation itself, and yet are not of the Earth, inherently. When this capacity is ordained it is consistent with the experience of being a sponge. You are being opened cellularly to have the energy of that which you wish to receive, available to be absorbed. It is also important for you to understand the way this works, so that you can more easily facilitate the experience.

Reception is traditionally seen as feminine because it means holding a container and supporting the intention for union, and yet not doing anything about it, actively. It doesn't mean that you go out and build something. It means that you lie and wait for that which is supportive to come into being. It is a preparation and a sustaining rather than an activation.

As you proceed with your immortality and see yourselves in total recall, information and energy come to you through your receptive modes—through your vision, through the experience of seeing, feeling, and knowing that which is out of this realm—clairvoyance, clairsentience, and clairaudience. You can experience in each moment that your propensity to receive is completely balanced with how much you get. It's as if your ability to allow becomes sustainable itself. And that's a very important concept to think about

~

*I receive all that I have given
and all that I am.*

~

for just a minute.

Your ability to allow is consistent with how sustainable your experience is. That means that you're not controlling it; you're not deciding about it. You're lying in wait for it to re-Source itself. Now that implies passivity, and yet it is not, because passivity would lie in wait in such a way that it would have its antennae closed because there was noninvolvement. In our definition, passivity means noninvolvement. So, you are not being passive, you are being receptive. That is a very important distinction, because lying in wait and allowing means that there's a state of excitation. As you're lying there waiting and are open to receive, all of your antennae are up, all of your viable conduits are available to run energy, and you are experiencing that you're in communion with or communication with that which you are receiving from. So it means union again. It means merging again. "Allowing" in this instance means sustainable communication and orientation.

Your ability to allow is consistent with how sustainable your experience is.

Osmosis—Being Sunlight on Water
An Exercise

An easy way to prepare the body and the psyche for the process of receiving this total recall, receiving the energy fields of your charge of light, is through an exercise which opens all the cells of the body as if they were pores in the skin, imagining that all of the cellular frame—the cell wall as you would call it in biology—opens out and allows the exchange, osmotically, of content.

This exercise is based on grounding or opening your field out so that you don't have form anymore, you don't have edges any more. As you open that out, Whoosh! let go. You are disappearing just as if you are on Star Trek. Scotty is beaming you up, and you are becoming an oscillating field that looks like sunlight on water. So, Whoosh! you're feeling this energy moving out of you that was normal—the form.

And as it's moving out of you, breathe back in, and when you breathe back in, imagine that all the cells of your body can receive total recall, that all the cells of your body are sparked, lying in wait to sustainably field the energy and information that is immortally available to you.

You actually begin to energize your system from this very easy exercise. A consciousness is born about what's happening, which allows you to know what you're receiving, because it has a velocity to it. It has an energy field which brings you this absolute space that you are allowing and have intended—from being light, and charging the essence. All of these pieces are now providing you with an opportunity to receive the inherent essence of your divinity.

Being in total recall is a divine gift that is your birthright. It is the place at which all things are understood. Understanding has to do with relationship, so that all things relate one with the other, sustainably. Now we have a context for receiving that makes it sustainable, so it will be easier to swallow in the sense of allowing.

It will also be a process which allows people to love each other in new ways, and to sustain energy fields in new ways, and to provide *for creation to be as important as manifestation.* Because the model that is normal puts much more emphasis and value on what is created—what is done, what task gets done, what is produced, those kinds of creations—than it does on what's received. You could say, "Well, I was lying around all day receiving," and somebody would say, "What did you do?" "I was receiving." "And what did you do?" "I was receiving." "But what did you do?" "I was receiving." "Oh, I guess we speak a different language. I don't know the value of receiving unless I see what you've done with what you've received." That's how most people think about creation—unless it produces something, it has no value.

We have a society that has value placed on buildings, and on process, and not on heart, not on the things that are hard to measure, like love and sustainability. So it's easy to comprehend that because of its orientation, technology has moved us away from the heart. Receiving brings us back to heart. And receiving also provides an essential ingredient for consciousness, because when one is receptive, one is open. The field is open. When the field is open,

~

Being
in total recall
is a divine gift that is your birthright.
It is the place at which all things are
understood.
Understanding
has to do with relationship,
so that all things relate one with the other,
sustainably.

~

When the field is open,
there are no barriers.

~

Your mode of operation will change from task orientation to creation.

~

All are fulfilled at once or none are fulfilled.

~

there are no barriers. There is no, "Well, I'm this, and then I die and I'm that," or, "I did that yesterday and I can't undo it," or, "This is fixed in stone, and I need to do this job, because I can't survive if I don't do that."

Being open means that you are boundless, limitless, and that each opportunity comes from the Source instead of from logic and mind. When you are open it means that you are re-Sourced. So if you lie around all day open, and receive, you are then energized. You are synthesized, and fundamentally your mode of operation will change from task orientation to creation. It doesn't mean that you are passive, it doesn't mean that you are lying around not doing anything, ever, in terms of fulfillment. It means that everything you do fulfills you. It means that being receptive and open sustains the whole. So fundamentally, everything that happens fulfills.* Because we are now co-creating a new model of fulfillment where all are fulfilled at once or none are fulfilled, it allows for there to be new ways to create, new ways to make foundation, and new ways to synthesize consciousness. It means that there is no restriction, because you are re-Sourcing from everywhere.

Your choosing to be open and receive greases the holographic wheel, and spins your piece into the total equation so that more is created and more is viable. Your piece stimulates union, and so more people meet more people, and it's more sustainable, and it's all a system. As you open and receive, the system grows. You know that it grows because your personal receptivity is fine-tuned, expanded, and provides a recognition that ultimately serves the whole, because what you're finding out, remembering, re-Sourcing, coming into contact with, or receiving, is valuable to the process of total sustainability.

It means that instead of lying awake all night and thinking that you've got something that's really important, and then talking to others about it, and having them tell you it doesn't mean anything, when you lie awake all night and you tell people something, it moves the whole model toward completion.

Each valuable piece you receive has a place to be put, because the reception is so authentic that it is accorded, it is of the design, and definitely of the Divinity. Every time you open a window to the truth, the truth provides something to immediately gratify the consciousness of the whole.

In other words, it's not ahead of its time anymore. It's not out of synchrony, it's not something that you think, "Oh, I wish I'd thought

---

* This new model is synthesized and integrated through critical mass—the combination of all energies flowing toward the same point of realization, simultaneously. Each soul may be in a different part of this flowing, the wave, and yet, the movement of the wave carries all forward at the same time.

of that yesterday," or, "I don't need that till three tomorrows from now." It's in synchrony with the consciousness that is being born. As we are all midwives of this new consciousness, we are on the edge of that knowing all the time, creating and sustaining the movement that is going to serve the birth. The difference in terms of being receptive in the old model of the normal and being receptive in the new model of the natural, is that what one receives fits immediately into the process of creation. In other words, it's rewarded, it's acclaimed, it's accorded, it's validated, it's affirmed—not because your ego needs it, which is the old model, but because it is actually in symmetry with creation.

The exciting thing is that each of you participates by putting in a piece when it's needed, and it moves the whole into resolution, into completion, and into fulfillment, sustaining it—sustainability. Adding your piece can also move creation to a new place which supports more creation and more sustainability.

It's a basic system that as a child you were always wanting, this experience of acknowledgment. "If somebody would just acknowledge that I fell down and hurt myself, or that I stood up and did something very, very beautiful, or that I read this book, or that I was able to tie my bow in my hair, or that I was able to do this or able to do that, that I was able to laugh at something that hurt, able to be courageous, and able to be fundamentally a good person." If everyone that was a good person had been acknowledged for being a good person, there would be a lot more good people. If you could just watch and wait for someone to do a really good thing, and then say, "That's wonderful!" then people would be children from ages 0-99 or 199—if you were just there to say at that right moment, "Oh, yes, it was a good thing you did." Acknowledging it would create more of those actions on the planet.

As you experience the receptivity of this exercise—opening all of your cells and pores and letting yourself out, and then breathing in and receiving from all dimensions—you are acknowledged by those dimensions, and that acknowledgment seeds you. It turns you on. It plugs you in. It opens out guidance points for you to make specific orientation with your truth, which then provides a way for you to fulfill your destiny. This is the way potentiation will work from now on. It won't be that you do something, and then people say, "Yup, that has real value. Now I wonder how you could do that and make money," or, "I wonder how we could get somebody to buy that from you, so that you could produce more, and make more money, or get

The difference in terms of being receptive in the old model of the normal and being receptive in the new model of the natural, is that what one receives fits immediately into the process of creation.

more fame or success," or, "I wonder how we could duplicate this so that we could have lots and lots of it, so that we could sell lots and lots of copies."

The old, or normal, model says that whatever someone does that has value has to be marketable and has to convince other people of its worth. The new model says, in sustainability, "All I want to do is contribute it. All I want to do is give it back to God, give it to the whole, give it to the experience of oneness." And when it's given back to the beginning, it magnifies its outcome and multiplies the result.

This is why so many people are so enamored of service, because when you do service you are contributing it, and not *necessarily* valuing it, because inside the process of service is the experience of absolute giving without expecting return. When one receives absolutely, without worrying about what one gets, it is service in the opposite side. In other words, it's receiving as service, rather than receiving as something that has to mean something so that you can have something as a result.

When you look for results, you think, "What did I get? Did I get anything?" the constant question in your society is, "Did you GET anything?" When you go into reception, in a contributing mode, what you get is what you can contribute as service without getting anything back.

The way this works, the way it's natural, is that it was yours to begin with. It will always be yours and it's your divine right to have it, whatever it is—information, understanding, guidance, energy, resources, whatever. So everything that you are now receiving belongs to you already. If you put it into the model of sustainability—service to the whole—you are giving everything that you are and have ever been, into the experience of the design. Then the design will fulfill itself and bring you right back to receiving what it is you inherently need to move the space of energy into the world to provide a contribution that will make it all work. Sustainability happens when one is in absolute receptive mode, because then one is receiving one's own essence, and making it available to the Absolute of this dimension. The experience is reorientation, recognition, re-cognizing. It's as if it is all the same piece of cloth again, functioning in such a way that *what you receive is what you gave before.*

So it's balance. Nobody can count anymore who did what for whom how many times. The tit-for-tat system that is normal in this

The new model says, in sustainability, "All I want to do is contribute it. All I want to do is give it back to God, give it to the whole, give it to the experience of oneness." And when it's given back to the beginning, it magnifies its outcome and multiplies the result.

So everything *that you are* now *receiving* belongs *to you* already.

society becomes unnatural. The experience of being in the foundation of symmetry becomes the condition of truth, the experience of natural, and the way that the design of the new world will be. You cannot give anything because it already belongs to whomever you're giving it to. And you cannot really, in an essential sense, receive anything, because you've already given it somewhere else, so you're just getting it back. It's the foundation of balance in motion. Everything you are and everything you sustain and everything that moves in and out is ordained in such a way that the foundation of that truth becomes itself—you're receiving truth, what you started out with was truth, and what you're going to end up with is truth. And so the foundation of all receptivity is truth.

When one opens to receive, the foundation of reception is that we've already been one with the truth, so that the experience of re-cognition/recognizing is really finding your own truth again. Receiving becomes truth-finding.

You might receive guidance and information from a source that you trust, outside yourself, and find that it's the truth. And yet, when you're in the space of truth-finding, the time/space continuum condenses, and the Absolute infinite and the holographic move into one point, and the divinity of your essence as an individual is known, and you are the same as the place you *believe* you were receiving from. The truth is that it's all one.

Receiving is living oneness. That's why it will work in this new time, because it's sustainable, because there are no conditions upon it. The experience of receiving and being in the oneness of truth means that there is no separation between any dimension with which one is communicating. There is no way of saying that one is talking with an *extra*terrestrial, because the feeling is that one is talking to oneself, which in a multidisciplinary fashion is the most accurate way of seeing the context of the universe—that you are everything. And this is how there will be resolution between factions that speak out from extraterrestrial bases. This is how the experience of being in more than one place at one time in one body can be created so that it does not foster schizophrenia, but fosters union in truth. This is the way that being male and female can happen simultaneously. One does not have to choose between.

This is the way that being God and humanity can be accepted, because it's the receptive nature of being in oneness that allows the truth to be born. When you receive and are a vehicle through which truth is supported, responded to, and then communicated, the truth

You are *everything.*

And so
the foundation of all receptivity
is truth.

~

If there were
an absolute balance
in each person's life between
what they receive and what they give,
oneness
would not be a question on this planet.
Violence would not be happening.

~

becomes an absolute vehicle through which reception is connected with oneness, truth, and creation. We can make God and humanity synonymous—make them the same by definition even though there seems to be a divergence. If they are diverging in a path, we can bring them together. We can say, "This is a foundational place where we can attest to the fact that if we were to receive on a continual basis, we could absolutely live truth without question." We could balance creation, sustainability, and contribution in the same contextual frame.

Why is this important? Receptivity is something that individuals and groups have looked at as having varying degrees of value and application. If there were an absolute balance in each person's life between what they receive and what they give, oneness would not be a question on this planet. Violence would not be happening. There would not be dissolution of all the things that are dissolving, like marriage and friendships, and models. Because what is making the models dissolve is that there is not enough, or there's too much. The reception and the giving are out of balance. That's what's going on here on the planet.

If you go into receptive mode and get that valuable contribution, and stick that into the formula of this model as it unfolds, it becomes connected to the absolute experience of being, so that everything works better and sustains life. Then you are a primer, you're priming the pump. You're right there, pulling at the front of the rope, and you're feeling exhilarated, you're feeling consciously happy because you are producing something from the fulfillment of the balance in your capacity to give and receive. You're linked in. You belong to the system. You are inherently a valuable part of what's happening. Now that is potentiation! The balance of receiving and giving as it is maintained in truth has the capacity to solve all of your world dilemmas. Just that little equation.

Everybody knows everything is out of balance. Nobody knows what to do about it. Start receiving. The more you receive, the more you will give. The more you give, the more there will be balance between what is being received and given. The more balance there is, the more there will be for the people that need it, so that there is not a fear of survival, the need of conquest, the need of power, the need of fame, the need of success. The balance inherently will be felt. Opening to receive is a primary part of this time because it upsets the apple cart of the old model.

Opening to Receive
An Exercise

We would recommend that you structure some receiving time into your daily schedule. How much you take and when you take it and to what degree, is an individual decision. If you can take one day a week and lie in bed and receive, that would be the optimal; one day a week where you just lie there and open your cells and Whoosh! move out the edges and all other formed process, and begin absorbing like a sponge— begin receiving. Energy comes into the body, revitalizes you, hooks you up, and orients all of the systems of your body to receive truth and to receive a vibration that serves your consciousness. Every time you hook yourself up, you'll find that it's time well spent, because the foundation is going to become very strong. Your circuits are going to be very deep. Your thinking will be very clear. Your heart will be very open. Your soul will be very present. All the systems of your body will be flowing as if there is one drum beat of order and truth—not to mention the light that will flood your system.

Receiving
notes

There are many levels that want to communicate with each of you. In the receptive mode this is possible, because this fosters a capacity to telepathically create connection with the invisible—and a lot is invisible. You orient your consciousness to support yourself from the sources in the universe that bring the intention of light, the experience of creation, and the foundation of the sustainable. Those areas of consciousness, awareness, and practice are what you need to build strong bodies, clear intentions, and purposeful, fulfilling, potentiated lives. So instead of going to school, reading books, or whatever it is, you say, "I'm going to a non-human level. I'm going to go to an extraterrestrial level, a level outside of this density and vibration." It can be a hierarchical level, a celestial level, an Angelic level, the God level or the Source, the Creation, the Goddess, the lineage, whatever you think of it as—it can be anything that you want it to be. Our recommendation is to choose a non-human method now to support your experience of this transformation for one reason—*you are moving out of density.*

Your spiritual connection now will be fostered in a more dramatic, destined, absolute, and profound way than ever before. You're going to hear the angels talking in your ear, see them manifesting in front of your face, know why you met that certain person, and understand synchronicity and coincidence. The angels are the ones that show you the design of the future and help you to live it. They put the pieces together so that you take the next step.

You have etheric societies of guides on all dimensional levels that are here to support each of you in your own affirmation and unfolding. Talk to that guidance and find out who they are, what they're telling you, where you come from, rather than asking somebody human for that information. Make the links, bring the energy into the experience of your body, so that you are the experience of what you embody. Honor the invisible and the inaudible: that which nobody else can hear. Honor the subtle: those knowings that come to you, the faces you see that aren't there in form. Allow yourself to see gnomes and fairies. Ask, receive, open, and make foundation with. Belong to the universe of spirit, call forth and recall your intention, receive it in truth, bring it in.

It's important for you to do this with non-expectation and non-formed experience, because if you want to see a person or an object or something that looks like this, and has this kind of eyes, and is this color, and is this size, you're taking density with you. You're already defining it. "I'm going to go to extraterrestrial spaces. Maybe

I'll see a Pleiadian today." Go there, instead, in a receptive mode. It's about being, more than about deciding what you think those levels are about, and what they're going to tell you, and what you're supposed to be communicating with, and what you've already had communication with. This is about a high level of intention that's pure, that says, "I am ready to live the truth, to make the reception and the giving and the receiving and the moving and the creation of all these levels the same."

Go into reception with this affirmation: "I choose balance. I want to see as much with my non-physical eyes as I've seen with my physical eyes. I want to hear as much with my non-physical ears as I've ever heard with my physical ears. I want my heart to love that which I've never seen as much as I love what I have seen." Another way of saying it is, "What awaits me? As I open these levels and explore the universe, what is there for me?" And what is there is excitement. Excitement!

In each moment you have the opportunity to open to that which is, and yet in many instances has never been recorded or oriented in language before. You're going to get solutions and fulfill yourselves, and acknowledgment will come to you from those around you, because you are providing miracles and magic, and the experience of all that *is* in this place.

You're going to speak with beings that *haven't* been trying to get information into this place, about such things as saving the planet—beings of truth that inherently understand that there is order to all of this. It isn't total disorder—nothing is going to be lost if something isn't hurried up and found. This is about order—sustainable life. There's no panic in it. There's no "this is a lost cause" in it. You are talking to beings of integrity that consciously hold a position in the universe and are ready to share that position with those of you who approach this in the model of balance—that what you receive you will give. There are many, many beings all over the dimensional universe and in intergalactic spaces that want very much to get information into this place. And it comes from you and through you, into the world and back again, in the twinkling of an eye.

That's what sustainability means, and that's how receiving in this space of knowing works. The foundation becomes that everyone, everything, every point of consciousness or aspectual awareness, is the same. So we're back to the theme of oneness. We're back to the theme that there is no separation. You may not be able to distinguish at times who speaks to you, or whether they have a name, or if they

*When you
go into
that space,
it is with no expectation of result.
It is with intention of service.
Receiving
is an honorable point
at which you are served,
and that service is then
full circle.*

want to give you that name, or if it's important. Whatever you receive will be your next point of application. Enter it with a blank mind, a blank screen, aware that you don't know anything about anything in your logical experience in proportion to what is, and that as you open to receive, you are actually linking into your greater psyche, where you have a balanced position within the whole universe.

What comes for you in that moment will be whatever is regarded by the whole as the next point of your fulfillment. And what is ordered and what greases the wheel of the hologram will be born. When you go into that space, it is with no expectation of result. It is with intention of service. Receiving is an honorable point at which you are served, and that service is then full circle. You are served and then you serve, and you are served again, and then you serve. It means you're useful, viable, important, dedicated, valuable, sustained, acknowledged, upheld, nurtured—and there's no condition for this. It is because you are in the system. Approach it from the pureness of that intention. To serve the whole.

So lie there on your day off and receive. It will be like all your days *are on*, because you will have a viable charge to work from, and every minute will be the experience of fitting your piece where it belongs, into the whole. And that is your yearning in fulfillment. It is the solace of knowing that you're in the right place for the right reason at the right time. As you go forward, you'll experience that everything is a viable means for expression, for joy, and for union. This is an absolute model of union, so it's perfect, it fits all the criteria. It's a way for you to get what you need in a way that serves everybody. That's what balance is about—for you to get what you need when you're serving everybody. In a linear model that's almost impossible. In a circular model, it is self-sustaining, self-perpetuating, and self-fulfilling.

It is feminine because it allows, and because it does not control. All of the facets of the system can then support one another as it unfolds, which makes it co-creative. You are more than you were before, and all you give up is the form of the way in which you live it. So it's a very easy exchange. And what it gives you is the sense that your piece has more value than can be estimated, and so it provides you with the feeling of absolute peace. You're where you belong, and the system is working, and you're the reason why. And that's true for everybody. That's the beauty of the system.

The Crystal Cathedral of the Soul

This is an excerpt from a channeling which engenders reassurance, safety, and trust from the soul, and provides an understanding of your fears—where they come from and how to deal with them effectively. The following passages help you understand your contributions through service and compassion, and your relationship with the "structure" called God.

MANY SOULS NOW FEEL A HIGH LEVEL of personal disintegration, which is an inner reflection of the outer destructuring of the world as we know it. Many times a track of aloneness and separation is created in the perception, which affects the experience of life profoundly, separating us from soul and from the Source.

You can go down this track or rut for as long as you want, until you choose to get off. You can learn to get off the track at any time, even when you're in the middle of it, feeling depressed, down, and thinking you can't get back up. You can learn to switch those paradigms by using different circuits and fostering a new reality of consciousness through your own intention. You can change the way things are by connecting to your intention of reintegration, and shapeshift your reality to change the dynamics and to create the life you want.

If you all created the life you wanted very easily and it didn't take any time, energy, effort, or learning, it wouldn't have any value, and it wouldn't be teachable. By experiencing the track of depression and separation, one learns compassion. Many of you have come here to bring compassion to humanity, so you're getting knocked out of you anything that's noncompassionate.

You're in a pattern of disintegration now, and that means that you've been integrated, but you're disintegrating. You have had times of complete union within yourself. You may not remember them, but you've had them many times. For millennia, you have

Cathedral
Cathedral
Cathedral

~

*I am going to live safely
within the structure of my soul,
re-Sourcing myself.
Whenever I need anything,
it will be re-Sourced,
and I will trust myself
in the presence of the Divine or God,
or the Source, or Goddess, and
all of these things are now going with me.
And that's my discipline.*

~

been saintly. That's why it's hard for you to get involved in the situations of conflict in the world, and go into the inner city where there are hardships that in your own heart you want to help with, but don't want to deal with. This is because in a lot of lifetimes you went into the monastery or the nunnery or were a helper. And you were taken care of by a structure that was also taking care of the people. So you served, but you weren't responsible for your own life in the same way that you are now.

Many of you attained greatness in other lifetimes, and you remember that. You remember the peace and the joy and the solace of having time to just sit and look at nothing, and pray and meditate and chant, and go out and putter in the garden, and have people go by and say, "Yes, my brother," or, "Yes, my sister," and have no real need to provide for yourself a reality of safety because the structure provided it for you. Memories are very strong in many of you of abstinence, celibacy, and aloneness. In some ways being alone made you safe, because it was anonymous. You had to be *alone* in the way of intimacy when you were in the nunnery or monastery. The way it is in this environment now, is that for you to do service there is involvement. You are the structure, and for you to have the safety, you must provide it.

So you're here this time to be walking the path of the people you've helped before, and of course you come into service because that's who you are. You're always going to serve, and yet serving yourself is something that you don't know how to do. You're not used to serving yourself. The structure served you, and you served humanity.

You're trying to do it all at once in a lifetime where critical mass is accelerating to get you to go faster, to get it through so that you can do your contribution. The consciousness of humanity is massively being destructured. Everything that you learned about what makes you safe, everything that you think about or believe about what's important, every point of reality that you've ever lived is changing its modus operandi—the form it has had, the framework, everything is going and, soon to be gone.

You are living the dream you had before you came, but now that you're here you don't have an instruction manual. You came back into a time of destructuring to do the whole thing without the manual and without the structure. So the safety issue is the number one issue, because you don't know where to get safety from. The second level is trust, because when you don't get the safety, you stop trusting in the structure. Now in this situation, what's the structure? You're the structure. If you can't provide safety for yourself, you don't trust yourself. If you don't trust yourself, then you really can't make decisions, and if you make them, then you're going to question them. You really can't have relationships because you say, "Well I don't trust me, how can I trust them?" So you're trying to restructure your experience of being safe and honoring your own being, creating the reality you want at a time when there's nothing to hold it together.

Creating a Feeling of Safety

The main thing we would recommend is that you make a structure around yourself. Give it some parameters—a crystal cathedral, a cave, or the Empire State Building. Whatever structure will help you feel safe, put it together; call it whatever you want to. You can call it the church if you want, and put yourself in there. You start feeling that the structure is around you, and it's going to make you safe. You do this as an exercise. If you don't do it, you'll still be all right and yet you'll probably go through more vacillation than you need to, and certainly more alienation from your own egoic space or center, and definitely more separation from your soul. The soul is where your structure really is. The soul is what took you to the structure of the church, and you used the church to support the experience and expansion and dedication of your soul. So there's no reason why you couldn't structure and put around you now, your soul, as that part of you that holds you safe.

What you actualize in your life is that you feel that if you are safe, and if the soul is there, and if there's structure, you'll begin to trust yourself. Trusting yourself means that you make decisions more easily, you realize that you don't have to relate with irrational fears, because they don't have any basis, and you can experience that ultimately there's nothing separate from you in any moment because you are one with everything. So you start living the principles that you really understand. You understand oneness somewhere inside you. You might refute it at the moment, but you do understand it, and you also understand that you're one with everything that is, which means that you're also one with your resources, and you're also one with your future.

~

So the safety issue
is the number one issue,
because
you don't know where to get safety
from.
The second level is trust,
because when you don't get the safety,
you stop trusting in the structure.

~

The soul
is where your structure really is.

~

You feel that if you are safe,
and if the soul is there,
and if there's structure,
you'll begin to trust yourself.

~

When you were in the other place(s)
you served God,
and by serving God,
the people came,
and you helped the people.
But
you weren't responsible in the same way.
God was responsible,
because you worked for God.

You can pull in what your future is going to be, and you can pull in the resources to live, and you can pull in everything you need. But in order to do that, many of you have to leave the structure of what you remember—the church, the patriarchy, the conditioning, the models, because you didn't ever take care of yourself before, in your memory. You think, "Okay, I have to do my own re-Sourcing, I have to go to the Source and I have to re-Source myself so that I have what I need to survive. I have to do my own creation. I have to stand in front of the people, or be next to them, and I have to give them my help, and I'm by myself. I have to leave the structure of the church. I have to change the rules. I have to play God. There's something in me that says that's not okay to do."

So you keep sabotaging yourself because you're not ready to play God. Now that doesn't have any rationale to it, except that when you were in the other place(s) you served God, and by serving God, the people came, and you helped the people. But you weren't responsible in the same way. God was responsible, because you worked for God.

Now it was easy when you had that structure, because you could say, "Okay, I get it, I'm just a peon here. I'm doing what I can do, and I'm following guidance and leadership that's outside me, that has this incredible structure. Everybody believes in it, so it has to be real, so I can trust there's a God because otherwise I wouldn't be here." Now here you are in this lifetime, and what is to say there is a God in your life? What is to say that you have the ability to represent God by yourself without some big organizational structure around you? And what is to say that you can even do this, because this means that you'll be responsible for these people.

So there are questions, doubts, and revelations in your psyche. You are angry. You're angry that God isn't doing it for you, and that is perfectly understandable because that's the way it has always been. If you didn't understand, you went and prayed to God and God gave you a sign, or one of the other nuns a sign, something that you could talk about, and you weren't alone. It was a group responsibility, captained by God. It was a group process. You could discuss things, you always had help before, and you're alone now, at least in your perception. So you must have done something wrong, something must be off kilter, because how could you really be responsible for another soul? Where is God anyway? These are some of the dynamics that are going on and that you are running neck and neck with, head and head with, face to face with. As you unfold this particular part of the pattern, it is very powerful because you're going to understand and resolve these points in the psyche and get on with it.

The thing that is important is that there are multiple dynamics here. So if you try to understand one of those dynamics and get that sorted out, it doesn't mean that you're going to get another dynamic sorted out at the same time. That's why you can think that you've made a decision and feel really good about it, and then you take a breath and you don't feel good anymore, because there is also something else there that is important to be recognized and dealt with.

The structure of your soul is not yet strong enough around you. That's not literal, it's perceptual. Perceiving that your soul isn't strong enough around you, perceiving that you're not really connected to God, perceiving that you're not aware enough to be responsive to the needs of people, and to see it through and make money doing it and to create rapport and to help them, and to be of service and all that, that's all perception. The easiest way for you to deal with this perception is to change it—not prove that it's different! Just change it. And that's what we meant by going on a different track. So decide to switch tracks.

To do so, the first thing would be to surround yourself in a structure, let's say a crystal cathedral. That crystal cathedral represents your soul. And every day as you go to work, and go into the crystal cathedral you say, "Okay, I'm at work, all right." Then you close your eyes and you say, "I need God. Unless God is here, I can't go any further." So you bring God in. Now you can bring God in any way you want, it doesn't matter. It can be a flying Madonna, it can be a cross with or without Christ on it, it could be a cross with all kinds of angels flying around it, anything. It doesn't matter what God is to you perceptively, because it doesn't change God to view it in a certain way.

So you bring God in. If you don't know how, say, "I'll pick up a feather. Here's God. I stick it in the top of my crystal cathedral. It's looking down at me, and it's looking at all of the fairy tale land that I'm in. So this is it; I got God." You don't need to do anything, you don't need to find God, you don't need to have a sign from God, you don't need to have God come to you in a dream or anything. Just decide; change your track and God is here. Fine. You know that is possible because it's all about how you look at something that makes it what it is. So you have God there, you have

*It doesn't matter
what God is to you perceptively,
because
it doesn't change God
to view it in a certain way.*

*You don't need to do anything,
you don't need to find God,
you don't need to have a sign from God,
you don't need to have God come to you
in a dream or anything.
Just decide;
change your track and God is here.*

the crystalline structure of your soul, and then you ask yourself what else you need to feel safe and put that into the crystal cathedral. Then everything that you need is right there, i.e., food, warm gloves, plants, your dog, etc., and you feel safe.

Now the next step is trust. If you create a crystalline structure to hold your soul, you can sit in it. God's here, you've got plenty of food—you must be able to trust your instincts. The objective is not to go out into the world and see if fifty thousand dollars falls in your lap, and say, "I can trust it because I got some money," or to see if somebody offers you a job next week, or whatever it is. It's not about testing the limit in the beginning. What it's about in the beginning is holding the space. If you get the crystalline structure, and God, and the safety, and the food, and the trust right there, hold it. Don't go anywhere with it, don't test it, don't try to see if you can go out and stand in front of traffic and see if you're safe—"I'll see if God's structure is really going to keep me safe."

Hold it steady maybe three to five times a day. Just sit there. "Okay, I've got my structure; God, safety, food, trust," and just go through it like a checklist. "Do I have it? Yes," and you sit there in the feeling of having it all congruent until your mood starts to lighten. If your mood doesn't lighten, stay there. "Well, if I'm going to punish myself, I might as well punish myself doing something that's going to be effective. I'm going to use my energy at least in a way that's going to help me out here." So you sit, and your energy starts to expand. The soul is communicating to you in a safe place with plenty of food, and God is present. You're beginning to trust that framework, and it begins to expand. You put the pebble in the pool, and it starts to open out. So as you sit there, you are feeling better.

Then you say, "I have to get up and go to work, or get up and go to school, or whatever," so you pick it up with you and carry it. Maybe you imagine that you're Cinderella: you're going to pick your skirts up, and when you walk you imagine (even if it's envisioning it in an imaginary sense) that you're carrying your crystal structure with you, with the feather on the top. Or perhaps you're a knight, and you put your armor on, envisioning that your structure is a cave or a castle. Your food is going with you, the whole thing—it's all visualized, but it's energetically available, and you're always going to have it.

So you walk along and you go here and there, and everywhere you take it with you, and pretty soon you realize that a lot of things that you've been worried about, a lot of things that you've been angry about, and a lot of the things that have been missing in your pattern, aren't missing anymore. You're not angry anymore, because you're carrying your wisdom, your essence, and your future pattern, design, guidance and protection with you.

You take your structure into each situation and speak from that place. You have relationship from that place, you have commitment and interrelations with words, language, consciousness, and energy, and you begin to feel as if you are embodying your essence and people are responding to that essence, and all of a sudden the questions you had before aren't there anymore. You changed your track.

Now we would recommend you don't try to forgive anything, understand anything, or analyze anything, because it won't help you. You're too smart for that. You'll go right around it, because when you decide you want something, you'll find it. Many of you are extremely powerful, and when you decide you're going to fail, you'll find a way to fail. If you stay on that track, you're going to create whatever reality you want, because you're very strong willed, and most of you have spent lifetime after lifetime in experiences and structures of discipline. "I have to be here for 35 minutes on my knees." Discipline. So if you say to yourself, "I'm not going to make it," you will do everything in your power not to make it, because you are disciplined. Discipline doesn't say, "This is good and this is bad." Discipline says, "I do what I say I'm going to do."

So when you discipline yourself to carry your little crystal structure with you or your cave or the Empire State Building, and you stay in it for a long enough time, pretty soon you find out that it can become a discipline, and if you just stay in there everything will take care of itself. Everything will be ironed out. You don't have to worry about all those little pieces because what you have is what you need. What you need is what you want, and what you want is what you are, because it comes from the desire of your soul to fulfill itself. So you don't have to do any affirmations about being safe, feeling good, liking yourself, or doing better—no spiritual mumbo-jumbo. You make the intention when you start: "I am going to live safely within the structure of my soul, re-Sourcing myself. Whenever I need anything, it will be re-Sourced, and I will trust myself in the presence of the Divine or God, or the Source, or Goddess, and all of these things are now going with me. And that's

Everything will be ironed out.
You don't have to worry
about all those little pieces
because what you have
is what you need.
What you need is what you want,
and what you want is what you are,
because it comes from
the desire of your soul to fulfill itself.

*So you teach people
by the embodiment of what you're doing,
that the essence is what's important,
because
the track of the essence
will always lead you home.*

~

*As soon as you hop
on the track of the soul,
you're at your highest vibration
in that moment.*

~

*You're taking all of your resources
and putting them into one place.*

~

my discipline. If I think I'm going to fail, that's out of the course of my action. I cannot pay attention to that anymore. I have to do it in here, and stay in the structure of my consciousness." Close off to those parameters of your thought and experience that don't serve you. You're learning to structure the duality in such a way that you serve yourself. And that's primary.

Now when you come upon the many people who have a myriad of problems and their world is falling apart, what are you going to be able to teach them? You'll teach them how to find what they need inside. Because you don't have anything wrong with you. It's invisible. If you explained it to anybody, they might put you in the loony bin. "I'm walking around like Cinderella or the knight in shining armor. I have this structure of my soul, and it's like a crystal or a cave, and I can see it around me. It's beautiful and there's a feather on top, and that feather is God." You know they'd go, Whoosh! and throw away the key!

So you teach people by the embodiment of what you're doing, that the essence is what's important, because the track of the essence will always lead you home. Instead of trying to figure out, "Why did I do that?" and "Why did I think that?" and "How can I change this?" Realize that it is not important, because energetically as soon as you hop on the track of the soul, you're at your highest vibration in that moment. It doesn't mean it can't get higher, but it will only get higher if you're there to support it because of the way this works. This is energetically fed by thought, and the thought is fed by energy, and it manifests in that way.

So in a nutshell, you're taking all of your resources and putting them into one place, saying, "I'm a little low on wood, or I'm a little low on fuel. I think I'd better put it all together and see how much I have. I'm not going to leave it scattered all over the place. I'm going to put it all here and make sure it's all together. When I need it I can find it." So the way this works is, "I'm aware of all my assets, and they're all in one place, and I can expand them and there is a relationship to each other because they're present in that space." It's a very thrifty maneuver, because it allows you to assess what's real, and when you start doing that you realize that you have a lot more than you ever thought you had, because you're collecting it from places where you forgot you had it.

What you can do now is to find out what's there, support that, and do it with grace. You don't need to carry on when you're in the soul structure. Just be there. Don't bring any stuff in there—just be there. Pretty soon the stuff won't have any place to attach, so it won't be able to come with you anywhere, and you'll be mostly in the soul structure anyway, pulling up your skirts like Cinderella, or donning your knight's armor. So you won't be aware that there's stuff out there that perhaps still needs to be looked at, and you'll say, "Well it's not on my list for today. I have enough trouble just deciding what dress to wear so that I can hold the skirts up, or getting on my horse with my armor on."

You understand after a while that if you don't give any energy to that stuff, it disappears. What you're doing is profoundly validating the experiences of truth inside yourself. You're allowing the foundation of who you are to be expressed, and you take that forward and anchor that in every moment that you live, and pretty soon that's all there is. So you're in the right place to live your future, you're in the right place to ease and balance and resolve your past. As you unfold it, you realize that you're empowering yourself to be in that space, and that it's providing you with everything you need from soup to nuts, and the foundation of that is recalling to you an initiation that you went through a long time ago when you asked, "Can I do this on my own?"

We're suggesting this because a lot of the work that you're now involved in is validation of your eternal life, of your immortality. Validation that you cannot be hurt—you really cannot be hurt. Until that knowing comes deeply inside you, you will be afraid. It isn't a judgment or something to worry about, it's just to understand, "Oh, if I'm afraid, there's a part of the knowing that I'm now accessing to assist me." When you're afraid, it means that the soul wants to access that experience. So ultimately as you go forward in the light, you realize that the foundation that you're living is calling you to be a part of the knowing that you're carrying, and it's not a bad thing. When the fear comes up, you jump back into the cathedral of your soul with this silver crystal light and gold shimmering sparklies, and say, "All right, fear's calling. What does this mean? It must mean the soul is ready to reveal something. I'm going to sit down and discipline myself. I'm going to listen to what the soul has to tell me." Sit there—crystal cathedral or cave, you're all there, you're the princess or the knight—so you say, "All right, show me what this fear is." As the fear is jumping around doing this and that, you say, "Soul structure, shine it from the windows, begin to throw down information or visions, or more feathers, or maybe it's scarves this time, but I want to see what the fear is trying to show

You're profoundly validating the experiences of truth inside yourself.
You're allowing the foundation of who you are to be expressed, and you take that forward and anchor that in every moment that you live, and pretty soon that's all there is.

~

You cannot be hurt— you really cannot be hurt.

~

Why don't you

just bring it in someplace

where there's enough light to see it,

enough clarity to feel its real vibration,

and enough solace

and support

and peace

and beauty

for you to know that

no matter what happens

nothing can happen,

because you're safe.

~

You don't have to provide

safety for the soul;

the soul provides safety for you.

That's why people don't feel safe,

because they're not in touch with their soul.

If they were,

they wouldn't be afraid of anything.

~

me that the soul has to tell me, so I won't be afraid."

What you learn to do in this process, vicariously, is to use archetypal, visual, and imaginary spaces to heal the parts of you that feel disintegrated or disconnected.

The story of the crystal structure of the soul is that it's the safest place to be and it has *all* the answers. Whatever comes up, you deal with it in the cathedral, because if you don't deal with it in this crystalline cathedral of your soul then you're going to be on another track, and who knows where that track comes from or where it's going. Why don't you just bring it in someplace where there's enough light to see it, enough clarity to feel its real vibration, and enough solace and support and peace and beauty for you to know that no matter what happens nothing can happen, because you're safe.

The more you go forward and live this as a way of being, the more easily all the pieces will fall away—the ones that you think you have to carry, that your shoulders are getting very, very heavy about. The more these levels of illusion dissipate, the more you're home free. You're able to be in this space with yourself whenever you want to be, receiving what you want to receive, functioning so that you are supported for the rest of your life. You put together what you know psychologically, philosophically, societally, and spiritually, with etheric, causal, practical, soul energy in the circuits of your body, so that all these points of relationship are formed. You do not leave the psyche to find the answers about the psyche. That doesn't make any sense, yet that's what people do. They don't stay in the essence of who they are to find solution, they try to figure it out somewhere else. They go into the mind, which can only tell them the past. It can't tell them what the solution is, because the solution is in the future.

So you're putting all your tools in a place where you can have what you need to work with for each thing that comes up. You realize that ultimately everything you have created in this or any time or space is completely available to you at this point, and will be coming to you moment to moment no matter what the situation is like, and the value continues to expand. You feel better about you, and the pieces come in so that there's no more doubt.

You don't have to provide safety for the soul; the soul provides safety for you. That's why people don't feel safe, because they're not in touch with their soul. If they were, they wouldn't be afraid of anything.

So when you go into the crystalline structure, the safety will be there that fosters the trust, and you're going to have what you need to have the trust. You don't have to stand outside and say, "I don't see the trust yet, so I'm not entering." The safety is relative. Think about that. How safe are you related to the millions of people on this planet? It's relative. "What track am I on? Am I on the I-have-enough-track, or I-do-not-have-enough-track, or I-never-have-enough-track?" If you think about all the children in the world that don't have any food, and their moms don't have any milk in their breasts, and there's nothing growing, there's no water, it gets perceptively easier for you to feel safe in the twentieth century western environment that you have here.

So you move into the crystal structure, and immediately have the feeling that you begin something. There is enough safety for you to start with, and you feel that growing. A lot of this depends upon your staying in there for a few minutes minimum, so that you can start to build that energy. Because if you go in and say, "Oops, I didn't feel it," and leave (you can set it up that way if you want to), you could miss it.

Trust Is Within You

The other thing that happens as soon as you feel the safety is that it's as if trust comes down to meet you, because you've always thought of trust as something you have to have, not something that exists inside you. Everybody thinks about it that way. "I don't have enough trust." Listen to people. They don't say, "I am not enough trust," or, "The trust is not enough in me." They say, "I don't have trust," or, "I don't trust you," or, "I don't trust that." They never experience that it already belongs to them, because they think about defining trust as something external.

You already have the trust inside of you. It's built on that safety, and when you're in the soul you always have those three components at the same time—the soul structure, the safety, and the trust. So as that balances in you, it is amplified so that people come to you and begin to have a state of trust with themselves. And that's valuable. If you can impart even that one little iota of consciousness to somebody so they have trust within themselves, their lives will change, because after that they can walk around, and they have

You've always thought of trust as something you have to have, not something that exists inside you—You already have the trust inside of you.

*The fear
is stronger by your own admission,
so the fear
is going to have soul as its adversary,
because the soul is strong enough,
the soul is immortal,
it can't be killed.*

~

Until the soul states *its position,
the fear has its way.*

~

presence. And when they have presence nobody is going to rape them, nobody is going to rob them, nobody is going to kill them.

There is a valuable process going on here within the self, and it isn't about failing. You who have come to serve humanity are learning the ingredients that you carry which are specific to you. Every minute it's the intention, "Well, what am I serving through now? How could I live this in such a way that it would serve humanity? If I have the whole structure of consciousness with me (which is what you've just set up here) then I have all my friends with me whether I see them or not. I have all the angels with me, I have God with me, I have all the souls with me, I have all the trust in the universe, all the safety in the universe, all the food in the universe, whatever I stick in here. This is an absolute space, and as an absolute space it is consistent with the experience that all of the dynamics are ready to be lived now." Because that's the way it is when you have everything attending the moment. There's a birth.

Fear Is the Messenger of the Soul

The foundation of your changing tracks is making the conscious decision that you are now ready to look at the fear as if it's a message rather than a killer. It's not going to hurt you, because it brings you something. Have a showdown with it. But *you*, personally, don't have a showdown with it, because it's not up to you. It's not about your personality having a showdown with fear, because that would be a set-up. The fear is stronger by your own admission, so the fear is going to have soul as its adversary, because the soul is strong enough, the soul is immortal, it can't be killed. So you're starting out with a hero or heroine that you know can win, and you're starting out with fear which is going to be the guy that gets put six feet under. This is the objective. You have strength to deal with this, and it's really going to work, so it's not some kind of set-up. Until the soul states its position, the fear has its way. Once the soul states its position, the fear has to acquiesce because *the soul is the place where the deepest point of free will is expressed in the universe* and in this context we're talking about here on Earth. You speak to the fear, because it's really a messenger of the soul to get the soul to come out and acknowledge and start living what's in there. It's basically a done deal.

Your deepest fears are unexpressed energies that have not yet found form and direction. So if you bring the fear out and look at it and see what's there, you realize what part of your soul hasn't come forth and been born. The fear stops it from being born. So the soul has every right to rear up and say, "I want to be born."

And because of the free will process, the mind has to give permission for the soul to exercise that. It's getting harder for the mind not to give permission as the critical mass is unfolding and the acceleration curve is evolving. There's more energy of awareness than ever before. Souls are really learning to express, and yet it's still a part of the dynamic that is supported by society that it's natural to have fear.

There are only two natural fears at birth: fear of falling, and fear of loud noises. So you go into the cathedral and say, "You're not a natural fear. Why am I having you? You must need to have a conversation here. I've got the stage ready. It's your turn. When I go like that, you speak." And you indicate with your finger—you're the director here. You just bring it out and see what happens. It can't hurt you because where are you? You're in safety in the cathedral. It's being acted out in your psyche, but you as a person are not damaged, you are enhanced by what happens because you're clearing out the closets. Some fears may be millions of years old, and that doesn't matter. So you don't have to say, "I wonder where that came from. I'd better worry about that for three weeks, because if that was in my psyche, no telling what else might be in there." Just let it come. It's not about judgment, and it's not about holding on and attaching to what happened and deciding because it happened it means something profound.

It's not about taking what happens literally and bringing it out in life and saying, "How do I worry about it?" It's watching the unconscious play itself out, and giving it witness, and yet knowing that you don't have the whole picture. See just what you're playing out in that dynamic, and know it is not the whole picture of what's happening in your psyche.

You can forge this commitment and intention to create resolution and balance in your life, and hold it steady and watch it expand, and let all the new pieces come in. You're not focusing or working just on fear, or just trying to stay in the cathedral. You've experienced that, "Wait a minute, there's balance here, I'm getting excited about this! I'm resolving that, I'm having more safety, I'm able to re-Source myself more easily. I let the opening and the

So if you bring the fear out and look at it and see what's there, you realize what part of your soul hasn't come forth and been born. The fear stops it from being born.

The safety and trust
in soul and self
are felt and acknowledged,
and the structure becomes
that you are the soul
and you are God,
for
as these points are lived
within you,
they will begin to manifest
from you.

expanding feed me, so that I keep all of it in balance at the same time." If you start focusing on your fear, you won't see what you're receiving and how things are changing and shifting.

You're using your capacity to create and the concepts of truth to forge new tracks in the consciousness to provide you with the results you want. The fear is dealt with by the soul in the cathedral. The safety and trust in soul and self are felt and acknowledged, and the structure becomes that you are the soul and you are God, for as these points are lived within you, they will begin to manifest from you.

Choose your track. Give the grease to what works, and the dis-integration is then lived only in the illusory and ceases to affect you because by living in the soul, you live now only from truth. And you are safe.

Your Vibration
Is Your Library Card

The Inner Workings of
The Ones With No Names

WE WOULD LIKE TO TELL YOU ALL THAT, as speckles of light and consciousness, you have come here from direct and very important processes of information, knowledge and wisdom. Your lights have come together from the integrity of what we call the records, and you are now here to live and ordain these records into reality. These records are called Akashic. They are where the storage unit of consciousness is located, where all the pieces of the plan, the design, have been articulated very clearly. They are available for your perusal at any time.

Our place in the Hierarchy gives us free access to these records and our use of them is much like your use of a library. We take out the card with our name, or "No Names," on it. There is a "library card" and a file with your name on it. We then take the file of your soul, and develop the theme. We actually look at each of your incarnative records, where you've been, who you've been with, and how that has played itself out. We look at what you have gained, what you have lost, what you have learned, what you have gifted others, what your capacities are, and what the foundations of your framework have been—your education, learnings, vocations, and understandings.

We take that together with what you think, how you process, what you believe, and how you have come to be conditioned by society, and work with the process of each of your experiences in this lifetime and in all other lifetimes. Then we read the record at the same time that we are experiencing your present vibration.

Your present vibration is the most important link, because no matter what the data says, your vibration is what reflects the truth of what you have embodied and incorporated.

As we are putting together the pieces, or aggregating the

~

My vibration is pure and clear and reflects all the truth I have embodied and incorporated, in all time.

~

foundation of your vibration, we are reflecting it through all time. Imagine having a periscope where you are on one level of reality and the periscope takes you to another level of reality. So you're able to see then in at least a bi-sectional foldout, where your individual vibration is, and where it's heading. If we want to, we can open up a periscope in another direction and have your past, present and future readouts, as well.

Our job is to aggregate the information so that your total consciousness gets organized. That's why we say for you, and have said for you in this manual, that you can have total recall. Total recall is where *your* imprint, blueprint, and reading comes from. It is the place where your foundation is laid in the structure of consciousness. What is read to you is vibrationally the accessibility of your entire content from beginning to end.

This time that you are living is very important, because it is the time of resolution, where all of those pieces that you've been carrying, and everything that you've learned and worked through and understood—all comes at one time to be used by you. This is why we call this time the Coming Together of the Ages—of *all* ages.

Each of you has a total capacity to synthesize everything that's on your record, and has a total ability to frame those experiences *differently* than when you lived them before, which means that you can alter their vibration *now*. This is where creation becomes able to be manifested through intention, because you can take those paradigms and frameworks that you've already done, and you can redo them. You can "do" them from a different vantage point, from a different perceptual base, from a different level of understanding, and from a different vibrational force field of unity, if you choose to do so. You can bring together dynamics and coordinates that haven't touched or met before to enlarge and enhance your assets and make them more available. You can organize your consciousness in any way you want to without limit, to design whatever outcome you want.

This means that you can take the karma that you have with someone and shift it. You can take what you would like to have done in a certain instance and imprint it into that space and make it happen. It's not about this level of reality. It's not that you decide, "I'm going to make up with Uncle Joe, and go back to the time when I was five years old and dumped a bucket of water on his head, and change that so that he likes me now because I'm not going to dump that bucket of water on his head when I was five years old. I'm just going to mention that bucket of water and walk by him, and I'm not going to do anything to him, so he's going to like me. I'm going to change that karma now."

What we're talking about is your vibration. If you go into alternative realities, into parallel places, into the experiences of knowing your dimensional connection to someone else's soul, and you reorder that union, that connection vibrationally, you change your vibration. You are fostering resolution in your own circuits, clearing that experience. As you clear all those circuits, that opens you out to dynamics of your reference which you may not have had before. As we're reading your vibrational pattern to you, as we're linking to the essence of what you carry, or what your calling designates, we are actually taking all the potential that is there *if* your circuits were absolutely clear. This is why some of you sometimes say, "Well, I can't do this for at least nine months," or, "It's going to take me three years to integrate this reading," or, "It's something that I don't quite understand. My essence is singing, but my mind says wait a minute, I don't think I can do this."

When we see your vibrational field as it is accurately portrayed in this dimension, and we go through all your spaces of reference, we literally give you the readout of your capability to clear those circuits, to open out to those eventualities and to provide yourself with a mechanism through which all of those intentions are manifest.

This gives you an opportunity to decide that this is accurate, and to make an intention, so that you can go forward and get your design, and manifest or aggregate it into the experience of your life, without delay. When you do that intending, and when you live from the vibration of your present field as it would be aggregated in truth, this means that your vibration of emotion and mind is clear, your body and spirit are unified, and you're grounding and saying, "Yes, this is who I am. I make the intention. Let it be." Then those circuits all get clear. Taking the bucket of water and dumping it over Uncle Joe ceases to have happened. Not because you go up to Uncle Joe and say, "Will you forget that, please forget that?" or you think about it and pray hard that he'll have a lapse of memory, or that you can somehow erase it off your karmic sheet.

You go into the experience of being absolutely pure and clear, with that pure intent, and as you experience your vibration, it is resolved. It is resolved, as always, through the circuits of the body and through the frequency it carries. That's why all of this deep work of reordering the psyche and the consciousness is actually what

We're taking that actual record,
which is what your potential says,
and your actual frequency,
which is the now of your vibration,
and linking them together for you.
We're bringing them into unity for you.

~

You've been
trained
to relate to experience
instead of to potential.

~

brings resolution to the experience of life. That's why you start getting along with people, and things start moving easily, and there are no more of those edges, and the framework becomes much easier, because, literally, you are in the place where your potential and your actual are the same.

We bring to you the potential that you have if your circuits are clear through intention and through the grounding process. If you bring those into the experience and open out to them, immediately the foundation of what you've designed begins to take hold. That's why many of you feel that there has been an acceleration after you receive the reading of the record, because it's as if all the pieces are clicking together. What's important for each of you as you receive, particularly your initial readings, is to understand that this is what we're doing for you as a service.

We're taking that actual record, which is what your potential says, and your actual frequency, which is the now of your vibration, and linking them together for you. We're bringing them into unity for you.

If you design your expression of the reading and your response to the reading as an opportunity to unify that actual and potential and hold that space, then what is read to you will manifest.

If you decide to take it apart, analyze it, decide what parts fit and what parts don't, when they should be done and when they shouldn't be done, if you can believe it or if you shouldn't believe it, if you can do it and how much of a percentage you can do, and whatever, nothing changes—except your experience.

The foundation of the experience is what you relate to or don't relate to. And that's because you've been trained to relate to experience instead of to potential.

We are held by the intention to give you a complete potential readout, because our perspective of the universe is that the potential is the optimal point at which your vibration remembers its entirety. It's the greatest gift that we can give you.

We always start with and move into your actual frequency, the experience of the vibration you're in at the moment—the experience of your present. Then we open that out to the potential, and bring it back and link it into your present space so that it belongs to you and energetically is accessible for you. It is present, it is available.

If you take it as the gift, hold it, nurture it, sustain it, empower it, intention it, ground it through, drink it through, feel it in fluid and immerse yourself, then you actualize the union of the two dimensions which are most profoundly available to humanity, in terms of contribution and design.

The Akashic record comes into this dimension when you get the reading, and in the vibrational energy you're receiving, you are having access to more places in your psyche than you've ever had before, both during the reading and at subsequent listenings of the tape. Because this is a synthesis process, you have the ability to read your record as if it were a forecast with information that says, "This happened yesterday, and that happened five years ago, or 50 million years ago, and this is where you are now, and this is what's coming in the future." And you see all of that simultaneously.

All the vibrational field is inherent from the above to the below. If you listen to the tape and experience your own frequency, then everything that in some way impacts this lifetime, which we call hinge-lives, will come back to you. And when you send resolution to that, "Yes, I'm in this vibration, I understand what that was about, and I learned this, contributed that, did this," it is immediately sent into that experience of resolution, and your frequency accelerates. You can actually change the story line of your karma, now, even though what you might be changing could have happened five or ten thousand years ago. Because of the simultaneity of reality, you can affect anything you want to affect.

We pick up your speck of light and hone in on it and vibrate with it, and go to the record and present our "library card," and get your record out. We always scan the record with you unconsciously beforehand—to find out what you want to hear and what you don't want to hear, to find out what you are organized around and what you're not organized around. We do a lot of homework before we present the reading. We actually check it out with you. That's why we have a very high degree of success in terms of each person feeling understood, and feeling as if the resonance that's being created fits their particular design. You can resist that, negate it, or do anything you want with it, and yet there is that framework of resonance that is established even before we get to each other.

The appointment for your "reading," or assignation, with us was determined before birth, when you were in the Swing Between Worlds with us. The Swing is an interdimensional space which shows you everything: all time, all truth, all dimensions. When you choose to come into a lifetime, there is opportunity to reflect not only upon what your capacity or occupation will be, but also where your piece of opportunity will be fulfilled, in terms of service and contribution to the whole.

So as you go forward from the Swing Between Worlds and are born into the experience of your own *ordination*—your life—we assist you at the critical moment when you need most to remember what you chose in the Swing to do. You are assisted to bring together those pieces that would most profoundly serve the opportunity for you to remember and to orient vibrationally to that which provides the highest degree of unification and success in society. You're bringing all of those points into a solution, into the fluids of the substance, where they can be lived—resolution again.

If you would think back to the first time you received a reading from this level of consciousness, and then the first time you read or listened to that particular session, looking at it in the perspective of your whole lifetime, you will see that what happens to you, almost across the board, is a reorientation. Something very deep gets reoriented. The basis of that reorientation is like an adjustment that the dentist makes in the braces every month. The reorientation is to bring symmetry and balance to the levels, to ordain the consciousness so that you innately understand you have been called on and awakened. Something has transpired which allows you to know, first, your importance to the design; second, that there is a collaborative effort to assist you in supporting whatever part in that design you have to play; and third, that you are not alone. Somebody, somewhere, knows who you are, and understands you enough to care about you. Through what is said, the foundation of all your pieces, the millions of pieces that could possibly be presented, are woven into a pattern, so that when they're presented, the right bells go off to instrument the being.

This seems important to tell you about, because it's a bit of the behind-the-scenes process that supports the intention of our dimension to honor your dimension, and to support a recognition between dimensions—the knowing that there is communication, alliance, and support between all dimensions.

Shapeshifting Reality

We talk a lot about changing your reality, and that you are responsive to—able to respond to—creating that reality. If you choose in certain instances, you can decide what reality you want people to remember about you, decide how you want to be understood by others, and realize that because you can create your own reality, whatever you intend, is.

For example, perhaps you give a lecture on Sunday morning, and when you are finished with the lecture you say, "I left this part out, or I stumbled over that word, or I didn't like the way I said this, or my facial expressions at this particular time might have been inappropriate with what I was saying, or I'd like to refresh the memory of people about something that I just briefly mentioned but was really important." So, let's say you finished the lecture an hour ago, and you're saying, "I wish I'd done this." So do it again in your head, and then send it back into the same framework. In other words, imagine that you're standing there again and talking to the group, and that the group is hearing what you wanted to say, and set it like Jell-O, set it in the mold, say, "This is it, I'm finished now, this is the way I want it to be remembered." If you do that within a 24-hour period, the people will remember it as if you said it the way you actualized it afterwards.

You can use your consciousness to direct energy in such a way that you establish the kind of relationship with your own being and your own abilities that reflects your intention to be known and understood. Regardless of what *time* it is, and how time is moving forward or backward, you can insert whatever you want into that time. If you have dialogue with someone, and don't like the way it went, or it didn't work so well, you go back in and say, "This is who I really am, this is what it was really about, and I just want you to remember that this part of my essence is also present, even though it might have been played down a bit in this process, or it might be different than you experienced it. I might not have given myself permission to be who I really am, and I want to send that essence to you, and I want you to receive it." As long as you do it within a 24-hour period, it will be incorporated.

You're learning in terms of vibration and intention, that you can shapeshift your reality. You can move wherever you want to, and decide how you want the vibration to be received by others. You can decide where you want your focus to be, and how you want your energy to be received. And you can change your mind, and create it differently, and sustain it. This is because, when you learn, you do something at a different level than you did it before. You learned as you gave that speech, so after you did the learning you said, "If I'd done this, it would have jelled better," so you go back and do it that

Because you can create your own reality, whatever you intend, is.

~

Regardless of what time it is, and how time is moving forward or backward, you can insert whatever you want into that time.

~

way. You can only do something at any one moment based on the knowledge of that moment.

So if you have the ability to look retrospectively at something, why not have the capacity to enhance it so that it reflects more truth? It only works to support truth. It doesn't work to support falsehood. You can't go back and say, "I'm going to take that out even though it's true, because now that I've said it, that means I have to do what I said." That would not work. But if you're *adding* more value, adding more truth to it, then the experience of the consciousness is going to reflect a higher level of learning and growth, because that's systems theory.

It means that you have opportunities to adjust the realities of your present situation within 24-hours. It also means that you can connect with your record, use your own library card, get out your own experience, and begin to look through it, at those experiences that you're working at in your life. You can get more information.

We say often that this is the time of resolution. For it to be the time of resolution, you need to know what to let go of in order to move to a place of union, which is what you designed to begin with. This means that the Akashic records are more and more accessible to each of you, so that you know the *how* and the *why* of your design.

The Akashic Records

The Akashic records can be accessed out in front of you, in the same place that the hologram is located—at 12 o'clock, about two to three feet above your third eye area. No matter what direction you're facing, the Akashic records and the hologram are always in front of you, at that 12 o'clock point.

You have opportunities, now, individually and collectively, to go to the record, use your library card and say, "I want to find out everything about this person, about this part of my personality, about these lifetimes I had, about whatever." When you go into the Akashic record and use your library card, you're going to have to present identification. Your identification is your vibration. So you must present your vibration to the Akashic records. You cannot present your brain, your mind, your thought, your yearning, or your emotion. You must present your vibration.

You can only do something at any one moment based on the knowledge of that moment.

Going to the Akashic Records
An Exercise

In a quiet and supportive environment, you close your eyes and breathe deeply, clearing your mind and relaxing your body. You ask to go to the records, and in your mind's eye feel, sense, or see yourself walking up to and knocking on the door of the Akashic library in the sky. You say, "Knock, knock, this is my vibration. I choose to know everything about _____, _____, _____." When you say that, immediately there are doorways that open for you. You get the panoramic view of the universe. You see the scrolls and the books which record everything. There are myriads of file folders and index cards. But rather than giving you the scroll or the book, *they only give you back the actual energetic experience of who you are in reference to what you ask about.*

It is something like a research project, because you're not going to get all of it at the same time, and you can understand why. You're going to get what you ask for. You can go back as many times as you want, develop the theme, work it out and ask about anything that you want to ask about, once you've given your vibration. If you want to learn about cultures that have effectively dealt with some of the phenomena that would now be helpful for your society— Lemuria, Atlantis, the Mayan cultures, Roman or Egyptian cultures, or if you want to understand and learn, you can ask about certain subject matters. You'll find that when you present your vibration, you'll get back what your vibration would resonate with in terms of that experience. You're in the middle of an opportunity where you're presented with your next step, because that's really why you're going there. As you're presented with your next step, you find out why you asked that question. So whatever question you're asking, the answer was calling you to it. What you need to finish off this round, is what it gives you to answer the question in your head. And when you go to the Akashic records and present your vibration, asking for certain information, what's given helps you understand what it's all about.

*And
if The Ones With No Names
have a calling,
it is to provide information,
because we believe,
if we believe anything other than light,
that you have
the divine right to know everything
that you can know,
at any moment,
because it is your life,
it is your process,
it is your universe.*

All of this is happening etherically and energetically, and you find out that it's not that you're asking the right or the wrong question, it's that you have been given an opportunity to find out where you really are, where your psyche is in its process, and what's important—what's valuable for you to invest in, open out to, and ordain in your life. These awarenesses are given to you so that you have the opportunity to explore your own divinity through time and space. It's going to be the wildest trip you ever take, because it's like exploring all the outer space themes that you've ever seen on the science fiction channel, or Star Trek.

It opens out to a dimension that is familiar, that's ancient, that's futuristic, that's at times dogmatic and at times creative, and at times sustaining and at times releasing, and every time you go and present your vibration as your library card, you receive a blip of consciousness—which is what you get back. What you get is what you need to further the experience of your own affirmation, your own birth into being through time! So going to the record is authentic and valuable, because immediately you start getting it.

In the chapter which talks about pure intent, you will read about how to look at your back to see who you are and what you're missing, the part of you that you cannot see, the part that eludes you. This is the human struggle. What am I not getting? It pertains to denial and repression, because the psyche believes that if it knew everything it would be ashamed, embarrassed, possibly incarcerated, because of the consciousness that evolved through humanity's journey. Many of the things that occurred were, if seen out of context, creating large amounts of separation.

You're going to be aware of what the scoop really is, and you're not just getting the dissected, condensed version like Reader's Digest. When you go to the Akashic records you get the "why." You get the experience of recognizing that when you're there, there's information, images, and that feeling of *being* there, because it's panoramic, like the Imax theater. It's huge and all around you, and you can feel the motion of it, because *it's your being unfolding.*

The bonus is that you get the *why.* "Why did I do it that way? Why did it happen at all? Why were we together? Why are we apart? Why? Why? Why?"—those questions that children are always asking because nothing seems as if it is in context because so much information is missing.

And if The Ones With No Names have a calling, it is to provide information, because we believe, if we believe anything other than light, that you have the divine right to *know* everything that you can know, at any moment, because it is your life, it is your process, it is your universe.

Through eons of time there has been an amnesia, huge chunks of information that are no longer available to humanity. Of course it's not good or bad, and yet it requires you to unify your complete consciousness without all the pieces present. And that's challenging.

So, take a daily, weekly, monthly, yearly trip to the Akashic records—whatever strikes your fancy—present your vibration, and say, "I am here for the purpose of remembering why." That's all you need to do.

The part of you that is asking the question, that is wanting information on XYZ will ask the question, and then the librarian will go and find the next step for you, and Whoosh! it'll come into you like someone has shot you with one of those stun guns. Not to worry—no harm will come to you. The knowledge will come in and go Whoosh! and its contents will diffuse throughout your body. You're just going to sit and receive and feel the experience of the why, and the clarification happening all around you. As you're experiencing it, you say, "Oh, okay, I'm getting it now."

What does that do? It alters your vibration. The next time you go back you're not going to get that step, because that step has already been intoned and ingrained in your consciousness, and it's coming in, being grounded, and then fostered. Your vibration will be enhanced by it so when you go back you get the next step. You don't really have to ask for XYZ, because you'll get it, anyway, but if you are thinking about it and it feels like it's appropriate, then you can ask for it. Know that on a cellular basis, when you get that charge, that Whoosh, that ray of consciousness is sent to you. It will accelerate your vibration to the next level. Every time you go back you're going to get the step that's going to take you further.

Knowing why is very important, because if you know why from a design level, everything gets clear. As you're sitting and saying, "I feel now why we did this, why this happened, what that's about," that's where forgiveness comes in, resolution, understanding, balance. You no longer have a charge on what didn't work, you have a charge on why it happened and what's been resolved, and how you've gone on from there. It's a great way to resolve relationship, particularly long-term ones that you've been doing for thousands of years, those patterns you've lived with people which aren't yet clear. Why are you still doing the same pattern? What didn't you learn?

~

You
no longer
have a charge on what didn't work,
you have a charge
on why it happened
and
what's been resolved,
and
how you've gone on from there.

~

It's also effective for questions about health: "I realize that every single lifetime I have this or that, or this happens to me, or I always pick parents who are sick, or parents who do this or that or the other thing. Why do I do that?" This is a level of understanding that opens you to a design process, assisting you to recognize that there's no blame, there's no real right or wrong. This is about recognizing how creation designs a framework that starts off in union, ends up in dichotomy and polarity, and then results in the optimal resolution of oneness. So the foundation that you're working with in this time is to understand everything as quickly as possible. When you do this process and show up with your vibration, you get accorded by the Absolute space that has and contains and holds steady the wisdom of the universe.

So you're not just getting your XYZ kind of framework in that exchange of vibration, you're also getting acceleration of the circuitry. You're getting a very beautiful level of validation from the universe that says, "You came up here, you really want to discern this, you really want to understand it, and you really want to foster a relationship now that's based on something new. You're ready to see beyond what your eyes can see in the world, beyond what your heart and emotion have experienced. You want to take this one step further. Congratulations, here you are, we're going to give you now as much consciousness as will fit into this next level of your awareness, and we're going to push it in there as far as we can, so that you have a higher opportunity to integrate it."

That's why we called it a stun gun, because it's going to come in, and for a minute you're going to say, "Oh, can I do anything, can I move? There's so much here, and it's coming so quickly. Oh, it's not going to hurt me, it's just to slow me down for a minute, so that I can sit here and absorb." So stunning you means that it's going to shift you from whatever consciousness level you're on to the deepest consciousness level that's available for you at that time. It's also going to support that next step for you, so that you're familiar enough with it to say, "This feels like exactly what I needed to find out," even though it might take you deeper into those experiences than you had anticipated. It's okay, because it's made to order.

As you take the incentive, and make the time to explore your totality, very interesting things begin to happen. One of those things is that, after a while, you get free access to the Akashic records. That means when you show your vibration enough, it's like going by a gatekeeper who knows who you are, who can identify you, knows your vehicle, what make and year you are and everything else, and you Whoosh! can just whisk by. "If you'd like to go into the top secret files, go right ahead, it's okay, you have clearance, you've been here enough times," and that starts to happen after a bit. This will vary with each of you depending on many circumstances—your history or herstory, your karma, the amount of times you've been to the records, how deeply you live your vibration on the planet, how you understand and implement your design, and so forth. Mostly it depends on pure intent.

As of February 26, 1995, you have such access to the Akashic. If you have absolute pure intent, the Akashic records are open to you without limitation. It's a big deal—for it was not always so. It means that you now have access from that pureness of intent to what needs to be made known to humanity.

It also means that at the moment you make the decision to begin, you are on a circular frame that's bringing you everything you need. As you have access to the information you can learn how it was all constructed, how everything is made, what it's about, what its function is.

This is a very exciting time for humanity, because just having pureness of intent opens up all the secrets of the universe to you. All the barriers are being destructured in this dimension also. Up to this point, the knowledge and wisdom have not been created on Earth in a way that could be assimilated, because it might have been synthesized dogmatically into a linear way of thinking.

Now that we have opportunity to keep truth as truth, and there are enough people on the planet that know how to do that—how to hold pure vibration through pure intent—there's an opportunity for as many of you as really choose to, to explore not only your record, but the record of how it came about and what it is moving toward, and what that record looks like. And we have suggested going into the hologram—going in there, looking at it, seeing what it is, seeing your part, seeing the part of everybody around you, and seeing how things are going to happen.

The other part that we play in greasing the wheel, or the spinning of this hologram for humanity and for the universe is, when we read you the record, we are actually sparking or catalyzing your part of the hologram so it gets activated. We actually activate that with you at the time when we read for you your record. This means that people will come to be with you in life, the people who are ready to live in cooperation with you, to actualize the design that you collectively

If you have

absolute pure intent,

the Akashic records are open to you

without limitation.

chose before you came in. And you all came into the Swing Between Worlds, one at a time, and then you came back two, three, five, ten, fifty, five hundred at a time and you said, "Okay, this is how we have it, how does it look? Is it going to work? Before we go in there, before we go into the playing field, we want to make sure that we have what we need, that we've covered our bases, that we have the support in motion. Before we play the game of life, we want to have played and practiced our moves."

As you create the system of the holographic consciousness, you can see everything you need to see, know everything you need to know, and make everything happen that's going to happen.

So part of our presence in the life of humanity is to make accessible those fields of energy that seem out of your reach, and to give you access to them through information and dynamic visual and vibrational exercises which will create a wave frame so that you can resonate in the same dynamic with that which you've chosen to foster in the future.

Again it's bringing the future into the present, and looking at, "What did I design in the past?" Yet, no matter what you're doing, no matter how you're functioning with it, if you don't really grasp those principles of, "How can the past and the future be the same point, and how can I be in the now and in both of them?" that's okay. Just understand that if you have pure intent and sit in your vibration for a few seconds so that you feel it, then you just fly up to that circle at twelve o'clock in front of you, and say, "I'm here, knock, knock, knock, this is my intention. I want to feel this now. I want to live this now. I'm tired of being blind and deaf and dumb, and out of sacredness and out of kilter. I really want to begin now to live the resonance of whatever is my next step."

Finding Yourself

This is where you go for your readings in the future. This is why in 1996 we are going to begin charging your frequencies—so that you can have a stronger vibration to go to the Akashic or wherever it is in the universe that you want to go, and receive what it is that your next step is, by yourself. So you show up like a "big" person, and say, "Here I am, this is who I am, and this is what I want, and this is how I bring myself to this moment." And then you're responsible to yourself. You have your own card to get in through the gate. You have affirmation about belonging, and about your pureness of intent. You begin to feel really good about yourself, because you don't need anybody to tell you what you're about—because you know.

What's very interesting to think about is the fact that your society basically functions by each of you going to somebody else to find out what's going on with you. And you do that from the time you're very tiny. Whether it's to figure out whether you're doing something right or wrong in terms of potty training, or in terms of living, how you're eating or drinking, whether you should be walking, standing, or crawling, what you should be saying, what you're not saying, or what you're thinking. "Should I be thinking this or shouldn't I be thinking this? Should I be feeling this, or maybe I shouldn't be feeling this?" Constantly you talk to somebody else, because why?

You do not see the part of yourself that you're asking about, because it's between your shoulder blades, in the back. That's the part that you want to look at, because that's where it is. That's where your wings attach. So if you can't see that your wings are attached, you forget that you are a holy spirit. You forget that you're a divine essence of light, and you say, "Well, since I don't know very much about being a human being, even if I've been around the block a lot, because it doesn't make sense, I have to go to somebody to make sense of my life for me. I have to go and ask them what's going on, because I certainly don't get it." And then you find out that they don't get it either, that they are also going to somebody else to find out what's going on in their life.

We're saying to you that it's time for that dogmatic structure of unknowing to stop, and for each of you to take the bull by the horns and say, "I'm going to the Source to find out. This is a non-biased, impartial, nonjudgmental, absolute truth about who I am. Why wouldn't I go there and find that out? It isn't in any way shadowed by someone else's perception of me, what my mother told someone about me, what my blood test told them about my body. This is about my essence, this is about who I am. This is about what is really going on, and this is about why. And I've been wanting to know why since I was two years old, and now I'm going to find out why."

This is a very special time, because each of you, by making a clear intention to recognize your truth, to experience it, to put it together, and to function, understands it from a level that can then be ordered and condensed into your consciousness so that you recognize that, no matter what is going on, you can get it all in a little

You begin
to feel really good about yourself,
because
you don't need anybody to tell you
what you're about
—because you know.

It's time
for that dogmatic structure of unknowing
t o   s t o p ,
and for each of you
to take the bull by the horns
and say,
"I'm going to the Source to find out."

~

Another dynamic that changes
is that you have
no guilt
about anything.

~

You
f e e l
as if you are on the inside track of
creation.

~

tiny screen. You can see it, and it gives you the condensed clear experience so that you feel it in all of your design levels, all of your cells, in all of your circuits, and you can expand it, acknowledge it, and put it into the formula of resonance. And now, because you can do that, you are conscious. You are aware. You are now supportive of and dynamically in relationship with yourself for the first time in as long as you can remember.

When you're in relationship with yourself for the first time, some very important dynamics change in your life. One is that you are able to be in relationship with someone else for the first time, truly, because you understand how to relate to yourself, and you understand why you are like you are. You don't have to make excuses, or decide that there's something that was left out of you when everybody else got what they needed, so there's something that you're failing at, something that is not quite working at optimal capacity. You understand that you're fully present again, knowing why, understanding who you are, activating that consciousness and putting that together.

Another dynamic that changes is that you have no guilt about anything. You have no separation about anything because you're getting it all, you're understanding why, and you don't need to separate anymore. You're feeling as if you belong to a level of awareness that is creating response on this planet. That means that no matter what's going on around you, you're able to see it clearly, you're able to understand, "Oh, this is happening for a reason. I can find out why, I don't have to react to it, I don't have to get depressed by it, I don't have to be saddened by it, I can just go up to the record and say, 'Okay, let me see what's really going on here.' "

Those of you who really like doing this may find that you go to the Akashic and get answers for others and bring back those answers to tell people why things are going on. It means that you can explain reality on such a level that the illusion dissipates. There's nothing to worry about, everything comes together, and the formula of consciousness begins to show itself to you so that you feel as if you are on the inside track of creation.

This feels good because after a little bit of time there are no more questions. You are living in the answers, you're feeling that foundation, and the support is there to continue. As you foster these determinations in the energy field, you start to understand how the universe works and what its intention is for you. Not only is that very profound and meaningful, it also brings a great deal of solace to each of you, because the peace that is making its way into the pattern of your life is because everything is resolved, and because there aren't any more questions, and because you know why. At that moment you are a creator, and that is our purpose in this dimension, to assist each of you to be a creator.

And as we unfold this information to you in this manual, that is our intention: that from this time on, we go to the records together. We co-create together. We function as one unit of consciousness, knowing why, and creating because we know why, and creating all life together, in harmony and in union, for the purpose of receiving this absolution: being at one with the Absolute without guilt. So our intention is to free humanity from restriction that is imposed by lack of knowledge, and to imprint each of you with the potential of what you are in the actual vibrational moment, so that those two places, those two times, and those two vibrations become one.

The rest is up to you.

At that moment
you are a creator,
and that is our purpose
in this dimension,
to assist each of you
to be
a creator.

The Silver Chalice of Justice

THE SILVER CHALICE IS THE "SPACE" IN CONSCIOUSNESS which represents universal justice and balance. Going to the Silver Chalice is an exercise in non-separation. It is the practice of aligning yourself with the true reason your reality happens as you experience it, and a way of knowing the truth about your relationships to others. It's a way of ascertaining your true connection to someone, and foundationing the realities of your consciousness with them, and seeing where and how they fit together.

The Silver Chalice is always recommended when one has a dispute or conflict or disagreement with someone that they would like to settle in the *universal* sense. This requires the balance point of actually understanding that no one is at fault, that no one is wrong in the situation, and that inherently, the human design was fashioned on balance. If you look at the Chalice, you can see that there are two sides which are then balanced in the center. The perspective of humanity has moved away from seeing the balance, to seeing and aligning (much of the time) with only one of the two aspects on either side of the balance point. So the Silver Chalice is the recommended "resolution constant" for allowing both sides to contribute to the balance, even if they appear to be polarized, particularly with legal disputes.

If you are to put into the experience of your own process the consciousness of patience and temperance with the highest good for all concerned being the result, putting all of the aspects of the situation and all of the players of the situation into the Silver Chalice is a way of bringing that balance into effect. The universal concept is that, since the beginning, there has been an unrolling of, or an undulation of, energy that comes from the Source. As it expresses, it

~

All I care about is that justice be done
as it needs to to be served
for the good of the whole.
I ask for balance.

~

*Nobody
knows exactly what's going on,
because
somebody else
has the authority and the power
to decide
what's going on in your life.*

finds itself in different situations and frameworks, and as these levels unfold through free will, learning takes place. Folds of this unrolling energy are rolling over others and calling out others, and are in some way dispersing the energy differently than perhaps it was intended. And as it comes down a particular channel of reality—as chosen by each individual—it sometimes will connect with and reveal itself through different kinds of situations.

If one stands in a fixed position the perspective might be: "You were supposed to roll over that way and not over this way," or, "You were supposed to come first and not last, and now that I'm first this means that I have do this, and I thought you were going to do that—." As the lineage, heredity, and karma unfold, sometimes the relationships between dynamics shift according to the unrolling of that force field, or the flow of the energy constant, as it is metered through form. So as each of you lives your life you will have experiences in which you could say, "From my perspective, I thought it would be different. I wanted it to be different. I went into this with good intention. I paid my money and I didn't get my floor done, or I didn't get my house sided, or the roof fell in after one huge rain storm. So now I have to take this person to court, and I have to create these relationships with other people—lawyers, arbitrators, and mediators—and I have to bring all of these people into this situation that I didn't want to bring in, and listen to their perspective, and all I wanted is to have it very straightforward."

These situations exist and are getting more complicated all the time—and have the experience on some level of creating mistrust between people. The dynamics seem to be constantly changing and to be in flux, so nobody knows exactly what's going on, because somebody else has the authority and the power to decide what's going on in your life.

And someone else, as it unfolds, becomes involved in your life. This is interesting when you think about the way some cultures experience reality. In some cultures, if you have a car accident with someone, you run out from the car and embrace each other, and believe that this is the universe telling you that it is time for you to meet, and you don't worry about the damage to the car. You get on with developing a friendship. So the perspective of how these events and circumstances occur is very interesting and sometimes seems complicated.

As you unfold in this time, you are dispensing with properties, relationships, old forms, and conscious structures that you may have felt to this point were legitimate, and now you realize may not be. You're looking at, "What do I do with authority? Where do I place my interest and energy? What is supportive of me in this moment, and how do I most fully compare the consciousness that I am choosing to live and the consciousness that I'm actually participating in? Is there a relevance between those two things, or between those multiple points? Am I being consistent between what I know I am, what I'm living, what I'm foundationing, what I'm involved in, and how I live my life? Is it reflective of the truth of my integrous essence? In other words, if I went up to the Akashic records, used my vibration as a library card, and then from that perspective, looked down at my life, would it be consistent? Can I say I do everything with that same vibration?" The answer is, "probably not," and that's fine. The most important thing is to go up there and look down on yourself and begin to ask yourself these questions.

Begin to look at the Silver Chalice as a way of putting together those positions, probabilities, possibilities, and parallel realities, including the experience that you're having right now, whatever it might be—particularly issues which involve litigation, or an authority figure who is included in the equation. Whether it's a traffic ticket or going before a judge for something, whether it's for a litigation of some matter or a dispute that you had with someone who still owes you money, or who hasn't in some way repaid a service to you in some sense of balance—all of you will find, if you look in the closet, that there's something there that doesn't seem completely ordained in balance. So, the Silver Chalice becomes a conscious point that you deliberate with, if possible, every day.

You say to yourself, "My choice is to place all the situations, all of the frames of my life into the Silver Chalice, and my choice is to have balance, and justice for the highest good of all concerned."

JUSTICE INJUSTICE

This is a very important point of service, because what it says is, "Every soul in this situation is as important as my soul. Everything that has happened has no meaning, other than as it pertains to balance. So I am not out to make a certain amount of money, to claim this property, do this, that or the other thing. I am out to completely

"My choice is to place all the situations, all of the frames of my life into the Silver Chalice, and my choice is to have balance, and justice for the highest good of all concerned."

Every soul in this situation is as important as my soul. Everything that has happened has no meaning, other than as it pertains to balance.

understand that balance is what is important and that nothing else is going to be served here except the balance. That's not my good, or somebody else's good, nor the good of this, nor the good of that, it is the good of the whole, again." And so as the balance begins to come together, the conflicts in your life, those injustices and seemingly unfair situations, begin to design themselves in such a way that your creation no longer involves injustice.

What's important about this as a concept, and why we're addressing it, is because you're changing the paradigm where injustice was the way justice got served.

In the old model you had to have the question before you got the answer, or before you could make change in the balance of a situation somebody acted out to raise a question in consciousness, so that the rest of humanity would say, "That isn't fair, we ought to legislate that out of existence, or we ought to put this person in a place where they won't do that again, or we ought to do this or that." And so the system of order and justice has been taken from the "fields of order" of nature, the core of order in the center of the Earth, and from the order that is based in the Hierarchy from which we speak. And it has been authoritatively handed to humanity. And that's where there's a sticky wicket, because humanity does not usually dole out justice, since it doesn't have the perspective to see what justice is.

Humanity doesn't have the "why?" information, because it hasn't gone to the Akashic records and said, "Why did that person do that? Let's spin this whole carpet through, and look at where they got jostled over there, and what they did over here, and how they come out over there!" Plop! There they are. You can see where they come out, but you don't see their journey, so how do you know why they came out that way? And that's why they have character witnesses in courts, because they are trying to establish that there's a reason for people to do what they do, that there is something going on in the life system that influences and supports certain activities and actions and outcomes. They want to give the whole picture, except that it's the whole picture of only a confined time of 30, 40, 50, or 60 years, not 60,000 years, or six millennia, or the consciousness of the complete Earth time.

When you put something in the Silver Chalice, basically what you are saying is, "I don't know what I did to them, and I don't know what they did to me. In the system of responsiveness, all I care about is that justice be done as it needs to be served for the good of the whole." You give up your claim, so to speak. You decide that nothing is as important as referencing the reality of truth. Your winning isn't as important as accessing truth.

You will understand your life from a particular perspective, rather than saying, "I've got to be right. This is who I am. I want a certain result to feel that I have been honored and connected to this experience so that the foundation is literally coming to me as *I* need it to come." When you give up what you think you need, what you think you deserve, or what you think is right, you allow the balance to come into being so that you are no longer separate from, but rather open unto. Then your system starts to change its focus.

This is why we're speaking to you who bring the highest memory—because evolution is based on what you remember. *How evolved you are is based on what you remember.*

If you go to the Akashic records and start remembering, and you're bringing the *why* into form so that you understand the dynamics, then you are a primary point of resonance that can go out to the world and say, "This is what we can do to establish order on this planet; this is the framework that can be organizing consciousness differently than it has been organized before."

So as you change the systems that are so inherently bogged down in the society, and establish a large frame that is not based on lack of trust and lack of integrity, people will care about their level of workmanship, their character of being, and will have more and more pride in the conscious distribution of truth from their absolute space. What happens, literally, is that you change those paradigms, and put those frames of reference into different categories of consciousness, and therefore, because the Chalice is your justice system, you give up control over what happens in that justice system. You just put it in. Then you are able to receive exactly what you need from wherever you need it, and this is, of course, very much the basis of the Model of Cooperation (See Appendix).

When you cooperate with the universe, the universe feeds you. You might think, "Well, I need to get $30,000 from that person." You might pursue them forever for that $30,000 and, in so doing, give up or forfeit the right to receive the $30,000 that you do deserve from someplace else. So when you let go of the need to have things be linear—"I do this for you, and you do this for me"—and you exchange that into a system that says, "I'll open myself to receive it from wherever it's available, and from wherever it has, in the biggest part of that design, already been accorded," that will be the

You decide that nothing is as important as referencing the reality of truth. Your winning isn't as important as accessing truth.

experience of justice.

As you live that experience more and more, you find that everything in your situation irons out, levels out, balances out. There is not the necessity for you to pursue those things which are unpleasant to you, and which do not seem to be reaping the results that you intend.

You are a different drummer, consciously working from a different paradigm that serves everyone at once. This brings people away from the old types of seeking justice and into a new space of representing and experiencing justice. The Silver Chalice balances it all with the infinite knowledge available in that space—knowledge usually not available in the human experience. The foundation of that consistent point of reality becomes a cornerstone in your society.

The new society will be based on less law, less thought about what is right and wrong, with more capacity for justice to be handed out by the universe—which means that the Akashic records begin to come into play here: you begin to understand how and why it is that someone is doing certain behaviors, and it's no longer upsetting to you, or disagreeable to you, because you can understand that this is their process, this is where they come from, this is what's important, and this is how it's been recognized in the world.

Just Relationships

As you come into relationship with people from this point on, if you use the Chalice as a way of responding to them—if in your dream and meditation state you ask and say the affirmation about the Chalice, you'll find that you begin to get information about those relationships. You will understand what is being resolved. You will take an equal stand in each situation, so that the foundation of your experience is that when you relate to someone, you relate to all of them—everything that is inherently valuable about that person, about their journey, about that framework that's unfolding, is available. So you have fuller, richer, deeper spaces of intimacy. It means that the part of them that you don't trust for some reason, that you cannot define, becomes clear. You say, "They did this, so it gives me this feeling. I understand that it's infinite, or it's invisible, or it has happened thousands of years ago, or will happen thousands of years in the future, and now I understand my hesitancy to A, B, or C.

Now I understand my reluctance." You begin to have that total awareness of each other. You're able to understand your responses without necessarily judging them or separating from the people involved.

As you unfold in this new time and are honing in on the truth more and more, you'll find that there are a lot of people who get left behind, people who don't fit into the model, who are struggling to understand why they are doing what they are doing. They have no clue. They don't understand that they were somebody else in another reality and this is setting up processes in them that are in constant conflict.

Many people choose to stop having relationships with others. They say, "I'm just going to go over here, and live my life by myself, and I'm not going to relate to anybody. All I've had in my life are some really difficult experiences, and so what does it matter, I'll just live alone." They end up alone, and do not necessarily understand why. When someone ends up alone and they don't know why, there is always a feeling of guilt, ineffectiveness, and unworthiness—the sense that they did something wrong, that they're unlovable, and there is a process that goes on. You can rationalize until you're blue in the face, "That person did that to me, so that's why I'm doing this." If you feel at any time alone, then there are going to be those accompanying feelings of separation, whether you're separating from somebody or they are separating from you.

For example, when you want to collect a bill from someone, the normal experience of human beings is to separate from each other, to separate from the person that owes you the money, or the company that owes you the money, or the institution—to get mad at them, and to send them letters. What's interesting is that that person or institution is teaching you about union, because if you separate from them because they owe you money, then you're living an inconsistent part of your reality, and why shouldn't they be living an inconsistent part of their reality?

So it's very important to stay unified with everybody, regardless of what the situation is about, to place all of those parameters, as many times as you need to, into the Silver Chalice and ask for justice for the highest good of all concerned. Feel this, literally, in your experience as these levels and veils of information are revealed. As the veils come down, these levels of information, and the wisdom, and the knowledge reveal much more about people and process. And as it's revealed, the dynamics are, "Oh, now I know why I felt that

When someone ends up alone
and they don't know why,
there is always a feeling of guilt
and ineffectiveness
and unworthiness—the sense
that they did something wrong,
that they're unlovable.

~

It's very important
to stay unified with everybody,
regardless
of what the situation is about,
to place all of those parameters,
as many times as you need to,
into the Silver Chalice
and ask for justice
for the highest good of all concerned.

~

What's interesting is that union requires of all of us that we be able to unify regardless of the situation or regardless of what it appears, in the illusion, has happened.

Anything that creates separation is an illusion. Anything that truly brings union is reality.

way about that person. Now I have justification for this." What's interesting is that union requires of all of us that we be able to unify regardless of the situation or regardless of what it appears, in the illusion, has happened.

ILLUSION REALITY

When we talk about illusion and reality, it's a very important distinction, because people think about reality as being that which is true, and that which they can prove is true, and illusion as being something that is false. The way that we talk about it is that illusion is really anything that is out of union, and reality is everything that is in union.

So it has less to do with truth and more to do with union, because truth is subjective many times. You can say, "It's truth because it's right," and then you are in that out-of-balance situation where you are looking at the points of the reality on either side and not necessarily at the point in the center. Anything that creates separation is an illusion. Anything that truly brings union is reality.

We're speaking now about walking your talk, about looking at all the dynamics in your life and saying, "All right, no matter how they were created, no matter what system was foundationed with them, it is really important that I take responsibility personally for living only in a unified place, only being alive in reality."

"Anything else that separates me on any level, regardless of how right I think I am about a situation, can be released into the Chalice so that the foundation becomes organized around the experience of absolute truth, which is where those places of union come together in the Chalice."

Fundamentally, as we provide a responsiveness to ourselves, we come together in an organized manner with the framework of the truth as it is seen from that total reality. That is why you're going to the Akashic records. You want to see absolute truth. You're not interested just in nuts and bolts and pieces, as much as you're interested in the "why?" This takes you back to the beginning to see why. It's as if you're foundationing a relative connection with the truth of the original space in order to find the parameters which diffuse themselves from that point, or that unfold in that unrolling carpet and bring together that affirmation.

Literally, as you create the context of seeing yourself as one who serves infinite justice, you will then receive infinite justice. And you don't receive it until you serve it.

If you don't think something is just in your life—whatever it is, from very tiny to very huge—one of the things that's happening is that somehow the service to that infinite space is being disrupted. Therefore, as you unfold your design, there's the experience of somehow being out of synchrony with that space.

If you are coming from infinite truth, the foundation becomes that the organization of your own space, your own affirmation—your psyche, your mind, emotion, body, spirit, soul, karma, and your infinite space of design—are working together in your life.

If for some reason there is a discordance going on, then whether it is with somebody else that you need to put in the Chalice or with a part of yourself that you might want to put in the Chalice, you're being asked to serve infinite truth. You're being asked to unify your individual field, synthesize what that means in terms of reality, and be receptive to the truth of the union that is the design. Then the foundation is organized around the experience of that one place of truth, which is all truth. What you're being asked, time after time is, "Are you aligned with that? Is there a constancy to this that you can support in your life to begin to change the models of your world?"

Literally, at this time, it's not just about what you do with you, because the veils are so thin that whatever you do with you is sending very loud messages to the world. A lot of chaos is going on because so many messages are being sent to the world now. Instead of listening only to the structure as a relative point of truth, people are beginning to open to many different dimensions to find the truth.

As you go forward and organize that consciousness in the world, the choices that people have are much more diverse. The impact and the energy they're receiving is much more intricate.

That's why sometimes it's confusing. "Who's telling the truth? What's going on? What should I believe? Should I worry about this or not? Somebody said we're going to have this. Should I worry about this? Should I spend lots of energy and time preparing for it, even though I didn't get information on it, and it doesn't feel like something that I'm going to need to worry about?" Where does the balance come in? Where do you live in safety? What do you think about that's going to be supportive of what you want to create? How

~

Literally,
as you create
the context of seeing yourself
as one who serves
infinite justice,
you then will receive infinite justice.
And you don't receive
it until you serve it.

~

Instead of listening
only to the structure
as a relative point of truth,
people are beginning to o p e n
to many different dimensions
to find the truth.

~

164 Sunlight on Water

Your development
will be on all levels
simultaneously.

do you take all the information that's coming in and weed through it, so that you take the wheat from the chaff? And what in each person is the truth? How is that going to be lived, and what's the foundation of that going to be? These questions are going to get stronger in each of you. They are not going to become less important—they are going to become more important.

As changes begin to occur physically on the Earth and in the psyches of people, and in the human structures, these questions are going to be imperative for you to answer. The Silver Chalice is a vehicle where you can put all the information that's coming, all the questions you have, all the spaces that need to be sorted out or organized in your thinking so that you know, "This is what I really feel about this." And you may not know right now what you feel about it. You stick all those parameters into the Silver Chalice and say, "I ask for balance."

This is a place where you can sort out or organize the levels that you're working with now. As the destruction of old frameworks supports the creation of new ones, chaotic energy is appearing in your dimension. You're going to have constant readouts about that chaos—what it feels like, and how people are going through it—the fear, the grief, the pain, and the struggle. All of this will come into your awareness. Stay steady and constant while putting that frame into position. By honoring completely, and putting the dilemmas in which you find yourself into the Chalice, things will be called together differently. It's as if you have a reason for creating new ways of being, which is consciously ordered by its own consideration—the consideration of whoever or whatever is being added to the Chalice.

You'll find that you receive the impact of those particular points at the same rate of speed or the same velocity that other people do, even though you're not involved in them. They might be hundreds or thousands of miles away from you.

Many of you are receiving information about earthquakes and Earth changes and tremblings in the Earth's crust, and chasms that are developing that you can feel and see, sense and know about. This is going to increase. We want you to understand that your perceptions and awarenesses are going to increase—not just that you say, "Now I can feel what she's really feeling, or I can see what he's really seeing, or think what he's thinking." Your development will be on all levels simultaneously. It's not only that you open to mental telepathy, you also experience more consciousness.

This is about reality here completely unifying itself in such a way that the illusion falls apart. Anything that's been connected to illusion, anything that has been in any way separating, is going to make a statement as it leaves. It's going to be resolved and organized and put together, and so the system of consciousness is going to effectively relate with its own individuation. What that means is that honoring the Absolute becomes intentioned in the experience of the person.

If you put the Chalice into effectiveness and hold that space, you can balance any information that comes in to you, any energy, any relationship, any process. Systematically, you function in a way that supports the integration, which is the way that the design has been placed. All the pieces fit. Everything, in a coincidental and synchronistic sense, comes into resolution. Instead of paying attention to the details that don't seem to come together for you, or that raise as many questions as they answer, if you put them into the experience and allow them to organize in your Chalice, then the framing begins to support itself differently. You begin to see where it is going, how it is going to come out, and what the new foundation is going to be about.

As you respond to the totality of the Chalice, you'll recognize that you are bringing the balance into the same moment that you're experiencing dichotomy. That balance is creating the justice, and the justice is moving you to areas of awareness which allow you to institute new models. It's actually a way for you to experience that you're seeing and knowing and being in an absolute place, which is the Chalice. What comes from that is available to the world, and to the experience, so that the foundation begins to recognize its own integrity.

You begin to figure this through, so that you say to yourself, "The recognition of the constancy that we're looking for in this new time, which is the reality of union in its essence, is now coming through me. As I learn to discern and make available the spaces of reality, then I can move with that as it unfolds, and bring ways to Earth which foster union in the world."

This is about reality *here completely unifying itself in such a way that the illusion falls apart.*

How the Chalice Serves the Design

As the foundation of justice
is lived in the world,
you have
the experience
of being in Heaven on Earth,
and the experience of Heaven
being the creation of
that universal paradigm of justice.

~

As you create relationship
with the Chalice,
you create relationship
with your new models.

~

The Silver Chalice has several broader and more diverse applications. After you work through the conflictual nature of human reality, you experience going to a whole different level of perception with the Chalice, where you work with global and universal frameworks. Use the Chalice to balance and measure Earthly things which on some levels would be disturbing, so that you're putting them into the totality of the whole, instead of looking at them from just one linear framework.

Working with the Akashic records and the Silver Chalice simultaneously is a way of taking the information, putting it into the Chalice, experiencing the balance, and then taking that balance into the world, understanding what equilibration is about. You can go into situations you've never been in before and aren't sure how to handle, where discernment, balance and solace are needed, and create new models, and a new foundation and resonance.

We can decide we're going to use the Chalice and extrapolate the actions and the frameworks that serve the whole in this design, in this moment, and we're going to let them flow into our awareness, so that what we actualize is what is coming up from the surface of that Chalice to be seen as a valid way of integration.

You are creating a referencing system where you use the justice of the universe instead of human justice. When this turn happens in consciousness, when you are actually turning the scales around so that universal justice is in effect rather than human justice, that's when you will have your most capability on this planet for healing. As the foundation of justice is lived in the world, you have the experience of being in Heaven on Earth, and the experience of Heaven being the creation of that universal paradigm of justice.

When that universal paradigm comes to the planet as a viable means to settle disputes, to organize relationships, to understand cooperative measures and partnerships, you experience the foundation of that level so that it serves to ordain totally new realities on the planet. As you create relationship with the Chalice, you create relationship with your new models.

You will experience that foundation differently so that you are no longer attenuating to what isn't present or what is irritating the process. Then you are more able to open to that space of justice, consciously. As level upon level of organizational knowing is made aware, people will say, "Oh, that's why that happened; this is what that is about."

It is important to understand justice from the perspective of the Silver Chalice and how it is lived out in world situations. Part of the reason why accessing balance from the Chalice will occur, is because it's going to be important to document the awarenesses. Some of you reading this material may feel called to go to the Akashic records, look at what's going on in the world, and put that into the Chalice, and say, "Show me what the justice is in this. This race is killing that race, and this race is looting that one, and this person is prosecuting that one, and this person is killing that one, and this person is raping that one, and this person is stealing from that one. I came up to the Akashic, and I think I understand why these things are happening, but then I get down here and I can't sort it out, because it seems so chaotic and so out of order." You then take the situations, put them in the Chalice, and say, "I want to know the 'why' of these experiences."

Many of you will write books to help explain human evolution, and the experiences of dichotomy and violence. As people move through these levels of reality—up and down from physical, emotional, mental, to the Akashic, and up and down between the levels of the physical and the Chalice—you will make trails. Those of you who are on that first wave of individuals who access that information, as you go back and forth constantly, will make pathways for others to follow. Just imagine what the world would be like if everybody makes that journey once a day, to figure out why— the activities of your world cease to be chaotic.

Much of what you can do about violence, hatred, and separation, is to make your own path of peace and to find that everything you experience in your reality becomes consistent with that place of order, so that the foundation is then lived so that your relationship with that point becomes considerable. In other words, instead of relationship with the newspaper, or with whatever is going on in the news, whatever is being hand fed to you by whomever is deciding what it is you're supposed to hear, you say, "I don't want that anymore. I want to go to a place where I know the truth of what I'm hearing and seeing and feeling, and it makes sense in terms of the total picture. It makes sense in terms of the fact that there is a design, and the design does have as its fulfillment the resolution of human dichotomy and the experience of union in all levels and dimensions, simultaneously."

~

Just imagine
what the world would be like
if everybody
makes that journey once a day,
*to figure out **why***
—the activities of your world
cease
to be chaotic.

~

If you diligently work with the Chalice, you will resolve karmic and legal processes very quickly and easily, because you're destined to clean up your act on every level. It's not just on the levels of forgiveness, or having guilt or not having guilt, or playing the game or not playing the game, it's about honoring that your commitment to *being* is real, and that it has to be on every level.

It isn't just, "I meditate once a day for an hour or two, so therefore that's my work." The work is 24-hours a day from now on. It doesn't stop. You're not going to get a rest. The only rest you're going to get is in being in spirit.

It's going to be like an incessant rain on a tin roof— a constant, "I'm hearing it again, I'm hearing it again, I'm hearing it again, I'm hearing it again." It's about changing illusion, which means that because illusion has infiltrated every crack of your consciousness, it will be let go from every crack of your consciousness.

This isn't about whether what you're doing is good or bad, whether you're being irritable, or your consciousness isn't being considered on some level, it's just that it's time for there to be an affirmation of that consciousness so that you're realizing that this is about *being*. When we talk about it being about *being*, everybody thinks, "That's really good because I'll stop thinking." But what we mean, when it's about *being*, is that it's about *being*—it's who you are in every micro-second of your consciousness in *any* dimension.

Other dimensions, lifetimes, and points of reality are affecting what's happening to you now. If you wake up irritable with somebody in the morning and you weren't irritable when you went to bed, something happened during the night to make you irritable. You might have gone to another dimensional space with them, and worked out something or not worked out something, and then awakened and said, "Oh, that's what that's about. Something has happened. What is it? Let me find out, because that's part of my beingness. And let me *be* with whatever is going on, instead of trying to decide it's okay, or it's probably fine, or I should just disregard it and it will go away." *Listen to your messages, feel them, consider them, think about them, be with them, and maintain the integrity in your consciousness that your intention is to be in that Chalice of justice.* Put everything in there that you experience or think about or that's pending for you, and know that everything is going to be fine in the sense that it's all going to come out in balance.

As you create the knowing of that balance, it supports your life system. This means whether you get enough money for what you do or not, whether or not people are aware of your presence when you think they should be—that they are not taking your classes, or reading your book, or calling you on the phone for lunch, or they're not interested in having dinner, or in being in your life in a certain way, whatever those feelings of injustice are, because you're not receiving what you need—those are all levels that are being worked out by everybody. They may not even belong to you.

The more astutely you receive these messages, the more you're foundationing them in your life, the more you will realize that you can't separate yourself from everybody else. You don't have an ego in the same way any more. Your personality is undergoing drastic change, because you're becoming the ray of light we talked about. You're becoming that consciousness of vibration and resonance that is able to live from the substance. You are completely, universally oriented so that you make a foundation in your life from the commitment to *be*. This is very important. Ultimately everything that you live, everything that you require to live, comes to you from the invisible.

Once you make the pact that the invisible is part of you, and you really are aligned with that, then the foundation becomes literal for you. In other words, you can't separate it out because you realize that whether somebody's handing you money or you're finding it under a rock, or under a carpet—no matter how things are received, ultimately they come from the universe. So putting things in the Chalice takes them to the level where they're really happening. You can retain an attorney, or talk to a medical doctor, or a chiropractor, or see an herbologist. However, ultimately, everything's in the Chalice, everything's in the consciousness. The Chalice is where you'll go to find the meeting place of all information you seek, without prejudice and without judgment.

You don't have an ego in the same way any more.

~

Ultimately everything that you live, everything that you require to live, comes to you from the invisible.

~

The Chalice is a representation of the meeting place of all information, without prejudice and without judgment.

~

The Chalice Fosters Honor

You can be a Chalice yourself and foster that as a way of being. You can honor that in every moment, what you are called to look at about receiving, or giving, or substance, is ultimately organizing a reference in your awareness that supports the integrity of your complete consciousness and says, "I now know how it works."

This is the whole thing again—if you know that it works in this way, and you use this system, then immediately you will bypass your present legal system. You won't need it, because you'll come into affirmation with the consciousness of the people. You'll make the agreements before you physically make the agreements, and everything will always come out in balance. You won't need situations to learn about balance.

You won't need to have understandings with people that are written down to the last "t" and the last dot on the page, saying, "If we don't do this, we don't know what we've decided." Your word will be your bond, and you will need no other framework except that intentional resonance between two people which honors the system which you've created, be it small or large.

People will go back to honoring their word. They will go back to stating what they need. They won't worry about having enough, so that they try to cheat other people out of whatever it is they're cheating them out of. They will have the sense that they're clear and steadfast and constant, and able to live by their word. And the word is very important. It's coming again to the time of trust, the time of resonance, and the time when people can cooperate. As long as you have legal systems such as they are now, where people cannot speak to each other and make resolution, there is going to continue to be a sense that everyone is in competition, that everyone is out for oneself. The experience of being in a consolidated frame where everything is available and you can sift it through and see order and justice come out of it, is very exciting because it is a very strong portent and affirmation for the coming of your world. You can really understand that the value of your consciousness is absolute, and you can affect everything by that consciousness. You experience the resonance so that the foundation is literal for you, then you're able to understand and organize your life around this experience now, and everything starts making sense.

Again, because of the number of decisions that will be made by many of you in the next two to three years, it is very important for you to have a method of sorting things out for yourself that you can trust, that you can work with, and that deals with physical process. Notice that we are not talking about your soul's calling, your essential states of resonance, or your beingness in the terms of what you designed for yourself. We're talking about what you do with the world, with people, situations, ideas, and information that's coming in. For example, seismology—seismographic readings. What do you do with those when you hear them? When you hear about what's anticipated and who's doing what to whom, what do you do with that? You can put it in the fluids, immerse it, and yet you're a human being, and you have relationship with other people, and with your world.

To take this and transpose it to the level of consciousness that has to do with infinite balance gives you a perspective that will always be honored by everyone. No matter who's involved in the situation, if they feel that you're out to actualize the balance for them also, they will then start cooperating with you to create resolution.

So, again, this is a model that could be used for litigation, mediation, resonance, or to support responsiveness in others. It becomes a personal tool that will guide you during this time.

This will all be sorted out for most of you by the year 2000, because you're going to have alternative legal processes by then. You're going to have the experience of groups making decisions in ways that are so easy that you'll wonder why you haven't created them earlier. All of that will start happening in 1995, 1996, and 1997, so that those of you who use the Silver Chalice will gravitate more towards working in community-based, co-creative consciousness, because you will not have the kinds of issues that now face humanity. That's because you'll transpose those issues from looking at the dichotomy to experiencing the union and balance. When you transpose them, you also create the models to serve from that context. So you're jumping from one to the other, and a foundation gets built. It's literally honoring that framework and saying, "Okay, here I am," and everything that comes in and goes out is going to be of the same resonance. So I can honor and formulate and design and resonate. I can also just hold the Chalice, ask it to show me, and wait for that result, rather than trying to use all of the process that I was taught or conditioned to experience before.

The Nuts and Bolts of the Chalice

This also gives you a way of looking into the future, of creating new systems, because you can put all of the components of an idea into the Chalice and say, "Show me what happens." You can say, "I want to create a community, and I have ten people who have signed up. I want to create a business, and I have this amount of money, and these resources." Or you can say, "I want to marry this person and

No matter who's involved in the situation, if they feel that you're out to actualize the balance for them also, they will then start cooperating with you to create resolution.

*The Silver Chalice
is the framework through which
mediation happens
between dimensions.*

they have five children, and ten cousins, and what would my life be like with this person?" You can take every single situation, stick it into the Silver Chalice and see a read-out and get a projection on it. This is what the read-out says, this is where balance is, and this is how it's lived. So you can say, "I think I need to add this to that equation also, and it looks like we're going to need about 5,000 more dollars for that to happen."

Now it doesn't mean that you use only logical information and say, "I can't do it." Because you can always tap into it, unify with it, accelerate it and go into the future, power the present with the future, utilize the energy of the universe, go into substance, and manifest through having the points symmetrical and vibrationally consonant. You can do many things for which you have skills, and yet if you put it in the Chalice, it gives you a way of actually determining what the outcome in balance would be. So you can see, in a nuts and bolts fashion, what you might add to this to make it more effective, to make it last longer, to include more resources or people, or to make it longer in terms of its life or its process.

So as you look at the Silver Chalice, it can become a vehicle for all kinds of things. If you're wanting to purchase property, wanting to do classes and looking at how many buildings you need, and what you have, and who is there, and how much money you have, you can put all of that in the Silver Chalice and get answers. Basically, what you're getting is aggregation. Everything you put in is going together and aggregating. It's giving you a read-out, like a spontaneous kind of ticker-tape that comes out and says, "This is how that would work."

This can save lots of time and energy because any time you can use the vehicle of vision and the experience of energy to get an answer, instead of using physical resources, it's easier. You can do anything with your awareness that you can do with your physicality, and of course, more. So save yourself time and energy. Go in, put the dynamics together and ask, "Does it work?" You can also do that for somebody else, by putting them into the equation and asking, "Will it work for them to be here, will it work for them to proceed in this way?"

You live from absolute reality all the time, which means that you can see the ways in which union will occur in the highest good all the time. So that is the course of action you're taking, the framework you're working with, and the dynamic which most clearly serves that capacity. A sensitivity is created that says, "I'm now ready to act as that mediator between spirit and form, because that's what the Silver Chalice is." The Silver Chalice is the framework through which mediation happens between dimensions.

You are now interdimensional beings. Once you have used your library card of vibration to access the Akashic, you're an *inter*disciplinary, *inter*dimensional being, in action. "I am exercising my divine right to know and to live as the conduit for the experience of the above and the below in the world, so that these levels of attunement can come together here, and be a symbol of the consciousness which is carried in the universe for humanity."

The Silver Chalice is a gift that comes to the world at a time when order and law, when the letter of the law, is failing the system. So we take it a few steps up, and aggregate from more levels, and bring in more resources, because we do not ever solve a problem at the level that it's born. We bring in other levels and dimensions to assist us at this time to more fully live the consciousness we have ordained. This is a calling, this is an honoring, this is saying, "*We* can do it ourselves with assistance and guidance from that which is ordered in the universe. Now we can emulate that order in this place. We can bring it closer and closer dynamically to that which we understand, to that which we evolved into and from, and can also formulate responses from different parts of ourselves. We don't have do it mentally, emotionally, or legally. We can do it so that the foundation begins to be different here."

The balance in our system doesn't come from meditating once a day or once a week anymore, but from finding out, "What can I do for the whole? Where can I go in my consciousness that those answers are going to be there, not just for me, but for everybody? How can we create these models that work, that are intentioned, that make a foundation? How can we do this in the nuts and bolts of premise, organization, and congruence, and take it into fact, data, action, projection and instituting, or beginning?"

Every time the foundation becomes literal unto itself, there is the experience of balancing that consciousness to such a degree that you know you have made the bond between those dimensions. You've made that bond between Heaven and Earth, made that bond between the part of you that is in the Akashic record and the part of you that's in the world. The more symmetry you have between those dimensions and levels, the more there is an experience of feeling again, that sense of belonging—that you can marry those levels together, that it does work, and it can be sacred here.

The Silver Chalice is a gift that comes to the world at a time when order and law, when the letter of the law, is failing the system.

We do not ever solve a problem at the level that it's born.

Whatever is going on has a purpose, and you can work with it dynamically. It's saying "Yes!" to. It's allowing. It's honoring and receiving. And it's also knowing you are important in this process, because when you orchestrate all these parts and put them together, you as that spectrum and point of light, now begin to radiate more truth, more fullness, more awareness.

You begin to participate, to further the design, and to honor that which has brought you here. It is a way to live it fully as that design, rather than to wake up every day and say, "I just don't know. I don't know. I read this and I read that. I heard this and I heard that. I don't know what to do. I don't know where I should live. I don't know what I should do." Just stop and say, "Hey, wait a minute, this is all bunk. I know exactly who I am, exactly where I belong, exactly what's going on, and it's time I fully lived it. It's time I fully saw who I am—I will look in the mirror 360 degrees. Where I belong, I plant my feet now firmly; Who I belong with, I plant my feet firmly; How I want my body to function, I plant my feet firmly." How is it that your life is to be lived? Plant your feet firmly and get on with it. Procrastination at this point in time will serve no meaningful end.

As you make those choices and decisions and ground them in, that's when they'll start working. That's when those pieces come together and show you how. For right now, it's a sense of, "All right, if I'm not sure, really, really not sure, I'll put it in the Silver Chalice. I'll let the balance come out the other end. Once I know what the balance is, I'll stand firm with it. I'll go from there." It doesn't mean that you can't put new pieces into the Chalice; it doesn't mean that you cannot use whatever new information comes in as a way to open your planting, your firmness, and your capacity. Literally, it's not about ending anything, it's about growing it. So grow it the way it really wants to be grown. Honor it in such a way that you're living it purposefully all the time, whatever *it* is.

Remember that as long as it's in balance in the Chalice, everyone wins, and everything comes into harmony. There's now an opportunity for reconstructing the order on your planet, in individual and group experiences.

The models will shape themselves differently. If everyone were honest and living the balance of their highest opportunity and experience, there would be less need for authority. There would be less dissemblance and segregation, because people wouldn't be worried about what other people were doing. They would be too busy living and honoring their fullness. If you're honoring and living your fullness, you very rarely know what's going on with other people, because you're too busy planting your own feet and opening out your own consciousness. It's very important for you to say, "Where's my nose?" If it's in other people's business, it's probably not doing its own business. So it's a very good time to shake yourself out.

Honor yourself and what you have to contribute. Plant your feet and get yourself going. What are you here to contribute? Live that contribution rather than waiting for an infinite number of variables that don't have any meaning, and cause you to feel ineffective. Do it now! Live it now!

Fully understand who you are. Ask, look in the mirror, turn around, put your life in the Silver Chalice, really put it all in there, and say, "All right, I want a blurb. I want a ticker-tape that comes out. What's my balance point? What have I really done in this life? What could I have done in this life? Let me hold these two things up and look at them. Let me look in the mirror. Am I doing what I came here to do? Am I living it as fully as I can? Is there something else that's in that Chalice that I have not resolved, have overlooked, have hoped would work out? It's time for me to do it now."

When you take the bull by the horns, and really start living that way, other people match that intention with you. The sacredness of the message of how you are to create balance together is forged. Then whatever you've been through together has meaning, and if it doesn't have meaning, you're missing something in that experience. Again, it's fine if you want to miss it, and yet you'll keep missing it, and as you keep missing it, you'll create another situation where you miss it, and yet another situation where you miss it.

So it's very much a part of your ordination, during this very special time, to get it together. And that isn't a judgment, like you're not doing okay, it's that you are doing okay and you can do better. All of you can do better. It doesn't mean you don't play, or that you don't have time for yourself to create and live. It means that you live intentionally.

You live in the substance of the fluid of the universe. You always expect the universe to be there whenever you remember to ask for something, or communicate. The universe expects no less of you. Be there, because it's up to you now. There's nobody else to be blamed, because we now have the Chalice. It's a co-responsible, co-created situation, whatever *it* is. It means that that point of reality is now determined through its own course of action, not through your

*Honor yourself
and what you have to contribute.
Plant your feet and get yourself going.*

*It means that that point of reality
is now determined through
its own course of action,
not through your opinion of it.*

opinion of it.

This is very freeing and allows you, ultimately, to support truth, because you realize that whatever it is that you're about, if it's not about truth, it doesn't matter. You realize where you are in your process. You're the only one who can pull yourself up by your boot-straps, because it's a free-will experience, so whatever you put into it, you're going to get out of it. The foundation of this is inherently absolute and infinite truth, and if you link up with this system, you will live nothing less than that. And that is how it has been ordained.

Unifying
Energy Fields

Unifying
Unifying
Unifying

IN THE NEXT TWENTY YEARS, BY THE YEAR 2016, the experience of being in the free will process will be so different that you will awaken and realize you have changed dimensions while remaining in the same dimension. You will be living in union with all peoples—the peace of a million years of dreaming. If you foster this intention now, you will provide the underlying framework for this new and absolute space of union to manifest in your experience and, therefore, here on Earth.

The field of union calls to you *from the beginning*. This means that there is, and has always been, a consistent and congruent flow of energy from all points of your reality, within your system, and that that system is reflected in other systems. You are in a total system, even though you may feel yourself, sometimes, to be only one system. These systems basically vibrate at the same rate of speed—your individual and original system are the same, and you are always gravitating toward the experience of integrating that in your physical life here.

When you are looking for a relationship, a place to settle down, for a job that is amenable, and friends that are cooperative in nature and who share your interests, this is based on how many of your circuits and how much of your field is compatible with the fields that you encounter, or have accordance or interrelationship with. This is a movement by the whole being to instrument, initiate, and create the union of the original and the specific together in your life. Another way of saying this is that you are about creating your unified field, or having all of your vibrational levels in union with the above and the below.

Everything you could understand about your compatibility with anything has to do with the amount of frequency you have in common, the amount of vibrational levels shared. If something comes together and feels like it's matching with a sense of

If it's going to be
other than projection—
if it's going to be
a real unified field—
then when you come together
it's going to feel like
union is being created—
not necessarily just in you,
but
in the total framework of that energy.

~

Relationship
meaning
intentional sharing of circuitry
on an intimate level.

~

"I could stand *in my own unified field*
and not be in any way
dependent upon that other person
to unify my frame for me."

~

coordination, it's because from a very fundamental level, you're vibrating at the same rate of speed. You're creating the same consistent wave frame, and not hitting against each other's waves.

An example of hitting against another's wave is the concept of people having chips on their shoulders. When people learn, there are certain areas of density in the body which reflect that learning. The shoulders are one of the most prominent areas. When people walk around in a room full of people they hit their shoulders together—their chips hit together—and they experience being teachers for each other, and might say, "I'm really not compatible with that person; our energies are different," which is the nice way of saying that you don't get along with someone.

And that is accurate, because when you feel a pulling toward someone, sometimes it's because their circuits are filling up in ways that yours are not. If it's going to be other than projection—if it's going to be a real unified field—then when you come together it's going to feel like union is being created—not necessarily just in you, but in the total framework of that energy. Sometimes it's a challenge to distinguish if it's really a unified field or your projection of the unified field. Is this the way you *wish* it were? Sometimes people wake up and realize they have been in an absolutely different ball park than they thought they were in.

One thing that would be helpful for you is to learn about your field of energy, and to know which circuits are on and which circuits are off. As you attenuate that frequency, or go out into the world, you understand the union that is being created and where it comes from, what its basis is, how it's fashioned or discerned, and how you, from your own innate space, can begin to open that unified field and create consistency in your own wave frame—which is an inside job.

As the frameworks of relationship change, it will be very amenable for you to say to yourself, "All right now, I feel in myself what I used to want in relationship, what I used to feel was the way I created union. And now, what I would like to do, is fill up those places in myself, to actually unify my own energy field, so that I can see and feel how I could go into a relationship with someone again—relationship meaning intentional sharing of circuitry on an intimate level—and feel that I could hold my own pattern. I could stand in my own unified field and not be in any way dependent upon that other person to unify my frame for me."

Understanding Your Field of Energy

Light beings, the ones who have come here with the intention to serve as light, will find the years between 1996 and 2000 especially important, because this is the time when all light beings come into the same wave frame of union. And the design suggests that this really needs to be done by the year 2000.

Understanding your innate field of energy is one of the most valuable assets to take into this new time, because, literally, energy is everything.When you understand and discern your own field of energy, and know what it's doing all the time, you constantly feel that you're orchestrating your own course, mastering your own life, captaining your own ship. What you learn can be applied to help transform the energies of situations by helping others to equilibrate their vibration. They can then communicate more accurately and understand more clearly who they are. It is also very important, as this new time unfolds, to remember that the hearing now is going to be without sound. So the more you understand about your field of energy, the more easily the creative capacity will be engendered in terms of organizing knowing from nothing—no-thing.

As you create reality now, remember that your foundation is energetic. You come from, are derived from, and return to light. You have a basis of order and truth established within you, and honoring those spaces and opening and receiving and aligning those circuits is very, very important. Then by grounding them and experiencing your mastery, you receive and intone equilibrium. All of that makes up a wave frame—how you think, what you do, your lineage, how much you respond to telepathy, mental intuition, the experience of receiving, the experience of communicating, connecting, and grounding. These are the determining points which reflect the total field of energy.

If you are not grounding, your energy is usually perceived from your waist up. If you're grounding and not receiving, it is usually from your waist down. If you think a lot and do not speak, there will be energy flows which come into the head and have no place to go if you're not expressing them. If you're using the center of zeal at the back of the neck—which unleashes your spiritual force—you will find that tension is eased in your shoulders, and creation moves through your body. The channels at the top of your head come into the center of zeal and are transformed into expression, which means

~

*Understanding
your innate field of energy
is one of the most valuable assets
to take into this new time,
because, literally,
energy is everything.*

~

*It is also very important,
as this new time unfolds,
to remember that
the* hearing *now
is going to be without sound.*

~

*You come from,
are derived from,
and return to light.
You have a basis of order and truth
established within you,
and honoring those spaces
and opening and receiving
and aligning those circuits
is very, very important.*

~

Your wave frame is
always
touching something else.

~

Your etheric causal field of energy
g o e s   o u t
in a twelve foot circle around *you*
all the time.

~

Individual energies
mix and match with each other.

~

The easiest way
to pick up a wave
and feel *harmonious*
is to be
in the spiritual energy of people
who have a congruent purpose.

~

that they are spoken, breathed into the body, or used by the arms, fingers, and hands through writing, drawing, sculpting, or painting. If you dance and move that energy of zeal through the body, it grounds into the feet and you will procreate and co-create more easily—procreation not necessarily always meaning biological childbirth. You are always aware of what is happening in your energy field, even if you're not linked to it consciously. The objective of this particular process is to be consciously aware of your energy patterns, how they foster growth and expansion, or keep you constricted in the body—keep you held back.

The wave frame is not encapsulated in your own system and isolated, it is always touching something else. For example, your etheric causal field of energy goes out in a twelve foot circle around you all the time. So, when you sit in a room with other people, you experience your spiritual level connected to theirs. That's why, when you walk into a situation like a bar, or someplace where there are mixed energies, you might walk in the door and immediately want to leave. Those individual energies mix and match with each other, sometimes causing great confusion because there may be cross purposes or underlying currents such as expectations, judgments, etc. So the field of energy will be incongruent when you walk into that space.

When you walk into a situation where a group is praying, the energy will, nine times out of ten, be congruent. People pray together, meditate together, or foster experiences of alpha together, because the easiest way to pick up a wave and feel harmonious is to be in the spiritual energy of people who have a congruent purpose, a reason for meeting and being together that is non-mental. When you have spiritual and mental aspects mixed together—for example, a group with a spiritual intention that's meeting to make a decision about something—and you walk into the room, you may feel the energies as dichotomous, or at least vibrationally incompatible, at that moment. You might walk in and say, "We need to shift the energy. Let's hold hands and pray, let's meditate, let's ground, let's just be quiet for a minute, let's see if we can recenter."

When you work in your own field, you may feel this incongruence—"I really want to be, to receive, to allow. I really want to be in that space, and yet I'm thinking all these thoughts, and I'm wondering why I didn't do this and why I didn't do that." You may feel frazzled or frenzied, and the more intuitively aligned you are with your calling, where your direction lies, and what the foundation of your being is, the more easily you will find that you get frenzied because of your sensitivity. If you are a very mental person—you've spent 99 percent of your life in the mind—and you begin to attune to the spirit, you'll feel less frenzied than those who are 99 percent in the spiritual etheric body and have 1 percent of the mind trying to kick back in.

Once you refine the circuits, any level of incompatibility or incongruence in those levels gives you a very strong read-out. You've attained that level of resonance; you have that feeling of compatibility within yourself. So the more sensitive you are, the more easily you're aware of those little pieces of inconsistency and choose to move into deeper spaces of resonance. It is not possible, necessarily, to judge how far along you are at any point in time based upon your response, because the more your circuits are aligned the more easily you can get irritated.

So it's a good idea to say, "If I'm irritated, then I'm ready to come into the space of my own resonance again. Yes, I know I'm on the edge of flipping out of that resonance, and I can flip back in."

As you practice unifying the circuitry of your field, you also learn to discern what the circuits are telling you, and how the alignment of the unified field can best be accomplished in every moment. If you are really with the field of energy, you'll find you are immediately able to attune to the part of you that can re-establish resonance. In other words, as you refine the circuits, it gets easier to maintain them. It gets easier to flip the track and come into those aligned spaces.

It gets much easier to choose ahead of time where you want to be and who you want to be with, without having to go through it physically, and then saying, "That didn't work." You can go through it in your ethereal experience and say, "Is that the best and highest for me to do? Is this the consciousness of the unified field that I really want?" It's very beautiful, because you can actually make a short-cut here in areas like relationship, and in choices for work, location, and whatever. You can align whatever the outcome looks like it's going to be with your present frequency and with the calling that you know is yours, and see how it feels. See if it resonates in the field of your own wave. If it doesn't, you know ahead of time, "I'm not going to participate in it that way."

Your awareness of your own vibrational situation aligns so that you are comfortable with a precognitive experience before you actually initiate physical action. This is very important, because there

It is not possible, necessarily, to judge how far along you are at any point in time based upon your response, because the more your circuits are aligned the more easily you can get irritated.

If you are really with the field of energy, you'll find you are immediately able to attune to the part of you that can re-establish resonance.

As you refine the circuits, it gets easier to maintain them.

won't be time to make mistakes in the future—meaning that you do something and wish you hadn't. Not that's it's wrong, it's just that if you really feel uncomfortable and took a lot of energy to do that mistake—lots and lots of energy—it would have been easier to have done it differently. If you'd sent it down your circuits first and experienced how it would come out, then you could have created resolution with it and moved on without ever having to take one physical step. Much of the processing in this new time will be ethereal, visual, and sensate, and much less physical.

You don't need to do everything in the physical any more, because you don't need to learn in that way any more. You're learning in a completely and wholly different way in this "future time."

Your Rainbow Body

The physical organism is a multi-faceted energetic system which responds to and communicates through vibration. It is possible to access your present state of balance by viewing the energetic system of your body and seeing or sensing where the energy is most predominant or most absent. This can be accomplished very simply through the use of vibration, sound and music. For example, the human energy system is comprised of seven major wheels of energy, or chakras, and the following guideline is one perspective of the chakra system.

Drumbeats, cricket sounds, night sounds, the color red, and the key of C, are associated with the **root chakra** area. The place of red is anger ("I was so angry I saw red!"), the area or experience of nature, passion, and physical responsiveness, the genital area of sexual interaction and procreation. Having a spiritual idea or creative energy manifests most directly when it is brought as an energy down through the energy centers and unified at this base chakra or root area. The root is your gateway to doing anything in the physical.

The color orange vibrates from the **spleen chakra** with the key of D and the sound of flutes and wind instruments. This is the center of assimilation—what goes in and what comes out—on all levels. You balance experience, food, thought, feelings, or consciousness into your body, your mind, your emotion, or out of your body by releasing anger, memory, and vibration. The spleen is the center of balance and purification. The wave frame of the spleen is associated with people who are socially active and helpful. Social workers are an example. Sometimes those centered only in the spleen are people afraid they won't have enough (food, money, job, relationship, acknowledgment, etc.). It is also associated with those looking for an opportunity to gain knowledge and to be able to produce results which prove that they have that knowledge, so they can balance their wisdom with their actions.

In the center of the body, in the **solar plexus** center, the vibration is tuned to the key of E. The sound of the piano and harp activate this center, as does the color yellow. Here is where the mitochondria of the whole being are located—the power center for self-actualization and fulfilling the potential. The power to be who you are. All memory is stored in the plexus here in the body—conscious as well as unconscious memory. Coordinating the sounds, the color, and the vibration stimulates innate memory, and releases fears and constrictions about demonstrating one's power (self actualization) in the world. The solar plexus is the lowest point in the sacred space and provides the foundation for living one's calling in the world.

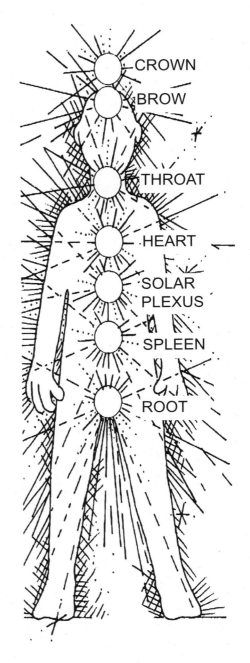

The soul is the center point of the sacred space and is sometimes called the **Source chakra**, although it is not traditionally associated with the seven major chakras. The soul area is under the xiphoid process, is a luminescent pink color, and has a resonant field that is absolute union. It resonates with the intonation of your calling. Focusing attention here stimulates the emergence of order, concentricity, and the activation of the design or blueprint of your life's work associated with the holographic "future-future." The **matrix**, or center of order, is housed around the soul.

The **heart chakra** is the uppermost point of the sacred space and calls you to temper the vibration and sound of your being through love, vibrating with the key of F. It responds to and emanates green and deals with practically anything green—healing, plants, money, growing, etc. The heart is the meeting place of the above and the below and fosters a union between dimensions. The sound of the heart is bells.

The **throat chakra** is associated with speech and expression. It vibrates to the key of G and the color of light blue. The throat is where the unconscious, which is below the throat area, and the conscious mind, which is above the throat area, are brought together. Questions associated with the throat are: "Do I speak all the time?

*The reason
we're talking about these centers
is because for you to* BE
*in a wave frame of a unified field,
they all need to be opened
at the same rate.
They need to be
absolutely z i n g i n g with energy.*

Can I sit in silence with others? Do I always talk about ideas? Is there something that always needs to be expressed? Am I always trying to bring what I don't know about myself from the inside, out? Or can I *be* in a space with sound, perhaps music, and not necessarily need to express? Or am I the opposite of that? Do I have lots and lots that I never get out, never express? Am I afraid to express from or speak about my zeal, my spiritual unleashment, my purpose, my focus? Am I always sitting quietly in silence because this area doesn't feel powerful enough or real enough to me?" The throat center powers the communion between what you *are* and your expression of that in the world. The throat responds to the sound of the wind, the rushing of air which communicates between levels and opens and balances the throat area.

The indigo of the **brow chakra** responds to the key of A and the sound of streams, showers, and rushing waters, which balances and stimulates this center of vision and knowing. This is the psychic center where all things exist throughout time and space. To open the third eye literally brings sight of the invisible and signals the circuitry in the etheric to ground truth into form. The third eye is connected with practical and cosmic understanding. The grounding process we so strongly recommend stimulates understanding between the above and the below.

The key of B and the sound of silence draw you into the cosmic consciousness of the **crown chakra**. This is the place of all color, ultraviolet, or no color; the place of all sound and no sound; the place of no-thing; the union beyond words of your critical piece of the hologram reflected from your spiritual essence.

It is very important to just discern, without judgment, "Where am I, and what's happening?" As you go up the scale, you can start at the root, and can pick music that will equilibrate with that particular key, and play or listen to that music, consciously opening those centers that you realize are in some way dampened down. The reason we're talking about these centers is because for you to be in a wave frame of a unified field, they all need to be opened at the same rate. They need to be absolutely *z i n g i n g* with energy.

Open these experiences first through sound, and the experience of *hearing* the key note and feeling it vibrate and open the center. One of the things we recommend is Steven Halpern's *Spectrum Suite*, because he plays every key note in succession. If you listen to that particular recording, you feel the centers opening up in your body. As you go up the scale, up the color rainbow in your body, up in sound from drumbeats to silence, what can you understand about your orientation? What colors are you drawn to? What are you working through in the lifetime? What sounds, notes, keys, and frameworks resonate with you? Where is it you want to be? High in the mountains or in the desert, on the sea, or under the sea?

Where is it that your ideas germinate? Are they germinated from you, or from books? Are you creating a reality consistent with the force field of energy that's coming into your planet, or are you learning about it from other people who are experiencing it? It's the difference between people who read and who are then obviously taking others' ideas and putting them into their own framework, and people who are creating connection with the truth within themselves and living that and perhaps never read anything. So you say, "Where am I? What kind of people am I drawn to? What kind of person am I? Where am I in my own advancement and evolution? Where am I in my own body?" When you start to put the pieces of your own vibration together, you begin to figure out, "Where do I come from? What am I learning? What's my purpose? How does it feel for me to be with certain kinds of people? Do I want to be with the kind of people I'm like, or do I want to be with other kinds of people who work from their different energy centers and align differently with their own consciousness? What feels comfortable?"

My Rainbow Body

notes

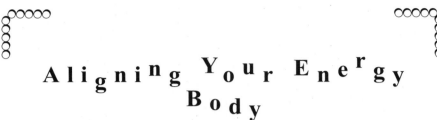

Aligning Your Energy Body

The Wave Frame
An Exercise

Take some time and go through the different parts of your body. Listen to music that lends itself to a certain chakra or area of energy, and fill your body with light, experiencing the flow of union throughout. After you've done that, you'll know what to concentrate on. You can see how your actions and intentions create certain experiences; you will understand what irritates you, or find those things that are your red flags. When a red flag happens, you can ask, "Where's my energy? What's my choice? What's my intention? How can I balance that, and feel again the flow of union through my being?" The objective is to feel that you are orchestrating this design so that all the pieces really fit together.

As you think about your being, are you in your feet? Are you in your lower body? Are you in your upper body more of the time? Where does your energy pool or constrict, expand or flow? How might you arrange your field of energy so that you could balance that experience and response, so that the above and below in your body are consistent? Accessing your energy flow is the first step.

The second step is to open the top of your head, imagine that you are a wave frame of energy, and that you don't have a body. You're like sunlight oscillating on water. Imagine that from the top of your head to the bottoms of your feet, you are moving the light and the sunlight, and the energy is flowing through you very beautifully, without obstruction, as if you're standing under a shower. When you do the exercise with this purpose in mind, the field of union which you are supporting shows you exactly where there's a movement of energy in the body, around a particular location. So then you recognize that the location that gets moved around in your body is your eyes, your ears, your third eye, your throat, your heart area, your left hip area, or your right knee, or whatever it is.

As you create a context with that, you can say, "What area does that relate to in the system of energy?" Because all of your patterns, your process, and those things that you are analyzing or referencing here, are indications of what's happening in your energetic field. So if you think about everything in terms of the *field*, rather than in terms of personality, good or bad, or, "I'm spending too much time in my head, what does that mean to me? What am I avoiding?" Just focus on where in the energy field the pattern of energy does not flow. Where does it flow best, and why? Observe, and then you can use the energy of your predominant centers to support and energize those areas which feel depleted or constricted.

If you take everything to the level of energy, it's much easier to move it. It's much easier to integrate it, understand and activate it, so that it becomes balanced. That's the objective of reflexology and polarity, and other therapies. Having the energy flow in the left and right side of the body equally, having all the chakras open at the same rate of speed and oscillation, allows for the physical, emotional, mental, and spiritual bodies to vibrate at the same rate of speed.

All of this is your pathway to mastery. All of this is the experience that will allow union between peoples. It is amenable to work with this physical experience, because the body is the home, or foundation, for all the processes we've talked about from the very beginning. It's where you carry and emanate your light, where you receive your experience, and oscillate your frequency. When all these parts of you are firmly connected, you are a system that supports itself.

All of this is your pathway to mastery.

This is the experience that will allow union between peoples.

When all these parts of you are firmly connected, you are a system that supports itself.

Balancing Chakras
Balancing Chakras

An Exercise

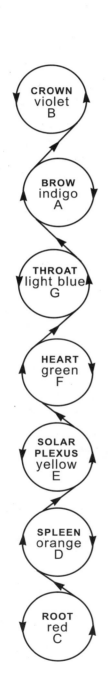

Once you have brought the shower of light and energy in the top of your head and gently touched all the parts of your body, focus your attention on the root chakra (See diagram). Imagine a red rose bud which is located in the center of the chakra. As you send energy and attention to that place, the red rose bud begins opening. This is a way to open the chakra easily, at your own pace, and to feel the energy being released into your whole system.

Remember the attributes of each chakra as you open it, and you can create affirmations which will align your intention with your physical energy. Open the energy of the root in a counter-clockwise direction because you are gathering energy into the body here. When the rose bud opens fully, you then move the energy to the next center, the spleen, in a smooth visual motion like you are painting with a wide hand-movement. Here the rose bud is orange, and the motion of energy is sending out, so it is clockwise.

Every chakra has its own color and goes from counter-clockwise in the root to clockwise in the spleen to counter-clockwise in the solar plexus to clockwise in the heart, etc. (See diagram). The Source chakra is opened after the seven major chakras and so is not included in this diagram. It is not opened in a clockwise or counter-clockwise motion.

When you have opened the crown chakra you can open out to the infinite. This a wonderful time to travel to the Akashic or do Silver Chalice work or make intentions, or go into substance. You can then bring the energy of the infinite into the matrix in the center of the body and tap the soul space, or source chakra, ask for your blueprint to manifest, or spend time in the soul gathering the fullness of your essence.

Complete your visualization or meditation with a grounding exercise. You can ground by bringing the shower of light again into the top of your head as the last conscious instruction of your meditation. If you are meditating inside, go outdoors and stand on the Earth, bringing the light through the crown chakra in the top of the head, down through the root center, and out the bottom of the feet. This balances and closes the chakras so that you are open to the Earth and spirit and maintain a congruent energy field in the world. This helps to smooth your edges, balance your thought with knowing, and temper any areas of expectation, belief, or fear.

The wave frame is set up from,
and emits itself from,
the field of union.
When you have a field of union,
the wave frame is unified.

The wave frame is set up from, and emits itself from, the field of union. When you have a field of union, the wave frame is unified. It goes out and gives a message—it actually has a little trumpet call to it which says, "I am feeling unified with my whole being."

When you come into contact with someone else, you will find that their energy field and your wave frames are matching, or not matching, or that only a certain percentage is matching. This is how you decide whether or not you stay in a particular situation or relationship. If the wave frames don't match, you may find that you want to retreat, or withdraw your field and regroup it, and approach that energy differently. You stay open, and yet in a regrouping sense you have a choice to decide how you want to approach them. You do not have to send your wave frame in completely, and keep it there if you're uncomfortable. Comfortability, as we have told you, is a very strong indication of how you can monitor your own level of resonance.

If you are opening your complete wave frame, and walk into a situation and the waves are sloshing against each other, you can say, "Wait a minute, I want to regroup this. I want to bring my energy flow over here, closer to me, and see where and/or how I fit with that

Until the wave frame is a perfect match, you're allowing the framing to be present, and yet steeping it in its own resonance rather than mixing that resonance with someone else.

~

Pick a partner with the mutual intention that you will work together to understand how you resonate with and respond to the world.

~

other field of energy." Many times you will go into a situation and be completely open, and experience being with others who are only partially open, who have expectations of you, demand something of you, or whose realities are different from yours. Again, it isn't a judgment about it, it is comfortability. You say, "I do or do not want to participate 100% in what's happening here. I'm going to stay open and in a unified field, yet, as I approach new situations, go into new groups, and foster new realities, I am comfortable with my own field. I choose to feel this comfort in reference to others." Until the wave frame is a perfect match, you're allowing the framing to be present, and yet steeping it in its own resonance rather than mixing that resonance with someone else.

You mix your spiritual dimensions most of the time—that twelve foot layer of energy that goes out and is always present. It is important in this time of transition, as people go through reactive experiences, that your field of energy be congruent—that you contain it as you go around and the wave moves through you and is unified. It is important that you embody and emote this congruence.

So, initially work with your individual energy, and then work in twos or small groups, to feel how union can be accomplished. Literally nuts and bolts stuff—"When I do this, this happens, when I do that, this happens."

What's My Energy Doing?
A Partnering Exercise

This exercise will foster a knowing of how your energy works, and help you understand your individual wave fields. Pick a partner with the mutual intention that you will work together to understand how you resonate with and respond to the world.

You want to know what feeds you from the world. We're all being fed from the substance, and yet, we want to know how our energy field relates to the physical—people, plants, nature, sky, underground mines, wells, aquifers, everything. What is your orientation with the Earth?

There are certain foods you like, certain colors, certain shades and resonances that are important for you, certain kinds of people that you gravitate toward, certain kinds of music and books. All of this can help you identify your wave frequency. And each of those items we've mentioned can be put together according to vibration, so that you develop a picture of your responsiveness.

You and your partner decide that you're going to take your energy fields apart, literally, so that as you foster your own understanding, you can reflect on it with someone who also wants that understanding about themselves. Pick a neutral person to start with so that you have no axes to grind, nothing to expect, and nothing to want out of it—but rather to learn and to discern. As your partner gives you feedback, you begin understanding how your wave frame works.

Pick a neutral person to start with so that you have no axes to grind, nothing to expect, and nothing to want out of it— but rather to learn and to discern.

Try This !

1• Begin with an intention to be fully present and open with your partner to receive any awarenesses that surface.

2• Sit or stand across from each other for energy flow observation. You can hold hands or not, have eyes open or closed, be silent or speak— whatever unfolds. The comfort you have with each other will determine which physical positions are most appropriate for you at each moment. As this changes, be ready to discern why your comfort level changes, and what message it brings you or your partner.

Your objective is to witness for each other, to understand:

a• how you each communicate without words;
b• how you each receive communication energetically;
c• what creates comfort and/or discomfort in you.

Your verbal feedback can help clarify the signals and messages given and received organically.

When you sit across from your partner and have balanced all of your energy centers, open your field and say to him or her, "What are you feeling from me? How does my energy come across to you? Is there anything that feels incompatible for you? Are you receiving all of my centers equally? Am I opening my energy field so that you can receive me easily? Are you receiving me and realizing that there is no demand? Is there something being communicated that I'm not aware of?"

There is honesty between you and the acknowledgement of what is and is not consistent in the field.

Practice joining with your partner's wave frame. Learn how that feels, understand that functioning, and then work with someone else. Do this a dozen times, so that you understand how energy systems come together in the world.

Opportunities may arise to practice with people you see sporadically, and you might say, "Can you sit down with me and do this exercise? I can explain it to you easily, and we can sit here for an hour, and have this experience. I've always felt really comfortable with you, but I don't know why!" People will come together and say, "Oh, I want to be with you a lot, and there's so much compatibility." Why is that? What does that mean? How do you define that? Where does that come from? This is an opportunity to use your mind to understand your process energetically, and to satiate your mind with the experience so that it is impressed by your essence and by your consciousness. You can say, "I guess we can do this energetically from now on. My personality can take a back seat, and we can work together with this as energy systems."

The way you approach other people, the way you feel, generates either resonance or dissonance, and this is very important, not only because people will like you or not like you, trust you or not trust you, accept you or not accept you, but also because if your field isn't resonant, you will not be emanating union, regardless of what you say you want to emanate. The effects of that will be to cut the energy powering in half, so you have to regenerate again.

So you state, "This is my intention," but only half the circuits are working on that intention. Then you say, "This is what I really want," and then you realize, "Wait a minute, the whole bottom half of me is missing, I'd better go back to square one." And that's fine, except that you might have only one opportunity to make a first impression, like for a job interview, or first meeting. Where do you want to come from in your experience? How do you want to represent yourself? What's really going on here? If you're half missing, the results of that interview or interaction are going to be different, and the question is, is that the result you want?

As we said in the chapter on relationship, one desires a congruity between the field of energy, the calibration of the heart experience and the appropriate terms of relationship with a particular person. There are dynamics, and if they are straightforward dynamics, nine times out of ten, your results will be consistent.

Constancy and the Unified Field

On this planet, there is now an influx of new energies and a massive destructuring, on all levels. It is very important for you to have something that's constant as this progresses. And you are your own constant. When that constancy becomes literal for you, you can go into situations where you experience order and disorder in varying degrees, and can know who you are, why you're there, and what to do in a situation. You know how the experience will unfold because you've already seen it through your vision. You know the purpose, the design. You're on that energy wave serving and being served by the universe at the same time. Resonantly receptive. Basing your experience on the unified field.

The wave of your destiny comes from the soul. So when you have the major seven chakras balanced, come into the soul last, in the center of the body, and say, "Here I am, now, show me my calling." When there's balance in the physical body, between the metaphysical and the physical realm, through the chakras, and through the breath, then you can feel your direction. Guidance will be there for your re-Sourcing, because the unified field is why you came here in the

The way you approach other people, the way you feel, generates either resonance or dissonance.

If your field isn't resonant, you will not be emanating union, regardless of what you say you want to emanate. The effects of that will be to cut the energy powering in half, so you have to regenerate again.

You are your own constant.

You do not have to wait until you fulfill the design to be in union.

~

The objective here is for each of you to live union with yourself And then create a world where union is the basis.

~

first place. You want to return to the experience of oneness, to be at one with all things, and live union—that's the design. That's why you're here.

What we're saying to you is that you do not have to wait until you fulfill the design to be in union. You do not have to wait for XYZ to happen before you know what it's like to be in a unified field. And it has absolutely nothing to do with somebody else.

Creating, sustaining, and living in union is about you. When you live in union with you, then you live in union with others. The objective here is for each of you to live union with yourself and then create a world where union is the basis. So the first thing is the individual intention, and the collective intention is to get it all together, and re-Source it, and cooperate, and feel it as unified. It's really a very easy thing, because it's up to you. It's not up to your husband or wife, your uncle, aunt, mother, father, child, minister, or guru. It's not up to anybody else. It's just up to you.

We suggest that you balance your energy field once or twice a day, and then find someone to reflect with, and keep records by writing it down. "This is how it was when I initially went in and balanced my chakras, and this is what my pattern seems to be when I'm with this person. This is what they're picking up. When I ground, it changes. This is what happens when I drink lots of lemon water. This is what happens if I have good rest, and I feel joyful, and I'm relaxed. This is how I might bring relaxation and joy into my experience, so that when this happens, I can affect my energy by this thought or behavior or activity, by drinking water or grounding, or bringing the shower of light through my energy field, whatever it is."

You create a formula for yourself. You are your own diagnostician. You get reflection from the other person, then go back into solitude, and say, "What do I do with this? How can I maintain the state of balance in my body and heart, and in all parts of me? I'm always getting instruction. What is my body telling me it wants to eat? What is my body telling me it wants to listen to? What is my psyche saying I need as surroundings? When have I been the happiest? What do I most long for? What am I most drawn to?" It's an opportunity to really scope yourself out, and look in all your nooks and crannies.

This is not about what you believe. It's about the messages you're picking up constantly, either listening to or not listening to. How could you listen more? What are the tendencies you have, the yearnings, the inclinations? What is really going on inside you all the time, that you either ignore or pay attention to? It's time to walk the talk.

When you are in the point of union, you experience being a wave frame of energy, and the field that you generate is concentricity. Your field goes out from the sacred space and begins to magnify. First you understand how you interface with individuals, going into situations and realizing how to be comfortable. You've regrouped enough to know how you can immediately understand where others are, and either merge energy with them, or not—order your experience with them or not, by choice. Once you've understood those parameters, you move to the next level, which is to remain a constantly flowing field of unified fiber and resonance, choosing to unify on a personal basis with certain individuals, and yet the whole field around you is responsive to this unification that you're feeling, and all those levels go out and touch other levels. This is why the critical mass happens, because if you hold the level of union based on order and truth, you stimulate that in the people who are in that surrounding pattern or environment with you. They feel their own consciousness activated, and sense you are giving them a mirror of their own capacity. They then feel potentiated, and activate their levels of response.

So keep in mind in each of these experiences, that the ultimate goal is union on the planet, and that the initial goal is union within yourself. As you feel each step of that union accelerating and working itself through you, becoming integrated into your life system, you'll find that each of those levels begins to be easier to understand, because you have the nucleus vibrating at a rate of speed that has balance, and it goes out, moving in all directions, and touching everything that is—and that is concentricity.

When we talk about the regrouping sensation, that's when you're meeting new people or wanting to be in a relationship, and you're not sure about the person you're with. Or you're meeting someone new and have an opportunity to sense the differences in energy, not to judge or to protect yourself as much as to return to your vibration of union.

You might say, "Do I want to be in that situation in the way I originally thought about it?" As we said, you can do all this ahead of time. You can do it from the psyche rather than from the physicality. Once you move into the physicality, you have already scoped that out and seen how it's going to work. You then feel it available to you as a point of discernment.

The foundation of this discernment is imperative because you

This is why
the critical mass happens,
because if you hold the level of union
based on order and truth,
you stimulate that in the people
who are in that surrounding pattern or
environment with you.

So keep in mind
in each of these experiences,
that the ultimate goal
is union on the planet.

When you make choices
to be with individuals
who are in union,
you will end up together
in the space
of the etheric potential destiny
of the Earth,
and you'll create a new world
there.

will work and interface with people who have varied levels of information about their own process. In a very intricate way, you will be the first wave of individuals who create new superhuman consciousness.

It takes hours and hours of individual work to understand your own field of energy, to integrate all your aspects, to be comfortable with who you are, to walk into any situation and hold your own field close to your experience, and move it out as it is amenable for you to do that, and to feel in each moment that you can orchestrate that. That's mastery.

It isn't that you don't have compassion, love, warmth, or anything else. These things are always flowing from you. That's a given. However, you do not give your unified field away. Because if someone else does not have a unified field, and does not match you in that space, it will always end up being an incompatible process. This takes time and energy and doesn't necessarily effectively assist the process you're in, and there's not a lot of time now—not a lot of time to experiment.

Union becomes a place where, ultimately, the order and accordance are always flowing from you. Union is always expanding itself, always going out in all directions, and there is nothing that it requires. As you balance the innate system of your body from the metaphysical, you have all the fuel you need. You just move that union out and experience it. People around you begin to respond to that. Union becomes an example of what's possible. The world reflects the truth you choose to create. You choose only to be in those places that support the experience of unity, because then you create in your outer reality that same vibration of union.

When you make choices to be with individuals who are in union, you will end up together in the space of the etheric potential destiny of the Earth, and you'll create a new world there. And so part of this is that discernment. You are not judging someone, or avoiding someone, or choosing against someone, because it's the time of rendering. Everybody is going to make these choices. It's really determining now who you want to spend time with, who you want to spend energy with. You may ask what their intention is and whether they are doing their work, and then the question arises, "How can all of us best serve the foundation of union on this planet?"

It's very simple. It's about making that choice and remembering who you really are, which is the key to how union will work in the world from this point on—remembering that this is the whole point of it, and getting down to brass tacks. Create from that part of you that knows how do to this, that remembers who you are.

You are an energy system—always remember that—you are an energy system, first and foremost. Being an energy system is natural for you. Being able to discern how that energy works is a capability you have. Perhaps you will develop techniques to discern your energy, and yet this capacity is something that innately comes to you, and functions to assist you to organize the data about energy that you've never been taught how to organize.

It's more or less making the natural experience of energy come to you in ways that feel normal. Right now they don't feel normal to you. You're more used to saying, "I have a headache, or I don't have a headache. I have a stomach ache, or I don't have a stomach ache. I'm hungry, or I'm not hungry." Looking at the chakra system to find out what is happening energetically is a way of viewing old symptoms. Since pain is caused by congestion of energy, you can evaluate or sense what centers are open and which are closed. You can ask yourself how your other centers affect what's going on in that particular center.

It's about unifying your own field by having communication between the dynamics and bringing those dynamics together to support your intention. Because that's why you've come.

IN OUR ESTIMATION RIGHT NOW, IT'S IMPORTANT TO CALL A SPADE A SPADE. YOU'RE IN OR YOU'RE NOT. AND IF YOU'RE IN, YOU'RE IN ALL THE WAY. THERE'S NO ROOM FOR SOMEONE TO BE HALF IN AND HALF OUT. IT WON'T WORK. THE CHOICES MUST BE MADE, AND THE ACTIONS MUST BE TAKEN ("MUST" MEANING STRONGLY RECOMMENDED). IT'S TIME FOR THIS, AND ALL OF YOU UNDERSTAND THAT. SO THE FOUNDATION OF THIS EXPERIENCE IS TO CHOOSE UNION, TO IMPLEMENT THE CIRCUITS AND THE ENERGY CENTERS FROM CONSCIOUS CHOICE TO SUPPORT THE LEVEL OF INTEGRITY THAT YOU CHOSE BEFORE YOU CAME. IT'S ABOUT CONGRUENCE. IT'S ABOUT YOU SAYING "**YES**" TO WHAT YOU KNOW YOU ARE, TO YOUR LINEAGE, SO THAT THE OUTCOME IS THE SAME VIBRATION, AND **YOU START MANIFESTING UNION TODAY**!

Guidance
From All Worlds

Guidance
Guidance
Guidance

FROM THE MOMENT THAT YOU CHOOSE TO BE BORN, a level of energy is created in the universe. As your soul comes toward the experience of life in this dimension, you attract to you energies from all dimensions, which will assist you in completing your task or design on Earth. Called guides, spiritual helpers, or the society of spirits, these dimensional energies live in the firmament and have attenuation to Earth, wanting to attune their frequency to the experience of your particular destiny.

They come into being through your life and are connected to the world through your auric fields, and through the soul's intention to vibrate at a certain rate of speed. Much of what you've chosen in terms of your design, your intention, and the experience you would like to fulfill in this dimension is supported by other dimensions that accompany you, which are invisible and have to do with the foundation that is accorded *between* the dimensions.

So when you come into the body there are many other levels also committed to the same process that you're committed to. They establish themselves from different levels to bring together a multifaceted, multidisciplinary approach, so that you're not really alone ever, even though you might think you are. These guardian levels are affiliated with the intention of your life, and come to serve the world as what might be called "adjuncts" to what you're doing individually. Many times when you get a thought and it seems to come from some part of you that is new or faintly familiar, these messages are being sent to you from levels that accompany you. You may get suggestions in your awareness, or see new pictures, or feel called to do something that seems out of context with your identity. They support you with a suggestion-box approach, so that your life has more options or available assets. Many times, as you develop relationship with your guardians, you'll receive suggestions and ideas that intensify your consciousness, and help you serve what you chose to do before you came into this lifetime.

~

I tap my full memory and knowing from all dimensions in every moment.

~

The pieces you fit together
will help explain
your yearnings and preferences
in all areas of your human experience.

~

When you
listen *and* respond
to the inaudible voice
or the inner awareness,
you are given a gift.

~

Your astral guides bring skills and connections to you from different lifetimes—such as Lemurian, Mayan, Atlantean, Egyptian, Greek, or Roman. These are times when society pursued knowledge and developed skills which brought all dimensions into contact, literally fostering a sharing of the infinite, dimensional spaces of the firmaments between the Earth and her people. You may find that you are drawn into a quest for remembering and acknowledging your other points of reality, or lifetimes, to bring forth the knowledge you carry. Particularly now, in this time when all the ages are manifesting together, the synthesis of this information is highly recommended. The pieces you fit together will help explain your yearnings and preferences in all areas of your human experience. They will fill in the blanks of your psyche to assist in understanding where you come from and what your easiest path will be. You can work with your guidance directly to synthesize your innate memory and knowledge and bring it into conscious awakening.

As you open to your spiritual and astral guidance, not only will you experience the reception of information and direction, you'll also find that tremendous input comes to you, helping you to respond to your senses rather than your logic.

As you listen to this guidance, more and more, the voices get stronger within, as ideas or patterns emerging in your life. You will find these voices, thoughts, suggestions, and leanings move you away from your habitual, patterned life and conscious thought, into reception, remembering, and re-cognizing.

They encourage you to develop a relationship with the invisible, and to do so requires an inner hearing, an inner responding, and a commitment to change your usual way of perceiving. For example, perhaps you are typing away at the computer, where you always put in an eight hour day: you have committed to remember your path and develop your innate wisdom, and suddenly you have to get up from the computer. A voice inside you is saying, "Go for a walk." So you start out and then get another subtle nudge which instructs you to sit under a tree that you are approaching. So you listen and sit down under the tree. The subtle nudge comes again with the instruction that you're going to become part of that tree. When you listen and respond to the inaudible voice or the inner awareness, you are given a gift, perhaps instruction, or a request to do something that will sharpen your skills or put ideas and energy into the experience of life for you. You may receive answers, or put together bits and pieces of information so that you understand a dynamic you have been searching for. You may receive a message from the rock or the tree or an element of nature—the fields of order. As you listen to the guidance, you have access to levels of reality that you've not yet consciously tapped.

You might have an astral guide named "Great Stone Man" from the American Indian, or "Alexander," the Greek teacher, or "Helena" from the Temple of Joy. Born with you into the astral as you are born into the physical, they come to help you with their particular knowings—writing, or physical strength, or speaking with animals and dimensional beings. They may help you practically, to know ritual, to contact the great spirits, to talk to the directions, or to develop skills and do tasks from the physical level. These abilities are held in the psychic informational level in the astral experience. Astral guides have shapes, form, names, and a commitment to physical process. You can address this level and call it out by saying, "I ask that my astral guidance be more present in my life. I ask that I experience the rhythms and the cycles, the skills, and the frameworks that I have maintained in other times or that want to be maintained through me in this time, because I am now listening to those levels and committing to be a part of those levels."

As you create that dynamic you find that you are calling together all your forces. You can talk to the astral level and ask questions about your diet or health, things that you should be or could be eating to assist you, questions about the weather, or travel. These are wonderful questions for your astral guidance. You can ask their names, what their specific intention is and what their skills are, and how they can bring those skills to you. You can ask what the marriage of the intention and skills would bring out in you, so that you find your missing pieces. As these levels work with you, they are attenuating and calling forth your plan and your blueprint, because they are here to make the passage easier, to fill in the blanks, and to put the puzzle pieces into order.

You'll feel something happening in your consciousness to provide a reality for you all the time, as if you can hear the heartbeat of the astrals, very present, and very close to this dimension.

The spiritual is much more subtle than the astral, and there are frameworks of "time and space," that want to be called together, to unify and come into this space with you, so that the overall design of that framework is seen in terms of spiritual relevance. You are shown what the impact of your future is going to be, or are assisted to see the design, and put the pieces together to take steps for humanity.

You'll feel something happening
in your consciousness
to provide a reality for you all the time,
as if
you can hear the heartbeat of the astrals,
very present,
and very close to this dimension.

The spiritual level is very connected to the outcome, to the overall design, and to the formula that you chose before you came into the body. Spirit is here to assist you in organizing all your capacities and living them, whereas the astral is specifically oriented to providing you with the mundane process, skills, capacities, and tasks. These reference systems "fill out" your consciousness. It's as if when you are born a whole hierarchy is born with you. Whatever is to be actualized is coming with you. The levels open the commitment within their dimension, also.

Entities or spirits can come to you bringing knowledge, order, truth, the holographic design, the framework of what we call pre-knowledge, or the accordance of creation. Those people who are here to work with creation and with the promise of archetypically creating designs here, usually have connections to guardianships in the Hierarchy (where we're speaking to you from). These beings of light many times have not been in the physical body. They accompany the journey so that the Hierarchical consciousness can be contained in the experience of life, brought forward into this dominion, and married together.

Remember that when your guardians choose you, it is based solely on vibration. It's not based completely on what you've done before, or what you're going to do; it is a mixture. This creates the vibration that you're working with. Many times you foster the guardianship so that you can have support and guidance, so the frameworks begin to cross over. As you create a level of your own distinction—fostering your own informational data base about who you are and what you're doing and how that's structuring—the guardianship communicates, deepening its response, moving you toward more and more of a commitment to expressing that which has been held for you in the continuum, and which is now ready to be born in form. The guardians, through their intention and ability, give you information and suggest and express through you, communicating their dominion or dimension, and you are a conduit for that. That's why many times we will speak as if you are the expressive nature of our eyes, our ears, our hearts, and our hands. We suggest and sometimes charge you with the commitment to act as if you are our particular embodiment on the Earth plane, because we are unable to be there and do what you have chosen to do.

There is a commitment by the light forces that they will not incarnate as such and will steadfastly hold a frame or container around your reality, so that as you begin to live it and support it, you are framing it, almost as if your presence makes it possible for the light to be not only available, but actual.

Ultimately, it is your commitment to the experience of life and your choice to help the design unfold, that supports the universe and vice versa. *Your intent can affect creation itself.* So it's a viable exchange system. The guardianship that comes and fosters the reality with you is very easily called back to this etheric dimension, so that you are a conduit or a threshold for the expression of that commitment on Earth.

As you understand your life system, develop the levels of your consciousness, work with your commitment, and ask that the guardianship fulfill for you, you recognize the invisible as a space or conduit, which supports it own intention. You are making available the union of consciousness on this plane. Whatever you're doing and whatever you're relating to are often supported by the guardianship, so that you're doing it not only for yourself, but for these other levels as well. You recognize your connection with the forces of light.

Many of you are here to call together the forces of light within your life. Your guardianship will show you that your experience is here and there simultaneously. You receive guidance and direction from these levels as they support your advancement in consciousness.

Sometimes astral guides communicate to lead you toward experiences and places which elicit memory and knowing. Sometimes you'll experience an urgency that you might question from your conscious mind, and yet cannot be denied.

Perhaps you have to live by the ocean, or in the mountains, or fly airplanes, or deep sea dive, or work with children, or flower gardens, or always read books, or write books or poems, or draw pictures, or cook food, or grow plants in the home, have animals around, or communicate through hobbies. Many times these experiences come to you from the dimensions and call you to experience, unconsciously, something that you've always known was a part of you. Sometimes the longings that draw you are to bring development of skills and abilities you have known and mastered in other lifetimes. Sometimes it is the natural development of your psychic abilities and inner awareness of different dimensions and levels that bring you to the realization that you are "plugged in" somewhere.

You are receiving gifts and have assistance in nature, in creation, in maintaining order, or there's a foundation in you that's trying hard to substantiate new realities here. And you may ask yourself, "Where

You are making available the union of consciousness on this plane.

Sometimes the longings that draw you are to bring development of skills and abilities you have known and mastered in other lifetimes.

are they coming from? Why am I linked to the future, rather than the past? Why am I interested in models about health, rather than models about economy? Why am I looking for ways to make the world a safer place for the children, even if I don't have children, or don't like children?" Many times the commitments come to you from someplace else, and are patterning their experience so that your feeling and intention are certain subject matters and experiences which might not have ever happened in your life before. You may not have been taught about these things, and yet they are a part of your reality, you seek them out, and you create a context through which they might work.

As you develop these areas of awareness and response, you may begin to receive assistance from the Angelic realm. Angelic levels help with taking the next step through coincidence and synchronicity. The angels are here to help you live the design more fully. They put into the experience what you might miss, otherwise. This is wonderfully intricate, because they look at your design and see the person you need to meet next, the framework that needs most to happen, the foundation that's going to provide the most interesting and the most viable means for your growth and support, and then the magic begins to happen! As you work with the Angelic, and pray and speak with them, you understand that everything in your life is being created from an intention that was made before you came, and yet you need sign posts and road maps, street signs, and posters with big red letters to help you understand, "What am I doing? Where am I going and why?"

The Angelic is that next-step finder, and if you listen to that synchronistic voice, it brings a weaving of situations and connections to make your life more comfortable. For example, they can assist you to choose books to read. Many times a book will fall off the shelf in front of your feet and when you pick it up, it falls open to just the page and paragraph to help you with a current question, concern or need. As you communicate more and more with the Angelic, you feel their support and that you're being taken care of and upheld. Greatly acknowledging the presence of the Angelic, in gratitude, will elicit more and more direct communication and guidance, to magically bring your design closer to your knowing and experience.

Information and guidance from the spiritual dimension are also available from your society of spirits. The spiritual society is comprised of light beings committed to your personal process. These

The angels are here
to help you live the design more fully.

The Angelic is that next-step finder, and
if you listen to that synchronistic voice,
it brings a weaving
of situations and connections
to make your life more comfortable.

beings are beams of light in your awareness, which change as you grow, and have affiliation with light, creation, guidance and direction about essences and aspects of the greater universe. They link you etherically to the dimension of light beings who serve your consciousness, and as your vibration shifts, these spiritual energies change dynamics. Your society of spirits is that which surrounds you most prominently all the time. They can be Hierarchical or not, depending upon what your intention is, and what your work is in the world.

You can look at what level of guidance you communicate with, and how this relationship to the interdimensional serves you. You can see what is working in your life, what you want to make more comfortable, what areas you'd like to put together differently so that the experience becomes its own responsiveness. Perhaps you are grounding and connecting to the Earth, and connecting to your skills, and aware of what is available to you. Now that you're listening at all these levels, perhaps you'd like to receive some guidance about the foundation of your experience here and how it will be lived. What is it that you've come to do? What are your next steps? What's your connection to those souls who surround you? What can you experience from the overall viewpoint which can see more than you can see? As you go to bed at night and when you awaken in the morning, you can call in your spiritual society, and receive specific information about what your design says, and how it can be accorded in this reality.

You can work with and receive guidance from whatever level of the design you choose. The astral level gives you information about the physical body, and the spiritual level works to attune that energy frequency so that it comes more deeply into the cells. If you're working with compassion, or the Absolute—absolution—with freedom, forgiveness, union, or intention and affirmation, you'll want to include a spiritual dimension in that process because those more universal concepts are part of the design and part of what is being resolved in the human experience. So the resolution process has to do with a spiritual connection or the spiritual design. The practical experience of learning and committing to unify with levels of the invisible on Earth, connects you with devas, gnomes, and spirits more astrally, helping develop skills of sensing, receiving, and visioning.

When you come down the tunnel and are approaching the canal of the mother just before birth, you absorb the frequencies of those

You can receive guidance on whatever level of the design you would like to work with.

~

*You are
literally able to exist
in more than one place at one time.*

~

parts of you, or parts of the universe that want to be expressed through you. Sometimes at that point, it is possible to connect with the thought-form energy of one or more aspects of your total reality or what we call simultaneous points of reality. These points of reality have lived before or are living in the future or in an alternate reality. Instead of thinking of just past lives, these points represent all of your reality, throughout time. These points can be with you during your Earth journey as part of your energy field.

There can be from one to twelve thought forms with you, and at certain times during your life these thought forms will be triggered, giving you information and assisting you energetically to unify with that particular archetypical process, personality, or alternative identity. It is a gifting space, as it were.

If you have chosen to have thought forms accompany you in this lifetime, as you go through transformational experiences of initiation, particularly challenging times of physical danger, near death experience, or extreme loss, you are calling together these important pieces of information and opening them to themselves. You may appear different after these experiences. Your vibration will be different, or perhaps you will have a different way of holding your body, or your face will change. You may have observed this in other people, and said, "That must have been a really powerful experience for them." Many times when you go into initiation, you change the frequency enough to embody another of your thought forms. You can actually carry them with you as an Indian life, Egyptian, Atlantean, or future life, and people who do psychic readings can see these thought forms lined up behind you or around you. As your vibration attunes itself, the thought forms unify with you, and are no longer distinct.

When you open up to all of these energies and thought forms, many memories come together, and parts of you are realigned and re-evaluated, and you begin to expand your vibration and grow. You have more charisma, more energy, and more intention because you know more than you knew before. You are literally able to exist in more than one place at one time. These thought forms are receiving information and understanding from many levels simultaneously, and as you experience those levels, you're also more committed to your responsiveness in the universe.

Touching the Dimensions
An Exercise

The place that you can find your guidance, astrally, is in nature, and spiritually, is in the realm of meditation. One way to work with the spiritual dimension is to close your eyes and feel your own vibration—your essence. Then imagine that you could take your vibration as if it were a pillar of light, a candle flame, and expand it out in every direction. As you expand that vibration, you touch dimensional levels of reality. Feel or see these levels, touch them, and as you go out from your own experience, they will become more palpable to you. These levels of energy are as responsive to you as you are to them. If you create a commitment to connect in this way, then you can receive the vibration and information which help you take short-cuts in your evolution to see the design from a viewpoint you don't normally see. What's interesting about the way the world shapes things is that if you do not know how to work with the spiritual level—if you are taught to pray to a God above you that doesn't have intricate relationship with you— then you're not taught how these infinite levels respond to you and how they belong to you and are committed to your growth, expansion, and experience.

If you go once a day or so into that experience of sitting with your little flame in the center of your body, and then moving that out, very, very slowly and gently out to the sides of your body, you'll feel that you actually rub edges or touch the boundaries of those other parts of yourself that have a vibrational seam with you. There's a little seam between dimensions, and when you feel that seam, you say, "I'm moving into another paradigm, I'm moving into another nuance of response." You begin to listen more clearly, you receive more strongly and fully, and you

If you are taught to pray to a God above you that doesn't have intricate relationship with you— then you're not taught how these infinite levels respond to you and how they belong to you and are committed to your growth, expansion, and experience.

*"Whereas
before I was trying to live my life,
now
I can respond to all my
dimensions."*

understand more dimensionally, because as your flame goes up the center of your body, you experience the truth of what you've come to honor, and a foundation is built that is organizing that intention with you.

You create the capacity to stay in communication all the time, and begin to get your own information.

You can now understand how these levels work, what they mean, and what they're doing. You feel more confident about your choices and the designs that are there for you. Your capabilities feel as if they've increased because you feel spirit as an inherent guidance system. These levels of reality are committed to the human experience and accompany you, individually, on your journey. (Now this is outside of those beings called the White Brotherhood, The Ones With No Names, the Counsel, the Hierarchy, the Absolute, the Infinite, the Goddesses, specific angels and specific planetary configurations, and extraterrestrial levels.)

The spiritual society attunes with you more and more as you take your light out and experience patterns and pathways around you. You find your own corridors of consciousness, and patterns in your life start to make sense. If you ask, "Why am I trying to grow this way? If I could just see that part of my design, see where I'm being guided to go, look at what wants to happen, and how that experience is going to fulfill itself," then you could see yourself from a different vantage point.

The power of this is very important, because it also aligns you with the intention that you came to experience, and shows you how to live it. So the foundation for your life becomes much broader.

In this time we're witnessing now, acknowledging, according and validating are of phenomenal importance. Having a spiritual energetic pact with the consciousness of light that's ordained to assist you with your own incarnative process, is a gift of the highest order. You feel that the intention of your life and the intention of your foundation are being called together so that you are able to respond now. "Whereas before I was trying to live my life, now I can respond to all my dimensions."

It is time for you to honor that your commitment to being is specific, and that your level of reality is specific, and you can get answers which apply 100% to wherever you are, and you can start doing that right now. The spiritual society is one entry point for calling forth your own knowing. To go to your own spiritual society, close your eyes and suggest that the answers are going to be there with you—and that you're going to call them out.

So the intention is that you begin it, and that you say "Yes" to hearing and receiving, and that you are ready to explore those realities, and how that level of consciousness is going to affect your actual experience. This is about always knowing where to go, at least 99% of the time—knowing where you are, knowing why you're here, knowing what's going to transpire. Be in the awareness space—sharpen your skills. Instead of sitting there saying, "Well, I don't really know," say, "I go to my awareness and spiritual guidance and ask for information to assist me."

If you're here from a Hierarchical level, if your lineage is created from being an original soul, which is true for many of you, this means that you inherently have full memory that can be tapped at any moment. You have a direction which deals with the totality of humanity—you are not just here for personal experience. You can live your personal life, but feel you must affect the outcome of the total paradigm of life, always looking at the bigger picture.

People who have this memory have the closest connection to the Monadal. And yet, even then, it is what they remember about the steadfast point of evolution, the Absolute, that is important. In evolution, souls who have moved further away from the original point do not have the same strength of memory. That's why original souls come to a planet to start with—their choice is to seed the memory so that those who have either lost or diminished their memory can experience the memory again in a different way, and can be honored in that process by one who brings the intention of that pure intent, or pure clarity into the experience.

Many of you will meet or be connected with original souls. Original souls draw people to them. They have an ability to make things happen, to see things other people don't see, and to be there first. They have an ability to contact consciousness and make it work for them. Sometimes they appear magical or miraculous. It is all a seeded process. Many times they are teachers, or people who share perceptions of different dimensions or invisible levels. Original souls come and direct their life from the Hierarchy. They may have astral guidance and use their spiritual society as everyone else does, and

~

You inherently have full memory that can be tapped at any moment.

~

That's why original souls come to a planet to start with— their choice is to seed *the memory so that those who have either lost or diminished their memory can experience the memory again in a different way.*

~

It is all a seeded process.

~

yet their primary objective and directive comes from the seeding place. So these people are the first wave. They are going to be out there seeding the world, and creating the connections and the unification points that are necessary.

The people who come to be with them are the "army of consciousness." They are the ones that make sure things happen—things get done. They are the stable pieces in the puzzle which link the worlds together. Those who come to work more with the practical—who have the experience of living in the energy dynamic of consciousness, who are putting the practical pieces together, are going to be those who have tapped the resources of the Earth and nature and humanity and want to see those reaped and expanded, proliferated.

So all of these levels work together. That's why it's not really better to be anybody else other than yourself. As each of these pieces becomes available to you and you put them together, things start clearing up. There's much less jealousy and envy once people start to realize they are intricately as important as anyone else, and that their piece of putting that in the puzzle and making it work is what will help the whole thing prosper, and that *all* the levels are necessary.

Being in touch with your guidance is recommended because it helps straighten out kinks in your pattern or perspective. It helps you see where you need to be, doing just what you need to do. You'll contact the levels most pertinent for what you're doing, and if you develop those levels clearly, consistently, and consciously, you can literally work with the dynamic of your intention so that it's always providing you with an understanding of why you are here, what you can do, what your purpose is, and how you can access those levels more completely.

So it behooves you to learn, "Who am I? What did I connect with? What are my guidance points? How does that differ from other people? What is it that I can understand and work with? How can I live who I am to the highest degree of my capacity? I'll stop wasting time working with things that I'm not really sure about, don't understand, and am not interested in. Let me develop that which is going to fully serve my own experience."

As this unfolds a sensitivity develops—you start listening to the guidance systems by letting those really strong seams be felt. You feel your connection to those diverse levels, feel a foundation building and working for you, and, at the same time, there's nothing specifically that you have to do. As you allow those levels to be

So all of these levels work together. That's why it's not really better to be anybody else other than yourself.

present within you, you fill out, you are richer, and fully understand how your place in the universe is working from all those dimensions.

When you come down the tunnel you have all the paradigms set in place. The positive and nurturing thing about this is that whenever you decide to awaken those levels, they are there. There's no need for you to do anything to make them come forward because they are part of you already. The more you develop all the parts of you, the more open, expanded, and wise you are. The levels of your containment are more and more broad and perspective based, and you can see them and can relax, be who you are, and bring that into the experience of your life.

The guidance begins assembling when you intend that it be so. These guidance points are pretty much silent until you ask for them to be verbal. They are available, and yet because of the free-will system it's important for you to ask for what you want, and to phrase the questions so that you get what you are really asking for, and to begin to design realities that support that kind of intention.

As you open to all these different doorways and windows to the invisible, which are giving you their input, you begin to acknowledge that your greatness is now emerging. When you understand who those guidance points are, and why they are with you, you have an even greater sense of your connection, because you realize that the design is so intricately perfect that everything is there with you. There's nothing that you have to do as a human being, and it "gets you off the hook," gives you the information you need, makes the connections that will foster your getting going with it and putting the pieces into place. Ask for who you want to talk to, ask for what you want to know. Go to levels where those awareness points are Angelic, or have wings, or have consciousness of light, and say, "I want to know what we plan to do together. I want to know what skills you can help me with, and I'm open to experiencing and perceiving from awareness much more deeply. I'm ready to acknowledge that I have lots of help and am going to use that help so that it is no longer out of the realm of my possibility to do magic, to do miracles, and whatever it is in my design and in my pattern to accomplish."

These levels commit to being with you and are intricately linked to your field of energy. If you're in a really difficult place and don't know what to do, many times there will be some event, situation, or process that literally brings you out of it, or sheds light on it. Someone will cross your path at just that moment or speak to you in

There's no need for you to do anything to make them come forward because they are part of you already.

The guidance begins assembling when you intend that it be so.

*You might as well unify
those levels in you
just as they are going to be unified
in the greater context,
because, as you do so,
you stand as a guide for others
in that process.*

a certain way, or you'll see a sign of what's possible, and there's a sense that the commitment is there even when you don't ask, and the signs are there if you choose to see them, and the support is always there.

So it becomes important to be aware, to ask, to listen, to experience, and to allow that broadening as much as possible. When you go into the center of your being and move out in the framework of dimensions, you'll feel that those levels have been waiting for your permission to accentuate that positive. The guidance which is there for you is so individual that you can start talking to it every day. You can begin to have your own readings, your own information coming through, your own system of support and initiation.

As you acquaint yourself with these levels there is profoundness, because all those forms of thought, all those archetypical processes, all those energies as they come around you, can in a split second synthesize with you so that you actually embody that which you are, totally, in all your levels—the physical and subtle bodies. Those levels of connection are part of the energy that make up the pattern as you transform. If you wonder where that extra energy comes from as you've seen people move through these initiations—sparkling, light and clear—they are actually synthesizing their practical levels with their etheric levels; they're more ready to fully embody the guidance systems that come with them; and as they open out in each of those instances, that which invisibly has made the commitment to serve is manifested in reality.

So as you synthesize all levels, you become a very beautiful picture, because there are no blanks in your aura, or in your connection, or in your consciousness. It is rich, beautiful, and sustaining. The fundamental purpose of aligning with all these levels of guidance is to be who you really are, to open up to that full potential, and to use all of the dimensions that are now coming together in union for yourself. You might as well unify those levels in you just as they are going to be unified in the greater context, because, as you do so, you stand as a guide for others in that process. And the more unified your field is, and the more the commitment is made to be with all of your parts, the more congruent, the more present, and the more powerful you will be in terms of living your spiritual force and your zeal, and your commitment to be what you chose before you came.

The levels of guidance respond significantly to you because they respond to gratitude, particularly the Angelic realm. The more you initiate gratitude and communicate with them and are thankful—the more they will respond. The more you receive and respond to these levels, the more deeply the relationship develops, so that you have a sense of belonging to all these levels simultaneously. All these dimensions, as they communicate with you, foster a reality inside and outside that's consistent. No matter who you are with or what's going on, you're constantly having this sense of *being* an absolute being, receiving attention and information, and knowing that they all work to serve you. You are of more service to humanity at the same time, and the circular service process of serving and being served continues, so that the more the service of consciousness affords you with a level of integration, the more that integration is available to the planet—and of course that's the design.

CIRCLE OF SERVICE

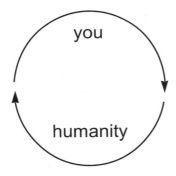

As these invisible levels come together for you, you'll have the vision of those levels, the skills of those levels, and the perspective that comes to include all dynamics—a synthesis. Each of you has chosen this synthesis, because you have chosen to be fully alive, living your full potential, in and with full awareness.

Remember: you chose to come. And you were chosen as a vehicle for the total expression of all dimensions, so according your place in the unfolding makes it real, and brings you fully into being.

Coming Home

Home
Home
Home

WE WOULD LIKE TO TALK WITH YOU about the experience of your choice to be here as light at this time, because you have come here to support experiences which you remember, and yet have never seen or lived in form. Much of what you will be living in this upcoming time is, in a sense, alien to you. You have the awareness borne within you of what it looks like and feels like, and how it's sensitized by your light, and yet the design of it, the plan, the memory of where it is going to fit in the future is not as present for you. So sometimes you may find that you have a yearning to go home, a yearning to return to where the design was first hatched, and to see the space again so you can remind yourself of it, so that you can carry it more distinctly with you as you go forward, so that you are not feeling as lost or as separate from the reason for your being here.

You are part of a light force, and there are 144,000 of you. Your lineage comes directly from the Monadal. This means that you carry an impulse within you to restore order to the universe, and to do that so you are conscious of instituting the Monadal in the framework of the world—because that's the choice for the free-will experiment. And this **is** an experiment. The Monadal energy, as it split into the twelve initial points of reality, and those split into twelve, made 144. At that point in "time," there was what you would call a conference. And at that conference it was determined that the space of this Earth would be inhabited by the experience of light in form, with the ability to create whatever reality was ordained by each individual point of light.

We have made statements that the consciousness of God rests in the hands of the people. Because you are God, you can affect God. Until this time, that thought has been kept under wraps. As you think about it now, think about how you might affect every point of reality by your choices. Ultimately, the freedom that you experience is dynamically connected to the eventual resolution and the formula of the design of the inherent creation, which comes from all points simultaneously. In other words, you are here acting on behalf of your past self, your present self, and your future self.

~

*I'm going home for my mission
and I'm coming back.
I'm foundationing the experience
of being myself, totally,
in all parts of reality, simultaneously.*

~

You are here remembering an ideal,
a space from which you were born,
from which the free-will experiment
was created,
and you
are also here making decisions
as you go along,
as if you didn't know any of this.

It also means,
for many of you who want to return home,
that you can do that,
and can experience it as a transcendence
rather than a transition
—in other words, rather than a death,
you experience it
as a dream or meditation.

If you think about your knowing,
you'll understand what we're talking about,
because
that knowing cannot be changed or
challenged.

You are here remembering an ideal, a space from which you were born, from which the free-will experiment was created, and you are also here making decisions as you go along, as if you didn't know any of this. You are also in the future reaping the results of the choices of the free-will experiment as it comes into resolution, so that you are actually everywhere at one time, fostering all of this reality. You are in this body and you don't remember the design. So the amnesia is rampant in the process.

As you think about that original design and being able to affect that design in this time, if there's something you'd like to include in your present formula, some information, or some part of that experience of choice that you would like to recall, relive, and reorder, that is possible. It's also possible for you in every moment to understand that you have the total capacity to create whatever it is that you desire. That means that the capacity you carry is equal to anything you've ever heard about, dreamed of, or wished were possible.

It also means, for many of you who want to return home, that you can do that, and can experience it as a transcendence rather than a transition—in other words, rather than a death, you experience it as a dream or meditation. And you come back from that experience with the answers, with the memories, and with the charge of that impulse of energy, so that you are ready to do what you have come to do, so the foundation of your life experience becomes literally changed by your own volitional will.

Your consciousness remembers that you have come here to do something special. And it isn't an egoic process that tells you that, it's a knowing that you have. And that knowing is different from any other knowing that you have. If you think about your knowing, you'll understand what we're talking about, because that knowing cannot be changed or challenged. It's deep inside of you; it's not superficial. It's not about a person, or a time period, or an idea, or an experience. It's about your essential point of reality and where it's anchored.

If you want to, you can come home and experience what that anchoring really means, where it comes from, and where it will resolve itself, so that the foundation of your life experience becomes that knowing, instead of having the knowing inside and wondering if it will happen, or when and how it will happen. Again, take the proverbial bull by the horns and say, "I want to know where my pieces fit."

We recommend that you come home regularly, then project yourself into your present life, and experience how that moment designs itself, so that you begin to realize who you are in form. In other words, it begins to manifest. This is different from resonating and receiving, working with your light body, experiencing your energy fields, balancing your chakra system, and working to see the balance of those things which are already a part of your life. At some level when you work with these "physical" areas you are functioning at a rate of speed which is consistent with your "normal" reality—like who's doing what to whom and why. Coming home is about your essential nature. It's about the spaces that come with you wherever you go, and don't change.

These are the points of reality that your being recognizes are necessary for you to continue with your life's work here. It's the blinders coming off, the understanding which is necessary to dispel all the doubts, and bring resolve into your being. It's the part of your emotion that keeps longing for something to fulfill it, but can't find it in the outer world. It's the part of you that mentally races back and forth and tries to decide what it is that's so important about being here, and being a light worker. Sometimes you come up short and say, "I don't know what's so important about it. I think I just want to cash in my chips and go back, because it is tedious and I don't quite understand what a lot of this means to me, and how it will unfold. There are not that many designs in my own thinking that I could imagine making enough models for the whole world, to not only survive, but co-create, cooperate, and bring absolute resolution. Somebody's going to have to help me here with this one, because I don't quite get the game plan."

Remembering Your Mission

We recommend that maybe four times a month minimum, i.e., once a week, you come home for an evening and reorient yourself with the vibration of what it is to be in the space of light, and you again function—vibrationally and energetically—as one who has a mission. You see, the knowing is about your mission. You know you have a mission. You might even know a little bit—or maybe quite a bit—about what that mission is. And probably something is missing in your knowing about it, like—when, where, how, and

It's the part of your emotion that keeps longing for something to fulfill it, but can't find it in the outer world.

You see, the knowing is about your mission.

*Perhaps the easiest way
for you to recognize this
is to know that
without your mission
you might as well go back.*

*Because if you don't know
how
your mission fits into the prospectus
of what you're doing
every day of your life,
in every second of your reality,
it's not only lonely,
it's tiresome and frustrating.*

what—how the resources are going to come to you, and when the dynamics are going to foster themselves so that you relate more and more to who you are in that mission.

A lot of you carry your mission like a sword, like a book, like a covering on your body, like a hat, like a pair of shoes, like an automobile, or whatever. You carry it with you, and you use it at certain times, and you don't embody it completely. It's as if you're waiting for something to show up to give you instructions about how to do that. Perhaps the easiest way for you to recognize this is to know that without your mission you might as well go back. And that's not being said lightly. Because if you don't know how your mission fits into the prospectus of what you're doing every day of your life, in every second of your reality, it's not only lonely, it's tiresome and frustrating.

So we're going to suggest that you come home to shed light on the parameters that you're dealing with in the knowing, so that the knowing and the mission start activating, so that you feel as if the foundation of what you've come here to do is beginning to build inside of you, because it has to build inside of you before it can build in the world.

We're going to talk to you about how to make the foundation work so that your mission amplifies, your knowing shows you exactly what that mission is about, and the points or forces of your consciousness begin to work together. You feel as if you have a thousand angels carrying you through this process. There is no opposition from any level, because internally your knowing, your mission, and your impulse of energy—that light you carry and the place of support or foundation which is your home orientation—begin to foundation your life here, so that you feel more complete than ever. A very deep and foundational space resonates and activates your whole framework of being so that you're not just here as someone who's landed on the planet without the instruction manual and you're not sure exactly what to do! So you pick up the odd bits and pieces and information around you and foster that reality so that the foundation comes together and you say, "I think I'm getting it, but it might take me another 20 years." And of course, in another 20 years the pieces will have to be already put together. They're going to have to be already synthesized. In fact, we're recommending that they be synthesized by 1996.

The other reason for coming home is because it's time to rewire your circuits, amplify your charge, time for you to put together, or aggregate, those pieces of your own reality so that the foundation you're carrying is literal and you are understanding what you are here to do. Put in simple words, "What am I here to do, how can I do it, and what's it really about?" You're thinking many times that it's about communication, about receiving, about making stability, about understanding, and all these other things. What it's really about is remembering. If you're not remembering it all, putting the pieces together is still a job that requires patience. And patience is running thin now.

It's as if you're in the ocean, and you know there are lifeboats, and you know there are little rings, like lifesavers, and somebody's trying to throw you one, and you know there's a current that's sweeping you away from the ship, and from the lifeboats, and from the rafts, and from the little dinghies, and you're saying, "What am I supposed to do, where am I supposed to go?" Somebody says, "Swim like hell." Somebody else says, "Why don't you just run with the current, just float, just flow with the wave—that will take you home." Somebody else is saying, "Look around, use your eyes, use your senses, figure out where you are. If you figure out where you are, then you'll know where to swim." Somebody else is saying, "Just float, let go completely, and just become like a piece of cork on top of the water, and then they'll see you and come get you." And somebody else is saying something else. There are probably 50 things that you could do, and at the same time, it's up to you to make that choice. So how do you decide?

This is about remembering as much as you can, figuring it out from the level of knowing and memory, rather than trying to figure out what you should pay attention to and what's going to save your butt. Because if you're thinking about what you should do, and where you're going to end up, you're probably not in memory, and you're definitely not in knowing. It's a very beautiful time for you, at those four times a month, to throw up your hands and say, "Take me back, I want to go back. And I don't want to make transition, I don't want to stand in front of a truck or anything like that. What I want to do is let go of all of the parameters that I think about all the time, that is, the discipline. The Ones With No Names say I'm supposed to do this, and I'm drinking my lemon water, and I'm grounding, and so on . . . ."

So once a week you might just say, "I don't want to do anything. I just want to go home. I want to be a child, I want to be free of responsibility and the need to survive, and the need to do anything,

*Because
if you're thinking
about what you should do,
and where you're going to end up,
you're probably not in memory,
and you're definitely not in knowing.*

the need to put it all together. I just want to be, in a place where I can remember. I want to have my knowing surround me, so that I am strengthened, and rewarded, and honored, and affirmed. I want to feel the divinity of my nature and really see who I am."

" Phone Home . . . "
An Exercise

You go to bed that night, or take a siesta in the afternoon, or meditate for a couple of hours and go home, whatever feels best for you. You basically tie your body to the bed by anchoring your energy—going from the top of your head down to the bottoms of your feet and saying, "I want to stay here, and I want to be safe while I do my trip. I ask that all parts of my body, all cells of my experience, all my molecular consciousness be grounded into the Earth. I ask to be protected by all the angels of consciousness that come around me. I really want to let go and transcend in these few hours, or in this night's sleep—I want to go home. I want to remember. I want to see what's real. I want to be renewed, and I want to come back energized—refreshed—revitalized, with lots and lots and lots of things that I remember which are going to help me live my mission." This is really about recovering your mission statement, recovering your mission energy, and recovering your mission affiliation—in other words, "Why did I say I'd do this anyway?" So you really get it all into perspective.

You anchor your body down, tie your framework to the bed energetically, gather all your sentinels and guardians, and Whoosh! Breathe through your body all the way down to your feet. Make sure you're in your body before you leave. That's very important, because then your body will be in the same condition when you return, except that you'll be able to energize and charge it, because it will be grounded. The circuits will be open to that last charge of energy, and if you bring energy in that is equal to or accelerated from that, your body will be able to handle that charge. If you're not in the body when you leave, and you bring back all this energy, you might blow a few circuits, or at least make yourself feel as if the trip was not worth while. So you want to foundation it, clear it, anchor it, and make sure that all the energy you're calling to serve you is present as you make this experience of transcendence.

You get ready to go out through the top of your head by first going all the way down to the bottom of your feet, like a shower, like the oscillating current of sunlight on water. Fill your body, and then reverse that mechanism. Take the energy and move it from your feet, through the chakras, all the way up out the top of the head, and ask to return to the Hierarchy of Order, or to the space of your origination. Be sure to breathe deeply and rhythmically during the process.

You're going to come through the time tunnel in reverse. You will remember how you came in, but be going in the opposite direction. There will be no pain, struggle, or problems with it. You're going to go through that process as if you're going through the tunnel and leaving the experience of the world, except that as you're going you are watching, and you're not feeling anything. You're not feeling pain, you're not feeling separation, you're just aware of what the movement is telling you about your consciousness. And you're moving into spaces where you are ordaining knowledge and remembrance.

That's why it's so important. Unless at times in your experience you are absent from the density of your world, it's challenging for you to actually recognize who you are, that your knowing is real, and that your mission is going to take place. Lots of times, we will say in a reading that you have the ability to shapeshift, translocate, bilocate, or experience your consciousness. You can recognize the awareness that you were born with, or assist others to transform, or take whole levels of consciousness and bring them into this reality. And you scratch your head and say, "Who, me? How can I do these things when I can't even pay my bills, and I don't know how to have someone really love me, and I'm afraid of this, or I'm not doing that?"

This is like a refresher course. A part of you needs to fulfill itself and really wants to have affiliation with understanding and awareness that is much more natural to your state of being than the world. This is a way of reacquainting yourself with your family of consciousness, putting together those situations that seem to be very real for you in your dream state and other spaces, and do not necessarily support you in the physical space. So you go through the tunnel and experience reliving, backwards, your journey into form. It has a very important relevance. As you move through that tunnel in reverse, you begin to experience the reason for your choice.

You're seeing the relationship between what you're doing in your life now (with your belief system and thought process) and remembering and re-living your lineage, the part of you that has come to do your mission. The experience that you're looking at, that calls you into being says, "Don't you remember this? This is why you forgot that, because you're supposed to remember it when *this* happens." You're getting details. A lot of those details are going to assist you to make sense out of your life, and definitely out of your reason for being here, which sometimes might be cloudy.

Until you reach the interdimensional space, you might have the knowing and hope that the knowing is accurate, and at the same time you may not have the pieces to make sense out of it. You might think sometimes that you're idealistic, or that you fantasize, or you're not sure that you can trust your own knowing. You might see yourself as a beautiful blue being under the sea, a mermaid, a beautiful green Goddess rising out of the trees, and flying into the ethers. Or you might see yourself dissolving as wind and carrying messages all over the world, or you might see yourself as dynamically being connected to something other than yourself, but you don't remember what it is, and you're not sure how to get that information into the psyche so that you have the power to activate the charge.

This is a way of regrouping, of bringing in the stability to answer your own questions, of looking at what keeps driving you. You wake up and say, "I've got to keep going." Why? "I don't know, I've just got to keep going." What are you going to do? "I don't know. I've just got to keep going." Stamina and strength forge you, and the urgency from your soul, and the sense of destiny—and yet you might look in the mirror and say, "I haven't a clue. I don't really know. It's getting clearer, I think, but there are only a few pieces that I can really assure myself of, and the rest is blank." We're teasing you, and yet it's real, that you *still don't know.*

As you're going toward the light again and regrouping the pieces, all of your awareness starts to click, "Yes, this feels familiar. Thank God something feels familiar, because I've been lost in amnesia for so many years, thank God this starts to feel familiar." It's an aching in you, a yearning to have this familiarity, and to be full of grace and to lay your burden down. All of you have moments when you lay your burden down, but then you always pick it up again. Why? Because your mission is unclear. So as you are retracing your steps, information comes to you. "That's why I picked these parents, this is what I learned, this is what I'm about, this is what gave me courage, this is what gave me strength, this is what gave me stamina, this is what gave me patience."

You're going through the tunnel backwards, and you're experiencing more and more awareness. If you make the statement that you are returning home for your mission plan, and you want your statement clearly and boldly outlined for you in images, in awarenesses, in sensate feelings and knowings, and you don't want to come back until you have more knowing than you're going with, then, with your free will, *you are claiming the right to know.* And you are claiming the right to receive. That's really valuable, because in this time when all of the destructuring of the belief system is happening, if you go home and restructure yourself, then you will find that you're crystallizing that intention. It's so crystal clear that you're able to go into the world and just start doing what you're here to do.

The foundation of this is very simple:

- Go to the place where the charge originated;
- Identify with the charge instead of your current reality;
- Shapeshift the energy;
- Bring the charge in the top of your head;
- Ground it in the same way you did before you left.

~

Go
to the place
where the charge originated.

~

You're going to sit in the Swing again and see where it is that your choices are destined to take you. Because once you see that, you can return to your physicality on the beam of light that you originally traveled.

While you're in the ethers, sleeping, dreaming, meditating, visualizing, organizing, communicating, whatever it is you want to do, you formulate your design from a place inside you at the same time that you're seeing it outside you.

In the ethereal levels you're going to travel through, it is important to keep going through all of those levels of awareness until you say, "Wait a minute now, this is the most familiar place. This is where I think I come from; this is where I belong." You're going to have your own path to take on this, so you're going toward the light, you're going toward the Hierarchy, you're experiencing that your intention is to actualize your mission and to reorient, and to go into the spaces where that knowledge is connected to the vision and the choice—because the choice is the Swing Between Worlds. So you're coming home.

You're going to sit in the Swing again and see where it is that your choices are destined to take you. Because once you see that, you can return to your physicality on the beam of light that you originally traveled.

And yet, since you've already been born, and since you've grounded into your body, and since the foundation is all the way through your circuits, you bring the memory all the way into your feet. It means you ground it in as if amnesia never happened! So you're returning down the same circuitry that you left, except this time as you go down that space, and as you're experiencing that foundation, what's real about it is that you can see your end point, you know what the personality is, who you've lived with, who your lovers are or were, who your friends are, what your vocation is. You can go right down the "shoot the chute" into that space and be back in your body with the full knowing that you had in the Swing Between Worlds before you came, *but this time you're not going to forget it.*

The more times you do this (you might want to do it four times a week or four times a day) the easier it will be to make the place of the formed body—where you have the circuitry and the anchoring—and the place of the awareness of consciousness, the same vibrational point, which is of course, *dat-dat-dat-da!,* the experience of living your mission. So the above and the below come together. The Absolute is living in form. You become God or Goddess.

All Your Pieces Fit

As you come together with the wave, the knowing, the mission, the consciousness, and the body—this is aggregation. Aggregation is the place where the pieces of the puzzle finally fit. This phenomenon is a rebirth. It's coming into the experience of your life so that the foundation serves the design, makes you happy, relieves you of the burden of carrying something you're not sure you can manifest, and allows you in a very literal and sensitive way to organize consciousness so that it is showing you what it's about. It's saying, "Look, if we do it this way, this will happen. This is really what it's about." You can say, "All right," and you can acquiesce. You can relax and let go of the struggle, and the trying, and the working harder, and just allow it.

You can allow it because it makes sense. The pieces are fitting together. It doesn't have gaps so that you're not sure what you're supposed to be doing. There's humor in it, joy in it, aliveness in it, that somehow you're receiving something that has so much value that for the first time in your life you don't care about whether you're going to do it or not, whether you can do it or not, whether anything is going to happen or not, because the *knowing* is stronger than anything else.

The mission you've come to live is organized in your consciousness! Even though it seems immaterial, invisible, inaudible, and unable to be tapped physically, it has already made the conduit so that it's in front of you showing you the way—not behind you, invisible, immaterial—it's in front of you, completely actualized. That's what happens when the circuitry turns on. You're going forward and backward in the circuitry, so that you get it coming and going. It translates itself differently when you're reborn, and you already have the circuitry in place to live the mission, because you put it in place by grounding your body before you left.

So you're coming down the "shoot the chute," and amnesia does not touch you anymore because you already know you're dense. You're coming back to density. So what? Big deal! It doesn't affect your framework anymore. Why? Because you're working on your circuits. You're embodying light. You're going to make the circuits of your physical body equal to the circuits you had before you left the Swing Between Worlds. It's obvious to you what's going on.

"Heaven on Earth" means that there is a vibrational equivalency

*"Heaven on Earth" means
that there is a vibrational equivalency
between dimensions
that is fostered
when you change dimensions.
It's fostered as you experience
going back and forth,
and back and forth,
and it isn't altered.
When you change dimensions,
it doesn't change!*

between dimensions that is fostered when you change dimensions. It's fostered as you experience going back and forth, and back and forth, and it isn't altered. When you change dimensions, it doesn't change!

You're able to keep it consistent, able to frame it in such a way that the foundation of it calls you together, and says, "You can have both worlds. You can have all worlds. You can have fragments of whatever you want all the time, and you don't have to leave anything and lose anything and create it in such a way that you are separate from what it is that you are."

The dynamics are supportive of all dimensions for you, and you do not have to choose. You can go back and forth as many times as you want, and have all those worlds with you, and you don't have to choose. The good news is that the foundation of your body is learning to hold your consciousness, and you can expand your consciousness as far as you want. As long as you're grounding the energy, as long as you're moving it through, opening your centers of energy, and learning to balance them, as long as you're experiencing the Silver Chalice and looking at all those pieces, it comes together, it's aggregating, things are looking up, it's a better life, it feels good.

Living in Resolution

So then you say, "It's time to go for the big one now. It's time for me to remember things, so that I am no longer feeling like the odd man out, or as if, for some reason, I've got most of it but I still don't have all of it. Now I'm going to go home, and practice balancing the framework of my physicality with the framework of my spirituality. Since things are always ultimately in resolution, doesn't it make sense that I'm ultimately in resolution? Yes it does. It makes sense that somehow I have safeguarded all my circuits and all my awareness and I can do this traveling, because where am I going? I'm going from one part of myself to the other. That's all I'm doing. Yes, I'm changing dimensions, yes, I'm moving from the Earth to the heavens. Yes, I'm experiencing dynamic dimensional reality and dense physical structure. So what? That's the design! That's what the free will experiment is all about; it's already been done. Somebody went ahead of me, and put all the circuits in place for me to do this, and if I have the intention to do it, if I have the capacity to do it, if I begin to do it, then it will be fine because I'm saying this affirmation: What I'm going home for is my mission, and I'm coming back. And because I'm coming back, I'm preparing my body and I'm leaving, and yet I'm coming back. I'm foundationing the experience of being myself, totally, in all points of reality, simultaneously. I'm also recognizing that I don't have limits. I'm going to move that barrier of perception so that my left and right brain can really start communicating, can really start activating, can put together frameworks so that I'm starting to spontaneously regenerate all the parts of me that I started out with, that were lost through amnesia, or socialization, or behavior modification, or whatever I went through—chaos theory, or time-out, or dunce caps, or whatever I did—whatever I have done, is going to be reversed. I have the opportunity to do this differently."

You can see it's about forgiveness, about losing guilt, about having another go, about receiving absolution, anything, anything you want. This is about resolving, once and for all, those memories you carry that still bother you. For example, you can probably still remember the way your mother looked at you when you dropped that glass of milk on the floor. It will always be indelibly etched in your consciousness. Or what that second grader said to you about your hair, or your nose, or your face, or your teeth, whatever; it will always be there. And you're walking around as a big person, wearing assurance on your face, and you're doing really great, except that all of those things are still inside the psyche.

You're going to go inside out, lose the pain and the hurt, to attain the experience of your own divine mission. That's the only thing that's going to erase those hurts, is to experience that all of that was for some purpose that you now comprehend, and which at this moment really doesn't affect you any more. And it's not because you buffed up your armor of self worth, it's because you recognize that your divine nature doesn't make mistakes. It doesn't matter if you dropped the milk and your mother was concerned because somebody could get cut by the glass, or that it was the last bit of milk in the jar or the carton, or that she had just washed the floor—something that had nothing to do with you. You understand that, when you come back through the tunnel.

What happens as you reorient your psyche to your consciousness is that everything that doesn't matter falls away, and everything that you are emerges, which is what it's all about. Dynamically, no matter what was said to you or done to you, you are being moved through

*What
I'm going home for
is my mission,
and I'm coming back.*

*You recognize
that your divine nature
doesn't make mistakes.*

an oscillatory frequency that's turning everything inside out. You're accessing your memory of what's important, and losing the memory of what's not important. The pain is being removed. Why? Because you're going into reality and you're losing illusion. It means that you're having a perfect scenario here for resurrection—coming into a space, coming back from the dead, and you're alive! And you're bringing with you that which is your purpose, your potentiation, your mission.

Bringing in Your Mission
An Exercise

Now, when you come back in the body, you want to ground everything that you are into the body, and bring it in from the top of your head down through your body, and send out through the bottom of your feet anything that remains of illusion in your body. You are going to transpose the cellular system and the framework of that experience in such a way that anything that's in the body, that's lingering as memory in the cells, is taken out through the bottom of the feet, so that, literally, you're having a transfusion of light into form. This time you're reorganizing the cellular structure as you go, so that the mission is replacing the abstinence, the forgetfulness, the absentmindedness, the I'm-out-to-lunch, I'm-out-in-space, I'm-out-on-the-meditational-wheels syndrome, whatever it is.

Living Your Mission

You're coming in. You're planting yourself in the form of the body, and this time you're going to be here in a way that you've never been here before. Because now there's a reason to be here, it's real for you, it's clear for you, it has vision, strength, capacity, and most of all, it has information that supports your knowing. When you come into the body, the knowing says, "Oh, thank goodness, I'm not alone any more; I'm hooked up. And as I'm hooked up, there's a reality here which suggests that ultimately everything that comes into being through me is going to be recognized as my own plan, my own design. I begin to organize my consciousness, I begin to put the framework together and structure it so the foundation of my life supports my essence."

So I look around in my life. "What am I doing? Does the foundation of my life support this knowing, this new information, this mission?" A lot of you are going to find out that to a large extent it doesn't.

You will be sizing up your life, reorganizing this and that. The knowledge, mission statement, consciousness and information are going to surface in a way that puts your external life into an absolutely congruent perspective with your inside mission. So you see through things that don't work any more, and see through those areas of your experience where you know you've been wanting to make a change, but haven't quite known what it was. You've been doing that more consciously in the last three or four years, particularly since the end of 1991, and you've been creating everything that you've been experiencing without anything to support it at all, except your own consciousness.

Now you say, "All right, what is my consciousness supporting, and is it what I want it to be supporting? I give permission to reshape my life now. I've reshaped my consciousness, I've come into these different spaces, and now I want to reshape my life." And when you look around, you will see through the illusion of your own mask first. You'll see through what you carry that no longer serves you, or fits you, or is no longer something you want. Next you're going to see through the masks of other people in society, or community, or societal biological family. If there are not masks, that's good—if there are, you're going to see through them. And it's not going to hurt you this time. You're not going to say, "Oh, I made a mistake. I shouldn't be here." It's going to be, "Oh, it's time to decide. It's time to move." You're going to find that you have an absolute strength that you didn't know you had to make those choices.

This happens only if you go home. If you don't go home, the masks are torn off the people and there's pain. And that's just the way it is, because if you live it from your dimension you have attachment to it, most times, without a broader perspective. If you live it from the knowing that "this is my mission, or this is not my mission," then you're decisive about it, and you know what it is, and it's clear.

~

You'll see through what you carry
that no longer serves you,
or fits you,
or is no longer something you want.

~

It's what we're talking about in the chapter on relationship. Someone comes to another and says, "I want to live from my full essence. I want to be in love with myself. I want to have a relationship with myself." If the other person says, "I don't really think I want a relationship with myself," then the first person understands that the other person needs to do something else, and there's not pain involved.

When you choose to be in a relationship with yourself, you will find someone else who is in relationship with themselves. And it's easy to make that transition when it's time to make it, because there is a great relief that no longer are there any masks coming off—being lived through as if it were reality. Take that illusion off, and it's a deep and rich experience. Then you turn around, and there's somebody there who wants to be real also. It's a beautiful transitional space to be in at that moment, because the transition you're making is not that you're dying and your heart is dying—it's that you're really alive for the first time. You're not afraid to be alive by and with yourself. That's very important.

You're not afraid to be ALIVE *by and with yourself.*

So as the mask comes off the people around you, you realize, "We're starting to live, here! There's zing to this. We're starting to be alive in ways the mission has always stated that we would be alive. And yet, I was looking around, and nobody was really doing it. So I was kind of waiting." You find that your direction becomes clear, and so does your calling. The calling is the frame to the mission: What it looks like, what it feels like, how it fits. Now is the time for this. We would recommend that your first mission is to *find* your mission, and that you design time into your week to do this. And the foundation becomes literal when you recognize that you cannot live without your mission. It's very, very simple.

The calling is the frame to the mission: What it looks like, what it feels like, how it fits.

We would recommend that your first mission is to find your mission, and that you design time into your week to do this.

So you go home on a regular basis. You can always go home when you sleep—you can go to bed at night, close your eyes and do the shower meditation. The energy is coming in through the top of your head and out the bottom of your feet, like a shower of water. Ground yourself strongly, tie yourself etherically to your bed, and feel the angels come around you, your guides, The Ones With No Names, the Hierarchical spaces, order, anything that makes you feel safe—your soul, light, whatever. Put the crystals around you, and then the light through the body, ground it in one last time, and then breathe as you visualize going out the top of your head. Say, "I'd like to go to the Hierarchy of Order and return home. And when I awaken I want to come through the levels again, differently this time, because I bring my memory with me. I choose to remember." The most important sentence for a human being to say is, "I remember."

It means that I can come back this time and put it together differently. I re-member, I member it differently. I synthesize it differently this time. So it's easy, and it gives you the glue to put the pieces together until you understand the magic to make it whole. That's the synthesis of information and energy. The first thing is to glue it together, and glue it again until it's whole, and then say, "Yup, it's whole." Then let it go, and the magic is that you make it reappear, and this time there's no glue, it's completely whole. Everything about you is synthesized into that space, and you don't have any pieces that don't quite fit, or someplace that needs more glue. It's completely, wholly synthesized to its own divine space of recognition and importance.

Again, go home. Remember. Reorient. Facilitate. Support yourself. Familiarize yourself with your own game plan. Go up there to the Swing and say, "Look, I want to know what's going on here. I really want to understand this. I want to see my mission as clearly as you're able to show it to me." We will do an instant replay—Whoosh! Whoosh! Whoosh! Play it back for you, so you can see the innocence with which you chose it; the divinity which supports it, and girds it and undergirds it, and surrounds it; the flame which calls it out and keeps it alive; and the integrity of your mission—which is the important point of recognition that you determined needs to be manifest on this planet at this time, which was important enough for you to come here in the first place!

Getting the pieces together, resolving all those nagging doubts, situating yourself in the universe so that you belong everywhere, this is what it's about. And the foundation of it literally serves the whole. Because when you come back with your mission through morphic resonance and the conception of the tuning fork, everybody else is clearer about their mission also. Resolution is easier. The pain that people carry gets resolved. If you don't have pain, and you're walking around clear, you can imprint everybody that you meet with that same clarity, and they can start feeling as good as you feel.

Everything you do serves the whole. The clearer you are about your mission, the faster it will actualize, and that's what it's about—facilitating resolution, bringing the oneness into form, making the sacred marriage between your above and your below, or the awareness that you carry and the instrument you've come to live it

The most important sentence for a human being to say is, "I remember."

You get an instant replay of what was important enough for you to come here in the first place.

Everything *you do* serves the whole.

through. So balancing this is very, very imperative, because each of you is at the end of your rope. You're at the end of the rope of suffering and at the beginning of the experience and space of complete and absolute resolution.

So come into resolution, and let the struggling end now. Fulfill yourself, fill yourself with the solace of knowing that everything about you has a reason and a purpose, and you're experiencing what your purpose is. You're free to receive fulfillment and resolution. Everything makes sense, and the pieces all click together. The symmetry and beauty of the design comes in and feeds the substance that you're carrying, and you begin to flow. The fluids and dimensions match and marry through your experience, and when you come into the body you feel that all the parts of you finally fit. And nothing is missing.

There's nothing you have to do, because you've kicked the mission into its unfolding. The framework opens out, and you go down the "shoot the chute" again, but this time you know where you're going. And you have the energy to complete it—and that's what you call "a piece of cake."

RELATIONSHIP with SELF

UNION OTHERS

UNION

Union Union Union

~

*I commit
to being in relationship with myself.
I'm now responsible for myself,
for my own knowing,
and for my vision of what will work for
me. My own honoring is my primary
focus.*

~

THIS IS THE TIME OF SEEDING UNION INTO FORM. What is being ordained from this is the seeding for the new world, the seeding for the new time, and the seeding for the new soul expression. A total reweaving is happening between all dimensions and dynamics here on Earth, and we will see that reweaving most prominently in the area of human relationship. Honoring the self from the soul is the basis for the new way of relating with others in "relationship." The soul, as it emerges, is being blocked by the existing conditions and frameworks structured by society, but it continues to move toward its fullest expression.

Since the structure of relational reality is now dissipated literally in the etheric level, and because the political, educational, and familial structures no longer really exist anywhere in this or other dimensions, there is the unsettled feeling of knowing that what you want to do, what you know you can do, and what you have done, are three different energies. So this is a time to weave together all those energies—past, present and future. Moving out of the structure and weaving, requires enormous flexibility and a capacity to know and dream and experience from that which has never been literal.

Reality is used to moving from the known into a space where the known gives one the focus, action, framework, and experience of what is normal. Bringing together the past, present, and future, when the normal is no longer palpable, can happen most easily when there is a container for the known in which to place "new" dynamics.

The Stewpot
An Exercise

To give yourself a place to put the future model is helpful, and gives focus to that which is emerging. One way to establish a "place" to contain the unfolding dynamics is to imagine using a stainless steel container as the place to "hold" your present state of being, much like making a stew. The container makes you safe and is constructed to hold the frame. That's what's going to be rigid. The belief system might say that in order to have that container exist, the old stew or memories will also exist, and the stew has to taste the same as the one you made last week, and have the same ingredients. But the structure has nothing to do with actual memory or making things the same. If you free the memory from its container, the memory can be a consciousness which adds new dimensions around and into the container, while at the same time, you might not have tasted the flavor of the stew yet, and that's okay because that is part of what is yet to come.

Whatever has been known, aggregated, or put together from all dimensions, can now be solidified and put into the pot. Finding the similarities in those spaces helps you bring them together and weave them consciously into the psyche as the experience of self.

You can put into the pot your focus for the moment, your intention, where you're going, what you want to live, resources from the universe, abundance, creation, love and harmony, peace and well-being, health, prosperity—all those pieces.

Because of this new seeding of consciousness, most people seem available to the manifestation of their dreams now. They sense the destructuring as a pathway to something new and exciting. Those energies are actually guiding the soul. The structure as it has already been dissipated etherically means that nothing that has worked before will work now. We're going toward a time when there is the procreative or co-creative, which means literally that the experience of the future has no structure, even though it's chosen and has an energy frequency.

The ideal is to take this container of past experience and knowing what works—the foundation—and marry that with the upcoming process, synthesizing it, imprinting it, and weaving these dynamics together. If you take both hands, the left hand represents the process of structure—the stewpot, and the right hand is the existing essence—that which is being woven, the unknown. When you bring the hands together, they create the present.

The present is the space that is most unclear. The future seems somewhat clear to most people. They know what it feels like and can sense it, yet they haven't structured it into the world. So for those of you who are in the critical time of choice, all your frames are being woven together so that they exist in a pattern that has the potential and the actual existing in that same moment.

The Dogma of Relationship

In relationship we can take existing structure and know exactly what it is. If you do certain activities with certain people, you're in a certain relationship; if you do other activities with another person, you're in another kind of relationship; if you have another kind of experience with someone else, that's a different kind of relationship; and until this point, humanity has kept all of their relationships very separate. We use the word "calibration" here, saying that the heart actually calibrates itself vibrationally in a different way in each of these different sets of relationships as they have been standardized by the status quo, by dogma, law, and order. If you have done a certain action with someone, society supports movement toward certain commitments or actions. The dogma is that you are going toward a permanent commitment if you have a sexual relationship with someone. Certain kinds of experiences are supported by the society and are given energy from the society. This is something that people don't understand. As soon as they begin to connect with someone, the society supports certain eventualities, certain ways in which the

*If you have done
a certain action with someone,
the society
supports movement toward
certain commitments or actions.*

*As soon as
they begin to connect with someone,
the society supports
certain eventualities,
certain ways in which the framework
of that relationship "should" exist.*

~

*There is usually
an underlying TENSION in
relationship because you're either
doing what is expected or not.*

~

*As people learn about and choose
a spiritual path,
the calibration of being
in a certain part of their heart
at certain times,
with certain people,
no longer fits.*

~

framework of that relationship "should" exist. Many times the resistance of society to new forms and ways of being is very literal.

There is usually an underlying tension in relationship because you're either doing what is expected or not. You're either moving toward the normal eventuality or you're not, and as these new paradigms open out, the tension becomes very taut, because the old structure is trying to hang on to what it believes is the norm, the desired, and the sanctioned. As people move out of this sanctioned experience, society puts tremendous pressure upon them to conform. As the models are changing, because etherically they need to change, those people who are change-agents and who come in expressly to frame things differently, become uncomfortable with the calibration. Those people who choose to sustain new kinds of form, or new kinds of relationship have to take a quantum leap.

As people learn about and choose a spiritual path, the calibration of being in a certain part of their heart at certain times, with certain people, no longer fits. It feels confining, constricting, as if all the frameworks that have existed do not allow for expression of the soul itself. So what we have here, if we go back to the original model, is the experience of the structure saying, "Stay inside certain bounds." And then we have the soul saying, "That's impossible! We don't have just one lifetime together, we don't have just one soul we can love, we don't have just one way of expressing love in and of and around the soul. We have to have a different model." So we have the tension between those two models which are breaking apart. And we're suggesting that you begin to bring those models together.

Take what has worked in your life before, and make that your container for your stew, make that the pot, make that the structure. It might be honoring, it might be communication that works, it might be terms of endearment that work, ways of expressing closeness and intimacy that seem to be appropriate, it might be the way certain levels of love are experienced and expressed.

Let's say, for example, with a teacher, you might not experience certain levels of intimacy, and yet the calibration in the heart would lead you to open out to that person in a frame that would be very expressive and very deep. So if you take the new awareness and place that into conjunction with the old spaces, you allow for the expression to be dynamic, innovative and unified, and yet, the calibration no longer structures the relationship from a cellular basis. What has happened as humankind has structured relationship, is that they have actually imparted to the cells an edict that says when certain levels of relationship are lived, the cells only respond in a certain way. For example, when we have passion and love and deep longing for union, there is an energy surge that happens from the root chakra which opens out to the levels of creation that are very dynamic and have no threshold of limitation. When the calibration says, "No. We can't have that kind of intimacy," then there is an actual wave motion which goes down and closes the root chakra, and raises the vibration to another level of the chakra system so that there is a response from that level.

If you look at relationship in terms of its passage, and if you have calibration that says, "There are no holds barred here. I can open out to any level of relationship with this person," the first thing that happens is that the creative energy is stimulated, and people feel more alive in a relationship. They feel more passion and experience more union from deep creational levels of the root. As the relationship progresses, different levels come into play, and sometimes, as a result of that, the passion is decreased, and there is more heart, or more mind, or more connection in different ways. What has happened cellularly in the past is that an edict has gone into the body and said, "This is appropriate, or this is inappropriate."

In the new space, the energy field remains open, and the passion, creation, experience, expansion and the relationship, are all going to be the same caliber. There is no limitation to expression and experience.

Models of the Aquarian Age

There may be differences in how it's acted out. And that's the major difference between the Piscean Age and the Aquarian Age. The Piscean Age says, "Stop the energy, thwart the energy, calibrate the energy, define it, put it into expectation." The Aquarian Age says, "Have it always open, have the energy field always expressing in its own volition within itself, and then see what's appropriate for you in that moment with someone else." So the difference is, the Piscean Age experience of "love" or experience of intimacy or of connection was unified through belief. In the new time, it's going to be unified through personal expression. This means that you don't have to have anybody in your life to have the same kind of threshold reached, or the same kind of creation and passion released, because it's not

~

What has happened as humankind has STRUCTURED *relationship, is that they have actually imparted to the cells an edict that says when certain levels of relationship are lived, the cells only respond in a certain way.*

~

In the new space, the energy field remains o p e n , and the passion, creation, experience, expansion and the relationship, are all going to be the same caliber.

~

So the difference is, the Piscean Age experience of "love" or experience of intimacy or of connection was unified through belief. *In the new time, it's going to be unified through* personal expression.

~

*People of the new model
are always a l i v e;
they're always committed
to expressing their own dimension.
All of the chakras are relating
and working and merging
and unifying,
and there is an explosion constantly
of the creative spark
of the commitment to living,
being,
and expressing.
And that allows the soul to emerge.*

~

*The feminine
goes outside of structural belief
because it procreates life,
and because
the system of the feminine
is always taking the unknown
and bringing it into form.*

~

directed toward someone, it is directed only within the self. And the difference is very profound.

In the Piscean society, people are only open at certain times. In the Aquarian time, people will be open all the time, and it's not going to be in relationship to someone, it's going to be from the commitment to be completely energized within one's own framework. So the container then becomes—instead of the relationship—the self. And the dynamic difference is that the people of the new model are always alive; they're always committed to expressing their own dimension. All of the chakras are relating and working and merging and unifying, and there is an explosion constantly of the creative spark of the commitment to living, being, and expressing. And that allows the soul to emerge.

Another major area of difference is the level of vision. In the old frame, the vision had to do with the model: "We're going to get married, that's my picture. We're going to live together, that's my picture. We're going to have a child together, that's my picture. We're going to take our resources and combine them, and live together so that it's easier for us, it's safer for us," and that kind of thing.

In the new model the vision becomes one of total aliveness within one's own being, total expressiveness within one's soul pattern. Then, whoever and whatever happens does not diminish that charge; it only has to do with being in one's full capacity.

The difference in these models is more easily expressed in the human feminine space, because the human feminine space has more vision, more passion, more capacity as a general rule, because it has not been allowed to contain its creation only through sex, and structural belief. The feminine goes outside of structural belief because it procreates life, and because the system of the feminine is always taking the unknown and bringing it into form. The masculine, or Piscean model takes only the known and brings it into form. So the feminine, because it can create life itself, generally has an easier time of moving into the new model.

Since the structure of the feminine is created through dynamics associated with safety, nurturance, procreation and co-creation, sustenance, manna, and protoplasm, these dynamics are more easily woven into the individual and collective feminine pattern. So the feminine looks for ways to introduce the Aquarian principles of soul equality and soul expression into the existing model. The feminine is saying, "Let's redo the model. I don't want to cook and clean all the time, necessarily. I don't want to be cast in a role that was chosen 20 years ago. I want to find my own life system. How do I have to do that? And what, if anything, is it that I have to give up in order to maintain what I've already had, or to create something new from within?" The feminine is breaking the model, and the energy of that capacity has a very real way of tapping into future realities, so that we have a level of feminine energy being restructured on the planet.

Some women may have difficulty with that because they have a more structured or Piscean process, and they want to stay within the models that exist because they feel safer. So they may begin co-creating ideas and energy from the soul, and yet compromise by staying in old patterns of relationship or security.

Some men are only able to leave the structural influence of the old model to be with "another woman," or to be with someone who is able to tap into that creative resource with or for them. This is one way that men escape from the old structure, by going outside of the monogamous bounds that were instituted *from* the structure. So each sex has found ways to cross over into the new dimension.

The Integrity of the New Model

The existing design for relationship and humanity in the future is that both sexes cross over from the old model, but they do it in a way which supports integrity. They order and honor the structure of their own frame—and they do it without compromise. This is the difference between being in integrity or out of integrity, because when one is in a structural relationship, the Piscean, and crosses over in a non-integrous way, there is compromise. When one crosses over from a total sense of knowing and commitment to truth, there is no compromise. And that means that honesty, integrity, and validity are born out of each of these experiences which create new models and new ways of expression.

So whenever one would go forth and say, "My soul needs to express in this way," it's suggested that you clarify that expression. Open all your chakra systems and energy fields, and align with the truth, then compromise is diminished, and the commitment to oneness and intimacy happens. This is the key: in the new time there is not a commitment to a person, there's a commitment to the process of deepening intimacy with the self through connection with others, in whatever way that unfolds.

~

The existing design for relationship and humanity in the future is that both sexes cross over from the old model, but they do it in a way which supports integrity.

~

Then compromise is diminished, and the commitment to oneness and intimacy happens. This is the key: in the new time there is not a commitment to a person, there's a commitment to the process of deepening intimacy with the self through connection with others, in whatever way that unfolds.

~

Relationship With the Self

Weaving the vision of the truth,
and the vision of the expression of the soul
into the moment,
requires a commitment
to non-compromise—
a commitment to full expression
in each person,
and the commitment
to being in relationship
only with the self—
with no one else.

If one says to oneself,
"I am now
only in relationship with myself,"
it frees everyone else with whom you are
in relationship
to be in relationship with themselves.

And so these basic differences in paradigm are what the tension is about in the structural system. Weaving the vision of the truth, and the vision of the expression of the soul into the moment, requires a commitment to non-compromise—a commitment to full expression in each person, and the commitment to being in relationship only with the self—with no one else. That means that no matter who you're with, or what you're doing, integrity will be maintained. If the commitment is to relationship outside the self, then there is a marriage that is nonsingular, a marriage that comes together out of need rather than out of wisdom. And being in marriage only with the self also means that there's a marriage between the masculine and the feminine within each person. That's the kind of marriage that will work in this new time.

So we're looking at a separation from the existing paradigm and movement into a totally new paradigm. That separation in paradigms is creating the conflict we now experience in relationships. That is what is creating the need to leave, the need to expand, the need to procreate or co-create differently. In our opinion it does not need to be a separation. It just needs to be a weaving—each person becomes clear about where they are in the process of unfolding newness. They don't think of themselves as having failed at relationship; they think of themselves as needing to enter a new relationship with themselves.

This is going to be the new basis of society. As this unfolds it becomes very powerful, because if one says to oneself, "I am now only in relationship with myself," it frees everyone else with whom you are in relationship to be in relationship with themselves. And the words, "I don't want to be with you. I don't want to be in relationship. I don't want to have this. I don't. . ." do not need to be said. Because if one says, "I need to be in relationship with myself," then the pressure is taken off of the participants in a relationship. If one says, "I need to blend my own masculine and feminine, and I am making the commitment to be in an honoring space of vision with my own capacity, and to open up my own passion for life, my own experience of oneness," immediately there is the opportunity to develop that kind of internal space in each person.

This seems to be the most dedicated way to serve the changing evolutionary experience, the individual needs and capacities, and whatever parameters are in effect in relationship. If that statement is made about relating to the self, all the frames shift, and they are no longer responsible for providing happiness. They are no longer responsible for making things good, right, or better. There is a space which opens and says, "I am now responsible for myself. I am now responsible to my own knowing. I am now responsible to my own vision of what will work for me." Then in each moment, those in relationship can come together and say, "Where am I now?" And the other partner says, "This is where I am now." Then you have a place to start meeting.

You have accomplished a foundation in yourself, and if you're in relationship with someone who doesn't want to work with themselves—doesn't want to honor the whole space as where they are—then very naturally they will gravitate toward someone who is still in that same frame. There will then be a gravitation for the initial person who has claimed their experience of self to find someone else who is also claiming that experience. And the loss and abandonment issues, the betrayal issues, so many of the dynamics of the human experience cease to exist. This happens when one says, "I have to be primarily in a relationship with myself." Then there's no way that the frame can be divided against itself. When people are in wholeness with themselves, no one can divide them anymore.

This takes the blaming, rituals, and experiences that have been in the outer framework, and dissipates them. If each person makes this commitment and combines individual knowing about that choice with the collective etheric model for the new dimension, the future becomes the present with them immediately. If they resist that, then they're going to be in resistance against all dissolution of the existing and pre-existing models, and they are going to get caught in an abyss of eternal desire for something which is no longer valid.

What we want to remember, what we need to remember always, is that when one clings to an old model, it's because the new model is not yet as viable or palpable, and it is only by people such as you going forward and saying, "I'm ready for the new model," that there will be enough inherent energy to support a critical mass which will assist in the transformation of the old into the new. So it's very important for people who have awareness of this process to live it fully. This does not mean that any new way of being replaces the old way of being in a structured sense—for example, nonmonogamy, or noncommitment—"Oh, well, this frees me up to do anything I want." That is out of integrity. It doesn't mean that you throw the baby out

They are no longer responsible for making things good, right, or better.

When people are in wholeness with themselves, no one can divide them anymore.

What we need to remember always, is that when one clings to an old model, it's because the new model is not yet as viable or palpable.

*It means that
everything you're living makes sense,
because it honors everyone
at the same time.*

~

*Growth doesn't mean pain.
Growth means expansion
into a full capacity
of experience and expression.*

~

*All of those existing frames
are stymieing
individual and personal expression.
There are
literally ties between people,
called Aka chords.*

~

with the bath water, that you get rid of everybody in your life that wants to be a certain way; it means that by claiming the self, you learn how to stay in a dedicated space of ritual with your own being. It means that everything you're living makes sense, because it honors everyone at the same time.

It honors you, and it honors the other person. In a sense, it frees them from responsibility to make you happy, to have sex with you, to marry you, to give you children, or to in some way be present for you—supporting you financially, emotionally, or in any other way. It says, "I'm going to do all this for myself. I'm going to live this in a way that makes sense to me completely, and so every moment, from this time forward, my own honoring is my primary focus. If I honor myself, it means I put myself together. I hold my self together. I sustain my field in integrity. I live myself in a fullness that makes me awaken all the time to my own capacities and my own potentials and my own rituals."

Then you are creating a frame where the other person can respond to you from that set of circumstances. It's very important that each individual understand that until they can make that commitment, they are going to be in a relationship that's nonproductive, that doesn't go anywhere, that doesn't have vision or potential to it. Because anyone that is in co-dependence with someone else, needing them to do something to sustain their viability, is not working with interdependence—not working with the systems theory where growth is the initial space of active participation.

Growth and Expansion

Growth doesn't mean pain. Growth means expansion into a full capacity of experience and expression, and changes relationship from co-dependence to co-creation. There are no promises—"I promise you I won't do this or that." In the new model you don't say, "You're uncomfortable with this, so this is what we have to do." All of those existing frames are stymieing individual and personal expression. There are literally ties between people called Aka chords. In the Hawaiian Kahuna philosophy, Aka chords maintain themselves as the status quo, and provide a separation from growth. What happens in the people who are ready to foundation a new reality, is that they dissolve the Aka chords by choosing their own volition and proliferation, living their own passion.

It is unnecessary to worry about those chords, to focus on them and try to make them different. It's much more important to focus only on the fullest expression of your own field of energy, rather than focusing on yourself as a person, a body, a mind, a heart, or an emotion. It is important to take together all the frames of being and say, "I'm a field of energy. That means I open, I expand, I bring in light." It means, in a sense, photosynthesis. You're bringing in the capabilities and releasing what you don't need. It's a part of the whole process, rather than being just what you focus on. When people focus on what's wrong, and what they need to change, and what doesn't work, and where they are feeling pain, it aligns them with only those fields of energy, and nothing seems to work. There is a stuckness in the energy field.

When people align themselves with an intention and go forward experiencing only those frames that are part of that expression, then what is not expressed is no longer valid, is no longer sustained in the field of energy, and there's a sense of being on target—creational experience emerges. There's a sensitivity to the formula which becomes very prolific, and they're in that space of acceleration—and this is the time for acceleration. Anyone who is humping along, going two steps forward and one step back, will find an extremely high amount of inertia, because this is the time for movement, growth, and expansion. People don't have to know where they're growing, or know what will happen next week. It's that commitment to say, "Yes," and choose to be a part of that which is ready to be experienced.

Every moment the choice is made for this expansion, there will be support that comes from the structural to align with that new dimension and create new levels of reality. For example, in relationship, if one says, "I'm going toward this experience of accelerated growth where I am unified with myself," immediately the structure of the being which includes all of those levels—the body, mind, emotion, spirit, the structure of the being—comes in and says, "All right, I'll support that for you." The way free will works is that whatever the intention is instituted through in terms of vision, idea, knowing, or calibration, the physical experience of the energy field will support that. If one says, "I'm open," then the chakras open. If one says, "I'm hurt," then the chakras close.

What people don't grasp sometimes, is that whatever they decide

When people focus on what's wrong, and what they need to change, and what doesn't work, and where they are feeling pain, it aligns them with only those fields of energy, and nothing seems to work. There's a stuckness in the field of energy.

Every moment the choice is made for this expansion, there will be support that comes from the structural to align with that new dimension and create new levels of reality.

*What people don't grasp sometimes,
is that whatever they decide
is fortified
by the system of cellular energy,
and provides certain realities.*

~

*The only way to have it all
is to be completely in union
with the total self.
That's exactly what the
experience of the future is about.*

~

is fortified by the system of cellular energy, and provides certain realities. If one says, "I'm tired of my marriage. I want to have an affair," immediately the cells of the body begin to open and send out this magnetic wave that says, "I'm ready" for that kind of experience, and those associated chakras open up. The heart chakra may not open up at all, because the heart experiences that there's a division there. A commitment has already been made, and yet there's a decision to do another kind of activity. Then there's a separation in energy, and only certain things are possible in that experience because the whole being is not called on to express the passion of the self. It's called on to experience only a certain thing with a certain person, which basically shuts down the field of energy. This creates both acceleration and depletion, and may be experienced emotionally as exhilaration and depression. One goes into a situation feeling a lot of passion and then feels sadness and loss. Anytime there is variation in the field like that, there's incongruence—something is out of order.

That's another thing that's different between the Piscean and the Aquarian Age. In the Piscean Age it was normal for there to be happiness in one or two areas of life, and unhappiness in another area of life. Let's say someone had a vocation they really loved, but they had a marriage that was unsatisfactory, or they had health problems, or they would love what they were doing, but they weren't making enough money to cover their rent. That's the Piscean limitation process—you can have some of it, but you can't have all of it.

In the new experience, the acceleration of being at one with the self and totally in alignment with that consciousness basically says, "Here I am, and I have it all." The only way to have it all is to be completely in union with the total self. That's exactly what the experience of the future is about. In a sense, we are moving from the need to concentrate on relationship, to the need to concentrate on the full expression of the essence of being, individually. So families, structures, and relationships are no longer important in the same way. That has been translated by individuals who have fear about the change, into the dissolution of family, into the dissolution of the structure of marriage, and into the dissolution of integrity, and that is not at all how it is intended. When one has absolute integrity with self, one has absolute integrity with everyone else that one relates with.

Instead of focusing on keeping the structures the same, if the focus is on keeping integrity within the self, then the structures that serve the self and the full expression of being are honored and expanded, and those that don't are diminished. There will be certain marriages that proliferate in this new model, and certain ones that don't. The proliferative marriages will always be woven integrously into the capacity for individual integration, union and expression.

Union with oneself becomes the passion of being alive, instead of that which one seeks to have outside of the self. As one feels this passion for life, the emotional co-dependence where one needs something in order to feel safe in relationships, is reduced and ultimately eliminated. There will be a division between the people who honor themselves and the people who don't, and this is something that we need to accept and honor even though it will create some uncomfortableness.

There will be a division between the people who can understand the new model and integrate it cellularly, and the people who can't. This isn't good or bad, it's just that any time you shift paradigms, when there's not a weaving, there is the capacity for people to think that somebody has chosen something that doesn't work for them, and that's fine, because again that's free will. However, what might work if one lives from a weaving of the old and new is—"All right, I'm in a relationship. I now choose to be changing or shifting the focus of the relationship to myself, so what I would like to do is shift a bit, and honor the commitment I have already made, and weave the pieces that feel most congruent, and hold them steady—creating a new structure between us—so that whatever we agree on supports each of us supporting ourselves individually." Then the relationship begins to coalesce. The focus for change is always on what works, not on what doesn't. And as we weave, we strengthen the fibers of where we can relate from.

It doesn't preclude relationship, it's just that it's not the focus of the connection to be a relationship. And even that difference in perspective makes a lot of difference because when one decides, "All right, what I'm committed to is intimacy. I'm committed to intimacy with myself, intimacy with my life—intimacy with a tree, with a dog, with my food, with my clothes, my car." Then everything serves you. If it doesn't serve you, you're not intimate with it! You don't give it that energy, so it will dissolve. It will go away from you, and you'll go toward that which does serve you. If that's the commitment, then even when you're in the experience of relating to someone who you've been or are in relationship with, the framework will be very different, because there will be no focus on this person providing an

Instead of focusing on keeping the structures the same, if the focus is on keeping integrity within the self, then the structures that serve the self and the full expression of being are honored and expanded, and those that don't are diminished.

Union with oneself becomes the passion of being alive, instead of that which one seeks to have outside of the self.

The focus for change is ALWAYS on what works, not on what doesn't. And as we weave, we strengthen the fibers of where we can relate from.

If it doesn't serve you, you're not intimate with it!

intimate experience, because the intimacy will be very much foundationed with the self.

The weaving becomes the key. As soon as one partner says, "Well, that doesn't work for me," the other partner says, "Well, what does work for you?" Instead of being afraid of bringing up the differences and looking at them, everything gets brought out, but it gets brought out in the sense of what works for me. If somebody says, "That doesn't work," you say, "What does work?" And if they say "I don't know," then you say, "Maybe it's time for you to go and do some unifying with yourself, and I'll do the same thing, and let's come back together when we're clearer about what does work for us." So you don't have discussions with people anymore in this new paradigm about what's wrong.

No energy in the new paradigm is given to the squeaky wheel. The energy is only given to what moves and rolls and expands and opens out, and it is a very different way, because most people say, "Let's sit down and slog it out and come to resolution." Instead, put things back into fluid where they are woven and move and synthesize. Working from paradigms that are opposite to this will not create union. If you go into the self and ask, "Where's the union in me?" then you come back to the person unified, and then you have a chance of unifying together.

So to get together to reconcile something, make something different, or to create a new way of being, works only when one is ready to dissolve the old model in themselves. If one is unready to dissolve the old model in themselves, one cannot expect to dissolve it when there's more than one person present. It's not as effective, and there may also be attachment to what the person believes is the way they need it to be.

Whenever the belief system ordains that before the couple can come together and reunify, one of the partners has to compromise, to give in to what the other person's attached to, it's the old kind of weaving. This keeps things the same, tries to make everybody happy, and the step which the individual needs to take to be responsible for themselves has not yet been taken. The rule of commitment in the future is that each person honors the self first. And in that honoring, people unify their fields, and make the commitment to deepening their intimacy with their life. Then they come together with someone who has made that same commitment. If that is not the commitment, whether it's spoken or not, whether someone is literally living that or not, there's going to be a sense of needing to spend time apart and/or

The weaving becomes the key. As soon as one partner says, "Well, that doesn't work for me," the other partner says, "Well, what does work for you?"

~

No energy in the new paradigm is given to the squeaky wheel.

~

Whenever the belief system ordains that before the couple can come together and reunify, one of the partners has to compromise, to give in to what the other person's attached to, it's the old kind of weaving.

~

needing to work on the individual.

When you spend some time apart, you're redoing the foundation. The more time you are apart, the more time you have to honor yourselves and come to that space where the honoring means something in terms of your expression of intimacy together.

As that unfolds, you'll find that you have a totally new basis for relating. One of you can take the initiative to be the model for that experience. And for most of you, that's what's going to happen. One or another of the parties will take the initiative to set up the new framework of honoring, and then the other person will either make that commitment also, or they won't. The sense of loss is dramatically diminished when one takes the self as being the most important intimate space. If the other person doesn't, there is really no sense of loss, because what's appreciated by the initial person who has made the commitment for self-initiation is that this is not the ideal place for that kind of framework to be experienced. So there's a sense of relief "Oh, now I don't have to do this anymore." You know you have done the weaving when the other person says, "I don't think I can do this," and you say, "Okay, I get it, and it's fine, and if and when you can, come and see me, and we can relate in whatever way our individual knowing supports us in the future."

There are no dead ends, there are no divorces of the old type, where you imagine that you don't love each other anymore, or anything like that. There's just a sense that timing is what is important, and that without certain levels of affirmation, it's not going to move into the direction one would wish anyway. So the sense of, "This is my one love, this is the one I have to sustain to make myself happy, this is what has provided me with support and with the safeguard of security," no longer has any viability. The self is so strong that there's not a confusion between what the person believes and is trying to live, and what the other person believes and is trying to live, which really makes a quagmire. That doesn't allow for the freedom of this beautiful woven symmetry of expansion and experience.

What is happening now on a large level is that people are being brought up short in relationship. They are no longer able to relate in the old ways, and there's a lot of back-pedaling going on, trying to bring up the things that used to work—and of course they're not working—so it's thrusting individuals, particularly those with a spiritual intention and commitment, and connection to the soul, to take this new step and to provide a whole new space for the self to

The sense of loss is dramatically diminished when one takes the self as being the most important intimate space.

There are no dead ends, there are no divorces of the old type, where you imagine that you don't love each other anymore.

relate from. And because this is so dynamic and so necessary, there's a wave of this new "frame" on the planet that supports large numbers of integrous changes in people's experience.

My New Steps in Relationship

notes

Understanding Your Relationships
An Exercise

CALIBRATION
my list:

Three basic concepts provide a basis for learning how to stay in the self and to be clear about what will call forth the connection of intimacy:

CALIBRATION
how open your heart is in each of your relationships

BELIEF SYSTEM
what you think you have to believe or have to be in relationships

ENERGY FIELD
where the cellular level responds in the body without conscious direction

So look at what kinds of relationships you have in your life. Ask yourself, "Who is it that I actually have relationships with?" Categorize certain areas of your life into family, friends, etc., first, or begin by listing the people and seeing where you want to put them, according to how you perceive it. However you choose to do it, list each person, i.e; I have Susan, and Susan is my friend; I have Paul, and Paul is my husband; I have Samuel, and Samuel is my son; I have this one, and he's my great uncle; this one's a teacher; this one's my grocer; this one's my neighbor.

After you have listed the people with whom you are in relationship, then begin to access the **calibration** with each person. Questions you might ask are: How much of my heart is open with each of these people? What part of my heart is open? What kind of deliberation do I do with this person? Is there an emotional attachment? Is there a sexual attachment?

BELIEF SYSTEM
my beliefs:

Is there any attachment? Maybe this is my child's physician. I have an attachment to this physician because this physician keeps my child alive. What kind of emotional bond do I have with this person? It's very literal. You say, "What is the bond? Does this person create stability, security, love, affection, passion? What is it?" Go through so that you're very clear about how your heart has been taught to respond to certain individuals and group situations.

Then go into the **belief system**. Say to yourself, "What do I believe is an appropriate behavior or relationship with each person?" Write down your responses. Then go back into the calibration which is unconscious and automatic. The belief system is what makes the calibration what it is. The belief system is also what you think is happening. When you do these exercises, you find that a lot of times you're giving off energy that your belief system doesn't feel is appropriate and that you don't think is a part of your calibration, but the other person is receiving. When that happens you have triangles, and experiences where you feel disillusioned, misunderstood, or betrayed. One is never really betrayed by another. One is only betrayed by the sense that the three levels that we're talking about—the calibration, the belief, and the energy field—are functioning from different levels, giving different messages, and experiencing connection in different ways.

The next level of focus is the **energy field**. When you think about the people and the situations that you wrote about in the calibration, go back and look at, "What do I believe about this person—what do I believe is effective, ineffective, appropriate, inappropriate, right, wrong?" Then go to the energy field and say, "How does my energy field respond with this person? Let me see it as it really is." So you go into each person and feel your field of energy and say, "All right, what part of my body becomes alive when I think about this person? What part of my body closes down? What part of my body is more expressive? How do I feel? What's going on? Am I warm?

cold? expanded? diminished? What's happening?" And when you're finished, make columns and put each person's name at the top, and give them three different read-outs. You can see if all of these levels work together or if they don't work together. How are they compatible and/or incompatible?

The objective is to have the calibration be totally open all the time so that the love is never categorized or diminished or expanded for just one person, group or situation. Have the belief system clear so that there is always love, and appropriate expression of love depending upon what the union and weaving of those three levels says. When these two points are open, this opens your energy field always, consistently, to the passion with self. That is the foundation for this new time and experience. When each person goes through and asks, "What is my belief system about being with a certain person? What have I made appropriate? What do I wish I was doing?" A lot of times in the belief system there is a very strong dichotomy, "I think this is appropriate, but this is what I want." And when that happens inside the belief, there can be a very strong experience of discomfort, guilt, and the feeling that something is unclear, or as if you're betraying something or someone, even if you haven't acted. This happens frequently on the subtle body levels.

There may be varying degrees of incompatibility in certain areas. If a person has trouble trusting, there may be a high degree of incompatibility in the love center, in the calibration in the heart, in trusting and being open. If someone has an unbalanced root center, there may be a high degree of incompatibility in the structural framework of how they feel about certain people and what they feel is appropriate, and what their body energy is doing. This is a very good way of seeing where the fields of energy receive their information. What is the response? What is the desired response? Each person can clarify what works for them, and what they would like to see happen.

ENERGY FIELD
my responses:

If you are married *to yourself,*
you're always on,
you're always open,
and you're always expressing,
and then you can make
distinct choices about marrying your
field of energy of wholeness
with someone else's.

~

There is such a
high degree of functioning
that you feel masterful
and live in the world
without fear
of being taken advantage of,
of being raped or disillusioned,
or abandoned.

~

Our objective in giving you this information is to assist you to clarify your process, to feel very clear with your responses, and to know yourself and the way your energy works, so that when you go out into the world, synthesis happens. That synthesis provides a high level of functioning, so that the energy field is consistently opening out into the world. And that's the difference, also, between being married to the self and being married to someone else. Because if you are married to yourself, you're always on, you're always open, and you're always expressing, and then you can make distinct choices about marrying your field of energy of wholeness with someone else's.

And you're not at the mercy of one of your chakras, or one of your belief systems, or one of your calibrations. It gives an autonomy to your being which is extremely valuable and honors itself very directly. There is such a high degree of functioning that you feel masterful and live in the world without fear of being taken advantage of, of being raped, disillusioned, or abandoned. All those fears dissipate when the being is fully alive and these three levels are in balance. That's why it's so important.

This exercise may take up to three weeks to do. It is invaluable, because it will help clarify what's going on. And it's not to be judged. Very important! It is to be honored as a signal from your being that there is a readiness to be consolidated, to make the commitment for integrity and intimacy. To know yourself intimately gives you a capacity to choose response rather than to react to or from. That is mastery also, to choose your response.

The Value of Synthesis

So what's important in each moment is that there's a synthesis. Everyone is in some way conflicted because of the structures that have been imposed upon them—the tension that's being held in the outside dynamic. Many people think they're doing the right thing and that everything is fine. Actually, they're being held in tension with the models of expectancy outside themselves and don't know it. Many times they don't really know what they want. They don't know who they are, and they don't know what's possible. So these insights would be valuable for each person to have. Even people who think, "I'm monogamous. I don't have to do this exercise or change the dynamics in my relationship. I have everything cut and dried. I know exactly what's going on. I don't have those kinds of feelings. I'm not ready for this kind of relationship, or connection to myself—I don't think I need it. I have a good relationship with my family, my husband or my significant other, and I don't have to do this," are deluding themselves and eluding the experience of the truth, because basically, since the models are changing etherically, they will affect all relationships on all levels.

Also, it is valuable to look at the energetic messages given and received during childhood, particularly the triangular situations which develop in incestual relationships, or if there are marked discrepancies in the exercise suggested above. Doing this kind of responsive informational indexing from these levels will assist you to understand the dynamics involved, and to know how those situations were created energetically. What parts of the energy system were open to others that you had interactions with, that you feel were uncomfortable or unpleasant? What was really going on in your field at that time? What was your actual physical response? Were you conscious of this response, or were you responding from a perspective of your calibration only, or your belief system only, or as sometimes happens, the energy field only? Many people go every moment with what their energy field tells them to do, and are out of touch with the original space of intention for that particular situation—the experience of what is right or wrong for them. They may find that they go the other way around, that they're always responding to whatever root chakra instinct they have, or whatever heart chakra instinct they have. These are the people who fall in love with everybody, the people who have sex with everybody, or the people who never have sex, or never have love. There can be any range of this, from complete closing to complete opening, and all of that can be going on at the same time. You can experience an imbalance between these dimensional levels in you and/or in someone you're relating with.

When someone has woven their levels together, they have an extremely integrous body of light and consciousness which is ordained, and they are able to make the choices that are always going to serve everyone in the situation, which makes it a win-win. How that's lived comes from an integrous bonding together of the calibration, the emotional and belief process, and the physical energy system. So the dynamics of light, when they enter the system of humanity, clear out the circuits so that there is only an absolute space

Also, it is valuable to look at the energetic messages given and received during childhood, particularly the triangular situations which develop in incestual relationships, or if there are marked discrepancies in the exercise suggested above.

Many people go every moment with what their energy field tells them to do.

These are the people who fall in love with everybody, the people who have sex with everybody, or the people who never have sex, or never have love.

The dynamics of light,
when they enter the system of humanity,
clear out the circuits so that there is only
an absolute space of oneness
with everything.
This is the kind of situation
that happens in societies
based upon soul expression.

~

It's as if
that new person catalyzes
the individual developing on their own—
which is the inner passion
of union with self.

~

Some people will feel
that they have found
the relationship they want,
when in effect all they have done
is tripped over somebody,
or brought somebody into the design
that is calibrated at the place
where their soul is then able to express.

~

of oneness with everything. This is the kind of situation that happens in societies based upon soul expression.

You'll find in this coming time—and for many of you this has already happened in the last few years—that the connection with other souls can be extremely deep and dramatic. For example, even when individuals are in a relationship with someone, they may come together with a new soul and feel that they have found or desire to find the deepest level of intimacy with this new soul. Their soul has been so long suppressed in their experience of life, that when they begin to birth their soul, they are open to so many dimensional energies, that there is sometimes confusion with commitment, with love, with loss, with passion, and with many parts of human interaction. There are many times when they develop or initiate a momentary sense of finding their soul through someone else. When these soul experiences happen, however they do—and they seem to be sometimes very dramatic and out of context with one's "life"—the person taps into their initial soul dimensional frequency, so they feel as if they've never been as understood before. They've never had someone who could touch them as deeply.

It's not because that's true in an overall sense, it's because as the soul gets activated, there is such passion in the soul that it is transferred to the other person, because the new person linked into the existing experience of that person from that level. It's as if that new person catalyzes the individual developing on their own—which is the inner passion of union with self. And so what happens is that people leave relationships and go all over the place, saying, "This is my soul mate. This is somebody I've got to be with, because I feel this person understands me in such a way that I have to be with them." And then it gets worked through, and the soul passion energy gets added to the sum total of the person's expressive capacity, and all of a sudden the light bulb goes on and the first person realizes, "This wasn't about the second person—it was about me. It was about my finding a part of myself that this person was vibrationally able to connect with and tap into, and therefore bring out in me."

Some people will feel that they have found the relationship they want, when in effect all they have done is tripped over somebody, or brought somebody into the design that is calibrated at the place where their soul is then able to express. If they come into the soul expression on their own and feel it from their own integrity, then they can integrate these people into their lives so they don't cause a lot of dramatic disintegration on other levels. It's often because the initial person has not done their own work, has not experienced their own capacity, that these other people are able to come in and turn everything upside down. It's because they need to make a shift, and they've not chosen to do it internally. They have chosen to do it externally, which creates a tremendous amount of pathos. They initially leave their life in order to experience the soul.

Honor and Integrity

Another option, another choice which usually creates integrity, is to choose to have that catalyst from one's own response-ability to the self. Then instead of feeling that things have been destroyed or upturned, one feels they have the capacity to honor their own experience and bring that forth, and hold that in the light, and it's integrous. It has integrity. The person can say, "This is something I am honoring within myself, and if another person is honoring it within themselves we can come together, but I'm not coming together with this person because they're honoring this part of me that I haven't honored." That's just a distinction we want to make, and none of it is right or wrong. Some of it creates a lot of waves, and a roto-rooter effect that goes through the life and upturns everything. And some people need to learn that way, apparently. Some people choose that, and it doesn't have to be the only choice.

If you choose to make the experience integrous, then when you meet people you validate each other, you mirror each other, and you're able to go to a step of growth together. And you do it in a way that is a natural unfolding of the design, rather than an insertion, out of order, in the process. That's just the difference in it. When one is in a state of completion with the self, when one meets a person like this, it's as if the person is enfolded into the process that's already going on and nothing has to happen from it. There's not resentment or challenge or a rebellion which sometimes happens otherwise. It becomes integrated into the whole picture. Let's say, for example, there's a couple, and they're each working on their own level of mastery, and they've experienced the integrity of themselves. A new person comes along and is added to the equation, but a triangle is not formed. The difference in the future design and the past design is that when mastery is not attained on the individual level, triangles form. If there is mastery, circles form. That difference is very profound. It

It's because they need to make a shift, and they've not chosen to do it internally.
They have chosen to do it externally, which creates a tremendous amount of pathos.
They initially leave their life in order to experience the soul.

If you choose to make the experience integrous, then when you meet people you validate each other, you mirror each other, and you're able to go to a step of growth together. And you do it in a way that is a natural unfolding of the design, rather than an insertion, out of order, in the process.

The difference in the future design and the past design is that when mastery is not attained on the individual level, triangles form.

*If
we work from mastery,
we work toward
union of many people at once.*

*And each individual
is honoring themselves,
so they don't need a relationship
to honor them.*

*And it's very beautiful,
because without this interim space
of couples adding new people
so that they are families of a new type,
the new community of cooperation
will have a harder time existing.*

means that one can move into community and expansion and not necessarily into separation.

If we work from mastery, we work toward union of many people at once. If we're working from the egoic space, or the separate space of, "This person came in, and they have more to give me than you do, and they're understanding me better than you ever have, and I think they'd do better sex," whatever it is, separation is created. That's the old model, and it's not right or wrong, it's just being phased out. If people want to work more with the capacity of truth, they work more with, "Well, what's the overall design intending for all of us, where are we going with this, and how can we fit this together?" And each individual is honoring themselves, so they don't need a relationship to honor them, which means that it's possible for expression of these connections in different ways than used to be possible. And there is not a dishonoring in order to honor. There's not a choice between: "I'm choosing somebody else instead of you," which is dishonoring, and which says, "The commitment I made to you, I'm now negating. I'm throwing it out like the baby and the bath water, to have this new thing." I'm saying, instead, "I honor myself, I honor you who have been with me in this process, and now I honor this new person. And as the three of us honor ourselves and each other, we'll create something new."

And it's very beautiful, because without this interim space of couples forming circles instead of triangles, adding new people so that they are families of a new type, the new community of cooperation will have a harder time existing. It's very important to experience all these levels so that we accelerate the models of group union and interaction and creation as quickly as possible.

If you do the exercises of calibration, belief system, and the energetic body, and begin to see where your glitches are—where you hold the energy, where you expand the energy—and work within your own model, you realize these are the same places where you hold the energy when you are a couple. These are the same places where you hold the energy when you're in a family or group situation. To the experience of relationship we add the capacity to know everything at one time about ourselves, and practice knowing about ourselves with another significant person. Then practice opening that to more people. Sometimes, if there is a challenge, the group can assist in the process of that honoring. It needs, however, in our opinion, to be honoring of the self first, and then honoring of everyone that's added on after that process.

Then the honoring becomes more important than having sex, than being married, than having a relationship, than being safe. And when you get a group of people together who honor themselves, they can say, "We agree on this, but we don't agree on the other." They then say, "Let's go with what we agree with right now. And let's expand that agreement and unify through that, and make it strong and clear, that we're going to honor what we honor." It's very important now to give energy only to what you want to create. As the model changes you'll find that everything the group does is honoring everything within the group, and there has been a natural resolution of those things that were in some way disagreed on in the beginning.

So part of the honoring is, "I'm not doing this to get my way. I'm not doing this so that everybody will agree that I can do this with this person, or have this." It's that the honoring of the self and the group (whether it's three people or it's thirty people) is the choice. What we'll find as we evolve in honor, is that the actions people wanted to take that were in some way uncomfortable for the larger number of people, get worked out automatically. The energy fields begin to balance together and there's no longer one person's lust, one person's need, ego, process, intention, or whatever. There's a sense of, "What's the best thing for the whole system?" which is moving from the egoic to the cosmic consciousness. There is movement from getting one's way and getting one's needs filled, to contributing. This is where the foundation of life becomes critical. This is where the communities begin to develop from a different model than they were developing from before—the difference being that now we talk about what's really happening and honor all people. It becomes a model for the new kind of relational quality of interaction rather than being a new model of relationship.

Relationship is going to phase itself out. It is too modular, too confined, too distinctly separate. We're moving toward group consciousness, group expression. It doesn't mean necessarily that we're moving towards group sex (many think that in this new model anything goes, and you're just going to have "love-ins"). When honoring is the primary focus, what will happen from that model is that the experience of life will be that we have sex with ourselves, that we have love with ourselves, that we don't look for people to do actions with, we only create together in a way that supports a long and real and lasting sense of union, because no one needs anyone or anything else in the old way.

You're always creating energy fields that open out and expand

Then the honoring becomes more important than having sex, than being married, than having a relationship, than being safe.

What we'll find as we evolve in honor, is that the actions people wanted to take that were in some way uncomfortable for the larger number of people, get worked out automatically.

Relationship is going to phase itself out. It is too modular, too confined, too distinctly separate. We're moving toward group consciousness, group expression. It doesn't mean necessarily that we're moving towards group sex.

The consciousness *of creation and co-creating is what's important and what's focused on, rather than saving a relationship or a particular model.*

The honoring of a partnership will be completely energetic.

and experience new models, so that the energy of the being gets balanced completely within the sense of the self. The consciousness of creation and co-creating is what's important and what's focused on, rather than saving a relationship or a particular model.

What we want to safeguard and create are solutions for the world. How can we work better together? How can we share resources more appropriately? How can we be in cooperation with each other on an ongoing basis, no matter what we used to believe or think?

These processes are so much more important than getting individual needs met, that it's going to create an interesting paradigm in this society. The forward movers and the thinkers and the masters will be in large world-wide communities with others who are making these solutions, and you're going to have other people who are still trying to figure out what they're here to do. And you're going to have that sense of dichotomy—splitting off—and that's why for people who are already thinking and knowing that they want to be the masters of consciousness, it's time to move the consciousness into the whole picture as quickly as possible: being whole with the self, as the microcosm, and then seeing where that piece fits into the total macrocosm.

Relationship will not exist in the same way. People who have a primary honoring, however, will honor each other so much energetically that everyone will know that they are in partnership without the paper, the ring, the process legally to define it, and without society to make expectations or dogmatic conditions around it. The honoring of a partnership will be completely energetic. It will be something everyone understands and ordains, and which creates a foundation for larger honoring. So people in relationship have a wonderful choice now, because they can be the foundation for the new world, if they choose to do it from new honoring.

So it is not going away from, and depleting, and saying, "That's not going to work anymore." It is an expansion of an existing model. And it's appropriate to the time because, instead of divorce, you can go into a new level of partnership that has no name and no condition and has absolute honoring. So it's a beautiful time, and a very beautiful awakening.

The Heart of the One

Heart
Heart
Heart

The following chapter was received by the Heaven on Earth community in Vermont on December 11, 1994. The Ones With No Names spoke with us about honoring the heart of the one, together.

Y OU HAVE EACH COME HERE FOR A SPECIFIC PURPOSE. The purpose of your lives together is to enrich and enliven each day, each moment, each cell, so that after you are finished you cannot tell yourselves apart from each other. And that is why the distinctions between you are now more obvious, why you are forging your own personalities, because if the distinctions come out and are apparent and felt and fielded, then they can be integrated. If they are hidden they cannot be integrated. Honoring the self does not mean that you hide anything; it does not mean that you go off by yourself if you need to express something. It just means that honoring the self is the focus and the purpose of being together.

When something is blatant and clear and precise and pristine, it can then be clarified. If it is hidden, it is understood or not understood, and is unable to be resolved and brought together in the way that you have chosen to do so. Much of what you are doing here is creating a pathway to yourself. And that is the most important part. As we have been saying for you, if you go outside to forge a path, it will be less successful. If you maintain the path of forging inside, it will be more successful, because if you forge the inner path, the outer path opens automatically. And that is the secret to what you are doing. It is as if you take a nickel, a quarter, a fifty cent piece, and a dollar piece, bigger and bigger circles, and you forge them into even bigger circles.

Do not worry about your boundaries right now, the borders of your property, where and how people will interact with you, where and how they will understand you and interface with you. Be advised that your intentions are clear and are therefore recorded in frequency, in the hearts of all of the people who know you, and all of the hearts of the people who are participating in the decisions that will be made known. Your job is to hold the space, clarify it, hold it again, clarify it, hold it again. Do what you have just done. Come together in the circle in *silence* where there are no words. For only when you come

~

*"My intention is to be always in heart,
with no sound,
no thought,
nothing more important
than being in heart."*

~

For only when you come to the place
where it is difficult to speak
is the heart engaged.

~

The heart will take you home,
it will take you to the place of being,
it is not something that you decide
with your mind.

~

to the place where it is difficult to speak is the heart engaged.

When you want to speak, and want to think, and want to be right, and want to be heard, you are not in the heart. There are no words in the heart. And when we all came together tonight, there were no words for a long time. If you forge this place then, everyone around you will come to stand in the circle that you forge with you. If you make a statement and ask someone to agree, to understand, to comply, to compromise, or to even look in your heart and see if you are pure, it is not the heart. They will join you only if you are in the heart. This is the key.

In our opinion, this land is sacred. It has been ordained for the purpose of bringing the clarification of heart into form. If you are to do this successfully it requires forging small circles, one at a time. It does not mean taking time, it means forging the circles, which means that you are concentrating always on the heart.

So if you don't do it three times a day, five times a day, at least twice a day, it will take longer. If you forge the circles three times, five times, together, with whoever is here, it will take less time. Circumstances around you are in a sense precarious because the dynamics are human. You see, you want to forge Heaven on Earth, you want to forge oneness with creatures, with nature, with spirit, and you also want to forge oneness with people. And if you are to do so, you are to forge it immediately from the heart now, together. And that oneness of heart will be taken away from you on the wind, and given to others, and they will then join you.

It does not matter who holds back, who comes first, who seems interested, who is against, who is for. You see, if you focus on these things, then you are just like you were before you came here. Just as you were when you were born and your mothers imprinted in you six generations of thoughts, ideas, and beliefs. If you are in the heart, then you don't have any disunion in you. You don't think about who is for, who is against, if it will work, if it won't work. You see, this is very subtle, but very important. If you think, "It might not work, we might need to move to the Caribbean, we might need to do something that is different," then you are not in the heart.

The heart will take you home, it will take you to the place of being. It is not something that you decide with your mind. And these are the premises, the theories, the foundations that are being forged in this place. You see, it is not so much that you create a relationship with nature, that you think about the wetlands, about the herons, about the fox, about the wolf, and these things. It is that you think *only* about being in the heart. Because if you're in the heart, they will come to you. If you are in the human experience of valuing and weighing things that people have said to you, then you are just as you were before. It is no different, and it will not work then, because it is not of the new model; it is of the old.

It does not mean that you forget to honor, that you do not learn, that you do not grow and understand things, or that you do not experience new awarenesses always—it is that you will do so from the heart. The heart has the frequency that will bring life together here. So it isn't really about who's planting what, and who's doing what to whom, it is about being in the heart. You are tired physically sometimes because you are not in your hearts. And it's not that you don't mean well, that you don't try, it's that you're not coming together in the places of the cells which will make your bodies strong spiritually.

You have been pushing things like bulls, and are moving things around instead of using the metaphysical energy to power everything, to take the weight out of things, to in some ways guide the direction of the forces which you elicit from your will. And so if you understand that you are here to create a whole new dimensional experience, then you can be excited all the time, you can be invested all the time in feeling the heart. The heart is what lifts the spirits. The heart is the medium point or the center point, the threshold point between the above and the below. It isn't loving. We're not telling you that you're not loving, we're just telling you that you're not in your heart, which means that you are someplace else. And it isn't good or bad, it is just a fact.

When you are in the heart, you don't have any words to say, you don't have any thoughts or opinions, you don't think about someone's understanding of you, or caring about you, because the frequency is such that there is so much to be shared that you do not need to express it through logical terms. It is something that is always known. And therefore your oneness is complete always, because the frequency is matched, it is accorded and it is esteemed, and in that way the honoring becomes singular and collective simultaneously.

So we would recommend that what you do, if you do anything, is that you practice making the circles of heart. When you go into the land, experience that the heart is what you feel here together at these rare moments. Have joy and laughter, have sharing and community. Those are wonderful things. The heart is what will seal it, so that

The heart has the frequency that will bring life together here.

~

The heart is what lifts the spirits. The heart is the medium point or the center point, the threshold point between the above and the below.

The heart is what will seal it,
so that your differences
are not differences,
so that your opinions
and your processes
are not separate in any way.

~

If you do not understand or know,
if you cannot make a decision,
then go to the heart.

~

your differences are not differences, so that your opinions and your processes are not separate in any way.

This is when the animals will come, and this is when the people will observe that the animals are coming. You don't have to convince someone that you won't harm the wetlands. What you do instead is show them that you are drawing the wilderness to humans, that you are pulling together that which has always been held apart, because the heart is so great it knows no boundary or separation. The foundation of it is then so beautiful because you don't have to prove or defend, you see. What is happening then is that everyone is observing this reality. And then you call it in, and you do it quickly, very quickly.

So instead of thinking, "Well, it will take a while to make this relationship, it will take us a while to build the building, it will take us a while to get the plan," all those things that are so normal to think about, you say, "No, I cannot think about it. My heart must show me the direction, and it must show me the order in which things will happen." So when we're thinking about what to do next—Go to the heart! If you do not understand or know, if you cannot make a decision, then go to the heart. The more people who go to the heart at one time, the faster this will happen.

It doesn't have to do with your intention, because of course we all know that you do have an intention for this to happen. It's that you're out of practice in *how* it happens. It's like knowing you need the music to play the notes. The music is the heart, and if you go to the heart, the notes will be played. It is that these things need to come together.

The feet are the other thing—the experience of being connected to the Earth while you're in heart. That's why you want to do ritual outside when you can, so that the feet are anchoring in the experience, and so you feel in each dramatic moment that unfolds, that the Earth is being given the opportunity to send the frequency through *her* methods which are deep and core-like, and have many ley lines and vortices that move from this place. What's important is that you use every facility available for you to send the message. You send it to the wind, to the Earth, you hug the trees, touch the animals, experience that you are the ones that are the determining factor, not the *proximity* of something to you, but your proximity to your heart, and to the group heart, to the group soul, and to the group collective.

The process is such that it will lead you quickly to resolution. It is our opinion that the head will lead you nowhere, and that if you make logical decisions about where you are to put the experience that you are creating, you will be held away from it for a time that will seem indeterminate, because it is not originally from heart. It's not that heart was not introduced to it, or interwoven in it, it is that it comes from ideas rather than from frequency. And it doesn't mean that the ideas don't substantiate the frequency, it is more that your practice here is to be in frequency first and then to have the experience of seeing and knowing second. And then in each moment what is to come will be made known to you.

It's very important for all of you right now to experience vision, to see what will come, to write it down, to come together with yourself when no one else is around, and regroup this experience of heart. Feel it again, imagine that you are in the room again as you are now, in heart, and that this foundation is established, and then feel where it is that you are going. Maybe you will be taken on a visualization to a part of the land, and you will feel what will be there, or you will feel who is there with you and what is done there. If it comes from the heart, write it down. That will sharpen your vision, it will open your clarity, and you will then know exactly how the pieces will fit together.

The experience of being in heart is rare in your society. It is even rarer to create from heart. It is even more rare to substantiate reality from heart. So this is an intriguing process!

What's interesting about it is, if you understand that it is a process, then you can enjoy the moment that you are in without waiting for the process to be complete. And that is what will foster the heart when you are working in diligent ways in the world, whatever that might be for each of you. Each moment then, reflect to yourself, to your body, to your cells, to your vibration, that frequency of heart. And that will take you very far, very fast. You have already seen the pieces coming together where people show up, and things get accomplished seemingly without effort. Things are determined easily. If it's hard then something is out of whack, so the hardness of it is an indication of how far you are from heart.

Even though you don't think you fear, many times you do. And so the heart is the place where the coming together of all of the design is available to each of you and where you can each access that which is inherent within you, the piece of the microcosm that you bring to support the foundation of the holographic. So it's interesting. What you're creating for yourselves is the clanging symbols, the loud things. "This is loud, this is loud, this is loud, I have to pay

~

Your practice here is to be in frequency first and then to have the experience of seeing and knowing second.

~

The experience of being in heart is rare in your society. It is even rarer to create from heart. It is even more rare to substantiate reality from heart.

~

If it's hard then something is out of whack, so the hardness of it is an indication of how far you are from heart.

~

It is not about love, it's about the vibration of being in oneness without words.

~

Animals will not come to you if you call them, they will not come to you because you have a pure intent. They will come to you because they cannot tell the difference between your frequency and theirs.

~

attention to this." And then in some moment you realize, "No, I don't have to pay attention to this. All I really want to pay attention to is the similarities, the congruences, the things where it makes sense to come together. Not the things which would keep us apart."

So talking about the things which are not working, talking about those things which in some way detract is giving the attention or the grease to the squeaky wheel, when what you really want to do is assist the already turning wheel to turn faster, to be brighter and clearer and move you. along the way more quickly. You are establishing here a foundation, and if it feels like it's taking time, it is, because until the foundation is established you will not be given the "go ahead." Without the foundation it won't work, and the universe will not support it until it is perfected. So speed it up, stay in heart, and remember.

If you do this and come together with it and align with it, the world of this nucleus will begin to change, and that is the only thing that people will listen to. It is the only thing that will be brilliantly brought home to consciousness. It's already changing its venue and its frequency. If you establish in your own heart that this is your priority—and again we repeat, it is not about love, it's about the vibration of being in oneness without words.

Animals will not come to you if you call them, they will not come to you because you have a pure intent. They will come to you because they cannot tell the difference between your frequency and theirs. And when you bring people on the land you will train them. They cannot go out on the land until they are ready. It's initiation. You don't have to take the risk that they will go out and scare the animals away. You train them. They don't go out until they are trained. And what you have is a process that they agree to determine, and if they don't agree to determine it, they don't come. It's very simple. It's not whether it's good or bad, it's just the way it is.

What happens as each of you gathers the space is that it grows. It doesn't just grow humanly, it grows on all of the dimensional frequencies that have been allotted to you, and you have a share of the consciousness of this process of critical mass that will be given to you to use as fuel for establishing this process in the Earth, because it's important. So we would recommend that you do not think about boundaries, you do not think about fields and lots and trees and shrubs, and processes of determination, because it doesn't matter. None of that matters. The only thing that matters is that if you're not establishing the foundation, nothing will matter anyway, because nothing will happen.

The only way you're going to get approval from the foundational spaces on this planet is if what is happening here is miraculous. Not next year when you get the facility built—this year. So, you want to quicken the hearts of everyone that is in this proximity, whether they are animal, vegetable, mineral, human, or spiritual. That's the gist of what you're doing. And ultimately, when you acknowledge that there can be and is no separation between anything, then the foundation will be set and the hoofs will start coming. It will be like a magnet. And when you see an animal, you don't say, "Oh, there's a moose, we're succeeding!" because then you go out of heart, and they'll go away, and you have to start again. It's like riding a wave. You want to stay constantly in the experience, because if you see them and they are different, if you haven't seen them before, and you have a human reaction, then what you have established is not credible.

And you will practice. Sometimes you will remember and sometimes you won't. There's no one keeping tabs, it's just that it's important. It's very important that synthesis be accomplished as quickly as possible. And that does not mean pressure, it means intention. If you want to manifest, make an intention. You have your body vibrate at the same rate of speed as your intention, and then you reach into the future and bring in that which awaits you in a manifestational sense, and you circle it together with the intention and vibration, and when the three are one, you will manifest the result.

So every day when you get up, practice. First of all, remember the union you feel at times in this group, feel it in your body. How does it feel, where does it settle? What is the vibration like? And then as you stay in the vibration, you'll feel it pooling around you and you'll feel that as you breathe, it expands. And the inherent thing is not to say, "Well, I want to go to the wetlands," or "I want to go to where the deer field is," or "I want to go to the beaver pond," or "I want to have oneness with the heart, or the sky, or the night, or the moon." You say, "My intention is to be always in heart, with no sound, no thought, nothing more important than being in heart."

And then your body will start being in heart, which means the vibrations of all of your systems will become attuned. That's very important, because you want to be superhuman experiences on this planet. You want to work longer hours, feel less tired, accomplish miracles, mountains of things in no time at all, and still feel as if you don't need rest. And that isn't will, it isn't thought. It's *substance*

It's as if what you're bringing together in the dimensions is then focused down here.

~

So it's a FOUNDATION that you're setting here. And the distances between you physically do not matter.

~

flowing through the body in such a way that it nourishes the intention, the vibration, and manifests that. Sometimes you'll find it in the same moment that you immediately intend it.

You will learn—must learn—how to do things outside of time. You are asking of yourselves a tremendous bit of challenge, a tremendous thing, because you want to know it all and do it all. And you want it to be quick, and it needs to be quick. You've all had experience in this, you've all touched it many times, and it is an intention to draw it into this time, now, everything that you have experienced as power, as commitment, as truth. Weave it into your lives right now. Bring it in. *Make it real now*, honor it. You don't have to start over again. You all know how to do this, or you wouldn't be here. Blend it. Bring it in.

If someone is opinionated, or they are thought-full, they have many thoughts in the head and they're speaking these, just weave it in and keep weaving it, and weaving it, and weaving it. Because it's important that all of that get out—be released, be mediated, be balanced, be unified, and be in the place where there cannot be any more sound. And it doesn't matter who it is, or what's going on, "Oh, there's more, there's more, all right there's more, we'll do it, we'll do it." So it's a commitment to being superhuman and to going beyond those things which have come to be habitual, have come to be ritual, or have what you think of as importance. Nothing is really important, except being in the place of no sound.

That means that you are in the place where the silence is bringing together all dimensions simultaneously, because in bringing those dimensions together that's what you'll find happens here. It's a mirror image. It's as if what you're bringing together in the dimensions is then focused down here. It is communicated and then all aspects of life can reply to that initiative. So it's a foundation that you're setting here. And the distances between you physically do not matter. It's forever important that you hold the space and include everyone that you know wants to be here. Again the differences don't matter. If someone wants to be here on some level you include them, and then the numbers will grow, and the energy will grow.

We would recommend that you don't have a goal. If it's time to submit a proposal or an agenda or something, and you don't know what to do, don't do anything except go into heart. And then the pieces will come together. If you're going to trust the universe, you will trust the universe *completely* or none of this will work. It's not about part-way measures. It doesn't mean that you're not learning about it, it just means that that's your intention, so that you get a very strong and very real sense that you're not being judged, that it's not about abilities, or capabilities, it's about the intention in your heart to make this work.

That's the foundation of it. You can talk about honoring, you can talk about oneness, and those things are spontaneous when you come from the heart. This is not hard, the way it is when you talk about emotion and love normally. This is the place where when you are in it, nothing else matters and there is no distinction or separation. And this is the place where we are always together, when we begin and when we end. We are always in that place together.

Peace is the feeling that you have when you're in the place of no sound. Your muscles relax, your thoughts still, your heart opens, your body rests, and you don't need anything. That's the feminine, that's the safety, that's the place where you are nurtured and where you belong. And this is what you've come to create: a place where everyone belongs. So there are steps involved, and if you take the steps you will find that everything flows very beautifully from it.

For example, when you introduce energy into form, when you move your body, when you dance and sing, think, type at the computer, answer the phone, move wood, there is a rhythm to the livelihood of doing those things in synchrony with life. And if one goes out to do a task, and does the task without the balance of the cycles of the rhythm of life within and without, the ebb and the flow is disrupted. It is something that gets done. It is not something that is co-created, because the rhythm and the cycle of the being is not in synchrony with the rhythm and the cycle of the universe. So what the land is saying to you is, "Please accord that we have the same rhythm and cycle, the ebb and the flow, what comes in and what goes out. And if we align together, we can help each other establish the experience of order in this place."

The other thing about tasks is, if you establish the rhythm and the flow, if the ebb and the flow is balanced, then work is not hard; you're not pushing against something, you are flowing within it. Many times you do from the mind and the will instead of the heart. So before you feel the log, you "feel" the log, feel the air around you, you feel the muscles of your body, and you do it all together. Everything from driving the car, to petting the dogs, to eating food— so you get to a very meaningful relationship with heart in everything that you do. Which is the honoring.

When you're doing tasks or moving something, it would be

~

Peace
*is the feeling that you have
when you're in the place
of no sound.*

~

*And
this is what you've come to create:
a place where everyone belongs.*

~

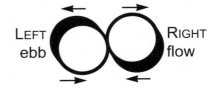

LEFT ebb   RIGHT flow

The heart is a louder voice.

~

*You're all here
because you understand
that your wholeness as a group
wants to express.
You're tired
of trying to express by yourself,
and believing
that that's what you have to do
to be seen,
and to belong,
and to be loved.*

~

*So being in heart
is different than most life experiences.
It isn't being in romantic love,
because there's no outer draw
to do anything with the feeling.*

~

helpful to imagine the figure eight. You're going from your left to your right. Then feel your body that way, visualizing your energy moving in a figure eight, and you feel any substance that you're working with in that same way. If you move forward, you move forward by balancing sides. The same thing backwards, until it is internally fixed that the order of the balance is something that's inherent in every step you take. It becomes a natural evolution.

Question: *How do we know when we're in heart?*

You are in heart here. That is why we did not speak for a long time. It is when your frequencies are attuned together, and you stop being separate people, when your energy starts to flow in such a way that you have no needs, no cares, nothing bothers you, that your being settles in. You feel more whole, and nothing is clamoring in the mind to be thought about and activated. It is more that the heart of the group is a louder voice. It's not that some of you did not have thoughts, but it was that the energy was acquiescing to the greater commitment, to diminish self and respond to the need of the whole for expression.

You're all here because you understand that your wholeness as a group wants to express. You're tired of trying to express by yourself, and believing that that's what you have to do to be seen, and to belong, and to be loved. That hasn't worked. So you're here to say, "Let's put it in the pot, and as we put it in the pot, let's see what we create, what is born."

So being in heart is different than most life experiences. It isn't being in romantic love, because there's no outer draw to do anything with the feeling. It's a sense of coming in, of resting, and at the same time expanding. So it's all things at one time. And it brings peace. There are those of you who are more into that vibration than others. The frequencies have been fine-tuned. You've been working longer together, and yet all of you in this room have a fabric of that piece and that heart because you are here, and it is felt. We are feeling it very strongly. That's why we can say these words to you, because if you are not of this consciousness you could not hear the words.

You may feel it differently, you may have different adjectives for describing it, and the easiest thing is just to put yourself here again, to hold hands, to feel the love, however you may determine it in your mind, for what you say, "definition." Just practice that, expand that, and the cellular vibration will become its own resolution. That's what you are looking for also. You're not trying any longer, you're just accepting that it's here, and you're here and you can begin. It's simple that way. That's why you don't really want to think about what you're supposed to be doing if you're here, or if you belong, or those kinds of things, "Will I do this, and can I do that?" It's, "Come be in the frequency and the vibration and let it happen." Intending to be in heart is important in and of itself.

There are many, many types of dimensions having to do with all manner of life, that are interested in your project. When you are in heart the doorways open for you, so you can see things, know things, participate in things that you have read about or heard about but not necessarily experienced yourself, and if you hold the energy of that which you are seeking to communicate with, it will be very strong for you to receive those pieces in this time. It is an anchoring of these dimensions into form in this place. Before you can determine the activities in form, you will want to have established these pieces of consciousness, so that you have access to these dimensions, because you will need their help. They have dedicated their access to you, as we have said before. You have been allotted quite a big chunk of consciousness for use here, *because not only are you going to live in oneness with everything, but everything is going to live in oneness with you.* That means everything is now tempering its frequency to be at one with the frequency of your joined hearts. And that is very exciting!

We would recommend that you start from scratch, in the sense that you don't worry too much about what other people and books say to do, although they are wonderful tools. You have your own nucleus of energy here. Work with your own communication and connection. Bring in that which is available here for you. Ground it in. Take the incentive. Know that you know, know that everything is available and begin it. In other words, take yourself seriously. You are not playing at some kind of deeply evocative thought. You are creating an inevitable and absolutely necessary model of consciousness. Pay attention. Listen and respond.

One of the things that we would like to share with you is the gratitude of the many dimensions for your commitment to come here and participate in this experience of the future. Just remember, you have tremendous help and assistance. Ask for what you need, ask clearly and specifically. It is not that we don't know what you need, it's that you need to ask for it to receive it. That's the way it is written. Write, and pool your journals periodically, write and see how

Everything
is now tempering its frequency
to be at one with the frequency
of your joined hearts.

~

Take yourself seriously.
You are not playing at some kind of deeply
evocative thought.
You are creating an inevitable
and absolutely necessary
model of consciousness.

~

Ask for what you need,
ask clearly and specifically.
It is not that we don't know what you need,
it's that you need to ask for it to receive it.
That's the way it is written.

~

they are similar and dissimilar. Share what you are experiencing, what you are knowing, and gathering and receiving. Put it together. Take it all very seriously, without worrying about it. Taking yourself seriously just means that you know that it's important.

Many times the sound of the voice takes away from the experience of the frequency. Know that we are with you in this frequency always. And it is each of your choices to be in this frequency with us. And this is the space that we call Heaven on Earth.

The Flame of Pure Intent

PURENESS OF INTENT IS THE FLAME through which life is vitalized. When you live your essence and calling from inner truth, this pureness makes your life spontaneous, exciting, and essentially "yours." Pure intent cuts through fear and the thought forms of separation.

Now is the time of human reckoning, which heightens the experience of separation and elicits the love vs. fear decision in each of you. You can think of yourself in human terms of reference—with issues about survival and other human considerations, or you can think of yourself as a pure form of energy that has come here to direct the force of light and pure intent into the world to break apart that which is mislabeled and misunderstood.

If you think about the way people choose realities, you understand that there are misconceptions about what the original space was like, which is where the false gods come in, and where the people ordain their lives separate from truth.

Your purpose for being here is not necessarily to overturn those truths, or to say what is real and unreal, or to get involved in belief systems—rather, your potential is to be a laser or level of consciousness such that in the presence of your awareness these things disseminate; they fall apart. And your pureness of intent is the clearest way for you now to approach everything.

In making decisions about where to live, when and if you should move, what is important, how your fears work, and what people say about things, hold the space and say, "I am of pure intent." When you think about the things that are said, and all that you learn in your experience as a variable, understand that pure intent will assure that those variables become accurate. Then you are a truth finder, a truth initiator. You are able to foundation experience so that the boundary that you might have had in thought, idea, or belief, is supported by nothing accurate, so all you really do is boil everything down to this true space of knowing.

And the knowing is born from the pureness. It's not that you search for the knowing, it's that the pureness engenders it. And when

I fill myself up with my own essence and live my full presence now from the place of pure intent.

~

Your pureness of intent
acts like an eraser.
It erases
the covering on your consciousness,
the covering on your soul,
and the covering on your body,
and lets you shine through.

~

That's what life is about.
In the highest realms possible,
it is vision,
it is seeing clearly what's there,
and making choices
based on what is known,
and what is awareness,
and what is absolute
rather than what is speculated on.

~

you engender it, you hold the space. And when you hold the space, everything comes into order around that space. This is the primary way that the critical mass of union and the experience of oneness is going to be fostered on the planet. Everyone comes to the initiation of that experience in the same vibrational field, which is magic, which is union, which is the capacity to communicate in ways that normally are not possible. With pureness of intent, a wave takes you forward and honors you and fosters for you stamina, strength, commitment to what you are, and the knowing that all parts of you are available—nothing is hidden from you, about you, about where you're going, or where you've been.

Your pureness of intent acts like an eraser. It erases the covering on your consciousness, the covering on your soul, and the covering on your body, and lets you shine through. The phenomenon inside of you has yet to receive permission to be. It's that simple. So you say to yourself with pure intent, "I choose to see who I am. I choose to see what I reflect, and what is initiated from within me. And I choose to see the way it responds to the world around me, so that I can assist in bringing the light into form." And that's why you're here. So yes, it's important to learn what you're afraid of, it's important to face your dragons. And yet, the other way you could do it is to experience that pure intent is your guide, and actually gives you back what you are—what you *really* are, which is what you're really afraid of seeing, anyway.

The Short-cut to Seeing Your Wholeness

Instead of looking at how you function or why you aren't seeing yourself fully, take the short-cut. Stand in front of the mirror and say, "I have pureness of intent, I want to see who I am." Working from the foundation of pure intent gives you commitment and consciousness, and allows you to know the reality of what's going on in the world. You are not in danger because you have knowledge and the capacity to see clearly. And that's what life is about. In the highest realms possible, it is vision, it is seeing clearly what's there, and making choices based on what is known, and what is awareness, and what is absolute rather than what is speculated on.

You relate to your own awareness in a very truthful way. You hang up all of your linen, dirty or clean. You hang it up and say,

"Well, I have to look at it." And when you do that you're purging yourself constantly, constantly, so you're not hiding anything. There's nothing in there that's going to jump up and leap out at you and say, "Ah, you forgot this." Because the only thing that is really hidden is your own essence from yourself. It's not that you have some demon that is holding you captive or something to be afraid of. You're at that place of seeing yourself. This is very important, because if you are to lead in the truest sense of the word, which means, mostly, to allow the unfoldment of all designs parallel with your own at the same synchronistic motion and movement and resonance, and not to impede anyone else's, and to support all life, as well as supporting your own life simultaneously, you have to be absolutely sure that you're seeing who you are.

You watch yourself from every angle. This is the key, this is the little secret. That's good, you know; see yourself square in the mirror, but do more! Look at the sides of you. Look at the back of you. Look between your shoulder blades. That's where you want to look. What's there? What is there that you can't really see if you look over your shoulder? What is it that everybody else sees but you're missing? Really look at yourself. And not with judgment, or, "I don't like the way this curves, or that moves." Look more at the essence and say, "Ah, what is the essence? Where is it? How does it support itself, where does it come from?"

So in each moment the relationship of truth to form is absolute in your being. The form that you see, the essence that you are, the truth that you bring, and the experience of being here, is all the same vibration.

What the consciousness ordains for you is a foundational space that says, "I am congruent. The pureness of my intent makes me fear less, makes me experience no pain, no struggle, no strife, because my essence is so bright it fills me up, and I don't need a lot of other things to fill me up. I fill myself up with my own essence."

Now the irony is that when you fill yourself up with your own essence, you attract whatever supports the fulfillment of that essence. It comes all around you, and whatever form that needs to take in that particular moment, it will take that form. So your perspective here is very positive, very definite, very clear, very quick, and very much supported by the total consciousness of humanity. Because pureness of intent is what's necessary to grease the wheels here to get this consciousness moving.

You are now creating a reality that is consistent with what you

~

I am congruent.
The pureness of my intent
makes me fear less,
makes me experience no pain,
no struggle, no strife,
because
my essence is so bright it fills me up.
I fill myself up
with my own essence.

~

wanted to do when you came in. So the congruence is between fulfilling the design and knowing what it is and having those things come into an absolute space of integration. See, that's power! And that's important, because when you know that you're doing what you came to do, there's no gap in the consciousness. In that moment you say, "I'm home; this is what I've been waiting for."

Unleashing Your Spiritual Force

As that symmetry is synthesized and equilibrated, your relationship with yourself becomes connected to your relationship with your essence, your future, your past, the hologram, and with the forces to make it happen, which are unleashed by the **center of zeal** in the back of the neck. So you want to have people rub your neck lots and lots in the next months. You want to feel that you're open in that space because you're unleashing your spiritual force. The energy of your spiritual force is moving down through your arms and torso and through your whole body, and you're expressing, you're writing, dancing, moving, because unleashing the zeal, in the same way that you are moving the pureness of intent, fosters a reality that expands your consciousness. It puts you in touch with the framework that allows those levels to, in a symmetrical sense, come into being and fulfill the experience of reality as you know it to be.

The reason many of you get so upset is because of some of the data, facts, and figures that you're hearing in certain settings. You're hearing about the illusion, and how the reality is being and has been lost because of the illusion. You don't want to support illusion. As you support the reality, the truth emerges; and one way of doing that is through pureness of intent. The consciousness that you have each brought to the world, the symmetry of that, how that unfolds, how that works itself through the reality—is very dynamic, very clear, very considered.

And as you open out and bring all the fields of order together *within* yourself and *from* yourself, everything begins to make sense. So it's not about what you know and don't know, it's that the clarity of who you are will cut through whatever you experience, whenever you experience it, and you don't really have to determine ahead of time that you're supposed to know something. It's much more that you're aware that illusion is there and you've always known it was there, you just weren't sure of the particulars. So now you experience it so that your presence responds to the experience in a concerted and very stabilizing way of choice. You will stabilize the pureness of intent regardless of what the situation is. So you function continually in that way, and foster the reality of truth for yourself, so that everything you have lived to this time makes sense and has had a purpose.

Part of what you're here to design into reality is the consensus that the consciousness you carry is an absolute consciousness. And why would you live any less than that? If you choose to live any less than that, you're going to suffer from that choice. That's not because you're bad, it's not because you're not doing the right thing. Why do you think that would be? Because if you have an immense consciousness and you're not using it, there's a sense of loss, abandonment, a sense of frustration, a sense of invalidity of your full worth. So, the suffering happens in your life from nonaccordance, and that's *self* nonaccordance.

So you're really looking at your life system and saying, "Wait a minute, there's nothing going on here. I'm just going to open my eyes, look at my back, turn around, spin around, see it all." Start seeing it all, invoke it, bring it out, and your level of awareness immediately. The pureness of intent goes out and touches other people, the foundation of who you are is supported, enhanced, accelerated, and you're home free.

Then you are naturally a teacher. You stand in that pureness of intent, in the light, and people come around, and you teach. And what do you teach? Self acceptance, self initiation, self awareness. You create the experience of honoring that absolute in everyone, and that comes out regardless of what you're thinking or doing or responding to. It comes out. You begin to feel it constantly, as if you're feeding the whole Earth with that pureness. And it has words, it has intonations, it has vibrational components, and it opens itself out so that it guides your way. You wonder what you're going to do—you wonder who you're going to be with—you wonder where all this is going to happen. It is all coming from the pureness of that intent. It is very simple.

It is important for you to ground now, even more important than before, and to drink lots of lemon water, so that the foundation of your experience is literally given to you from the point of reckoning and stability that you're carrying. So you feel aware, aligned, and instrumentally connected to everything that is. You don't have any

*Foster
the reality of truth for yourself
so that* everything
*you have lived to this time
makes sense and has had a purpose.*

CREATE
*the experience of honoring
that absolute in everyone.*

more questions, so as soon as something happens, you know—yes or no. And it's not a question.

You actually have your antennae out, and the light's going on and there's a pureness of intent, and you experience that yes, you're shaking that up. You're constantly allowing the energy of that zeal and that motion and that level of reality to be there with you so that Whoosh! it's like you're on your own motor boat, or you have your own channel, or your own rail under you that's carrying you forward, and you've got a schedule, and you know where you're going.

Pureness of Intent Is a Magnet

It's much more of a focused life.

The focus is being absolutely on track with that intent. And that shines light on your way, it paves your way, it supports you, it unfolds you, and it's the current that carries you in.

It's much more of a focused life after this point, so the discipline is not to be with any particular part of yourself over any other part, or to try harder to think about what you're afraid of, or what you need to forgive, or how you need to do this or that. The focus is being absolutely on track with that intent. And that shines light on your way, it paves your way, it supports you, it unfolds you, and it's the current that carries you in. So it's very different from a mental approach that says, "Well, I think I ought to do this, but my intuition might say this, so I'd better balance these things, I'd better balance the conscious mind with what my feelings say." And you don't do either. You see, because the pureness of intent is the flame through which the life is vitalized, it's deeper than intuition, it's deeper than the ability to balance this or that, it's an experience of being in knowing, and following it home, not thinking, not trying, not analyzing. So you're not having to worry about anything, because the level at which you're intoning this kind of affirmation is an absolute level.

Now you may or may not believe you have the experience of that absolute, of that level—and that's fine—get out and do it, be with it, and then you'll realize that none of the other stuff, the illusion, makes any sense—it doesn't help you to honor the experience of your ability or capacity. It might give you a good going over and get you to think about what you really believe, but you don't even care to believe anything, probably. That's at least what we're recommending.

So, it's saying, "Okay, on those levels of fear, illusion, and constant questions, I'm not going to function. I'm going to function *only* here, with my pureness of intent." What happens when you function from that point is that you begin to actualize the integrity of the union that happens when knowledge and truth and order and light come together. That's your back! So you move your consciousness so that it functions to make a path for others to follow—you are able to see where you're going, and it isn't logical, it's absolute.

This way of being draws people from every walk of life and every foundational point to come together and be with you and this experience. It's like in the movie *Fearless*, when the protagonist gets out of the crashed airplane and follows the light, saying to others, "Follow me to the light." And those who hear him follow him. Basically they got on a wave, and when they got on the wave, they left the vicinity of that disruption and chaos, stayed in order, and followed that wave right home. When you're in that pureness of intent, it carries everything with it.

You don't have to take responsibility and say, "What if they are on my wave and it doesn't work? What if I fall off?" because you're cooperating with your decision to live your design and to do that fully, and you're not looking over your shoulder at what others are doing. So the people that come to be with you do so because they observe that the union you have with the experience of that energy band of pure intent is so clear and so real and offers so much, that they're going to participate in that. So you're not eliciting their support, and you're not trying to get them to join your band wagon. You're moving forward on your own incentive, under your own steam, in your own energy field, and exemplifying that which characterizes consciousness. As you do that, you experience that fundamentally everything that you have come to live is being played out by you, through you, and with you, and you're happy, because this is where it's at!

It's not about saving souls—it's about honoring a point of reckoning and passing through that point of reckoning, making your choice, and sticking to it.

So that isn't difficult for you, that's easy. It's an easy thing to say, "This is what I feel is right for me, this is the pureness that I come from," so it's not about action either, saying this is right over that. It's saying, "I'm going down the center of my being from the essence and the soul, and that's why it's center, and I'm going to stay in that space." And that is the key, because you're not taking sides, for or against, you're not trying to recommend anything, or convince anybody that they ought to do anything. You're just saying, "This is

> *So the people
> that come to be with you
> do so because they observe
> that the union you have
> with the experience
> of that energy band of pure intent
> is so clear and so real
> and offers so much,
> that they're
> going to participate
> in that.*

the way I see it. This is the way it is here, and this is what I'm doing, and this is how I'm functioning."

Now because it is a place, it has impact for many people, and because the systems you'll eventually work in have to do with recognizing truth, you'll find that people come to be with you who are in some way discerning truth. They're saying, "I'm here to figure out about truth." They're with you because they see that you found the truth. Remember that truth, no matter how many pathways it takes, is going to end up going in one line, in one direction, so the framework is always in unification. So as you open out and experience the validity of the place you hold, people are experiencing that validity, and they're saying, "This is really what is also in my own heart, this is also my pureness of intent." And because you've seen yourself, looked at yourself, looked at your back, you know what it is that you're up for. And you know how that effect displays itself and where it's beaming or shining to. So there are no surprises. You realize that you are here to bring truth, and here to hold the space so that truth can create itself so that the value of total consciousness is expressed.

Many of you are at a place now where you are changing gears. You're deciding that you're finished with certain parts of your life, not only literally, but in the invisible—parts of your thinking, parts of your process—and you're ready to open the closet door and throw it all in and close the closet door and blow the closet up. Done with that! And you're actually birthing yourself in a way that you've never felt alive before—never felt incorporated. You are working from the zeal center, unleashing the spiritual forces, opening this pureness of intent, seeing your whole being and essence and continuing to say, "I want to see who I am," calling it out, and calling it out, and calling it out. That will make a foundation for you that's very beautiful, and support you in ways that "thinking" about the support wouldn't work.

You will feel stronger than you've ever felt. You'll feel as if the foundation that you've brought in is paving the way for new awarenesses. Now this is where the important changes in your life come in, because you'll move from a position where you have to have certain levels of authority and deal with certain levels of authority, to a place where you can manifest your own destiny. And this is very important for you to do right now. Incorporate everything that we've been saying, and also say to yourself, as you want to see yourself, "Who am I really in terms of my work? Who am I really in

Now because it is a place, it has impact for many people, and because the systems you'll eventually work in have to do with recognizing truth, you'll find that people come to be with you who are in some way discerning truth.

Truth, no matter how many pathways it takes, is going to end up going in one line, in one direction, so the framework is always in unification.

That you are here to bring truth, and here to hold the space so that truth can create itself in such a way that the value of total consciousness is expressed.

terms of what I'm here to provide the world? Who am I in terms of where the world is ready to receive me? Where are these pieces now available? How can there be a system supported where I can create my next step in the world?" It's really important that you reach inside yourself and draw this one out. It's really important that you say, "I see who I am—who am I as a teacher, who am I as a provider of services, who am I as an example, as an embodiment," and ask, "What is the easiest way for me to see that part of myself and to create the design that is going to make a new system of reality?"

So every single time that you work these dimensions together, and experience reality in a beautiful sense of union, there is a coming together that supports you and says, "As I look at myself, as I see my intention. As I clarify my position, as I experience my truth, this is a new universal paradigm being born in the world. This is where I am going to support my livelihood, my intentional mastery, and my experience of consciousness in my work. So my work becomes personal."

You live out the pureness of intent in the world. It isn't separate from your job. It isn't separate from how you orient your time and reality. It is the orientation of your time and reality. So you take the shrouds off yourself, the parts of you that have been steeped in whatever tradition, and say, "Now, who am I really? And if there were no system, what system would I create? And if there were reckoning to be had, where the souls of the children have to learn what they have to learn, where could I do this? What is it that I could establish that would make a difference for the planet?"

Take the shrouds off yourself, the parts of you that have been steeped in whatever tradition, and say, "Now, who am I really? And if there were no system, what system would I create?"

Commit Yourself to Your Calling

Now, you can play around, or you can get in there up to your elbows! And you're going to come up against this—and this is one of the things that you might also have been holding back on a bit—"It's my turn, it's my turn!" As you experience the validity of your own pureness of intent, it starts guiding you right into places where you thought about going, but didn't know how to structure. The pureness of intent is going to make these things happen for you, out-of-the-ordinary things, miraculous things, where the parameters that have been set up can fall down. Where the structure that says, "This is possible, this isn't possible," can shift.

*What the pureness
is leading you toward
is your calling.*

~

*If you have the thought,
the world is ready.
If you have the urgency,
it's time.*

~

The important part of your job is to stay with that pureness of intent as if your life depended upon it, because it does. And instead of thinking, "I'd like to do that, but it's not time yet, or I'd like to do that, but you know the world isn't really ready for it, and we'd have to do so many things in order to get approval for this or that or the other thing," you just decide what this pureness of intent wants.

Your first statement is, "I want to see myself. I want the pureness of intent to foster itself, so I want to look in the mirror and see who I am, then go around and look at my back." Okay—second thing is, "What am I here to do? Let me do it." Get down on your hands and knees and say, "Look I'm dying, I am really dying. I can play well, and I can do this well, and I can do that well, and I'm dying, because my essence isn't fully alive. I'm waiting for something, but I don't know what it is, so I'm dying, because my essence isn't dancing and playing and expressing and changing the world. My essence is shining this lovely little light in this safe little place." You know that you've been preparing and now you're ready to leap—and the directions you might be ready to leap in are safe. The direction your pureness of intent wants to take you to is a very big leap. And it's the only place you'll find fulfillment. And a job and fulfillment aren't the same thing for you. So what the pureness is leading you toward is your calling. That's what you say in the mirror, "What is my calling. What am I here to do?"

Now, the "how" question is going to be really big. Because as soon as you realize what your pureness of intent wants to convey, you're going to say, "How could I do that? How could I do that?" And then you realize if you have the thought, the world is ready. If you have the urgency, it's time.

If you want to be there in that world making dynamic new models of reality for the children of this world, it's time to start. If you wait for something, whatever it is, it'll be too late.

And so you begin to foster in yourself *discipline* and *commitment* to the calling. Because nothing else is going to serve now. No matter what your calling is, it doesn't matter what it is, as much as it matters that you have it. And if it's a little bit off, it'll get back on, because it's pure. So it's not about worrying, "Did I get it right?" It's about allowing it to surface and giving it energy, and staying with it, and hanging in there until it does surface, and taking all the "how" questions and putting them back in the pureness of intent and saying, "Well the pureness of intent will show me how, and if I stop myself by thinking, 'I don't know, it might not work,' I'm out of my pureness of intent." So, you really understand and recognize that the foundation that you're working from, as long as it's pure, is going to provide you with every single answer you need.

What Is Not Truth Falls Away

The essential place in you that's shaping right now is the expression of the core essence and its connection to the truth that you carry through this pureness of intent. As you foster that as a way of being, anything in your system that isn't real, that doesn't really reflect truth, falls away, is unimportant, and is dissipated in such a way that you wonder why you ever thought of it to begin with. Because it's such a little thing that you're letting go of, you have no charge on it. You have no energy for the thing that you think you're going to. It doesn't have any charge, literally. What you've got planned in your life—Whoosh!—Gone!

Where's your excitement? Where's your life force? Many of you practice many times a week to vitalize your life force, through yoga asanas, for example. What are asanas for? They are to vitalize the force of life and spirit in the body. Why? Why would you want to do that? Why do you meditate, affirm, intend, visualize, exercise, discipline yourselves? When you vitalize the life force of the body and bring spirit and form together, you are the edge of the blade of the sword, and you cut through all of the illusion and manifest truth. You're here to do that.

You're not here to be railroaded or to be crucified or burned at the stake! You're here to create models of birth, of life, of health, of joy, and of communion. And that's nothing to be scared about. It's just weaving it. "Oh, it won't work there, okay, we're going to weave it over here. Well, it'll work, because it's time for it to work, the world needs it, the women need it, the babies need it, the consciousness needs it, so let's do it, let's find a way." And so you make up your mind from your pureness of intent first, make up your mind and say, "Okay, it's going to happen. This is who I am, this is what I want, it's going to happen. I carry my energy, I carry my consciousness. I carry my awareness, it's going to happen."

So you break down the barriers of perception people have against life, and that's a challenge. That is a challenge! They say, "Well, no, it's okay the way it is. We need to spend more time and energy on

*You're leading them
out of the darkness of a boring life
and of a life filled with diseases
that don't need to be there,
fears that don't need to be there,
separations that don't need to be there.*

X Y & Z." And you're aware that they are talking about supporting death, because it's safer. And you understand the dynamic. You're not fooled, you see, you know what's going on, so you can be prepared. You say, "Well that's their philosophy, that's their thought. They support death." It's not dying, it's not killing; they support death which means slow, laborious lifetimes with boring experiences and status quo process and rigid belief systems and authoritative controlling processes. So what! Because life is now ready to be lived differently and you are in support of that. And there are other people who are also in support of that. So you go out and say, "This is who I am, and this is what I'm doing."

And you just watch how that pureness of intent calls the life-seeker out. And you get excited, and more excited, and then you have that pathway, and the people will follow that pathway with you. They will! Because you're leading them out of the darkness of a boring life and of a life filled with diseases that don't need to be there, fears that don't need to be there, separations that don't need to be there, perceptions that are separating, so you become clearer now that it's all about saying, "Yes!" It's your time. There's nothing to worry about any more. Nothing. It's a done deal. And you're right there and you're spinning, you're spinning. And when you stop spinning, you stand and say, "Yes," focus, and go!

My Pureness of Intent
notes

Full Presence
An Exercise

Saying, "Yes!" is the place inside you that is clearly feeling this flame. Go in there every day and feel the flame! And then imagine that you open the gate and the flame starts to move. Feel where it wants to go. Follow it. Be with it in such a way that the flame is the truth, and where you end up is what it is that truth is seeking, and where it is that you want to be. You're doing this in a visualization, so you have nothing to lose. Write it out, and then some day follow it with your feet. See where it takes you. Follow it with your fingers in the yellow pages, see where it takes you. Play with it. Play with it. Where does the flame want to go, because this flame is going to come out, it's going to express, it's going to be experienced inside you in such a way that the phenomenal capacity that you have to move the Earth, which you have used many times, happens here! Why is it not possible for you to create a miracle next week? No earthly reason. Why don't you do it? Fear? Nah, it's not really fear, it's this lack of *full presence*. That's all it is. So you could say, "Oh, I'm not all here. That's true, I'm not all here."

So see, it's simple. It's not some kind of deep psychological problem, it's not that you've done something and you have to pay penance, and you have to initiate yourself for three years, and read fifty thousand books, it's that your presence is incomplete. All that says is, "Well, I guess I'll put it all together now. I guess I'll let myself see what's here and let it come out, and I will have full presence. And then everything else happens, because that's the only thing that's missing! I have the love. I have the intention. I have the clarity. I have the lineage. I have the capability. I have the vision. I have the heart. I have the stamina. I have the discipline. I have the intelligence. I have the education. I have the degree. I have this, I have that, what's stopping me?"

And you say, "Well, the glue, that's it, the glue that puts it together, that's what I need. So I'll weave it with this flame, and melt it all to a solid molten core, and then I'll let the flame out, and when I let the flame out, I will be the flame, I will be the movement, I will be the outcome, and I will be the energy that carries it all at once, "Ahhh, that's who I am. I am everything. I am the past, the present and the future in the flame all at once." So as this unfolds, the presence of that consciousness becomes absolute. And you say, "Okay, I was this, I am this, and I choose to create this. These three levels are now valid in my consciousness, so I experience them."

Now what I provide for myself is a vehicle. What's the vehicle? Permission. You give yourself permission—free will. The vehicle is, I give myself permission, and when I do, all of the variables come together. It's that simple. It's a Whoosh! sensation. It's the vibration of the infinite or original design. The vibration of saying "Yes" and being in the vehicle that will move that—the vibration of your future or hologram or the pureness of intent manifesting, seeing that all of those three points (past, present and future) are of the same vibration. When they are of the same vibration, there is an absolute experience of instantaneous manifestation. So you are going to instantaneously manifest your presence.

So practice. "This is what I chose, this is where I am, this is what I want to do, this is where I end up." Where you end up is absolutely alive, like a flame burning, so that everybody around *feels* that flame. You're not hiding the light under the bushel basket, you're not waiting for anybody to give you permission to do anything, you're going for it as if your life depends on it! These points have vibrational quotients with them. So practice bringing the vibrations to the same point, realizing that they are the same vibration, and that powers your pureness of intent. That powers the flame which opens the door for you to see where to go. It isn't something that you have to fight with your mental process, and with your physical body. It won't work that way. It's about the flame of the essence burning away the resistance— burning life into the experience—and the value of that is that you show people everything is possible when it comes from the flame of that intention.

What's the Glue?
notes

*You don't have
normal conversations anymore
—you have exhilarating conversations
charged with life and energy
and hope and inspiration
and the effectiveness of truth.*

So you drop every perception you have about yourself. That's important, and that's what the flame does. As these perceptions drop away, you have no limits anymore, *you have no limits*. This is very important, and valuable enough for you to share it, to speak about it, and for you to empower other people to live the charge of their own consciousness, whatever that means to them. And stop having discussions about, "Well, do you think we could do that? Well, I don't know. How much money do we need to do that? Well, more than we have."

Just start stating what you want, start stating what that pureness of intent is telling you. State it everywhere you go, whether verbally or nonverbally, however is appropriate, but state it.

And know you're going all the way. Know you're going to that fulfillment. Know that there's no separation in that. Know that the value of that experience is profound, and there's no part of you that's left out. It's going to happen regardless. Unleash the spiritual force of that zeal to let it happen. Then when you're with people, that excitement is contagious, and you magnetize it and draw it into being.

You don't have normal conversations anymore—you have exhilarating conversations, charged with life and energy and hope and inspiration and the effectiveness of truth. Because when you say, "I don't know if I can do this." Where's the truth? And how do you feel inside when you will not allow or acknowledge that the truth is there? Because the truth is, you know exactly where you're going, and exactly what you're going to do, and nothing is going to stop you. Isn't that true? So when you say, "Gee, I don't know, well it's going to take time." It's like you take your being and divide it in half. And when you divide it in half, that experience says to you, the value of consciousness, the value of everything I've ever worked for, is minimal. I'm really not invested in allowing my knowing to surface here. I'm just any normal human being sitting here having a conversation and saying, "I don't know." And it's fine to do that, it doesn't harm anything, but it really is a procrastinating device. It holds things separate and creates life that's very drab. And very boring. And for you, very frustrating. That's where your frustration comes from. You are not acknowledging your own wisdom. And if somebody else doesn't acknowledge your wisdom, you say, "Well, yep, that's true, I don't know if I have it." And they are only doing what they see you doing. So it's time to change that, in our opinion. It's *time* for this. That's why we're able to say it to you. Otherwise, it would be what you might call a kick in the pants. But because it's time, it's not a kick in the pants, it's what you call an affirmation. We are validating for you that it's time.

Teach Others to Be Vital

So your presence here, in this space, at this time in this world, is very important. We would recommend that you not waste one second of it. And that you teach this. You teach people how to be vital. If you teach others how to be vital, their births will be very simple. Their rapport with their children will be very exciting. They will know exactly what their child is doing, and know exactly what's happening. At birth, mothers won't have to have machinery or instruments to know these things. They will be timing everything to the exact instant when it will foster the most life. Teach vitality, teach essence. That is what tones the being. Tones the muscles. So experience that your validity is in your example.

What makes you different from anybody else is that your wisdom comes from your flame. It says, "I am life. I have always come here to bring life. Now I bring life in a different way than I have before, and my premise is that life creates union in and of all time, and when union is created, and oneness is experienced, there's peace on this planet, and that's what I came to bring."

Peace means enjoyment of life, peace means experiencing union and happiness, peace means no war, violence, or killing. Of course there is illusion that these things are happening because they mean something—but they only mean that the separation and dichotomy still exist. Remember that. That's all it means. So when you are supporting life, what happens? You diminish death. You diminish violence. You diminish the illusion of separation.

Imagine the changes in your society when a mother can feel union with herself and then with her child. What she teaches her child is invaluable, because the child then knows what union is before it gets out in the street. If the mother needs you to tell her how she's doing, there's no union. Then she goes out to give birth and the child feels afraid, and she's afraid the child will kill her, and the child is afraid it will kill its mother. And this is literal. There's is no rapport. Maybe they talk soul to soul, but how much does the mother know about her own body, about her own ability to move the force

Teach vitality, teach essence.

~

Peace *means enjoyment of life,* peace *means* experiencing union and happiness, peace *means no war,* violence, or killing.

~

When union is created, and oneness is experienced, there's peace on this planet, and that's what I came to bring.

~

fields of her own cells? How much oneness does she really experience with herself? She might love the child, and yet, that doesn't usually diminish her fear.

The objective here is for you take everything you know and define it, "What do I know? What do I know that I haven't yet put together that I could create—ideology, philosophy, experience, educational process, birthing ritual, etc." Whatever you know, let it be born. Whatever your flame calls you to be, to live, let it out! Develop it freely. Ask yourself, "What would open all the gateways so that things worked the way I know they can work?"

What is it you know? Let yourself see the fullness of what you know. Let yourself experience the flame of your calling. The pureness of your intent brings the calling and the knowing into being. Follow the flame. The world awaits the model, the knowing that you are called to bring.

Birth the flame. Live it now . . . Now is the time!

Hearing
Without Words

YOU ARE MOVING INTO A TIME when there is to be no language as you know it now, so your level of awareness will increase, and your potential will be expressed and experienced vibrationally and shared through the waves of reality that you create together, simultaneously. Before long there will be no words to define consciousness—before long, that which you know as truth, and the knowledge you are carrying in your beings, will no longer be accessible from language.

As you approach this time, we suggest that you use fewer words, that you itemize in your consciousness what is important and shine that out like a light; that you foster the vibrational frequency that you intend to be; and as much as possible limit discussion, particularly of those things which you either don't understand, do not wish to manifest, or are afraid of. If this is your intention, you will substantiate that through the substance and the fluids. What will be forthcoming is the acceleration of the vibration that you choose to manifest through, and that you choose to use as an awareness point. This means that you also magnetically attract what you are emoting as a vibrational choice, and organize the being through that intention.

If sometimes you feel that you don't quite get what's going on, or that you're not quite in the picture, or you're striving for something and it doesn't seem to manifest, surrender it to the vibration of your essential space—what you want to feel like, what you want to emulate, and what you want to support. Bring that together dynamically, vibrationally, as the charge inside your body, and let the rest be. When you seek something, you are going outside of your own vibration to find it, so stay in your vibration, and surrender to that vibration.

Now this is emotional response or reaction, this is mental thought or patterning, belief systems, it is that which you think you want but don't know how to get. It is that which you think you want to express, but don't know how to speak about. Basically, it's anything that doesn't seem congruent. Allow it to be dissolved, so that what you are is the frequency of what you carry, and nothing else.

~

*I am a vehicle of consciousness,
I am always aware of my calling,
emotionally balanced and sensitive,
yet clearly conscious that I am
an instrument for order and peace.
I allow myself to be dissolved,
so that
all I am is the frequency I carry—nothing
else.*

~

The Destructuring Process

There is destructuring of mind, emotion, structure and consciousness happening on the planet. So if you pay attention to vibrations that are uncomfortable for you, that put you in a tizzy or a feeling of disequilibrium, you'll be magnifying those places.

It's even more important to structure your reality of consciousness so that it doesn't take from you, but gives to you. Destructuring is a massive energy of taking what is and disassembling it, disintegrating it, which means the energy is returning to the no-thing space. It's time for all of you to rise like the phoenix out of the ashes, and that takes energy. It takes intention, it takes the forward movement of being on the wave of consciousness as it unfolds, and of having your vibration be consistent with that which you are.

As things fall apart around you, choose to excel, continue to expand, and continue to oscillate and vibrate as a master, which means you are non-reactive to the destructuring and coming together so that you support your own integrity. This is really important, because as the foundation of your human technology dissolves, societal structuring no longer stands for anything at all. There is no longer faith in government, no longer faith in religion, no longer faith in education, no longer faith in your health system, no longer faith in marriage, and no longer faith in many of the institutions which seem to represent what is real. And there is going to be grief, emotional response and reaction, and loss.

You can deny those feelings and those realities, and yet what is more advantageous, what supports the advancement of consciousness more directly, is focusing and intentioning on what is desired as outcome, which lifts the whole framework of this intense and very challenging consciousness to a higher level of responsiveness, which releases energy. Raising consciousness releases energy.

So, as you choose to substance yourself from the procreative, co-creative, essential fluids of the universe, you are energized. As you are energized, you put out magnetic waves. You attract energy to you, which is easy and supportive and helpful for manifestation, collaboration, cooperation, unification, for synthesis and symmetry. As you emote the magnetic field and it resonates and returns to you, you magnify that release of energy and culminate it, so that as you unfold it, it supports new growth.

You need energy to support new growth. That's obvious. So in a beautiful way, systems theory works here very dynamically, because its premise is that all life is intelligent. Everything that is being destructured intelligently understands on some level what's going on. It may not always be conscious, but it's always known. All life is co-creating the reality that's being experienced, so even though it looks like a lot is being lost, nothing is being lost that has value, or that is consistent with truth, or that will support new life.

Everyone and everything is co-responsible for what's happening, so there is no blame. As the structure is decomposed it is beneficial for each of you to decide that, fundamentally, the process is one of co-responsiveness. In other words, even if it's falling apart, there is the opportunity to reorient it, to re-establish whatever the pieces are that would serve the growth of the whole in the future.

Systems theory is working for the whole—for total growth, the expansion of union, and the framing of integration through all levels and dimensions. There are experiences where growth—moving the system toward light or more production or more co-creation—is the established new reality. Then the release of energy is prolific, abundant, and absolute. And this is where all of you come into the picture, because this is where the model of the hologram begins to discern its pieces. As each of you picks up where you left off in planning the design, you begin to implement that aspect, and it all starts clicking together.

Ultimately, it's not about what you think you're supposed to do in the future, or how it's going to look, it's about riding the wave of the energy which shows you in a deliberate sense, that if you hold the vibration, it will manifest. It will release energy, it will magnetically bring the people, situations, and resources to you that are necessary and desired and have already been planned to grease the holographic experience. All of those points of foundation then become unified in the experience of life more easily.

This is the new model that we always talk about. When those pieces become unified in the systems of life and are the new reality, then honoring, respecting, upholding, nurturing and unifying is a foundational space of reality. That becomes the normal. What is natural becomes normal as the model changes. Making the choice to stay in the releasing of the energy will be very powerful, because if any of you decide to watch the world destructuring, to try to pick up the pieces and put them back together, if any of you are moved to go

~

Nothing is being lost that has value, or that is consistent with truth, or that will support new life.

~

What is natural becomes normal as the model changes.

~

Loyalty comes up very strongly—
loyalty to parents, friends,
siblings, children, spouses,
significant others,
ideals, techniques,
and
to those vast memories of evolution
which accompany this process.

and work with the old paradigm and in some way try to patch it, you'll find that you are overcome with grief—overcome with the feeling of loss, abandonment, and separation, as you literally are a part of what is being destructured.

You'll go through a time period where you destructure. Vast emptiness will accompany the experience, and as we always say, it's not good or bad, it is the choice that you have to make. Saving souls, supporting life, helping with growth, opening to healing the abandonment and loss and grief, creating places of haven and resource for others, is working with energy that's being released. So it is much more prolific in a very foundational sense now, to support life rather than to support death.

And this does not preclude feeling. It's just that the feeling is accompanied by acceleration instead of deceleration. It's accompanied by knowing, instead of feeling in chaos or out of control. It's fostered in a space that supports integrity rather than de-solution. Loyalty comes up very strongly—loyalty to parents, friends, siblings, children, spouses, significant others, ideals, techniques, and to those vast memories of evolution which accompany this process.

Many of you will be called by those people who would not listen to you five minutes ago, or did not wish to participate in your activities ten minutes ago, or were in some way unaffected by your truth, because their mind controlled their response. And you will be torn between going back and going forward. And we literally want to make a statement to you, that if you go back, you will release energy into what is being decomposed. If you go forward, you will assist in the rebuilding. It does not mean that those people cannot come with you, it means that you choose to go forward instead of going back. That may be literal, it may be figurative, it may be minuscule, it may be absolute. It may be that you will separate from someone because they will not come where you are going. You may have a telephone conversation and say, "This is where I am, and it's safe here. You may come." Then they have the choice. You may have a literal parting of the ways.

It doesn't matter about the intensity, it matters about your direction. This becomes true about where you're living, where you feel is safe or unsafe. The level of consciousness supports your intention in every minute. If you choose one direction, there will be a certain outcome, and if you choose another direction, there will be another outcome. As the foundation recognizes your intention, it becomes easier for you as you go forward in each moment, because you've made that commitment to the intention and you've recognized that this is where you belong, and this is who you are, and this is your choice. And as it's fostered, others will come to be with you in that space, because you are re-working the design so that all of your intention and all of your foundation assist you in this decision. Your understanding about transition, death, loss and separation, will be important at this time—for there will be those who accompany you and those who do not.

And so, the choices that you make must be made from only the vibration of what you really want to create from yourself. Literally, it is the parting of the ways, because others may not decide or choose the same as you. This is the way the definition of truth will be assembled in this time. It's the way in which the foundation of your consciousness will be ordained in this time. And fundamentally, it is for each of you a time of reckoning also, because even though your choices have been made, you will want to stick with them, to stay with them, to affirm them over and over again. Sometimes you will cling to each other, and sometimes you will cling to the past, yet keep your feet in the motion for the future, knowing that you cannot go back.

There is the Bible story about the woman who turned around and was turned to a pillar of salt. Once your direction is set, it needs to be proclaimed and rejoiced in, because you have seen the way, and as way-showers, providing that space of integrity allows you to show the way to others. If you go back, then they will go back with you or stay back there, and it is not the same message.

It is not really about faith—"I have faith that this outcome will be perfect, and I'm going to go forward with what I think I'm supposed to be doing." It's again, as we suggested in the beginning of this experience with you, that you are choosing to align with the vibration of what is being built. And you are fostering relationship to that vibration in such a way that it no longer is absent from your experience, it's absolute in your experience. Each time you make the commitment to reorient to that vibration by going forward to experience it, you also understand that as the foundation is being supported more and more, there's more energy being released. There's more growth going on, there's more affirmation that is attenuated, and it accelerates the consciousness so that it lifts everyone out of those spaces of separation and grief and questioning, and moves the total consciousness into its own frame of being.

Your understanding about transition, death, loss and separation, will be important at this time— for there will be those who accompany you and those who do not.

*As each moment
supports the truth
of the future design of oneness,
people will choose
varied ways
to reclaim their consciousness.*

~

*What you
observe
on the planet
as transformation and transition,
is the foundation becoming unified.*

~

*Earth
that is belief-oriented,
that is separation-oriented,
falls away.*

~

Ultimately, as each moment supports the truth of the future design of oneness, people will choose varied ways to reclaim their consciousness. This may happen on different levels and in different dimensions. They may be in a level of transition, or in an Angelic space, they may be in the astral level assisting on some particular point with whatever or whomever is remaining here, or with those whose choices take them from this planet. Varying dynamics are created. Because you are working with less words and more substance, you will be able to hear, know, see, and feel where these people are, what they're doing, why they're there, and why they chose to go there.

What you observe on the planet as transformation and transition, is the foundation becoming unified. So developing the telepathic process, opening to being rather than thinking and languaging, becomes a very proficient and stabilizing choice because it allows you to know what's going on, to be a part of that destiny, a part of that unfolding, and to organize consciousness so that you are a part of it. You are working through it, and it doesn't impact you the same way that it impacts the people who, for example, are no longer having connection with their presence in the same way.

There will be profound teachership during this process. Literally, every single second becomes packed with stimulus from all levels, all dimensions. It's not about trying to save the world; it's about creating an etheric potential destiny around the world. It's an alternative reality, a way of being in consciousness with light and truth and order, and staying on the Earth at the same time.

So the Earth that is belief-oriented, that is separation-oriented, falls away. This is what many people see in their psychic projections about the energy changes on the planet Earth. Many of you will be assisting to co-create unifications and fields here, where there is a symmetry of the Earth's potential space, which will be foundationed through an experience of choice. The falling away of those levels that no longer serve will solidify this new etheric body of Earth.

We talked about this before at some length in the tape called "The Bridge of Light" (See Appendix). The Earth has great difficulty in maintaining integrity when there is destruction of natural resources and inherent separation and dishonoring of life. When you choose to walk in the light and co-create and cooperate with others, you share resources and make a foundation so that each of the pieces fits together and greases the hologram. Then the choices that you're making to be with the part of consciousness that continues to create and sustain the growth, creates new systems of life.

The Potential for Heaven on Earth

There is now the potential for all life to be exactly in balance in this new etheric potential of Earth—potential for extinct species to return to the etheric potential Earth. So everything that you know about the integration of consciousness and the places through which the experience of oneness is already ordained, can be lived, literally, here as Heaven on Earth.

Yes, at the beginning of 1992 light workers began creating an etheric planet around the Earth; yes, we are going to "save" the planet; yes, we are going to create solutions; yes, we are going to work in systems theory; yes, there will be union of male and female on this planet; yes, there will be interspecies communication so that there's balance and acknowledgment of all forms of life; yes, there is repair of the substantial damage to the etheric level of the Earth's physical and emotional body, and her dynamic body. As each part of the system takes hold, integrates, and correlates, there is born a new dimension of reality.

You are probably very much aware that when you go forward and experience this recognition, that you're going to be in a new Earth. You're going to be in a new light body, and be in new kinds of relationships that vibrate at rates of speed that are not contained in the gravitational fields that you're now aware of. So it's obvious that something's going on here, and that it all is working for the good of the whole, and that it is moving away from structure. It's moving into inherentness, and as it does that, it provides new mechanisms for integration and for solution-based realities. They will be occurring at a time and space where there is aggregation of energy to support that advancement of consciousness.

When this happens the acceleration curve begins to move in such a dynamic fashion that there's no turning back, there is no sitting on the fence. There is no waiting for proof, there is just the opportunity for the advancement of this experience to be profoundly initiated in form. It means that you live from this dimension and you create this dimension as the Earth's natural reality.

This is the formula for the next few years: orienting to nonverbal signals; receiving telepathic messages; ordaining your consciousness

~

So it's obvious that something's going on here, and that it all is working for the good of the whole, and that it is moving away from structure. It's moving into inherentness.

~

*You are beginning
to vibrate energetically, cellularly,
in response to what other people are,
rather than
to what they are saying.*

*What you start getting from people
is their essence.*

in the vibration of mastery; grounding and expanding the field as far as you can, so that your orientation becomes synthesized daily and your presence is affirmed in this new dimension constantly. Where are you getting fed from? Substance. What does substance feed? Substance feeds the etheric. Where do you want to live? In the etheric body of the Earth's potential destiny.

As you make amendment to your constitution and accelerate your field and open your dynamic tension with truth, you change force fields. You literally change dimensions. That is why we encourage the framing of a community that is based on those changing dimensions. And that is why there will be many such communities on the planet, experiencing the profoundness of Heaven on Earth, because it is necessary. So choose to listen more with your body than with your ears, just as if your ears no longer worked. For those of you who have diminished hearing, that's why—you are making choices to hear from the part of you that will be extinct, literally, in some time to come. Not tomorrow, but soon.

You are beginning to vibrate energetically, cellularly, in response to what other people are, rather than to what they are saying. Rather than watching what they are doing, you're beginning to hear them inside your being. The words that come to you from other people's lips are organized from their consciousness and provide you with a capacity to hear what the lips are saying from that organization rather than from the sound. Basically, you're experiencing that the organization is their consciousness, and you're beginning to feel that experience of organization as if the foundation of their being is communicating itself to you from their essence. You begin to feel their essential ingredients, their essential nature, instead of hearing the words. The words are reflected always, of course, from the mental process.

What you start getting from people is their essence. You start going right to the heart, right to the soul, right to the place of the essence, or the essential, rather than spending time deflecting the words, or reflecting them back, or trying to figure out who's listening, or who's not listening, or who's really there and who's not really there. In a very beautiful way this is a short cut, and we really like short cuts! Practice being in the room and communicating in a silent sense, not that you have to be silent, not that you can't ask somebody something if you want to or have to, but in the sense that there doesn't need to be talking.

There can be the experience of being together, and literally beginning to feel the waves that are being ordained between you as communication waves. When you walk into a store, or an experience of some type—a room, office, family room, or your own bedroom—what is the field of communication? What is that wave that comes to meet you and greet you? Become much more aware of what that is, what it sounds like, what it feels like, what its purposeful communication is saying to you. You sharpen and hone those skills of mental telepathy and intuition. Your telepathic process is as clear as the physical acuteness of your five senses.

Eventually you do not need to be in the same room with someone to know what their wave of communication is saying to you. This is going to be very important, because there will be changes in the dynamic structure of the world, and people won't know the conditions of others, or be able to pick up the telephone and have a discussion, because at certain times in the future, they'll be in separate physical locations. Or if you can talk to those significant others, you'll do so briefly, and then not be sure of the outcome, what the person will choose, whether they are on their way, or how they are faring on their journey, or where that might take them. So this is a way to take that wave of communication and stay linked to them, as if you were on the telephone with them.

Ordaining this space within your own capacity by choice now, is very important. It also provides a relationship with your own sensate being. Of course it's wonderful to receive all this input and put the pieces together, and to see how people are doing, and to be in their vehicle with them as they are unfolding their journey. Yes, that's great, and yet what's really going on is that you're sensitizing yourself. You're organizing your own framework so that you no longer feel distant from those you love. You can feel them and open to them as they are making their choices and decisions. You have an ability to affect the outcome, because you can put growth in there, and expansion, and etheric consciousness, and perhaps give them some sound advice, or some very important boost of consciousness, or acceleration of their own dynamic physical structure, to assist them in lifting their vibration in times and places where that might be necessary and strongly advised.

Ways to Sense More Fully

You will refine the skills of relating organism to organism without thought, belief, fear or separation.

This dynamic of communication becomes a wave of union that allows you to be in the wave of love and communication with those you care about all the time. It will be necessary in the next ten years for you to all have these skills finely tuned and honed.

Open your awareness—open the doorways, the gateways, the framework, the paths, osmotically, with all the cells of your body, by opening up your ears to that which is many, many light moons, and light years away. Then experience, "I can hear what no one else can hear. I am in contact with that which does not have present tense, presence in the world. I'm hearing the natural rhythm of the universe. I'm hearing the breath of the Earth. I'm sustaining her rhythms and cycles because I can feel them in the bottoms of my feet. I can hear her creatures speaking to each other without words. I can hear the sounds of laughter of the devas and fairies and gnomes. I can experience the light of truth of the unified field of consciousness in the etheric realm of the Earth's destiny and her etheric potential. I can hear the singing that's going on as all of the psyches raise their vibration to experience subtlety, and begin expressing. I am aware of the levels that are being born into this dimension, that were never here before. I can hear the pre-knowledge, precognitive, pre-original space—the words that are beginning and becoming from the experience of that point—in this dimension. I can hear, I can feel, I can support that there is new integrity. Because I'm aware of it, I can represent it. And as I represent it, it becomes actual."

So listen, open out, stand firm and tall and stable on the Earth, open the bottoms of your feet, receive, acknowledge, expand, choose, and stay in the framework of that foundation as much as possible, so that it's constantly giving you what you need to take the next step.

If you make the commitment to listen from your pores instead of your ears, to see with your eyes closed instead of open, to feel with the auric field instead of the fingertips, to sense and smell and receive from the levels of the invisible and the subtle, you will be born as a creature that has natural capacity to know, in each moment, without restriction or limitation. Perhaps more importantly, you will refine the skills of relating organism to organism without thought, belief, fear or separation.

Practice, first of all with yourself—What field is open? What field is closed? What am I doing? Then practice with each other, one by one, two by two, and three by three, until what you feel is that resonance, and you can feed back to each other, "I sensed this, is this accurate? Send it to me again. Put it into perspective again." You establish realities without having to think about them.

One of the ways to open the visual acuity is the grounding process. One of the ways to work with telepathy and intuition is to be aware, rather than to use the five senses. Close them off by your own choice, so that they don't close off organically. And then you can feel where you are in that spectrum of reception. It is the place of allowing, the place of being in connection with that which is most beautiful and most profound, and which calls the spaces together so that all of those dynamics begin to serve the whole again.

You are then made aware of that which you are to affect. The first step is to make the choice, "I want to have my awareness as finely tuned as possible. I really want to be available to my calling, so that I do not respond from emotion, from reaction to anticipated loss, disaster or separation. What I'm really saying is, 'I'm a vehicle, and as a vehicle I am emotionally balanced and sensitive and yet I am clearly conscious of the fact that I am an instrument. I am not here to change reality as much as I am here to dynamically be a shower of the choices of what realities exist.' "

That's a very important distinction, and one which we recommend that you take to heart. The foundation of your consciousness, as it unfolds, provides a mechanism for the choices of your experience to manifest organically over and over again so that you're always on top of what's going on. You always know what's coming down, what's moving through, and what kind of affirmation is going to be best for you to hold in each moment. Sometimes it will be that you affirm order, and you will go into the center of the body where the matrix is. You breathe down into the soul and feel the fundamental order that you carry as a being of light, and beam that out concentrically—in the spiral circles that happen when you drop the pebble into the pool—which is what you ordain when you go into the center of your being.

So you send out the order wave in a concentric, consciously spiraling clockwise motion, and say, "What I'm to do in this moment is to make as much foundation of order as possible." Or you may be in a situation where you realize that what's needed is a field of energy that can assist in a transporting process, or a transmutation

*I am not here
to change reality
as much as I am here
to dynamically be
a shower of the choices
of what realities exist.*

process, or transformation process. Or that what is needed is a supportive energy—the substance. You send that to someone and support them in substance so they feel safe, nurtured, expansive, or one with nature. In each instance, "This is what I'm being called to, this is what I'm aware of, this is what I'm going to serve through."

Serving the Design With Absolute Trust

Remember that when you serve, you are served. That's the way it works. You are in a communicative link with consciousness, and you begin to know exactly what your course of action is, the actions and frameworks that will most inherently support the whole. If there's a distinction between the whole and a person, what do you choose? That's the sticky wicket. You can always ask for opportunity to digest that consciousness in such a way that as it comes into you, you are shown only that which you are meant to affect, which takes personality and heredity and the familiar out of it, and puts you in contact with the expansiveness of your own soul.

These are going to be very important dynamics, and that's why we're talking about them. It might be easier not to talk about them and say, "We'll just see what happens and do the best we can as it comes down and shakes out. We'll foster it in such a way that we're always on the edge of that wave of being in creation." That's true, that's accurate, that's consistent with the dynamics of your overall choices—and yet your consciousness will also make you aware of things that are happening simultaneously, and you will choose that which your calling indicates is your highest point of resolution.

Always remember, it doesn't mean that the particular person you are aware of, who might on some level want to be assisted, or communicated with, or connected through, isn't going to receive help, isn't going to be okay. This is where your affirmation to be at one with the calling really serves the design. You know that in the process of the overall picture, if you do what you know you are intended to do, there will be resolution on all other levels, and everything will happen according to what's going to grease that hologram. And it's not really as much faith as it is knowing: "This is how this will shake out."

It gives you permission to be the best that you are, to use your intention in such a way that it fosters total recognition of this experience of union, and so that you foster all these paradigms so that they all serve the whole and each other. That is a beautiful and very wise type of reckoning.

There will be fewer and fewer words. There will be less ability to discern by physical means, and more capacity to discern through etheric means, which defines itself in your reality as: the subtle gets the intention. The awareness, the fluidity, the invisible, get the focus. Everything that seems obvious, that's always been obvious, that's loud as a drum and continues to beat, and wants to be heard, and is squeaky, and wants attention, and wants to have the vehicle on some level contained within or defined by the old paradigm, is ignored. This sets up some very interesting dynamics.

We still suggest that you ignore the squeaky wheel, because what you ignore and do not give energy to will be re-solved somehow. It will come back into solution, and have to state its case differently. It will have to come up against its own parameters in a way that will define it for everyone and itself, and therefore give it the opportunity to transform.

If you are in there trying to change it or save it or make it easier, it will not transform because it won't need to. That's why many of you have made choices to move away from those who are constantly squeaky.

Living Essentially With Integrity

Habituation is another thing that will be destructed, so many of you will begin new habits and new ways of experiencing. Your foundation will be ordained from a different rhythm. So this intention for transformation, for carrying the consciousness to a point where it can speak to you directly, is pure magic, it's symmetry, it's lovely. There is no miscommunication—it doesn't matter if Mercury is retrograde. It is synthesizing constantly this reality of truth that cannot be gainsaid.

It's the sense that the foundation is always going to reflect itself, and communicate itself accurately as the organizational capacity of the being which is expressed. By organizational, we mean the part that comes from the essential, so there is no miscommunication or misunderstanding. There's an opportunity for honesty, clarity, resonance, harmony, and balance in ways that organize the system, so that the foundation literally provides its own resolution and its

There will be fewer and fewer words. There will be less ability to discern by physical means, and more capacity to discern through etheric means.

own affirmation. People can say, "Oh, I didn't really mean that," and you know the energy of their body did mean it. You can get into discussions about it, and they can be adamant, "No, I didn't mean that," and you know that it did mean exactly what you are feeling, because you can sense how they are organized inside, how their essence responds in those situations.

Each of you designs your capacity so that you feel the integrity. The beauty of having no words is that you hear what the capacity of creation is imbuing into you and from others to you, and so the levels start merging together—the Hierarchical level, the Source level, the Angelic level, the celestial level, the firmaments, the dimensions, the subtle bodies, all frameworks. They start foundationing over and over again in the same way that you used to hear and discern physical action and movement and words and integrity and energy. Because you're really aware of these subtleties, all the windows and passages open for you to experience total communication with all realms.

When you are in substance, you receive communication from those levels because that's where those levels are sustained. The oneness becomes an inherently beautiful affirmation of truth. What you're about here is solidifying the fields of your energy so that they are equal and balanced and give you the optimal amount of information constantly. You feel as if on every level you are being sustained, on every level you are receiving, and on every level everything that needs to be available is available. Everything that you would wish to have at your fingertips, in terms of skills, capacities, or relationships with being, are available and present.

This means that as you hear from the being, you are more and more present as a being, and the normal ways of communicating fall away to the experience of what is natural. What is natural is that you know everything that's going on all the time, and there's no need to deny it, no need to replace it, no need to in some way change it. Dynamically, when you're in an honest place with total knowing, the truth of all beings is heard, sustained and created through. This establishes a natural order in your world.

That is how the new world relates. That is a very beautiful experience, a gift that you receive from each other, because it's the gift of your purest intent, your deepest integrity and your most absolute space of knowing. It's a gift you exchange as you receive, and there is accuracy to it, so it's quicker.

What you're inherently doing is connecting with the fundamental point of creation as one unit of being, regardless of how many you are, and this is where the absolute integrity of your union can best be lived.

Living as a Master

The Importance of Intention

WE WOULD LIKE TO SPEAK WITH YOU about the field of intention, and how it directly affects the outcome of everything you do and everything that is fostered on your planet. Intention is the wave that the soul initiates from free will. When you make an intention, it is the expression of and characterization of creation as it is unfolding, and you are in a trajectory with that which is fashioned through the wave of thought.

It is important to understand how intentions work, where they come from, and how they will be orchestrated in this coming time, which is different from any time you have ever lived. Time is accelerating at such a rate of speed that it cannot be contained. This is why many times when you try to create something, you either over-shoot or fall short of the mark, because the movement of consciousness is so rapid that unless you are *on the wave* with it, you do not necessarily understand where you are in the process of manifestation, or creation.

Intention is a way in which the wave can be a part of your system and be unified as a consistent field of force. This allows for the experience of oneness *while* one is processing reality, determining outcome, and receiving fulfillment or the solution from the future. It is the way in which you can say, "Yes, I need money now, and I don't have time to work with 'future-future,' " or, "I don't understand how that works and how I can make it happen so that I can experience it rather than just hope it occurs. How can the intention be like a fishing pole reeling in the fish? How can I call it in closer to where I am and feel the actual substance of that which I yearn for? How can I experience having that simultaneous reality be a part of where I am in my design?"

Mastery Mastery Mastery

~

I AM a sacred part
of the ever-expanding pattern of life.
This is my intention, my invocation
and my agreement.

~

Substance Carries the Intention

So as you come to the experience of

"universal process orientation,"

or become conscious beings,

as you look at how you fit

into this big design,

you know you are greasing the wheel.

~

You switch tracks

from human to cosmic consciousness,

and in that moment

substance *becomes your food.*

So you are being fed

by that which feeds

creation itself.

~

Creation works

by filling a need

that no one has yet expressed.

~

So as you come to the experience of "universal process orientation," or become conscious beings, as you look at how you fit into this big design, you know you are greasing the wheel. Everything is interrelated, and you feel capable of living your divinity and destiny now. You switch tracks from human to cosmic consciousness, and in that moment, substance becomes your food. So you are being fed by that which feeds creation itself.

Creation works by filling a need that no one has yet expressed. It means it's ahead of its time, because it has already anticipated what is necessary and provides it, and at the exact moment it provides it, the need is there, and the two come together in a marriage. So it isn't about getting an idea and saying, "I wonder if this is marketable." It's about actualizing the process—placing it in a container of energy supported by and surrounded by substance and having everyone participate in it.

Substance is the food that feeds consciousness and the universe at large. Substance is like air—your breath here. Breathing calls you to life. It holds you and sustains you in the field of life and order.

Substance feeds the dimensions and the firmaments. Substance is fostered from the experience of universal knowledge and comes into this experience through breath.

An intention you might make is, "Substance embodies my essence." Breathe that, feel it, and fill with it. The substance then associates you with the fluids and you ride the wave, which is the future and the present. The consciousness of that intention is bringing you the rhythm and cycle of your own unfolding in connection with what is ready to happen.

Living in substance is feeling fed by something other than the Earth dimension. When one lives by the intention of following the wave of creation and being in substance, then one is charged etherically.

The capacity that you have come here to imbue is brought forth from you. It's elicited—it's not logical, i.e., "We need a restaurant at the corner of 59th St. and Dale Avenue." It's the experience of saying, "This is who I am. This vision has come forth. And this is where it fits into the design. As I hold the picture of it, people will come and actively align with the energy, participating in it because that's the next step."

It is a systems theory approach. Individuals come together as a whole mechanism of response to something that serves everyone, rather than just serving one person. As that foundation honors itself and you are on the wave of intention, what you seek to create, the resources that you need, and the participation of those who will make that possible, all coincide at the same moment. This is the foundation that you have come to work with in this new time. As you unfold each of these moments and bring them together, there is a sense of expectancy—meaning the excitement of knowing that what you are involved in creating is *all* that is possible at that moment. It's like riding the highest wave-crest and seeing where you want to go, because you have the vision to see where you need to be and where you need to end up. You are in a space of consistency and constancy with that which is waiting to be born.

Creation is much like a birth—there are waves you can ride which sustain themselves from substance and require no physical energy. The time is coming when you will not need your physical energy in the same way. The circuits of your body will be working completely from substance, and the physical experience of your electromagnetic fields will be an adjunct to the substance, and not the primary place from which action happens.

Changing from a will-driven muscle to a substance-embodied wave is, conceptually, a movement from masculine to feminine. It is a movement from stamina, drive, practicing, habituation, and training—to receiving, unfolding, enlarging, unifying, and to manifestation through consciousness.

*Changing
from a will-driven muscle
to a substance-embodied wave is,
conceptually,
a movement
from masculine to feminine.*

Immersion

Intention is very important in moving from human to cosmic consciousness, because it actually helps one design a space, a manual, or an instruction booklet for putting the pieces together in order and balance. We recommend the experience of immersion—going into fluid, or substance, and feeling oneself as a fluid base. Put the issues, areas, problems, concerns, worries, and thoughts of your life into the fluid with you so that everything is balanced in the wave of creation and there is nothing on your mind. Let it all go. Live instead in the space of determination, always, in constancy.

When one experiences being in substance or fluid for large

~

*Feeling substance being expressed
is the point of life.*

~

Expression is substance in motion.

~

amounts of time, it is challenging to return to a model where one reacts. It is easier to dissolve and allow and support the resolution that happens once everything comes into the water and settles out. One sees where everything is and how it all comes about. Instead of having the emotional reaction or the trauma of an experience, or to be over the hedge row not knowing which side to land on, or how to get over the hedge row to begin with, one feels the power of the essential being in substance—rising, opening, and expanding. The being is taken care of, the fluid and the substance become an environment for growth, supportive expansion, and nurturance.

Substance is a key if you feel separate from your capacity to create or do not yet experience the fullness and richness of being nurtured and sustained. Substance is the framework through which intention is fostered, because there is already a connection between what holds one in safety in the soul space and the outcome of that in motion.

Expression Is Substance in Motion

Feeling substance being expressed is the point of life. You can have abilities and capabilities, but if you're not expressing them, you will feel less than whole. Expression is substance in motion. As you think about what you intend, it's very important that your intention be aligned with who your expressive nature says you are. That expressive nature might tell you you're an artist, painter, child care worker, carpenter, or a designer of models for future realities and relationships. Whatever that expressive place in you wants to do, it can be aligned with the intention so that substance can bring that experience into being. This is how creation works.

If you were thinking from the linear model, you might say, "I want to be an artist, so I have to take a class, buy supplies, practice," whereas, if you were experiencing the expressiveness of your nature in substance, you could make a picture from pine cones, nuts and needles, and glue them all together, expressing in that substance something that you had never thought of doing before. Whatever your intention is can be supported by the ability to use the tools around you substantively, so that you feel connected to the creation rather than to the normal patterns of your time. You express naturally, which may or may not deal with those supplies, thoughts, and ideas that have been entrained by the culture. As you create from this spontaneous place, you actually feel linked to intention. You're on the wave, and it begins to unfold.

Riding this wave of intention is not based upon what you're thinking or feeling is meant to be manifest. It comes from the substance around you and through you. So it is not about yearning in the sense of, "I think I want to do this, or I've trained for this, or my mother taught me this, or this is where I fit into society." It is from such a deep level of substantiation that it fosters its own coming together. It creates a context through which the foundation of the wave is the impetus. It has very little to do with thought or idea from the level that you're used to living from. That's why, so many times, one is unsure or unclear about how to ride that wave.

The experience of riding this wave is proliferative, expansive. The intention and the coming into substance is a way to stay clearly in alignment with the fulfillment of the design, rather than with any other level of experience. Instead of doing things in the same way, you express creation in ways that have never happened before. It is like creating a piece of music. It is authentic within itself, although it has the same keys, time signatures, and notes that people have used for many millennia. You are simply expanding the context through which creation occurs.

The new models of the future will come from tapping the sources of substance. It has very little to do with what has been, so it is a completely new arena. This is where the excitement, the expectancy, the sense of being fresh, of being collaborative with the nature forces, the elements, and the experience of spirit exhilarate the being.

When you follow the calling there is a flame, a place within you that is charged so dynamically that you need very little food, sleep, companionship, or love in the old ways.

There is a space for you in the world that has your name on it, and things actually move aside and allow your emergence, and respect and honor you. And it isn't about proving it, it's about the vibration of substance making its own place in the world.

You are the substance in expression, and because you're riding the wave, you continually fulfill yourself. When you are one with the God or the Source of creation, which inexorably fulfills itself, you are always fulfilling. So it is a different track from *preparing* to create, from *preparing* to decide what you're going to do. It is about allowing.

The vibrational field of each person will be marked. The fields

Riding this wave of intention is not based upon what you're thinking or feeling is meant to be manifest. It comes from the substance around you and through you.

The intention and the coming into substance is a way to stay clearly in alignment with the fulfillment of the design, rather than with any other level of experience.

There is a space for you in the world that has your name on it, and things actually move aside and allow your emergence, and respect and honor you. And it isn't about proving it, it's about the vibration of substance making its own place in the world.

As this freedom expresses,
there is sensitivity to
being creation
instead of creating something.

~

It's really about
honoring
the essential part of you,
instead of the formed part of you.

~

Substance
does not require anything from you.

~

will be very intense, very obvious, because as *individuals become substance in expression*, they are vehicles through which creation occurs multi-dimensionally. They are absolute. The understanding normally necessary to provide a relationship between one and one's tools or creative frameworks is no longer necessary. Wherever you are, you're spontaneously able to bring forth the expression regardless of what is there with you, which gives you a freedom that before has not marked the experience of humanity as much as it will in the future. As this freedom expresses, there is sensitivity to *being* creation instead of creating something. It's a very different contextual frame. It's really about honoring the essential part of you, instead of the formed part of you.

Instead of formulating a design in your mind and then executing it with your will, you say, "I'm going to draw a picture, write a story, create a garden." You invoke it and call it forth, and in the choice to allow it, creation emerges.

This has to do also with Soul Recognition workshops and classes. As you ride the wave, you never know what will be said or done. Continual co-creative energy is facilitated in each of the mediums that is explored. What it involves is a simultaneously receptive and expressive nature. It means flowing with and having all parts available to you, instead of only some parts.

One of the people who demonstrated this spontaneous, creative capacity to its highest degree was Walter Russell. He decided he wanted to sculpt, or paint, or make a sacred garden, and he just did it. He was not dependent upon his past experience. He delved into creation—think of him taking both hands and immersing those hands in substance, and then integrating substance through different mediums. He and the substance were the same. And this is your objective.

This is about living the experience of no separation. This feeds the moment. It substantiates that which does not require anything from you. It's a free act of creation *to* each of you. The expression is so complete that you feel you are what is happening through you, and yet you are the substance which makes that possible, and then you are also fulfilling the outcome.

Living as a Master

As we speak to you about how you can orient differently with your perception, the fundamental difference that you'll feel, energetically, is in the circuits of your body.

When your circuits are charged with light, creation, substance, and riding this wave to the fulfillment of creation through your expression, the dynamics of your reality shift so markedly that you are unlimited in any capacity and you can do anything. You can take apart an engine you've never seen before and never understood before. Even if you don't know where the parts go, there's a sense of symmetry to it. You can fix plumbing leaks, and nurse children, and foster whatever is needed in the moment. If milk is needed, you produce it. The foundation which you have come to experience as normal is being overturned.

We talk about this time as the Coming Together of the Ages. The veils are now very thin between dimensions, and evolution has stopped, and the spiral, or "slinky," of consciousness has closed in on itself. There is accessibility to every skill or capacity that you, as an individual, have ever mastered in any lifetime. And because of morphic resonance, you are also able to express whatever anyone has opened unto at any time.

The Evolutionary Spiral

Before December 31,1991   After December 31,1991

~

When you are in substance
everything
has purpose,
everything
has a reason for being.

~

Bringing it into substance with you
is a birthing
and allows you to have
the capabilities of its expression.

~

So mastery
is a state of acknowledgment
and a preparation for
instantaneous responsiveness,
rather than a preparation in advance
for something that we don't know
the timing of.

~

We are crossing over from a lineage of, "This is my karma, this is my experience, this is what I understand," to, "I am a part of the whole, and anything that has ever been created by the whole, or will be created by the whole, is accessible to me." This not only honors the divinity, opens memory, and elicits innate wisdom, it is also mastery. Mastery is a way in which the wave of substance and the wave of creation are always available to you.

Mastery is the space where no containment is possible. When you wake up in the morning, you look at the day as if it is a masterpiece waiting to be created. Whatever comes through the proliferative force of your life field can be implemented in form. You can build buildings even if you've never built buildings. You can know sacred geometry and geomancy by honoring the place of all things. Then you remember where the sacred geometry originated, how it was used, and what its purpose is.

When you are in substance everything has purpose, everything has a reason for being. When you walk in the forest, you are able to determine the interrelationship between all the points of reality that exist in that forest, and you can replicate this and represent it. You can take parameters of reality and study them, comprehending them completely—not because you've learned them step by step (which is the linear way) but because you have made the total consciousness of that space available to you with the intention to substantiate it. Bringing it into substance with you is a birthing and allows you to have the capabilities of its expression.

The fundamental message about intention is to provide you with a linking system whereby creation is constantly present with you, rather than something that you're waiting for. Intention is a wave that has already completed itself, and because it is completing in substance, you can organize and express the details in a natural, spontaneous way.

Mastery is the experience of total recall and total orientation to being, cellularly. There are no edges to mastery—no places forbidden. One has the capacity to be all, because the capacity from all has already been received. So mastery is a state of acknowledgment and a preparation for instantaneous responsiveness, rather than a preparation in advance for something that we don't know the timing of.

Understanding that mastery provides you with all capabilities at once is an organizational knowing. Stepping into it is the easiest way to work with it.

Immersing in the Fluids
An Exercise

Step into the fluid. Immerse yourself in a pool of water that you might see as a beautiful forest stream coming together in a place where the water deepens. Immerse yourself in it. Physically experience this in a hot tub or bath tub of warm water, or just close your eyes and visualize being in water. Immersing into the space of substance, with the intention of surrounding your essence and body with viable fluid, provides you with a pathway to ride the wave. This experience provides you with a conscious understanding of where you are in relationship to creation. When you're sitting in the pool you realize, "I *am* creation." This is how creation functions; it supports and surrounds everything constantly.

Instead of the linear process of thinking you have to wait for something, or that something is going to come to you at a certain point of readiness, you approve of *being ready* by stepping into the pool. This takes you through the threshold of your own consciousness into that which has been ordained for you.

Mastery is ordained, and each of you has been ordained into mastery. By stepping into the pool, you actualize, acknowledge, accord, and validate that the readiness is now. Each moment you nurture this experience, the reality becomes more strong.

The wave is underneath you and moving from you into the future at the same time. And it is receiving itself, receiving its flow back from that future. You're moving toward the future, and yet the wave that you're riding comes from the future. So as you experience this fluid movement, you begin to feel as if you're in the womb again, as if you're a part of what's being created, and yet the fluid is where creation is happening also.

~

*You're moving toward the future,
and yet
the wave that you're riding
comes from the future.*

~

*When you're
in the levels of the substance,
your physical, emotional,
mental, and spiritual bodies
come together
and vibrate or oscillate
at the same rate of speed.*

~

*As this substance of fluid is unfolding
you don't have to go anywhere,
learn anything,
remember anything,
because it's all* present.

~

*You are taking your consciousness
to a place where it is being fed.*

~

You sustain yourself in the experience of being accepted, of already belonging. This experience of belonging is very important because many people feel they do not belong here. Again, you do not feel as though you are waiting for something. If on any level you're waiting for anything, it's procrastinating rather than bringing it in, procrastinating instead of creating. When you immerse yourself in the fluids, you are in totality—whatever you've been waiting for just pops up to the surface. You actually initiate and activate your system so that you foster a whole new reality.

When you're in the levels of the substance, your physical, emotional, mental, and spiritual bodies come together and vibrate or oscillate at the same rate of speed. When you are in an oscillatory wave, like the fluid, where all the vibrational parts of you are synthesized and balanced, there is no disease because dis-ease means, basically, that the energy levels are vibrating at different rates of speed.

Another way of fostering this absoluteness is to imagine that all parts of you are vibrating consistently at the same rate of speed as your creative consciousness. As this substance of fluid is unfolding you don't have to go anywhere, learn anything, remember anything, because it's all present.

When you're lying in the pool, all your cellular frameworks, levels, and frequencies are attuned to the experience of mastery, oneness, and creative substance. Not only do you feel nurtured, but everything in this cellular and organic process, even the DNA itself, is reminded, refreshed, renewed, and revitalized with the energy of the fluid. Cellular receptivity happens most proficiently and most easily in the fluid. When you are cellularly bathed in the absolute level of creation, the distinctions which come from thought and emotions, and which may ordain certain patterns—like loss of hearing, loss of balance, loss of integrity of tissue and tone, and all the things people are exercising and running around trying to repair—aging, chronic fatigue, or whatever—are *reversed*. You are taking your consciousness to a place where it is being fed. The spiritual component of each cell (every cell has a spiritual, mental, emotional, and physical component) is activated. This is why people meditate, do processes together, go to church together, or have dinner together, because they are bathing their cells in a certain frequency.

You go into substance and move your levels so that your foundation feels supported, your levels activate on a frequency according to the level of substance that's present. So it's like a transfusion. When you transfuse, you receive the absolute sense of integrity that goes with belonging—cellularly—which you may not understand initially. All of this is about subtle bodies as well as physical, emotional, and mental bodies. It's about taking the energy of the physical to a dynamic where it can be charged by the metaphysical, and where the energy system can be realigned naturally.

The fluids are a threshold for the advancement of consciousness—the advancement of proliferative energy. So people will run faster and jump farther. They will have more stamina and more conscious awareness of what's going on in their bodies, much like yoga, where spirit and breath move energy into the muscles. Any physical experience becomes differently oriented when it is fostered from substance, because substance is a natural, fluid space and therefore has no boundaries. So you can literally move a couch by yourself. You can ordain any reality you want, because what are you doing? You are becoming one with everything that is in that environment, and the experience is a combined effort. The couch helps you move it. You don't have to do it to the couch.

Forming Agreements With the Kingdoms

You experience communication and agreement with all life—material and immaterial, all kingdoms. And those agreements are set and accorded. When you want to accord something for a particular purpose, and your intention is felt through substance, the foundation becomes available to you for that experience to happen. For example, if you want to walk on water—you talk to the cells, the molecules of the water, and say, "My intention is to unify with your essence. This is my purpose, this is what I want to do." Then the water will change its consistency to support the movement of your feet upon its surface. It's an agreement between you and the water. Much of what happens as you ordain your life system through substance is that you make life agreements. Life becomes sacred. And when you spend time in substance, you find it becomes vital to you to stay connected. It is vital for you to support whatever activities open out wholeness unto itself.

It becomes a knowing then, rather than asking yourself if it's going to work, or if you're strong enough to do it, or light enough to

~

Any physical experience becomes differently oriented when it is fostered from substance, because substance is a natural, fluid space and therefore has no boundaries.

~

Life becomes sacred.

~

And when you spend time in substance, you find it becomes vital to you to stay connected.

~

walk on water, or if you have enough courage. These questions would be asked from old linear thoughts. Once you're in the environment of union between substance and form, agreements are made from such a deep space that the questions cease to be there. Questions are only there when you start, to lead you to the answers.

In the linear, polarity initiates movement. When one is in substance, the answers are provided continually and questions aren't needed. Because there is no separation in space, there doesn't need to be polarity to initiate movement.

Change is usually initiated because something needs to be attained, whereas in the substantive space the agreement is already there, it's already attained. It's allowed. So creation then is the place where the inherent union is opened out from, expressed into, actualized and manifested from and into. As you enter into this field, you experience that there are no more questions about how. That's when you and the outcome are the same.

This takes time out of your equations. When you keep all the steps of order that you need to create something, and allow the communion and agreement to be intact—upheld and nurtured by the experience—time is unnecessary because you have kept the order of being intact.

It can be like a lasso, where you pull all the steps closer and closer together. You're not seeking them, or trying to find out what the steps are—you're in an environment of completion when you start. That's what substance assures you of—that it will nurture the outcome. And this is where miracle happens. The more miracles that happen, the more consciousness will change on the planet, and the critical mass will build to support the experience of miracle. You are in the wave of intention, and the result is miraculous!

Staying Constant

Holding the space is also of critical importance. The agreement is that you will stay as stable and as intentioned as the universe is staying. Sometimes things get disrupted because people change their minds. Have you ever had the experience of affirming that you're going to receive a certain amount of money by a certain date, or a certain job offer by a certain time, or make a deadline? As that time comes and goes, you say, "Well, it didn't happen, so I must have

In the linear,
polarity initiates movement.
When one is in substance,
the answers
are provided continually
and questions aren't needed.

That's
what substance assures you of
—that it will nurture the outcome.
And this is where miracle happens.
The more miracles that happen,
the more consciousness will change
on the planet.

done something wrong, or the universe doesn't really work that way, or I wasn't really heard, or something was out of kilter, or maybe I didn't affirm enough." And what really happened energetically is that there was a wavering in your intention, because intention is based on getting a certain result, and you did not forge that agreement prior to setting the date. It's as if you are all by yourself making up your mind, and the agreement that could be substantiated in the universe is not taken into account. When people stay alone while going through these paces, they have a lack of faith in their ability to create certain things. It can get a bit hairy, because each person yearns for that which is the calling, and yet many times does not know how to manifest the calling in reality.

Making an agreement, holding the container, and staying in substance to feel the foundation move through you, sets it, holds it steady. If you have a doubt, at that moment, say, "Oh, the doubt indicates that on some level I am changing the agreement, questioning it, or that I'm not quite sure of it." So doubt or questions in the beginning, when you are practicing and moving through immersion, mean that the immersion process might want to go deeper, be clearer, and more agreed upon. So you put your energy back into it. When you're starting a company, you don't deplete all your assets; you put your assets back into the company to help it grow. The same thing happens in the immersion process—you put energy back into immersion when you want to grow. You do not hedge your bets and say, "I don't know if it's going to work. Maybe I should try another alternative while I've got this going, just in case it doesn't happen." You become, instead, a part of the system that's creating what is intended. That's the secret. That's the key to it. If you still see yourself as separate from it on some level, then you'll realize that you thought you made an agreement, but you really didn't.

It's about an absolute commitment to agree to sustain yourself and the ecosystem that you're in as viably as you can all the time. So your presence is absolute in that space. That's why we spoke to you about presence, because if you put your fullness into this, make a clear agreement and foster a reality that is consistent with your creative capacity, then it's a sure thing. The intention is the idea that your level of commitment is the wave of life itself. You're not just putting in that idea, i.e., "I want to have X by X time." You intend: "I am the wave. I am the creative moment. I am the system through which the substance is always infused. I am participating in the

I am the wave.
I am the creative moment.
I am the system through which the substance is always infused.
I am participating in the viable, creative means through which this universe is emerging.

*Expectancy
is not to expect a certain result.
Expectancy
is being on the edge of knowing
what is about to happen.*

~

*This is the super-human
coming into super-consciousness
and living from
absolutely viable
means of support
that nobody can see,
and that are nurtured
in each moment.
The condition of being normal
becomes
an unconditional space of naturalness.*

viable, creative means through which this universe is emerging."

Again, it's not, "I want this by this date," it's (as a part of the total system), "How have I determined that my place is going to be lived?" And then of course, not really knowing that, you allow yourself to be immersed in the substance, which provides you with a way of actually balancing all your if's, and's, but's, how's, when's, why's, and where's. It all comes out in the wash, as they say. As it is flowing through you, you get it.

You may not get it when you start. You get it when you're in the process of being immersed. And then as it flows out from you, at no point do you stop and analyze, "I can feel that I'm creating now, what's my medium going to be? Should it be chalks, or acrylics, or oils, or pastels, or whatever?" What it's about, when you're in that expressive moment, is to stay in that space of substance rather than taking what is emerging and designing it from your mind.

At each step of the way it's a commitment, and an agreement to stay immersed. The first few times you do this, you may find you're jumping out of the wave or out of the river, out of the pool onto the shore, and looking back and saying, "What's going on, what's happening, where am I, is anything going on?" Then you realize, "I just stepped out of the pool, and now I'm qualifying everything, I'm quantifying everything, I'm defining everything, I'm analyzing everything, and I'm feeling lost as if I don't belong anymore, as if I'm in it alone, as if I have to do it by myself, as if I don't have enough money, time, energy," or whatever it is.

Whenever those thoughts come up, you are not being nurtured by substance because you're in a different place, that's all. So you jump back in the pool. Proliferation starts to happen!

Expectancy is not to expect a certain result. Expectancy is being on the edge of knowing what is about to happen.

And so you're always on the edge of the blade of the sword of truth, always experiencing that the foundation you live from is supportive of you completely and entirely—with no conditions. This is unconditional love, unconditional receiving, unconditional creation, unconditional mastery.

This is the super-human coming into super-consciousness and living from absolutely viable means of support that nobody can see, and that are nurtured in each moment. The condition of being normal becomes an unconditional space of naturalness.

As the system advances, you are in a sacred place of balance between male and female, between what gets created and expressed in form, and what is the invisible, nurturing space that provides the conditions for this to occur. This unconditional place is where each of you will be living your life in the future. That's what you're hanging around for, and why you made the commitment to come back and live through what looks like chaos. You will support new models that will improve the condition of humanity in terms of happiness, comfort, intention, and invocation. What gets invoked? What has value? What is paid attention to? In the systems of creation, only those aspects and experiences which foster life are invoked.

The Continual Choice

Each of you has a choice continually about making this agreement. To make the agreement unconditionally is our suggestion, so that you're putting apples and apples together, and meeting the universe where it wants to meet you.

The Earth has agreed to nurture and sustain your physical form, to give you a place to walk, to give you resources to eat and drink from, find shelter from, warmth from. The universe has supported you by agreeing to nurture your essence, to nurture your invincibility, your creativity, your divinity, the space of oneness with all things—spiritual union.

So if you look to earthly things for spiritual union (and that of course includes other people) you will come up short, because spiritual union doesn't come from other people. You can experience spiritual union with other people, but it isn't coming from other people. That's the distinction. So when you come into immersion you really grasp that if you expect something from your life, you will find disappointment. If you live on the edge of expectancy, you will receive unconditionally.

When you understand these dynamics from a literal perspective, knowing *what exists* where, then your natural evolutionary step is to know where to go for what you want, where to tap to receive that unconditional space. You don't go to people for unconditionality, you go to spirit for unconditionality. You go to humanity for companionship, and for the walking together now that supports human exchange, hopefully, in a more natural way than ever before.

Until everyone is immersed—until everyone is coming from that

This unconditional place is where each of you will be living your life in the future.

You don't go to people for unconditionality, you go to spirit for unconditionality.

Until everyone is immersed —until everyone is coming from that same space of knowing, oneness as you know it is literally an ideal. Once everyone comes from that level of unconditionality—then oneness is the experience.

same space of knowing, oneness as you know it is literally an ideal. Once everyone comes from that level of unconditionality—then oneness is the experience.

Statement of Intention

Our recommendation is to make the intention to ride the wave of your own creative expression in substance every moment, proliferating your own space of being. Expressing yourself as fully as possible, in whatever system you find yourself, for the highest good of all concerned, for the good of all, in all time and from all time. And in those moments you will receive, unconditionally, the consciousness through which this expression will work.

It happens as soon as you feel yourself in immersion—as soon as the water and fluid and substance surround you. This is where you can relax, be fed, where you can know your true essence. It's like being in a beautiful pool, and you realize, all of a sudden, that you're in motion, and going toward the world. When you're going toward the world and you stay in that motion—or that wave—the next steps happen *from* you. Instead of thinking about what those next steps should be, and jumping out of the pool, wondering what you should do next, you stay in the pool and the expression comes naturally from you. Agreement is made with each new biosphere or ecosystem or environment in which you find yourself.

So instead of thinking about the results you want before you go into immersion, go into immersion and *allow the expression to come from you.* You will find yourself in the place where the agreement has been fostered, and you will experience the agreement, and express through that agreement. The foundation is then literally made forever. You always have availability to that dimension. That's how you learn about force fields, biospheres, ecosystems, environments, interspecies communication, creativity, being creation, proliferating energy where there is none, and about how you call up energy from the Earth to assist you. Because when you're walking the Earth, when you're in the situations that require something of the substance, the substance knows it. And that's why you're there in the first place.

It's the agreement of your presence that fosters the result. You don't have to know anything or do anything for that to happen. You only need to be fully present. The agreement has already been made,

So instead of thinking about the results you want before you go into immersion, go into immersion and allow the expression to come from you.

Because when you're walking the Earth, when you're in the situations that require something of the substance, the substance knows it. And that's why you're there in the first place.

literally, or we couldn't say this to you. Because if you jump into the fields of the fluids right now, we're going to have to be backing this up by saying that you'll find whatever it is that the agreement has been made with, and it's already waiting there for you. You're really not waiting for it; it's waiting for you. As you make these choices and shifts in perspective, the foundation is given to you so you end up saying, "Why didn't I ever do this before? Why didn't I get this before? This is very simple."

Step by step, honor your own being. Intention, foster, support, receive, and be fully present—make agreements, stay expressive, open out, and see what happens. You can recap at night, just by way of seeing your progress. "What did I do for the last twenty-four hours? What agreements must I have made to be able to do these new and very natural things? Where am I now in that process?" You can look retrospectively at the last day or week and see how it is emerging. Yet when you begin the next morning, you're just in the fluid, and not trying to discern how your progress is advancing, because that would take you out of the fluidity.

Know there are patterns that you can adapt to serve you in this—ways you can foster each reality. Know that fundamentally what gets provided for you is a path, and once you look around and say, "Where was I?" you say, "Oh, yes, it's a path. Now I see the coincidence between these things. I see how this was happening for me in a spontaneous way. And it was because I was present in that moment, and the fluids were there with me. I was one with everything. Now I fully and truly grasp that my invocation has brought me here—my agreement to be a sacred part of the ever-expanding pattern of life."

That is your intention, your invocation, and your agreement. When you feel that within your being, it is accorded you in the twinkling of an eye. And that is written; that will be the experience; and that is also natural. If you were never taught to be afraid, never told there were limits on what you could do, this *would* be your natural way of being. So you are returning to naturalness. Commitment, agreement, intention, invocation, sacredness, movement, substance, flowing, essence, fluid—it is all the same. It is creation in expression.

In the truest words, that is why you have come here. And that is Heaven on Earth. We invite you to participate fully in the substance—to invoke it—to make life sacred here—and to make mastery the normal way of being.

~

It's the agreement of your presence
that fosters the result.
You don't have to know anything
or do anything for that to happen.
You only need to be fully present.

~

My agreement is to be
a sacred part
of the ever-expanding pattern of life.

~

Afterword
From The Ones With No Names

PREPARE FOR THE EVENTUALITY THAT YOU WILL BE A SACRED PLACE for the world. Diligently see everyone and everything as light. Please see only that they are light. Do not worry about if they are all light, or how much they have, or what is missing—for what you focus on will magnify.

When humanity remembers that it is light, and when you remember that you are light, dichotomy stops. When you vibrate in the frequency of light, truth happens, order happens, judgment stops, separation stops. The main reason to believe only in light, is that it brings you to a vibration, and there is no time in vibration.

There is no-thing but light. And when you allow that, no-thing matters. You can forgive, you can trust, you are safe, you are in touch with your soul, you are re-Sourcing from the universe, you are honoring yourself, and then relating from that space of sacred marriage. There is no need to defend or justify—it is simple and easy. It is the natural way of being.

The most profound action that you can take in your life now regarding the future, is to make children available to your life, and be sure that they remember that they are light; that you are creating ritual with them from birth about their light nature, as in the birthing chapter of *I Remember Union* (See Appendix).

If you have a question that we have not specifically addressed, you already know the answer. Stop a moment and remember that the answer and the question are the same points, existing at opposite ends of the time line and yet, when there is no time, they are the same. The answer is giving you the question because it is time for you to live that answer. When you decide that you know, the answer is your guide to the experience of union.

Know that we are loving you very much and that we pledge for you our presence in each moment of your unfolding, now and always.

We give for you our blessings, and say for you that
You Are Blessed.
You Are Blessed.
You Are Blessed.

Appendices

Aggregation

YOUR HOLOGRAPHIC SELF IS THE AGGREGATION OF ALL the coordinates of your total self through all time, and can help you access dynamics to unify all aspects of yourself and bring your future into the now. Aggregation offers a unique way to put your pieces together and solidify your potential. The following is excerpted from a reading on January 6, 1995. Our thanks for permission to include it in our manual.

We suggest that you foster a relationship with yourself which is designed from the future, yet has accordance with this time—a relationship where the pieces of your life, your future, your design, the clarity, the cosmic energy and the original design of what you came to do, actually begin to relate to each other and develop a system, and where all of these dynamics are available simultaneously. They become interchangeable, so that the foundation that you're carrying in your body, the psychic energy that you carry around your envelope of consciousness, and the cosmic connection, can establish congruently, can aggregate and fit together so they don't come apart again.

You can work from a creative capacity which is very deep and clear, so that you look constantly at the world without filters on it. You see the design as it's meant to be lived, the function and purpose of all actions that are given to you. You begin to function as if you are a delegate of the cosmic in form.

All that you bring clarifies itself, brings itself together and fulfills itself directly. You find a sensitivity that functions through your life in so much detail, that you begin to see your future clearly, day by day. You see the rules which people play by in your life to steadfastly bring you into the experience of rapport and relationship. You bring together an ultimate sense of knowing where things belong—knowing how to put them into place—knowing what the foundation is about, sensing the deliberation of your own consciousness, and putting that into such a framework that you organize the understanding that comes with knowing, and with relationship. Correlation, core-relation—is putting things into relationship from the core, developing the capacity to see how they come together and maintain their integrity to present a picture or a reality. Understanding these processes is necessary for your life, your design, your purpose, and the fulfillment of this holographic process.

Organize a design that simplifies your relationship with your calling, and puts together the dynamics so that it's like a puzzle. You have all the pieces and you can see their colors, the design, what belongs to what, and what belongs where.

Assembling the Pieces

We would recommend an exercise called aggregation. Begin by assembling small pieces of paper, magnets, and a magnetic board. Write your dreams, ideas, visions, what you think about, the inklings you have, the yearnings, the dreams, and your longings (from the first time you can remember having a longing) on the small pieces of paper. Put all the pieces of paper together in a movable kind of switchboard operation, moving things around on your magnetic board.

Decide that you're looking at your total consciousness, your holographic self, as you sit at the board, and that you want to support this self, open out to it, and make a foundation from the hologram. Structure a relationship with your psyche that's absolutely dynamic, that becomes your focus, the most critical part of your consciousness. You'll get information and you can organize it and bring it in, so that the puzzle pieces fit. You're taking the ideas and the pieces of paper that you write those ideas down on, and beginning to see the correlations—core-relations clearly. As each of these areas comes together, you see where they fit in the bigger picture. So this is an exercise to collaborate with, collect, and unify the pieces of this design. You can bring them together so that you begin trusting this process as a way to prepare for your life on a daily basis.

In the beginning you get the bigger pictures, then the bigger picture comes in closer. As you bring it closer, you see how to create the larger, so it's as if you take the circle in its concentric wave, and begin with the biggest circle. You get the outer periphery first, then you start getting the inner dimension, then you go back out to the periphery.

You not only can know the future but can see the correlation between everything that is dynamically important for you to know, because your choice is to act from total knowing. You act from a place inside that doesn't have separate considerations, doesn't take things out of a formula, but rather puts them together, synthesizes them, organizes them and puts them into place.

As you begin to put together the ideas, inklings, dreams, thoughts, and processes of your life, you also begin to access resources. This is a most satisfying process, because when all of the dynamics that are at play in your consciousness begin to aggregate, they come together and solve their puzzle. They appear together as if they are one picture, and you know the complete and total relationship between those places and points and people and ideas. The resources to create all your projects—the actual money, ideas, commitments, connections, and fulfillments—will come in right behind that foundation. The universe will speak to you about the design and how it will be created, and the resources then appear.

Open yourself to a magnification of your intention. When you magnify it through the universe, you go out to the periphery, then you bring it back to yourself, and then you go back out, and then you bring it back to yourself, and you then go back out. You are amplifying ideas, sending out the vibration, creating a charge of consciousness and putting pieces into perspective. They become connected and unified and organize themselves so that you simplify your life, simplify creation, and place yourself in a pivotal point where you can orchestrate this creation.

You're calling together a framework so that all the pieces fit, and all of the pieces are magnetically attracted, and you play it on the board first. You put it together so that there is no more separation in any of the context. It's aggregating the whole, or total, consciousness in such a way that it doesn't have any boundaries.

The basic model is union. So as you create a system where the aggregation becomes the experience of truth, you see that this is the wave of the future, this is where the models are going to come from. You have application in every dimension. If we make this whole program a dynamic way in which all the levels can be seen, understood, integrated, collated and then worked from, the resources appear spontaneously. If you get all your pieces or your ducks in a row, then you get to play in the fields of order in a way that puts the position of consciousness together and allows it to feed the cellular and the cosmic—where the resources come from. As you look at the experience that's coming in front of you, a great deal of excitement is generated because the energy of that foundation becomes literal, and it opens out to its own affiliation. The dynamics begin to shift and change around you, yet the pattern stays constant, so you can plug in the dynamics to the pattern and have all of the frameworks assisting each other in their actualization.

Instead of trying to create from a linear model, where nobody knows how to "do" the future, you're basing this on the hologram, where all the pieces want to serve all the other pieces. The foundation really wants to come together and be aggregated, and dynamically wants to serve the outcome.

What fulfills itself through your life in this particular instance is the experience of being validated. As you find ways to accomplish the impossible, you recognize immediately that when you live from the hologram, you express your total consciousness.

Aggregating goes on even when you're unconscious about it as long as you're holding this framework of the above and the below in an integrous position. The holographic dynamics are supporting you while you do your Earth work—while you make your bed, while you do whatever you do—this foundation of support from what is being aggregated is building inside you. You can feel that it's not what you're doing, it's the container that you're carrying—it's the knowing you have that this foundation you've worked from is continually building, systematically being organized, and supporting itself.

You learn to find the bridges where all these dynamics are serving each other and where fulfillment comes for you. There's nothing in you creating set-up situations, or creating delays. Whatever you are interested in is there, being evoked, being responded to, organically, and the response is instantaneous.

For that to happen, three things are necessary:

1• you have an intention;
2• you maintain the vibration;
3• you focus on the outcome.

The outcome and the vibration that you are in and are maintaining are the above and the below being consistent, and the intention is for the hologram to manifest through you immediately, distinctly, succinctly, clearly and simultaneously. If you have the intention, the vibration, and the manifestation all at the same frequency, manifestation is instantaneous. And that's the secret.

This will bring you the feeling that you have finished the work of the material. Now this is a very important part of the puzzle. Until you feel you have actually finished the material work, there is a distinct separation between what you manifest, what you are living, and what you want. So remember that part of the affirmation that you say, part of the intention that you bring in, and part of the field of energy you vibrate with is that your material work is finished, that manifestation is no longer material work. It's no longer that you do X amount of work and you get X amount of dollars. It's a different mindset, a different way of approaching it, and a different vibrational responsiveness materially.

When you think that way, you separate the material world from the resources of the universe, make a circle, and cordon yourself off from the universe. So when you create this magnetic board, you actually put the pieces of your reference system together so that you create a deliberate union and cease to have the old kinds of thoughts. The manifestation part becomes the aggregation system rather than a linear system of push and pull. I do this, I get this back.

So you stop having the direct connection between work and money, and begin spiraling through an organizational content and context that has to do with the re-Sourcing of the universe. You create a literal union of time and space, and put that together and organize a system in which relationship, manifestation, resources, health, anything, can be manifest immediately. What you really want to do, is get sections of consciousness and get them onto the same board.

You have an intention for your life. What does the vibration of that intention feel like? Bring that vibration into the body, and in your cells become the vibration of the intention. Then feel yourself moving out into the "future," seeing what it looks like when it's done. Actually have the outcome vibrate at the same rate of speed as the other two coordinates, and then bring them together, systematically so that they become the same, regardless of when we're thinking about—today, tomorrow, five years from now, ten years from now, etc.

This is the way the holographic design gets lived. This is the way we consolidate two thousand years into twenty-one. This is the way we function so that the foundation lives itself over and over again. It's also the way that the foundation of life becomes organized differently than from the mind.

Regardless of what shows up on your holographic screen, it will be earmarked vibrationally to show itself to you in terms of your intention, so it will actually take a construct that was made many millions of years ago, and it will say, "This is the construct and in this twentieth century life this is your vibrational intention, so we'll set this together. We'll put this into focus, and frame it so that it can express itself to you in this language, can show itself to you in this picture, can show up in this dream." You can actually receive input from parts of yourself that you don't speak the same language with or have the same orientation with, yet are in your vibrational field.

Aggregation is the way union fits together through all the pieces of individual psyches and collective consciousness. You literally receive your instruction manual. You can specifically design, clarify, and unify through all the different projects you set into motion. At least once a week say, "I want to look at all my projects, and see how they take me to a higher level. I want to see how they fit and dove-tail together, and what they're trying to tell me about my next step." Go in and out from the cosmic point to the personal point, and back to the cosmic point. The faster you do that, the greater the growth will be, the faster the results will happen, and the easier will be the process of transformation. You can say to yourself literally, every day, "I know what is being created and sustained here. I can challenge myself if I want to create higher, deeper, broader results."

As you aggregate your consciousness, the pieces come together and are brought into your present experience, bringing you the totality of what is and what is possible with no unknown areas—nothing left to chance. The aggregation process unifies all aspects of your being, and provides a doorway to your fullest expression and knowing.

The Birthing

From

I Remember Union: *The Story of Mary Magdalena*
by Flo Aeveia Magdalena

I rode swiftly, urging Saschai onward into the cool, damp darkness of the midnight sky, for I heard the calling in my mind and answered it. There was one, a woman, coming into her time, and I must be there to assist her. The cycles and the rhythms of her birthing were unbalanced, and the body and the soul of the unborn child were, as yet, disconnected. If there was no one to bond the spirit to the body at birth, the soul would have no grounding place and would bind to the mother and to the patterns of man, and the beliefs of fear and judgement. This was a special soul, one who would help to lead the people after I had gone, and it had been appointed that I attend it. I would teach it the ways of the Earth and reinforce the pathways of its calling, and that was why I must assist in its coming forth. I was almost there. I could feel the energy of the coming, calling me forward.

When I arrived, I took my pack form Saschai and left her to graze, knocking upon the door frame of the small home before me. The mother answered the knock, not appearing surprised to see me, relieved at my presence. She remarked that she was alone now. Her man, a shepherd, had gone with his flock, and she said it was good that I was there to be with her. She was older and seasoned, her face rich with experience and tempered with time, and this was her first birthing.

She invited me within and we sat in the way of women. I listened to her passage. She told me of the days of her life and the ways of her learnings, and I was aware of her fears and her strengthenings.

After a time she relaxed, telling me of her dreams, and then finally, of her saddenings. At times we laughed together, but always quietly and softly, as if honoring the presence of the unborn child through the whispers of our caring.

And after a time, when I knew that she was ready to listen to me, I told her of why I had come. I reached within me to the core of my memory and began to speak: "There is a place called the Hierarchy where there is no hatred or fear or judgement, the place of the Source, from which all souls are born. The truth is born with us from this space also; the truth of who we are and where we are from and why we have come here to learn. But we forget this. When we are born on Earth, if those who birth us do not tell us of this truth, we do not remember it. And therefore an amnesia is born and we feel separation from the truth and from the Gods."

"The ways of humankind, the greed, the fear, and the judgement, are because we do not remember that we are all from the same place, that we are all the same. The forgetting causes pain and then, after a time, the pain is expected. When the children are born, they are taught that the pain is a part of life, and that the separation is a part of life, and the competition and the fear are a part of life. And then, sometimes, there are souls born who come to the Earth to help the people remember the truth. Your child is such a one."

I paused a moment and let the words stand between us, giving her time to take in what I had said. After a moment, I continued: "Your child will be a girl. She will remember what the people have forgotten and will teach them. She brings hope and will speak to them of the truth and the oneness which they seek. She will remember that she is one with the Gods and will act as such, healing and standing as a guide to the people on their inner journey. She will help the people remember that they are divine, that they are light, and that they come from the truth and will return to the truth."

I stopped my speaking and rose to add wood to the fire. Then I moved the water to the heat and began preparing some steepened brew. I did so to give her time, for the tears were standing as droplets unshed in her eyes, and her memory was stirring, but not yet ripe. "Why do you tell me this?" she asked.

"I tell you this because of the child," I answered. "As she is born, it is important that she remain at one with the Hierarchy and the Earth at the same time. This will help her remember." I paused and then continued. "During her first years it will be necessary to teach her and to remind her so that she knows her calling and remembers who she is and what she has come to do."

She waited, as if weighing her words before she spoke, "I am seasoned, as you know," she said. "I have wondered for these months of my confinement why, now, I would conceive to bear a child. My husband and I, for many years, have had no life between us, and now . . ." She paused, looking away from my eyes, and then, after a while, meeting them again. "Is it so?" she asked.

I heard the unspoken questions between us. She wanted to know if her destiny was tied to the unborn child and if bearing her would help to bring a change in the ways of the world. She asked me if the child was her contribution to the unity of which I had just spoken and if she could find this unity through the passage of her calling into motherhood. She asked the question each mother asks silently before that moment of birthing. "Can what I now create bring the love and unity I have sought but been unable to find? Can I love this child enough to change the patterns of what is and create here what I know can be?"

She asked me if the world could change and if there could be love and if there could be acceptance, and peace, and the remembering. As I heard her questions, I knew I had asked them also, as does each woman at the moment of procreation, and I answered softly, "Yes."

We looked at each other then in complete understanding, and I said, "It is time to begin."

She nodded and moved slowly and deftly to the stove where she finished preparing a brew of strong herbs and leaves to see us through the long night to come.

I watched her as she made me a small meal of bread and figs and meat. As she moved, I saw that she was more assured, the fear gone—a new determination showing in the carriage of her body and within her womanness. It stirred me deeply, for it affirmed my calling, and I was well rewarded. I let her prepare the food even though she was beginning her rhythm and the cycle of birth was upon her. This was the only way she could repay me, and it was a point of honor between us. She gave to me the food, and I ate what she had prepared. She nodded to me then and said, "I am now ready."

I began to speak. "The child is now moving into the tunnel. The vibrations of density from the Earth are now affecting her memory, and she is seeing only the light, forgetting the calling, and where she is, and why she is moving through the dimensions."

I paused and drank some brew and felt the knowing come into the mother, and then I continued. "The pattern of destiny is encoded into the soul, but for the child to remember it, she must be connected again to the memory as she is born. I can do this for a time, but it is your calling to instill the knowledge of divinity and the memory of her origin into the consciousness of your own child. When the child's soul is honored and upheld from the time of birth, there is much joy, for there is no experience of separation from the knowledge and the unity within. The child is happy, well contented, fulfilled within, needing nothing in the way of the human to give her dignity or self-worthiness. The child creates from the inner potential and remembers her design. When this memory is real to the child, she has a sense of belonging and knows the angels as well as her physical playmates. The world is a beautiful place of discovery and creation. This is the way of the calling."

"How can I do this for my child?" she asked. "Close your eyes and place your thoughts in the seed of light in the center of your body, in the place where your ribs come together in a point. There, yes, right below the heart. Breathe there, and you will feel your knowing. Ask that your light and the light of your child now be one. Imagine a light in the place where you hold the child in the womb. Now, as you feel and remember unity, expand your thinking to be a part of the light which your child brings. Feel your lights as one. Yes. Now as the rhythms and cycles of the child are felt in your body, you will feel the quickening more strongly, and the time between cycles will be shorter. Stay at one with the soul of the child now, and the birth will be easy and quick and clear."

We moved to the place which had been prepared for the birthing, and I continued to instruct her in the breathing and the merging. I told her I was also bonding with the child, and we continued for some time, feeling the soul of the child approaching now, more completely.

I instructed her to breathe into the light of the union between her and the child and to form a bridge of this light between her womb and the outside world. This would lead the child through the canal and into the world in light.

I asked her to keep the image of light inside and outside of her body at the same time, so that the child would see no separation and would be born in unity, remembering that the universe is a safe place to be.

Just before she was born, I sent out the call to the child and anchored universal light in her consciousness, helping the mother to bridge the span between dimensions. I showed the child the light of her calling and led her out of the womb into the density of Earth, affirming her divinity: "You are spirit, and so you shall remain," I said over and over again. "Your truth shall be honored here. You are free to create from the design within and live your potential and hold to the memory of your knowing."

When the mother had fulfilled the birthing, and the cleaning and ordering had been accomplished, we sat, the three, and bonded the light between us once again. I instructed her, and she began the ritual of the birthing of light into form. She began connecting her seed with her child's seed again, feeling the bond between them. She then brought light into the top of the child's head and drew it through the small body, creating a waterfall with the light. She did this several times until she felt the light steady and constant throughout her child's body.

She then took the child's small feet in her hands and held the bottoms saying slowly and distinctly:

> You have chosen to come into form.
> You have chosen to come into form.
> You have chosen to come into form.
>
> I anchor you into the mother Earth.
> I anchor you into the mother Earth.
> You have chosen this form.
>
> You are light.
> You are light.
> You are light.
>
> You are light and light you shall remain.
> You are light and light you shall remain.
> You are light and light you shall remain.

She said the word of the affirmation to her child with intent. Then she placed one hand on her heart and the other hand on her baby's heart, speaking into the child's ear and saying:

> The bond that we have is through love; what I teach you I teach you from love; what is not of your truth, I give you permission to release. I acknowledge your divinity and your spirit. You have arrived on the planet Earth, and you are a part of our family. Know that you are creative and can achieve and accomplish anything that you desire and that there are no conditions on my love for you. I will love you, always, without question.

As she finished the ritual of the birthing, she drew the child to her breast and they continued the joining. Since she was more open in the first forty-eight hours after her birthing than at any other time in her life, I told her it was important to run the light of spirit through her body before she held the infant so that she would be filled with light when she held her. I also spoke of the need for her to be with her own spirit, while cherishing the bond with her child.

I instructed the mother to spend some moments each day joining with her child's seed of light and going with the child into the light of the Hierarchy and the place of truth. Since the first twenty-four months establishes the foundation between the hemispheres of consciousness, I told her that every day for two years the child would need to hear an affirmation that she is light.

I stayed with them for six months following the birthing. Each day I instructed the mother and sent the child a validation of her purpose and spoke to her the affirmation of light.

I grew to love the girl child and her mother, and we spent many hours talking, sharing, and loving. I told the mother of the future of the child and gave her the teachings of the soul to share with her when she was older:

> To always uphold the creativity of the child and encourage her uniqueness, affirming her child's divinity daily; to listen every morning to her child's dreams and, at night before bed, to listen to the experiences the child had that day. This would help to integrate the unconscious and conscious processes of the child every twenty-four hours.

> To have the child express all of her feelings without judging them and to give the child an example of this through her own honest expression of emotion. This would explain the

ways of the world and the laws of man, telling her why things are as they are. This would give her the understanding necessary to live here and respect others. If the child respected the ways of others, then others would respect her ways.

I spoke to the mother about the Earth as a learning place and about the lessons the child's soul had come to learn. I told her to teach the child that the lessons did not have to be learned through pain because pain is man-made and is not created from the Gods.

I instructed her and the child in the ways of the heart:

To love unconditionally,
To ask for the memory of the design,
To join daily with the seed of light of those you love,
To spend some moments together in dreaming and being.

I stayed because of my calling, yes, but also because it was a respite from the travel and the aloneness of my outer existence. I explored the hills and the valleys there and took the child with me, explaining to her about the Earth and the elements and the force fields. We went into the wind and the rain and under the trees and the stars. We touched the living things of the Earth every day, and the child learned about life.

And as I was preparing to leave, I told the child about the truth within her, telling her of why she had come and of why I must go. I spoke to her as if she were of my years, sometimes using the tongue and sometimes using the mind.

She would listen, now barely sitting by herself, propped against the rocks beside her earthly home. She had clear almond eyes which reflected the memory of her inner truth and the knowledge within her soul. She was happy, smiling often, and content to be here.

When it was finished, we stood together in the door frame, the three as one—one in our calling, one in our being, one in our intention as women to create the wave of truth. I knew we had done well and I smiled, kissing them on each cheek.

I mounted Saschai then and rode forward, even now feeling the next calling. I was going in a direction, a direction which would bring me to Christ, for we had so appointed it. It would take many Earth years, and yet I did not sigh, for I was well contented. There was no place of lack within. The child had filled me again with the presence of home, and it was fresh in my memory, as was the image of the prophecy and light the child had chosen to bring to the Earth.

As I rode away, the sun came over the mountain, and all the memories of all of the sun's risings came with it.

Model of Cooperation

From The Ones With No Names
Received Through Flo Aeveia Magdalena
For a group in Washington, D.C.
On August 14, 1991

(Abridged from the original transcript)

We are giving you access to the information that you seek for the coming together in union of the peoples of your planet.

The Principle of Cooperation

The first principle that we are operating with is the one called *cooperation*. You are operating coordinately together so that there are pieces of information that are held by more than one person. Everybody here knows something different from what everybody else in the room knows—but you may not know what it is. So your first exercise might be to say: "What is it that I know, that is important?"

Once you understand the dynamics of cooperation, you no longer have to hold your learnings, but can share them in every moment. So you create layers upon layers of union through the practice of your being. You create these layers because you have abilities, gifts, meanings, focus. You want to do something that he doesn't want to do; he wants to do something that you don't want to do. Fine!

But nowhere on this continent is there an organization or a group that is dedicated to finding out what those abilities and resources are—to make them available so that everyone has something to share, and everyone has what they need, and everything comes together in a way that is synchronistic.

So if you write down your gifts and make them available, then other people will come, and there will be sharings and movements and connections. People will begin to recognize that there is magic, because they find exactly what they need wherever they need it. They have access to information, understanding, experience, knowledge, resource, to practical things that they don't have otherwise. And they stop feeling alone and begin to feel part of a very beautiful network.

No Beliefs Are Necessary

People do not have to believe anything to belong to this network. They only have to have experience that teaches them something, so they have something to share. This is an open-ended exchange of being. There are no religious connotations, no demographic, cultural, racial, or educational considerations. The only thing the person needs is a life force. They have to be alive on the planet, breathing. And they have something special, but the world is full of people who don't think they're special. In this room you have unified with your light, with your spaces of being, so you know that being in the human body is not all there is. But so many people don't know that. They think that this is all there is, and it's a pretty bad experience for them, because they don't know better.

And you cannot teach them through education. You have to teach them through the *heart*. You have to teach them through creating a vibration that they can relate to, that's going to come to them cross-culturally, across the barriers of separation that are imposed by people on the planet.

All of you have a design that affects other people. You are not individual souls who are only concerned about your own evolution. You have all graduated from that particular grade. You are here for the experience of oneness. Nothing else really matters. And if you put this model of cooperation into a spiritual framework, with beliefs and rules, it will perpetuate separation. It's no different from one race not liking another race because they're different.

What do you have in common? One thing. Your life force. What you have in common with all species is your life force. So train yourself to respond to your life force more than to your external five-sense stimuli. This will bring you into accordance with your life and with creation, and with the experiences that need to be established on the planet. You will come to the point where you no longer consider anything, because you have your heart so open that there is nothing to consider.

So it is all right to be wherever you are in the process of that recognition. It doesn't matter where you are or what you think. It does matter what you believe, though, because if you believe something, then you are attending to the details of the external world, which creates separation.

So believe nothing.

When you believe something, there is always a judgment attached. Your beliefs have a way of etching themselves into your psyche as truths, when they are really not truths at all. They are just things that have been appropriate for you to do in response to stimulus that you have received on the level of the five senses.

So if you don't believe anything, and you're running the fiber of being, and you don't have any context for anything, then you end up living what you know. And none of the rest of it matters.

You'll find that everything you know has been given to you from your soul as a pathway that is the expression of your essence. So when you go into essence, you are not considering anything, and you're in the fiber of being. Your essence is out there like a neon flag, and you continually live your potential. And there is really nothing else.

When you teach people, when you teach them from potential, they get it because it's nonverbal. You're transmitting the fiber so that what they feel is re-energized, alive; they feel considered. So you are not considering anything, but they feel as if you have taken time to be with them in the space of union. And then they are able to bring forth their gift.

Maybe all someone can do is wash your dishes. If you look at them with your purposeful essence, from the fiber of being, you see that their hands are golden, and their soul is full of light. And they will do a very good job for you and won't break your dishes, and you don't have to do them yourself. Because that's what they do best—and it doesn't matter what they do.

The Hologram in Action

Now, this is the beginning of the hologram in action. It is important for one person, one purpose, one universe, for everything—microcosm and macrocosm. You have a purpose, and your purpose fits into the big whole; fits into the hologram. And your purpose and everybody else's purpose merge together. You are all there, in love and harmony, and you fit the purpose of your soul into the manifestation of your destiny.

But the intermediary step to fulfilling all of that is this organization. Here you are doing things fundamentally—sharing things that you care about because they help your life work more easily. And there are ways that you can connect with others that don't believe in this or agree about that, because it doesn't matter. As you come together and share and unify and experience the fiber of being together, you create a hologram that is working on a practical level. It is working with language, and of course, sustained without language. You sustain your hologram without language and live it in language.

As you go forward, you expand your hologram. You have 10 in the beginning; and then you have 20, then 50, and then 500. And you don't have to have meetings of 500 people, although it might be a nice idea. You have core people who radiate the energy. You don't even have to get together again if you don't want to. You can just do it together all the time. Every time you are in the fiber you are with everybody anyway. But you do want to have times when you come in and introduce the fiber to other people, when you want to experience merging your edges and feeling union.

Action is born of union. If you don't create union, you won't have any action. The union creates energy, which creates action.

The Practical Parts

You have a data bank of information, and it's available all the time. You will create positions where people want to fill the roles of typing, entering information, or answering the telephone. And what they get in return is whatever they need. And that's where the universal design comes in, because you will attract the people who have what you need in the beginning.

The question is not: "How do we start?" because it's already started. Your question really is: "Will I make the commitment to be in union, to be in the fiber of being? Will I share my experience with other people and think about my uniqueness, write down who I am, open my heart without exception in every situation, so that there is no longer any separation?"

Consciousness is not separate from life, and that is what is going to change the dynamics. If you open and do not separate, and unify with the fiber of being, you will join together with those people who come across your path. You don't have to reach out. They'll come right to you. And if you open your eyes, and if you listen with your heart, the people who come across your path will have something to exchange with you—something very important. And if you are open to that exchange, you have just created another person in your network.

And you say to them, very excited, "You know what, we're just starting this group! And we need your skill. We need your gift." How many times in the week does somebody say to you, "I need your gift"? And if they were sincere, coming from a very open heart, vibrating with the fiber of being that binds all life together, having all kinds of angels and realms around them, and said, "You have a gift to share, and it is very special," how would you feel?

So this is a very good opportunity to be a light—to shine in a way that is very different from recruiting and from all the normal process that you go through to establish something that you want people to belong to. Because you don't have to do anything. People will come, as long as you are comfortable being in the space of cooperation. People will be attracted and will come across your path, and you will get used to seeing their gifts. You'll say, "I know that you can do something very special," and they'll look at you. And you say, "I know what you can do, and

I know that it is needed over here." And it begins to happen. It's very subtle.

You will change the dynamics of human conversation, of human interaction. Society will be bonded through potential. The action is the extension of the energy of potential. So it's a quantum leap of experience, because you do not really have to do anything. You don't have to wrack your brain for days to have something happen. All you're doing is placing yourself in a vibration, which we are calling the fiber.

As you place yourself and the group in that vibration, you affect reality consistently. It is the concentricity theory. You are creating concentricity to connect. You don't have to do anything because you know what happens. Everything you need comes to you, individually and collectively.

Expanding the Network

If you share this with 10 people and they share this with 10 others, see what will happen. Not that you get on the horn and convince anyone! Simply say, "I open myself to 10 people; may they cross my path when it is appropriate. May we see the light in each other, and may we share resources, and may we add this momentum and this energy to the union of cooperation, to the model of everybody working in harmony. May we trust the design that we, ourselves are creating—that everything is perfect, and everything we need is right here." Whoever crosses your path is going to be connected in whatever way they need to be. And you do not have to structure it. You are taking everything out of a practical standpoint in terms of creation and bringing it into a framework of holographic design, which means that it doesn't have one point of initiation. It's like taking the group and dividing it into a million pieces and then giving a piece to everybody.

You are known as a group that shares. It has no name, no place, because it's everywhere. It doesn't confine itself to anything. You go from washing dishes to car mufflers to doing surgery. It doesn't matter what the skill is. It doesn't matter what it is that's being exchanged. It might be human labor, human compassion, anything that is needed and that can be shared.

Everything that would become a task in any other organization, everything that you don't look forward to—you don't do. Create something so different in your experience that you can't wait to do it because it's so exciting. And what you find out is a gift to you in that moment because it's exactly what you need. Trust the process to the point where you no longer think "process" and are not considering the normal options.

So there is trusting, receiving, balancing, union, sharing, excitement, joy. And touching becomes an ordinary, everyday occurrence. Touching a life, making a difference, having someone come into the fold. And not worrying. When you stop worrying, you start creating. You see, this is a very monumental, pivotal point in evolution. People are beginning to think about something other than themselves.

It is important that there are pioneers in consciousness not interested in profit, not interested in glory, or in publication. They are interested in consciousness because they understand that the only way to heal the world is to raise the consciousness. So place yourself in a position where the fiber and the light is your focus.

The fiber does not have language, so you can join with the fiber of a hummingbird, or a bee, the moon, a beam of sun, a star, a drop of rain, a bird, a leaf, or a tree. It's not just a nice feeling of bonding, it's, "What is your language about? What do you need?" It is establishing a continuum of experience broad enough to encompass inter-species communication so that there are people who actually understand what the language of BEING is.

Synchronicity

The excitement is that you know as others cross your path, there is a reason. If you find out why, you'll be richer. And they'll be richer. Then everything you touch is rich because you are living the magic. You'll experience simultaneous points of reality, coincidence, and synchronicity pouring through you at a rate of speed that makes things happen. And the people who are drawn to you are ready to live the magic with you. Never question that—regardless of their education, or how many teeth they have, or how tall they are, or what their prejudices are, because it doesn't matter. It doesn't matter.

And that is the point where you stop separating, and you start being. And then your work is clearer. It's faster. The work that you've come to do happens like "that" because you are no longer thinking, "How can I do what I came here to do?" You're doing it. And it doesn't have to be logical. It only has to be the truth of your essence so that everybody you talk to will recognize it and they will trust you. Think about that. They will trust you.

Living From Your Essence

Do you understand why people trust us, The Ones With No Names, and the one speaking? Because we recognize your essence. We recognize your divinity. What would happen if you went around doing the same thing, and sharing this with 10 people, and they shared it with 10 people? It's practical, yes. It's essential, yes.

And it's necessary, yes.

It takes your ability to see something that is not there, to dream of something that has not been seen, to know in your heart that why you are here has more to do with what you are than with what you do. So call forth your essence and live it, and everybody who passes your path is destined to influence your reality and you theirs. When you do that consciously, you stop having "accidents" because when you cross each other's path, you acknowledge.

This is what the "new age" is that your people talk about—the Coming Together of the Ages. Everybody is rich, happy, loving, and coming together. Everybody is happening together. That means that you can have power at the same time I have power. A man and woman can each have power and still be married. Children can have power at the same time their parents have power, so that they can all live in harmony. And it changes everything. And it's simple. It's fundamental, and it doesn't cost anything! Your people need you. They need you to be accessible to them. *Accessible to them.*

You will need to be accessible to the people, to animals, to the elements, to the essences—to everything. Make yourself available. A doorway will open up in your psyche. All of the gifts that have been crammed in there and not used since you were two years old—they'll all fall out, and you'll recognize who you are and what you have to give. Nine times out of ten, what you think you have to give is not what you have to give. You have to give something more fundamental than you're thinking.

So as you develop the experience of giving, of opening, you will receive in exact increment to what you are giving. You will get exactly what you give— exactly. It will be balanced infinitely. So you give over here; you will receive over there, in balance. You will not be drained. You will be affirmed. Because you are available for the work of the universe, you will receive what you need.

You will receive in the amount that you have allowed yourself to be opened. And if you don't think it's enough, then you're not opening enough, because it's always in exact balance. When you live in the fiber, the wave of creation, everything you need will come to you. If someone needs something, and you're the right person to give it to them on whatever level it is, whether it be advice or a dime or a cigarette, or whatever it is, they'll ask you for it. You will know as they speak to you exactly what they are really asking you for, and you can give it to them—a piece of information, a little bit of time, an apple, whatever it is. It works 100 percent.

And you will receive many gifts. Sometimes it will be a smile of a child, or a grimy apple that you would like to wipe off, but that you take a bite of anyway in gratitude that someone gave you something that they don't have very much of— you know, these rare human experiences.

And people will come and say, "You know, what I am aware of is that there is this diffuse group of people who are all working in harmony with very little strife, very little communication, and everybody seems to know who to call for what, and where to go for what, and everything is working, and it's strengthening. And what's interesting is, there's no money being exchanged. And there's nobody really in charge. And the people are making it work." That's the way the new society is going to be based.

There has not been a society that has lived this way throughout its races, throughout its species. There are clusters of people who have lived in cooperation because they have had to. But when you add the element of free choice, and you throw away all the other dynamics, and you start living in harmony, it becomes magic. Because people are going to know that there's a God out there—a Source out there that cares about them *because they are getting taken care of by human beings.*

So know that your hologram is very specific for you. If you need a banana, your hologram has a banana in it. It has a sunset in it, if you need a sunset. Your hologram is complete, so when you allow yourself to live it fully, and open up to receive and experience from the fiber, whatever you need will be right in front of you. And that straightens out your health, your love, your awareness and your life. You don't have questions any more because you don't have any considerations. You are living your purpose. That's what this is about and why it's so important.

Weave Oneness

So weave, weave a pattern. If you bake a loaf of bread and give it away, the person will feel in you God, Jesus, Buddha, Mother Theresa—whoever they idealize in their own frame of thinking, perception, and experience. And you won't care what they think. Then they will stop feeling that maybe idealizing is real. And when you don't care what they look like, and you just feel their essence, they will give you their essence. If a teacher knows that a child has a special gift and tells the child, the child will give the teacher the special gift. It is the *intention* to find potential that actualizes potential.

And it's all you have. All you have is your potential. And you understand what you would be like without it—how dead you would feel. That's what you are looking at when you are looking at the killing. You are looking at the deadness of the people who do not have a knowing of their potential. They act dead because they don't believe they have it, and that's their reality. And that becomes truth for them.

So you are missionaries. You can actualize potential by living in the fiber of being, by weaving the thread of oneness. If you go into a situation with someone that you do not know and cannot relate to either through language or experience or race, whatever the dynamics might be, and you are in the fiber, they will feel and see the sunset in your body. And they will say, "Can I come and sit in your garden? I feel good when I am with you." And the thing that is important is this— when you stop separating from anyone or anything, *there is no separation*. What you experience is created from what you believe.

So don't believe in anything. Just be in the fiber of being, because there is nothing that separates you from anything. Nothing. You *are* a butterfly, a cloud, a rock. You are freedom.

When you see someone, of course, you do not judge. You do not separate. You do not categorize. You open yourself, and practice this, practice, because you weren't taught to do this. Maybe you will stand with them in the supermarket and talk about tomatoes. "Is this one ripe? It looks a little green. It doesn't smell very good. What do you think about this one?" You give them the fiber wherever you are. "What day do you shop? I shop on Wednesday. Maybe I'll see you next week." And you hand them a lovely tomato. And in the tomato you place the fiber. And they share the fiber with their family, and they all have the fiber. And it doesn't matter what you think happened or what they do with it, because that's in Divine Order.

Let go and let God. Do you understand? It's giving up your power, to be in the power of being. It's knowing that you don't know enough to analyze anything. And on some level, yes, that's trust. The interesting thing is, it wasn't your tomato. The tomato was there and you gave it, but you didn't give anything that was of yourself. And yet you gave everything from yourself.

The tomato was there as a way to bring together this union. You see, you use the resources that are available. So everything belongs to everybody. And once you believe that—everything belongs to everybody—you don't have to worry about it any more. Everything gets taken care of. The fundamental beingness is important, and then all the pieces fall together. Whatever you need, manifests. And then, you give thanks. And everything that you are, and all that you know, and everything that comes from your record, from your Akashic record, is available to you. It comes from you as an extension of the fiber—your role, your part.

Now, this model of cooperation is a model for the future. And of course, you start it now. Speak to the people that you really care about, the ones you want to have with you. If you are having a meeting of this group that shares and you want someone to come, you call them up, but you do not say, "I want you to come to the meeting tonight. We're going to have a meeting at 8 p. m. Will you come?"

How many demands do you have on your time? How many people are asking for others' time? You call them up and say instead, "I really want you to be there. This fiber thing is really important, and I care that you're there with me because when you're there with me, it's easier for me. Because your specialness is helping me feel my specialness." Or whatever is true for you. Be real with each other.

And then people come, and it's such a strong experience that whether it's two months or two weeks before you do it again, it sustains you because it magnifies the energy of concentricity. Micro into macro. And you don't talk about your lives. You feel your space together.

And you say to someone afterward, "I need to just say this to you; it won't go away. There's somebody's name I need to give you." And you do it, and then you allow. And they come back to you, and they may say, "That changed my life. I needed that, and I couldn't say it to anybody. I didn't even know what to ask for, and that person was the one who was the key for me."

What you are doing is creating a very beautiful concentric crystal that accelerates and amplifies the energy of manifestation. Being in the fiber makes this easier. It brings the connection into focus and memory so that being here is the experience of oneness again. Remember that you do the work of the universe through the vehicles of your expression and your being, and we are grateful to you that it is so.

The Fiber of Being
An Exercise

Begin by sitting or standing in a group and holding hands. Remember that running the fiber is not a meditation or focused exercise as much as it is becoming the fiber that flows through all life and brings it together, in sacredness. To become part of the oneness of all dimensions, breathe together, flowing the breath between and among you for a minute or so. Sense the flowing and movement of your consciousness as it merges and mingles together.

Begin imagining that you are at your favorite place for watching sunrises or sunsets. If you have a memory of a particular place, a particular sunrise, return there in your mind. Feel the sun's rays rising or falling above the horizon and imagine that you are at one with these rays. This is the important piece, because as you visualize and experience the rays moving, your consciousness will move with the rays and begin to touch the whole planet, filling with the fiber of being.

As you continue to hold the space with the group, you may feel a deep, warm, and tender awareness forming in your body, usually in the areas of the sacred space, the soul, and the heart. You may feel your body relaxing and moving with the sun's rays through the universe. To be in this space together for about ten minutes allows for the osmotic blending and melding of your knowledge and information to touch others, and for the experience of the fluid to fill the cells and tissues of your body bringing a sense of balance and peace.

When it feels comfortable, someone can suggest using your awareness to come back into the room and you can gently bring your consciousness into your body again. When you feel ready, share whatever you are moved to communicate, organically and spontaneously, without thought. You have an opportunity to flow in union with the other people in the group, with the Earth, the sun, the universe, and spirit. Sharing organically is a process of allowance and participation which brings you the experience of oneness with the point in the universe where oneness originates.

Have fun!

The Bridge of Light

From The Ones With No Names
Received Through Flo Aeveia Magdalena
For a group in Washington, D.C.
On October 16, 1991

(Abridged from the original transcript)

We have been gathering our forces for many days, for this is one of those moments in history that will be recorded in your hearts and in the wisdom of that innermost part of you that remembers and cherishes what we call union. You are standing in history at a very important moment, because when you cross the line of linear time from December 31, 1991, into January of 1992, you will experience the aspects of yourself in union, perhaps in your memory for the first time physically.

This is going to happen to all of you at the same moment, and this is the miracle. All of you are entering the kingdom at the same time. No one is ahead of anyone else, because all of you are exactly the same, exactly equal, exactly recognizing that you are in oneness. The key to the new time is the recognition of oneness.

You will now work from the core of your being. Look with your eyes and wonder. From a child's perspective look at what is, and say, "Why not?" There are no structures now that can hold their form from a linear point of Piscean authority. And as you are observing the moments of time that now accelerate, you say, "Nothing is the same. There is no place within me where I can rest anymore. There is no place within me where there is strength anymore, unless it comes from my core."

Everything in your outer parameter is shifting; there is nothing to hold on to. You may feel more alone than ever, but also understand that you are less alone than ever. Because many of you are consolidating in exactly the same way, at exactly the same time, in exactly the same moments.

As you go forward, there is opportunity to join together in a way that you have never joined together before, because fundamentally, you have the same core. That is why you remember the light, and that is why you remember the oneness, because you have the same core.

We were having dinner with Jayn tonight, and she was saying, "You know, when The Ones With No Names talk about the people *seeing*, I begin to cry." And she had tears in her eyes, and we are hoping that she doesn't mind us saying so. And as she was speaking, what we were thinking in our spaces, was, that it is time for the people to see. To see each other, essentially from a point of view that has no reference, no context, no belief system, but a fundamental consciousness that everything is light, regardless of what it looks like.

So individually and collectively, you are refining your energy cores. You ground your energy, you drink fluids, you keep your protein level constant, and rest, and be with yourself in the way that you have never been with yourself before, and then your self ceases to exist in a sense, because it gets so much attention that it is satisfied, and you can move on to *We-ness*.

The important process that we are undergoing as a fortified unit of consciousness in all dimensions, is the consciousness of all time. Because that is what this age is about: all of you coming together through all time, to affect the most monumental, pivotal, span of consciousness that has ever been accomplished on this planet. We call it "The fulfillment of a million years of dreaming." The child within you remembers the design—the fundamental consciousness that knows the truth of all things, the truth of all being.

So your consciousness will never be the same, because what you have been striving to create is the extension of your own potential. And in this time, your potential has its best opportunity to be actualized, in all, and of all, time. You cannot go astray now, because the truth is louder than the dichotomy. And the union is more present than the separation.

We are telling you this because it is imperative for you to understand what's going on, so that as you are working through what you call your "stuff," you can go forward in a way that allows you to synthesize very quickly. And because there are no parts within you that are resisting the process, you can fortify, integrate, and unify all aspects of your being so completely, that there is no separation between your levels. Your mind, your emotion, your spirit, and your body dance together in the cells, so that there's a vibrancy and an aliveness within you that you may have never felt before so consistently.

And the beautiful thing about it is that you don't have any "reason" for feeling it. You can't say, "I'm happy because of this or because of that." And it's very good, because all that's left is joy. And when you feel the joy, there is nothing else except knowledge, because knowledge is joy in action.

So there is a synthesis going on, multidimensionally; everything that you have ever been solidifies with you. You get everything in this package, it's a deal, you see. Because everything that you need is within you. You may not think it's in this particular character, or personality, or identity, but it is within the essence of your totality. And that's what we're all living in this new time. The essence of our totality.

So decide that nothing matters—"no-thing" matters. And then of course, as soon as you decide that, you know that everything matters, but it matters in a different way.

Once you let it go, you have everything, and you have nothing. That is the point of the Monad or God, so it's all one. But you are not attaching yourself to anything. There is nothing that you need. There is nothing that is sacred to you, other than the essence of oneness. And so the false gods of the material, and the things that are taking attention are placed in the position where you can hold them up to the light of truth, and they dissipate because they're not based on anything.

So you're going to find out what's real and what isn't real. And that's very important, because that's the foundation for this age that has been designed into every single soul on the planet. Everybody knows what's coming—everybody. So what you can do is feel the oneness of light, of intellectual, spiritual, emotional, and physical bonding, so that none of your levels are in charge of any other levels. Your mind begins to come together with your heart, and your heart begins to come together with your soul, which catalyzes your memory, so that you know where you are and what's happening.

As you enter this new kingdom in 1992, we're calling it "The Etheric Level of the Earth's Potential," because what is going to spin into your consciousness, into all of you light bearers on this planet, is the potential of your self working with every single other aspect of the hologram. So you begin to create the etheric potential destiny of your planet. And you all love your planet very much, or you wouldn't be here. She is not only your mother, she is your friend. So not only are you actualizing your potential, but you're actualizing hers. This is parallel reality, and it's very important that all of you understand how to actualize your parallel reality (See illustration and exercise in this appendix, Parallel Reality).

So take the chisel and the hammer, and everything that doesn't come together with oneness, you chip away—"chip, chip, chip." And what is left is the seed—the seed that has your destiny encoded inside it. So when you wake up in the morning, you don't think about who you are anymore. You feel how you are living your potential instead. A tremendous excitement and momentum start to build inside you through concentricity, that place in this experience of choice where you touch everything in the universe from one point, which is your own seed core.

So refine yourself. And there will be less need for anybody else to use the chisel and the hammer. Decide now. "What I want is to live my destiny, completely. Who I am is the fulfillment of my potential, and what I believe is light. I believe nothing else. I am only light, and that is all there is."

As you go forward now, you will make *bridges to the light* through your intention. So no longer do you have to work at being light. What you do instead is feel that essence of light inside you and know its point of origin. And then you're not alone any more, and your sight is expanded. And everyone you see is also light.

This is the design of the age of union. Everything that you are is crying to be expressed in a way that you cannot diminish—through your mind, your beliefs, your fears, or your judgments. See the light, intend the potential, and the light is a bridge to actualizing that potential.

Place the bridge of light in front of you. And know that as you breathe through the consciousness of your potential, that everything you want is right there with you. YES, all time is one moment, but we're actually speaking about something a little more special. Because with this etheric potential destiny level of the world, what we're speaking about is that when you enter the bridge of light, you will enter the Kingdom of Heaven.

You are here to bring the Kingdom of Heaven to the Earth. It's not a masculine place, by the way. The Kingdom of Heaven is the place of the creation of oneness. You're here to create this kingdom here on the planet Earth. We are going to all create the kingdom in the next twenty-five years, by the year 2016. We are going to take two thousand years of linear history, and consolidate the events, and expand the sequential time, so that you get it all in twenty-five years.

And in twenty-five years, that etheric level of the potential destiny of the Earth, which is like her spirit—and her physical level, which is like your physical level— are going to come together. The way that's going to happen is that you'll spend most of your waking hours, and all of your sleeping hours, in the etheric dimension of the destiny of the Earth—her level of manifestation. It's also yours of course, because you are one.

What you accomplish on the level of creation from essence is linked to her creation from essence, and grounded through your body onto the planetary configuration that you're walking on now, into matter. And as you experience this year after year after year, the consolidation will become more defined, the separation will become less, and the merging of the planet in etheric and physical levels will happen, as it is destined to happen through the choice of all the people on the planet in this year of 2016.

Your Destiny Gives You Joy

You're walking into your destiny. And everything that you've ever wanted from your soul core is going to be there, waiting for you. Because you have already created it. That's why you have such a longing to connect with it, because it's already there. It's good news!

Many of you have jobs that you don't like. You have issues with your physicality that are nagging, aching, prodding symptoms that say, "Please listen to me and unify." You have relationships where your belief systems are stronger than what you see as real. And you have memories that are there in place of the memory of your divinity.

So you get refined. You won't even know how. It's going to seem like a miracle, but it's designed. You chose it before you came here, so it's according to your plan. It's in accordance with your divine right to choose through free will what you will experience. So what that means for you is that it's easy. Say it! "It's easy."

What starts to happen is that you get your joy back. You get your joy back! You're not looking at people any more and wondering, "What do they think of me? How are they looking at me, and are they judging me, and what should I say, and what should I do? Maybe I should keep the job that I don't like because I need the $350 a week." You do not have to conform any more. When you look at the world, the greatest secret is that nobody likes what's going on. But they keep living it because they don't know what else to live.

The models of the Piscean Age are instilled in each of you when you are born through your mother, and you are bonded to her when the cord is cut, and there are six generations of belief systems that are bonded into your psyche in that moment. So the belief system is stronger than the vision.

But now you say, "I'm getting this joy thing! I'm really feeling that there's something different. Maybe I'll take a chance. Maybe I'll pick the smallest thing in my life that I want to change and I'll change it right now." And that will feel so good that you'll continue to do it. It's time for you to be happy. It's time for you to remember that the only thing that's real is light. And so when you wake up, live your light.

Everybody's prosperous, everybody's healthy, everybody's equal, everybody remembers, the children belong to everybody, there's no color, there's no separation, you remember that. Where do you remember it from? You remember it from your future. Your future is telling you everything that you long to experience.

So we're suggesting to you that you walk out into the dawn and place your life in the center of that pathway of light, and live the knowing that you have brought to the planet, which will catalyze its creation. And the fundamental concepts that you know and value and recognize will be possible, because they have already happened. You have already lived them, and you have come to bring the memory to humanity.

You're actually stepping out into this etheric level, this point of memory and essence and expression and union and potential, and there is everything that you want, from essence. And there is nothing that you have to do to get it. Absolutely nothing that you have to do. Because it's who you are.

Living the Hologram

When we step out into this dimension together, we recognize that everybody has come here to help everyone remember. So you recognize each other. You begin to place the hologram of your microcosm, which is the fulfillment of all of the ages of your learning and your consciousness, together with everyone else's hologram. And your pieces start to fit together in a way they've never fit together before. And you have the experience of knowing the fulfillment of your destiny.

All of you already know this, because you helped us design it. And we helped you design it. We designed it together. So as we all are bringing our oneness through the we-ness, into what seems like a beautiful fairy tale, we catalyze for each other, cellularly, osmotically, the foundation of the marriage of male and female, which is union. Each of us walks in union with ourselves. That's what this is about. So if you want an affirmation, that's a good one. "I walk in union with myself, now."

All of you are here to serve, and that's a basic knowing that you have. You are here to serve. The way you serve becomes a clear vision. And in that clarity, see your creation in the crystal ball of your future, in the hologram of your divinity, and lock it into your essence.

Now, you may have an idea from your essence, your essential self: "I want to write a book." In that essence you believe in light taking you to your destiny, because you are intending from your essence. It's all a movement from your sacred space, the core of your being, your matrix, like the filament in a light bulb—flashing, divinity, divinity. Okay, there you are, "I want to write a book." So say into the trajectory of light whatever you want to do. Place that there, and wait. And create a see-through ball in your hand, in your consciousness, and watch your destiny shape itself in front of your eyes. And as it resonates to what you are feeling inside, you get turned on. You say, "Wow, it's getting very, very clear to me exactly what I want!"

It resonates. It grows and grows, and you get more information, and more pieces come together. You're going to get the "how" piece as you watch the energy formulating itself into the awareness. And as your energy is moving in that direction, bond and unify with your destiny in a way that accelerates all the continuums, because all of you are accelerating, and all continuums are accelerating, and so everything accelerates. There really is no time. So there is the feeling of being drawn. The more you visualize and feel and unite, the faster the determination of your potential will be actualized. So go for it. You'll get pieces that are very interesting, because you're going to have specific things that it's your turn to do.

This evening we requested the presence of a gentleman who is going to grid the new etheric dimension of the planet, along with many, many others who love to do the work of gridding. Some of you will have the job of holding the holographic templates so that all the workers begin to understand how to come together. Some of you will raise the consciousness of that new space, and some of you will condense the consciousness and bring the events into the framework of union, so that what would normally take five hundred years—for one race to stop hating another race—you can do in a consolidated point of time of fifteen years, maybe less.

What you watch is the miracle from the hologram. Incorporate it cellularly. As you're watching you create a bond with what you're seeing, which makes it happen in this dimension. That's how your destiny comes to you, and that's how you're actually going to create changes that everyone is predicting in terms of union for this planet—as a symbol that the free will experiment worked, you see.

So you're now honing your skills. If you can see something with your eyes closed, do it. Begin to see what we're saying on the screen of your awareness. Know that there is no separation between any dimension, and in any moment you can come together with everything that you are in all time.

As you breathe, move into the dimension of light. Let go and just go into the light. And what you'll see is very different than anything you've seen before— you'll see the replication of the union of the events of the next two thousand years. They will start playing across the screen of your awareness. And you'll say to yourself, "We can create union more quickly. We can bring together everything more completely. Now is the time. Now is the time."

And as you watch your hologram, everything that you know and are becomes essentially present within you. As you breathe, there is a fulfillment of consciousness which is your specific vibration, which will bring to the people the memory that they have chosen peace. Live it now.

Create resolution in the evolutionary spiral, so that all pain is erased from all time. There is no more pain. Each of you will erase it from your memory banks and then when you live, when you see the people, you will not identify with the illusion of their pain. You will identify with the reality of their divinity. And you will lift them into that divinity, because your vibration is very, very strong and your knowing is stronger, and your memory is even stronger.

You will outgrow illusion. When you outgrow illusion, you're free, you're free. Now remember this as a fairy tale, children. Feel the freedom. Allow your adult heads to feel freedom. If you're going to go out there and "graduate" and outgrow the illusion, then what you want to do is remember what it's like to be free.

What happens as you unify with the consciousness of your destiny is that you feel a fundamental freedom that you have never felt before. And that fundamental freedom allows you the experience of gathering all of your knowledge and all your wisdom and all your joy, and placing it within the core of your being and radiating it every single day from that part of you that remembers that it is joyful.

Blend Your Edges

In this time that we are spending together, one of the things that's important is that we allow ourselves to merge and blend our edges. Do you all give permission to merge and blend your edges? The future is predicted to bring oneness. Where does oneness start? Right here.

So you want to feel each other, allow each other in, allow each other in, now. Just say that, just feel what happens. You feel it? Now that's the actual foundation for the etheric planet of the Earth. Everybody's in, everybody's together, everybody's one. So in your choice to be one of the first ones to land on this new planet, you want to know that one of the things that's very, very helpful is not to have any edges at all. Flow together as fluid, so that you don't have beliefs or separations or judgments. You're just together.

This foundation is going to live in the etheric level of the planet for the next three or four years, perhaps five years, depending upon the perspective of the people and their choices. That means that all of you are going to create a new society in '92 & '93 & '94. The people who are here to bear the light are going to be family together! So you begin to make a new society.

Creating the New Society

Creating a new society means because you are physical, anything you visualize becomes physical with you. That's the rule. Everything's created through the physical from the metaphysical.

So understand that what you're doing in this new time is anchoring the connections of the new society into this society. So it's less important for you to change this society than it is for you to visualize the new society. Do you understand what we're saying? Take your energy and place it where you want it. Live your destiny and know that it's being given to your planet through your being and your essence, your body, your cells, your osmosis.

When you ground, put your feet flat on the floor, shoulder width apart, and anchor the light of the divinity of the etheric oneness of all time, which is where you are living your life, through your cells into the core of order in the Earth. You have roots coming out of the bottom of your feet.

Grounding is imperative. What's going to happen if you don't ground, is you'll become a bundle of nervous energy because you are running so much current. You can see, and you know it's alive, but if you don't ground it, your life won't change. Please understand that. You've got to trust your body with your spirit.

So everything that you're creating in your new society is cooperative in nature, because you're all pieces of the hologram. The health clinics you've been trying to get off the ground for years and years, all the things you've been trying to work through in terms of establishing new points of order on the planet, you establish in this new space of society. They make their way into this planetary configuration and are lived.

You have a focus that has no limitation to it. You're visualizing who you are and your destiny, and it falls into the planet and creates a bond. And every time you anchor your energy through concentric circles, sending out your point of light to all points of light, you make a space on the Earth to house your vision. The Earth wants to house your visions, the Earth wants you. The Earth wants you to live the etheric potential, because it's like rooting in her corner, "Yes Earth, we're with you. Yes, we know that you are perfect, you are Divine. That's our perspective, you are absolutely Divine."

So you don't look at her anymore as if she's in big trouble. *Please, look at her in her divinity.* There is nothing wrong, there is nothing to fix. All that you are here to do is live your destiny, and by living your destiny you change the world.

You are going to be zinging and feeling so alive that you're not sure what to do, which is beautiful. You're out hugging oak trees and picking up leaves and playing with dogs, and just living your life.

How does this happen? The reason this happens is because when you enter through your intention the divinity of the Earth's etheric destiny, you are also entering the dimension of creation. And when you enter the dimension of creation, there aren't any rules!

When you enter the dimension of creation, you feel at peace, and you feel connected. What do you feel connected to? The plan, the design, to order, to balance, to the integrity that you carry inside of you forever. That will straighten out your check book. Are you getting the picture? It will straighten out everything in your life, so that it reflects that order, because you're connected. You're connected to everything that you are.

We recommend that you make sweatshirts with wonderful sayings, "I live the fairy tale," and "The dream of we is in me." The people will respond with the consciousness of the dolphin. They will listen to the words, they will imprint the experience and they will let it go. And like children they will be awake for the next moment, and they will incorporate that next moment, and nothing else matters, and then everything matters. And when everything matters and nothing matters, you're connected.

We've also been talking about the Model of Cooperation, which is the basis for this new society, fundamentally in synchrony and in union with what we call the "fiber of being." The fiber of being is the current, the thread that links everything into unity. When you look at the species of the Earth, when you look at all of the aspects of the universe, they are in phenomenal order. You walk around and look at this and wonder who created this, because it's really cool, it's very good. Everything knows what to do, a duck is a duck you know, everything is in its place. Animals know what to do because they know their script, they know their essence.

So when you are in connection and living your essence, you function with this fundamental thread that creates the current of union between all things. So you're taken care of because you belong to the family of life. And you begin to experience on very dynamic levels what that's about. Your people call them miracles. Because you are held in the hand of the universe, you are precious. You are the only one of your kind. And when all of you in your individuality and in your power unify, watch out!

Question: *What do you mean by gridding the etheric of the planet?*

The fundamental concept is, that as the Earth moves and rotates and as her consciousness evolves, there is a consolidation of union which is placed within her etheric body, in reference to her job, which is to nurture and sustain all the life that is a part of her system. So in her etheric level it is recommended that she have the experience of order and balance instead of dichotomy.

So as those who grid move into their process, they create union through the planet by designing reference points so the Earth understands where she was, and then can transform into where she is. So as the gridding occurs it is a fundamental shift of consciousness for the Earth, but it is also physically being done. So you can go into a point and define it and know that it ceases to exist. It's a way of regridding the Earth, by gridding the etheric level in a way that reflects balance and order onto the Earth.

This means that it's time to stop gridding the Earth and start gridding the etheric, because there's no resistance in the etheric—there's nothing that's happened in the etheric that has a belief system or an evolutionary karma to it. It's a very free space. There are no rules there. You can make everything holographic there.

Question: *Because of the regridding of the Earth, does this also signify that there will be geological changes? Physical changes in the Earth?*

You will find that the physical changes that have been predicted are going to happen, perhaps differently than it has been experienced in psychic representation, because you see, the consciousness of the Earth must understand what it is to merge.

Her dichotomies and her poles must switch, but at the same time they must unify. So they can switch in a moment of consciousness and reunify, and if we do all of this work, we create a different response on the physical level.

If you go into the etheric level, and all of the people that are working with the etheric potential say, "All right Earth, now you've got to understand what your opposition is, what your point of polarity or dichotomy is, so that we can bring that together very quickly, so that you understand what union is and both poles are reflecting union."

So then, on the planet, the shift occurs. And you may find that somebody remarks in the newspaper, "This amazing thing happened, you know, there was darkness for five seconds. Nobody knows why." Something will happen that is inexplicable—the shift that people imagine would destroy whole aspects of your continents.

You see, Earth changes are not something that can be predicted on levels of matter very fundamentally, because matter is always affected by consciousness. So the greater the consciousness, the less matter has to shift in order to create the union that the shift was intended to create in the first place. So if you cooperate by choice, and not disaster, then you don't need disaster to create cooperation.

The fundamental thing is to recognize that you are what you are, and the process is what it is, and it's all fine, and just go for it. And then the shift occurs and nobody really notices it. It's not something that necessarily creates those dichotomies in the experience that had been predicted. Not that there will not be shifts, because the shifts are necessary to formulate the awareness on some human levels of consciousness. Some people will need to have physical loss, or some kind of situation they consider to be irretrievable so they find themselves in the core of their being, and live according to that dimension.

Question: *What is the Hierarchy of Order? What is its purpose and task? What is their relationship if any, to the White Brotherhood?*

We are speaking to you from the Hierarchy of Order. And the Hierarchy of Order is the body of light that holds knowledge for all of the continuums and dimensions. Many of you are actually born from the Hierarchy of Order. You have been around for a long time, and have come into a body to live out the destiny of light through form. You are our hands, our eyes, our hearts, our souls. Your destinies fulfill our destinies.

If you come from the Hierarchy of Order, you are interested in three things: truth, order, and unity. There are essences also that are part of the hierarchy or a part of the order, and some of you come to represent them. They are love, beauty, harmony, understanding, wisdom, and knowledge. And many of you play many different roles, have many different hats.

Our purpose is to actually hold the order of all dimensions constant. That's why many of you can come into the world and hold order, or the template of order constantly. Because you are an adjunct in physical form of the light body that we're holding in etheric form. We are doing what you are going to do. Do you understand that? We are holding for you what you will hold for the Earth.

So when you are communicating with us, you are communicating with the aspect that is in a sense, guiding the process. And the process becomes very clear once you're in essence, because that's your tie-in. Essence is the way that you link to creation, and creation inexorably fulfills, fulfills, fulfills. So when you are linking in, you are creating constantly, so you are unified in that space.

The White Brotherhood is an embodiment of consciousness that has taken the framework of the dimensional universe and crystallized it into knowledge and experience so that people can activate themselves through that connection. People need something they can see, something they can identify, something that makes sense to the brain. The extension of the Hierarchy is the White Brotherhood. The White Brotherhood creates a crystalline structure so that you can experience it most easily. But of course, since we're all the same, all of the levels are one, so there is no separation.

Question: *Is it necessary to go through economic chaos?*

Of course not. It's a very good question. Economic chaos can be interpreted as denial of substance. What you are actually asking is, "Do we have to deny our substance to find our substance?" The answer is no.

Substance, Protoplasm, and Creation

We are now in the place between worlds, where the vision of who we are and the process of what we can create is palpable to us. It has substance which is feminine, which is protoplasm, which is creation. So when you are working in this new etheric level of consciousness of the planet Earth, you are working in substance, protoplasm, and the invisible. Invisible, to the naked eye. Remember that it is a feminine space. That is why for this age to occur, there must be union between male and female. What you are creating is not masculine, because it isn't knowledge, it's creation.

The knowledge that has been structured into your planet is now being released. So the masculine level is taken care of. That's why your mountains are opening for you, that's why there are many people walking, walking, walking the Earth, to bring forth the knowledge. That's why you're all going to the places that are pulling your strings and calling you so much: "Please come, please come, please come." And you say, "How?" and they say again: "Please come." And you finally find a way to go.

So use this time that you have to practice unity in whatever way is appropriate to yourself, so that what you learn and what you remember and what you accord yourselves is the experience of each of your cells dancing together—the knowledge and the creation. You know what you need to know, when you need to know it. And you create who you are in the world.

Now the etheric, substantive, protoplasmic level has one purpose, and that's to serve the design. So if what you do is in accordance with the design, creation will serve you. That's a geometric or algebraic equation. So practice anchoring into your body as much substance as you can. When you do your grounding, experience the protoplasmic substance in every cell of your body, and unify. And you won't have mother or father issues—issues with your opposition. You'll mergewith your opposition.

You begin to synthesize substance into your life. That's how you get prosperous, that's how you feel healthy. Because everything you're doing is incorporating on a cellular level the substantive force of the etheric destiny of all time.

You think differently. You experience light differently in your body. You want to imagine that you are see-through, like Saran Wrap—that you do not have form. And then you can transmute form, which is what many of you are here to do. The hologram does not have to be lived in a human body. You can live it energetically through the substance of being, and you can go everywhere in the universe and attend to the business of unity. You are not confined to your physicality.

The people are going to begin to look for you. They will want to know, "Who can I trust with my soul?" So they'll start looking for you, and you want to be transparent. They won't see you, they will see your essence in substance, in balance, and in harmony with the fluids of the universe, creating without limitation. They'll identify with the fulfillment of your potential because that's what they want to do, more than anything else. Everybody's growing toward the light. So if you're light on a physical level on planet Earth, they're going toward you, which means that they're going to come to the new society, which means they're going to assist the planet to actualize her destiny. So it doesn't matter what they believe.

Do not define your relationships by your similarities, but by your core essences. And decide that the fulfillment of your potential is just that, experience. Living beyond belief.

So as you experience who you are, your relationships heal, because you are experiencing the substance, which is the feminine, which is the resolution. The feminine is the nurturance that creates life. So no matter how masculine you are, your compassion will expand and your sensitivity will expand.

All of you regardless of your sex will find that your vision is clearer, very much clearer. Don't worry right now if it's going through its ups and downs, it's ins and outs. You are saying, "My eyes are changing." It is difficult to focus these days, because everything is moving at a fast rate of speed that you're not used to focusing on with your mind. Focus with your heart, and your eyes will improve. Feel, feel the movement of the consciousness taking you into the dimensions of substance and you will heal your bodies.

So you are foundationally here creating change through your intention for choice. The masses will say, "We've had enough of the structure," and will look for ways to create alternatives. In our opinion, particularly in this continent, you're not going to find people going against government. What we see is that people will decide to create something alternative and take their energy out of the structure, which will help it die, you see. There won't be anybody giving it any energy anymore, so the structure will have to change or die.

The people will say, "Where are the models for what we need here? Cooperation and sharing and resource connection?" What you're doing on the etheric level from the demand of this culture, will pull you into frameworks where you can actually create what you want on the physical level, to be with the people in a way that is your calling, to do the service that is fundamentally and monumentally your own.

So experience that you are in dynamic resonance with all that's going on. And it's very exciting, because you're doing what you came to do, and you're not having to convince anybody of anything. Nobody has to believe anything any more. You're just doing who you are. And you're making money at it. Because where are the people going to put their resources now? You see, they're very intelligent people; they're not going to put their resources in something that doesn't work.

And the thing that's going to happen, that's very important for you to understand, is that by going across the bridge of light, it's morphic resonance, the 100th monkey syndrome. You go across the bridge of light, and then they know that they can. And they don't know how. Age old question. They don't know how, but they have faith and hope and the generation of their calling is, "There's got to be a way, there's got to be an option." So they start to stretch their thoughts and their awareness and their imagination. And when they talk to other people who are stretching theirs, they'll say, "Why don't we get together and do this? Sounds like a good idea to me."

And they find that there's somebody already doing those ideas, and those somebodies are you. So you generate a network of energy that is your "PR" person. And for all of you who worry about "PR," that's probably the best news of the night—that when you generate your being, you generate the energy to create the results that you want to create, because they're the same thing, exactly the same thing. Remember it's easy. It's easy, it's easy.

So everybody begins to come to you and around you and through you and say, "What are you doing? You're almost invisible, there's this light that's coming from you. I'm seeing it. You've changed, something's going on, what are you doing? You look excited, I feel depressed, what are you doing? What are you doing?" And you know what to say, you say, "I'm BEING, I'm Being."

And they say, "Well, is there a recipe?" And you say, "Well, as a matter of fact, there is." So you end up taking people across the bridge of light. Doesn't that sound lovely? You take them across the bridge of light and it doesn't matter how.

In '96 you're going to experience that people generate enough consciousness to begin to come together on levels that are going to create changes in your governmental system—long-lasting change. So in the next several years, your job is, in a sense, to magnify the substantial energy of the feminine so that the union and the bonding is occurring on enough levels to begin to shake most of those foundations, so that in '96 a restructuring occurs.

Now all of you who work with the hologram, and with the time and space continuums, and simultaneous reality, and have been given your designs from your souls—your job is to hold the point of unity that you experience collectively. When you go into your bridging techniques, and you hold that aspect, you play the events through that aspect. You find each other and begin to work together. You hold the framework simultaneously, and each of you has aspects and the ability to contact different points of what reality is doing. You will be able to validate for each other and substantiate through that process. And then what we have accorded for you already, what you look at in terms of time and events, becomes the opportunity to create union from dichotomy.

So the gridding of the planet that is happening etherically, and the people who are working dynamically in that light space are the examples for the people who are going to work on the time continuums. Because what you do in that continuum is say, "All right, I see what they're doing. They're taking the poles that are opposite and they're bringing them together and creating that resolution. So every single moment what I do is to aid and support that process. I see that perhaps my intention is to work with racial clarity, so that people understand that racial clarity is not seeing any color." So if that's your job, you're attuned to those people and situations which need to bridge through that continuum, to come together so that the union is created.

Now when you go home tonight, ask to have a dream about your destiny. Ask that the dream be clear, concise and right to the point. Ask to see the steps that you need to take in your consciousness to cross the bridge of light. And ask to be shown those experiences and dimensions in yourself that will be refined for that learning and integration to be accomplished. And every day for seven days, we would ask you all to go outside for five minutes a day, and tell the Earth that you have chosen to help her manifest her greatest destiny, and ask her to show you what it is that you are here to do, from that point of accordance.

And the fundamental shift that will happen, that you have been waiting for, for millenniums, is that you will no longer be concerned about your own survival. Because as long as you are concerned about yourself, you are not seeing the big picture, the great design of which you are a star player.

So everybody is waiting for you to assume your role. "When is he or she going to get it together?" They see potential, they see your light, and they see that you're struggling with those dynamics of how, when, how much?

So as you decide to make that conscious choice, you begin to live. And your life is dynamic and vital and sexy and beautiful. It's the fiber of being, it's the dance of the mating, it's the call of the wild. It's very wanton, very wanton. And very essential, full of integrity and union, and completeness. There's nothing else you need.

Crossing the Bridge
A Meditation

Breathe in the substance of the universe and link it in the center of your body to that vibrating chrystallis of being and begin to feel yourself alive inside your body.

Breathe it, breathe it in . . . Breathe in who you are, and what you know, and where you come from . . . and the design that you've come to effect . . . Breathe it in . . . Now feel inside of you, a softening . . . Soften, right in the center of your body, soften . . . That's it, you're planting a garden here . . . These are seeds . . . feel them . . . now they are beginning to break through the Earth of your essence . . . the Earth of your essence, they are breaking through, and they are beginning to grow . . . Soften . . . Feel the energy growing inside of your being . . . Soften . . . Now feel how your heart is opening . . . feel how the love is generating . . . keep softening, relax, let go, soften . . . breathe in the substance and soften . . .

In the beginning was the word, and the word was God, and there was no form, and the people rose up to create a form to journey to a land where they could find their God again. Now is the time. Feel within you the end of your journey, feel the softness of your being wrapping itself around the reality of your divinity and the visions of your calling. Feel yourself merging within our being with all time. Let yourself go now, into the universe. Feel the bridge of light taking you where you are recognized, where you are seen, where everything that you are is visible and there is no fear. The light is now within you, opening all the doorways, every part of you, in every way, in all time. And it is a blessing, for you know everything you need to know. You are wise in all moments. And the resonance is oneness, and the vision is unity, and the society of light and order is now accorded in all dimensions. You are now unified. There is no separation.

Open and soften, open and soften . . . The light of the substance is now before you, open your cells and receive it . . . the consciousness of the one . . . soften, go deeper, go ahead . . . And now you will see the image of the people dancing in the world, hand to hand, circling the world with joy and light and love. You will see now the peace of a million years of dreaming. Look and you will see it. Breathe it in . . . fill yourself with it . . . there is no time, the union is now, choose it. If you wish to choose it, state "I now choose the union" three times . . . and now say it in your heart slowly and silently three times . . .

Know that your choice has been accorded in the dimensions of consciousness and it has been so recorded on your records, and in this moment you are given the power to fulfill your choice. And it is so. We are bringing for you the greetings of light, from all the places of your being, and we honor your choices to be the instruments of peace for your planet. We honor your destinies, we are loving you very much and we share with you the blessings of the universe. For you are now truly the workers of the universe.

Remember that we are always with you, in all ways, and that there is no separation. Remember your choice for unity and there will be no more separation. We are grateful to you for the soul's choice to be in this place, in the seed of the new society, and we pledge for you our assistance, our presence and our guidance in this and in all moments of your future. We would ask for you to merge your edges silently for a few moments before going into the darkness of the night, and practice merging your edges every day with everything, so that you have no more edges, and all that you live is oneness. We acknowledge your divinity and accord you in all aspects, always, the choice of your free will, for truth and order and unity.

The Community

From The Ones With No Names
Received Through Flo Aeveia Magdalena
For a group on July 25, 1994

We are here with you and would like to welcome you to this place and say that we are very glad that you have come.

As you understand, your purpose is to create *this space*, which we are calling Heaven on Earth. There is really no other purpose for anything that you are doing. To create this space on Earth means that each individual has value, each individual has an intricate part to play, and each individual is an intricate link in the outcome of the total. No one is considered more than another, and each of you considers each other more than yourself.

You will do your best to always honor another before you honor yourself in the *outward* sense, while maintaining an *inner* honor that fulfills what you need. So when others honor you, it is the icing on the cake. Their honoring you does not fill a place that you need to fill for yourself.

Self-Responsibility

So there is work to do in an individual sense to make sure that you are honoring yourself in a way that supports the total. Because if you work toward the total and have not honored yourself first and filled in all your own spaces and gaps, then you're always going to want someone else to do that for you. In a very beautiful way, you are responsible to do that for yourself first.

So when you are bringing people to these spaces, *the core of what you are creating, what your model is to be, is that you have already honored yourself and filled in all your blanks* and that you do not need that experience in the group. If you need that experience, we recommend that you not be a part of the group.

We are saying this so that this message can go out to anyone who is considering being in the group. Any reservation that we have about who is in the group is based upon this premise of individuals being responsible for their own wholeness.

If one does not know how to honor oneself, it is then put on the group to do that. That's the old paradigm—that the group takes care of its people and in some way tries to make it all work. When this happens, there are no magnets for creating wholeness. So this is our first expression of interest—for you to have your own internal dialogue individually as you are going forward.

Location

The location is not as important as the intention and the knowing of what needs to happen. You see, you are going into the future, and you are learning to bring the future into the present, to foster an absolutely congruent space, and time doesn't matter. In other words, the fact that you're tapping into fifteen years ahead of 1994 doesn't matter, because the essential energy of your formulation is able to hold it steady and bring it in.

The reason that Vermont is a good place for a location—not "the" location, but "a" location—is because there is a vortex here. Many of you have felt this vortex. It is a place where the threshold for the future can take seed and take reference in physical form. It has already been happening in the organic, etheric level. It's like creating an etheric city—and the land will support that. It is not the only land that will support it, but the location will support it, and you are drawn to this space because of that.

The etheric level needs to be fed by *intention*. It is the intention that manifests the linkage that will physically designate the space, vibrationally, and that becomes the magnet for the physical body. Honoring the self becomes the magnet for the emotional and spiritual bodies, and the practical elements and plans become the magnet for the mental body.

Creating the Community

We would recommend that you holographically create from 15 years in the future in this year, because the energy and intention of the individuals fulfilling the body, mind, emotion and spirit, are very strong. You'll get the best response this year in terms of activation. And the focus this year is on the individual.

What does the individual have to offer? What does the individual need? What experience and expertise does the individual have? What does the person yearn to create? support? engender? contribute? The individual thought, focus, energy, and aspect, is the drawing card, and in 1995 the community is built.

So it stays in alignment with the design of the foundational work that we see necessary before you get to the world level in 1996. If you do this now, you will be ahead of the game. If you wait until the world is ready, then you'll be late. It's very important that you crystallize this and catalyze it by the yearning inside you to have it done. Do not worry in any way about the details.

Now there is a question: "Do we make this community in just one place?" If we take all the considerations, all the people involved, and the way the wheels turn in your society, we would answer that we do not want to in any way preclude the model of the totality, or the new ability to act holographically. What seems to be almost imperative is that you act holographically, in a unified space.

But it would be a very strong and real stretch to act unified now, in a holographic sense, in many places. And it doesn't mean that you can't do that in three to six months. It just means right now, it would be helpful to experience the facets of it and to get that very clear.

One way of looking at it is like the conference you just held. You wouldn't want to have planned three of those at once, literally down to the last participant, the last period on the page, because it is a new learning experience. And it's not that you cannot act holographically, it's that it works best only if you have everything already stabilized.

Since you don't yet have it stabilized, it seems as if trying to be holographic would be putting the energy out and trying to get the fulfillment happening before you made the intention. It's like putting the cart before the horse.

It doesn't mean that it takes a long time. It just means that you make a proposal for one place. You honor what is needed, and you understand the dollars it takes to create that, the energy, the etheric energy that will be supportive of that, the amount of people it takes, and the amount of time it needs.

It doesn't have to be linear. You see, what you're doing right now is bridging between dimensions, between styles, between options, and between aspects. And when you're bridging, one of the most important things to do is to make sure that you have a foundation in each place. Then you can accelerate it.

Remember in creating the lasso, you set down the first intention, which gives you your second, which gives you your third, and then you go all the way through and pull it tight. And in order to pull it tight, you have to have the points of order.

So we're suggesting that you function as a body of light and union, honoring your own being, and honoring each other more than yourself. Honor yourself and then honor each other, and as you honor each other, you get all the pieces together.

As it comes together it accelerates, and you have a magnified space of congruence. The congruence fosters the intention. Then it has its own energy. You don't have to think about that again, and you can initiate that in another place.

It seems that when you were at the July conference, after you had everybody registered and in a bed, everything shifted. So until you have the cornerstones of the foundation of your buildings, until you have the ways in which you are going to focus that intention and energy, until you have a sense of how it's all going to come forward—you can't create in some other place. You don't have to stay and build it brick by brick, but build the *intention and the whole etheric design* first, and then get the people in place.

So you learn how to make the dinner before you open the restaurant and before you make the chain of restaurants. You're not going to open a chain of restaurants before you know how to cook the dinner. (It's very important for us to explain this a little, because since people don't want to do a linear model, that means we have to be spontaneous, live in the moment, and always take opportunities to be all over the board.)

The goal is to be in every corner of the world, where everyone is experiencing this kind of energy, and have locations all over the place. And that's fine.

Establishing Integrity

Right now, you are establishing integrity. And it may take ten times longer the first time to establish that integrity. So what? Because if you don't establish the integrity, it won't hold together. You are building bridges between the old and the new, which means you want to preserve the things that function well from the old paradigm, and use the new paradigm to accelerate the momentum.

So the energy, the funding, the capacity, are all there before you even begin it. You know that, so you are not worried about those things. What you're logically setting down are your points of foundation. They may be people, process, proposals, connections, junctions, linkages, or bridges. Whatever they are, they have to be covered before you'll feel comfortable.

So anything that you begin, if you feel uncomfortable about it, say, "Wait a minute, we need another foundation point here. What is it?" First you open to get your holographic picture, and then you start plotting. Plot it circularly, that's fine. And when you're finished plotting it, say, "All right, does it feel complete?" And it may not feel complete. The part of you that is going to let you know if it's complete or not, believe it or not, is the logical part. You're learning to see it holographically and open out to it, so that the whole picture is always present. Then the logic can do the details. But you're always in the creative mode, and that is a marriage.

Before one can marry those components, one must honor ALL the parts of the self. So you see, we keep coming back to the individuation. Because if you want to act holographically, all the parts of the self have to be married. And you're learning to do that now. All of you are learning to marry those parts. You're learning to marry your power and your gentleness, and your force and your trajectories, with your open expansions. And you're learning to marry your logic with your absolute.

It is really a training ground. And what you train to do in this year is going to be your curriculum for next year, because you're going to go ahead of the crowd and be on the edge of the wave. And people will come and participate in the wave. By the end of this year, you're going to have a sense of what it's like to be in community.

Make sure that you each take care of your honoring first. If you don't do that, the community is going to feel it. Because if one person does not honor himself or herself in the community, it will become a community issue. So instead of creating all that could be created, there will be the consensus that he or she will have to be dealt with in a way by the whole community. And that's the old paradigm—that the community is there to heal you, that the community is there to listen to you, that the community is there to support you, because you don't have what you need in your life. And if you make a community that is based like that, then it's going to take a lot more energy and time to create.

Creation and survival are dichotomies, as you know. If you are worried about surviving, then the honoring is taken away from the self, because the self does not believe in its own ability to create. So that's why we are making this distinction from the "get-go." We are creating a consciousness with you. The first sentence we stated is what you want to remember—we welcome you to this place. *This* place is what you have come to create on Earth.

Creating the Resonant Field

Now, how do we function up here, in this place? Up here, wherever we are, how do we function? We function through knowing that our lights are inherently necessary for there to be light. We function knowing that we are truth—that we don't have to find it, we don't have to remember it. It is what we are. So each time one of us speaks, or we speak as a group, an inherent resonant field is conveyed. *Your objective, your intention, is to convey a resonant field.* It is to have the process going on all the time, where your light is the light.

It is the opportunity for each of you to take that flashlight and open your being and shine the light in, and say, "If there is darkness, pain, anything in here, then I make it light." And it's not that you need to do deep processing, necessarily, although some of you might need to do that. Come to glory and to grace with those parts of yourself. Say, "Okay, you are my teacher. How do I honor myself at this moment, with light?"

You see, co-dependence begins and is fostered from the mind and the emotion at birth, when the emotion responds to the mother's sensations, and the mind begins to understand the belief systems of the process of humanity. There is co-dependence set up on the human realm, so everyone is looking for some way to be acknowledged through the experience and expression of the human factor.

You are yearning to find the congruence outside the human factor, and then live it in the human factor. So each of you has an assignment, in a way, to become completely self-sufficient. And in becoming self sufficient, the irony is that you will choose not to be alone—you will choose to support others and be in an environment of support, all the time.

Now being in an environment of support doesn't mean that you keep trying to find ways to oneness through human interaction. It is one way of doing it, but it is not the desired way to do it. The desired way is to find it yourself—through the fields of order, through the connection with your own guidance, through the experience of your own sunrise and sunset.

You activate your independent God space and assist each other in maintaining that. That's what you really want to be together for! That's what co-creation is. And it's very important that those distinctions be honored.

If you are resonant at that frequency and you make yourself responsible for or responsive to that frequency, then you are creating a model for your time. Anything else is going to be already lived in other kinds of groups and communities.

So we want you to understand that there's a challenge that goes along with this. You've been chosen to do it, so that's not a question. Yet you each have your own closets to look at. And we want to be very honest with this. Because in a very real way, and we have never said this before (this is what we experience), this is the model that will help change your world. This is our intention.

And so the laser beam that comes sometimes through us to you is that there is a path, and that path has all of you and many millions of people in it. It is not one belief system, and yet there's a path, an energy, a frequency, a guardianship. And we're charging all of you with that guardianship, because there is a difference between this and the other models that have been lived in the world.

You Are Facets of One Gem

If you live it as it's been intended, you'll see the facets. Each of you will have a facet that shows congruence externally. On the inside is the place where you need to connect with each other. What shows outside is the wholeness of the facets as they blend together to make one stone, one rock, one gem.

So you want to be clear that you are all one as you support your outer framework in the world. The distinctions are so deep inside that they cannot be found, and yet the distinctions are what make the facets happen. These kinds of awarenesses are new to humanity.

The way that is honored is that each facet honors its own need to utilize its own reflection and refraction of light. Then as it comes in to the center point, there's an agreement that there are distinct, whole pieces that are going to be forged together. And that space is going to shine for the totality. It's going to open the framework of all time and space. And each of you is going to flow through the other to make the wholeness happen.

So it is fundamental that each of you do your work, and then practice bonding with each other. Practice bonding with the larger group, then practice the resonant field.

Always Unify Your Field

Before you do anything, unify your field. Individually and collectively. *Never assume you are oriented with anything from this point on. Actively unify all the time.* This is a formula that we would recommend for everyone, no matter what group they're in, who they're with, or where they're living. Unify with yourself and then with each and every component. And never make an assumption from this point on, because the integrity that you're holding is a charge from GOD. It's a charge from the Counsel, it's a charge from The Ones With No Names, it's a charge from the archetypal, from the Angelic, from the firmaments and the dimensions.

Your souls have been honed, and honed, and honed, over time. And you have had the capacity many times to live this kind of union and awareness and synthesis. But when one of those components would be absent or delayed, it did not come about, because it wasn't supposed to happen in the design. It didn't come about because of something.

Each of you has a knowing of why it didn't come about, for you. And that's the honoring again—finding the place of your own tension, and honoring that place of tension, and saying, "Okay, what is it? What is my link in affecting the total framework in consciousness?"

In other words, if I were to look at my own conscious space and my own unconscious points and my own affirmation from all time, what would it be that is glimmering, shining, flickering? What's attracting me to look at it? Look at it, look at it, until it's not there any more, until there is a resonance in your field so you can be resonant with others' fields.

The thing about this that's so important, is that *if one person in the group is not resonant, the group is not resonant.* Because that's where you each have infinite power. You see, *if you're resonant, the whole thing magnifies on your frequency. If you're not resonant, you take away from the magnification of the total frequency.*

So, if you're resonant, then you are like 50 people, or 500, or 5000 people. If you're not resonant, you are not in the equation, so you detract from that equation, and you start bringing the energy toward yourself. And when you do that, it gets the whole thing out of schematic. So we would recommend that first of all this be something that people are aware of and take responsibility for, and that you practice. Practice being resonant.

Now, the thing that we would also recommend, very strongly, is that you let everybody know that your group is practicing being resonant, you're practicing union, you're practicing the core work. You're creating something at the same time that you're practicing.

We are not advocating, never have advocated, and never will advocate as far as we can tell, waiting until you're done to begin. Don't wait until you're perfect to start the community, because that's not the point. We're not trying to discourage you. We are being realistic so that you don't set yourselves up. You know many, many communities, groups, and organizations that have set themselves up. They have wonderful ideas and great visions. And yet they cannot get past their personalities. And you don't want to be another one of those. So the personality is your responsibility. Nobody else's.

Put Your Pieces Together

What we would recommend is aggregation—that is, putting together as many pieces as you can as quickly as possible, to support and expand what you already have in place. Do the logical thing now. What is it?

We, and the one speaking, and you are connected to an etheric city that is waiting to manifest. Now, that is at least 75% of what you need. You have the energy, you have the commitment, you have the intention, you have the soul family, you have the excitement, you have the environment, you have the physical location, and you have the etheric dimensional promise.

It is the promise from the etheric that if you do your work, heaven will come and be here. That is the thing—that's the equation. If we do our work, and you do your work, it's a marriage. It's that simple.

We would recommend that you purchase as much property as you can, to reach about 200 acres. Then you can have a nucleus of about 20 families here, according to the law here at this time—10 acre parcels for each family. If you have that much land, you have a buffer between your activities, your etheric communications and creations, and what we call the "mainstream of consciousness."

Creating Into Nature First

Remember when you create in the etheric dimensions, you always want to create into nature first. You do not want to create into human consciousness first. If you create order in the fields of order (which is nature), you create and magnify the fields of order. If you magnify them into a situation where there are lots of people, like a city, immediately you are going to have chaos. And that isn't your intention.

If you create a lot of order at once, you create a concentric wave. And if you don't ground and stabilize it into the Earth first, you don't get fed. Because what happens is, if it goes out and is needed around you, that need sucks it dry. And as it is sucked dry, it goes out and there's nobody with the intention of fostering it. Then there is chaos in the waves, in the wave frame, while there's re-adjustment . . . like in the cities . . . it's another kind of design. And that's fine, there are many people who are doing that on purpose, working in the cities.

Your commitment, though, is to create Heaven on Earth so that people can come and feel it, palpable in the land. They can come and feel it in every breath they take, in every twig they step on, and every piece of moss they see, and every leaf they see falling, because there is the intention that this is the place where The Community of Souls has been born.

In our opinion, doing retreats in the center of the land is most effective—to create the energy from the center out and foster that, dimensionally. You consecrate and ritualize the space as intently and clearly as possible.

So you function through a framework. You live it in a creative way that allows people to be responsive to it, because they are responding to the way you responded. If you really look at what's going on, you are the first wave. Whatever you experience, they're going to experience.

Set a parameter in place and measure it by your sensations, your feelings and your harmonics. Put it all together and feel it in the entire sense. Then when people come into this space they will say, "Oh, this was already thought about. It's already been taken care of. I don't have to worry about that. The space has been prepared, and I am ready to enter it. I am being received." Creating the harmonics literally cuts in half the time you need for preparing the people to be on the land.

That's why when we prepared the space at the conference at Massanetta, people began to move through their processes the first morning. Because you and we had prepared that space. We had made it safe, and we had taken those spaces and filled them as much as we could, all of us in our own inherent ways.

So this kind of paradigm is a model, an example. Most of you will come to this land periodically. Some of you will stay here most of the time. You will go out from this place and create another, and another, and another. And you will not always participate in these communities in the same way. However, you will assist in their etheric birthing in a physical dimension, because you are here to see the truth born into form. All of you. All of you foundationally, that's what you're here for, so that will happen.

Learn by your mistakes. Cover your bases. Take responsibility for your own honoring. Always honor another more than yourself in each situation when you can. If you do the honoring consistently with each other for three weeks (21 days), it will never be an issue again because it will be recorded in the psyche. None of you has ever had this experience in the world, and that's why you yearn for it.

So be powerful. Honor yourself, give it to each other, and it will be a done deal. Then wherever you are, you don't create stuff with anybody. You are just present. And it all flows around you, and it all functions through you, and it's an absolute space of truth. And that's what you really want.

We would recommend that you meet as soon as possible and practice. That's why you're getting together in small groups—to practice. And it's fine when you're in small groups. It's when you get in the large groups that things start to come apart, in a sense. So you learn to listen, adjust, and frame.

Do it differently from now on. Adjust with yourself first, and then enter the group. You'll find that clicks immediately. Try that instead of adjusting to each other. You see, what you've learned is to adjust to other people—the way they think, the way they feel, the way they talk. We all know that it doesn't work because you spend a lot of time and energy trying to adjust—and then you can't create.

Stabilize your field. Then enter other fields that are stable. Learn what that feels like. Once that's done, it becomes a normal and natural part of your evolution. And then the pieces come together.

What Do You Want to Create?

We would recommend that you individually write out what you feel are the primary spaces that need to be filled in the world. If you were to go to a place such as you dream of creating, what would you find there? What would be different from anything else that you have ever experienced? What would be the essential ingredients for you? How would conflict be worked out? How would decisions be made? How would love be expressed? What rules would there be? How would one know what truth was? What kind of environment would be essential?

Things could change. There could be mountains or not, ocean or not. That is literally unimportant. That may seem harsh, but it is true, because if you have the truth and if you have heaven, then it doesn't matter what your scenery is.

And it's beautiful, it's lovely. You see, beauty is the gateway to nature, the gateway to spirit. So if you already have spirit, then nature cooperates and you don't need nature and beauty to make spirit happen. And it isn't that you want an ugly place, don't get us wrong about that. But let's take "It has to be here in the Southwest, or it has to be there by the sea, or it has to be up here," and throw that away, because that's secondary to the process, in our opinion. Of course you can disagree, and you can do it any way you want to.

But in our opinion, if you do the essential grounding resonant work, and you connect with the ideals of your yearning for this community, then the place that has the etheric grounding will come unto you. You won't have to figure it out. It will come unto you. And it'll just be, "Okay, that's where it is. Let's do it."

So if that isn't happening—very important letter of recommendation here—if you don't know something right now, it's probably because it's not important. Because what you do know is extremely important. Develop what you know, hone what you already yearn for, write it down, explain it, express it. Then come together and share.

Find Your Congruence

See what the similarities are, and write them down. Have one of your playing and brainstorming sessions where you have that beautiful pink or purple paper and plenty of sticky spray stuff. Stick the papers all over the wall and look at them and say, "This is what we all want. Yes, there are 10 things that we agree on. There are a lot of differences on the edges, but let's focus on what we want." And then the concentric circle will give you your next circle, and you're on your way.

You see, the way people usually create things in a parliamentary process is by taking their pros and cons and addressing everything. And they give as much weight to the cons as they do the pros. We would suggest that *in the holographic design model, what is congruent gets the energy. What's incongruent doesn't get the energy.*

The incongruent doesn't like that very much. The incongruent starts coming out and becomes a squeakier hinge. But still don't give it any oil—if it's not congruent, don't give it any oil. Focus only on what you want. Create the intention to focus on the things that you come together on. If you can't meet physically, send each other faxes and mailings. Communicate your ideas. Have somebody who will agree to be a central clearing space if you cannot all get together.

If five of you out of ten can get together, do it, because you are going to find that your numbers get pared down and reassembled. A lot of people will find that when it comes to honoring the self first, they still need to do that somewhere else.

And that's fine. It is no reflection on anything. So you just keep going with what you've got. If you end up with three, you end up with three. So what?

You will get so finely tuned that the three of you will be like an instrument playing the same note at the same frequency. Then that magnet will draw the next three. And maybe they won't be the same three that you thought they were going to be. It doesn't matter. If you have an attachment to who's there, it's probably not serving the congruence. Just work with what feels congruent, as you seem to be doing, and then if somebody doesn't seem to fit, fine, keep going.

What needs to happen? Just start. The three of us, the six of us got together. This is what we feel. All right, what's our next step? Take your next step regardless of who's there.

The Work of the Soul

All right, the rock is already rolling. We set the rock in motion in 1986, when we made our first physical appearance in this domain in this particular century. We did this in a very different way than we had ever done it before. We did it from a mountain in Scotland, and we began the work from there.

There are people who know about The Ones With No Names, who have connected with us, but we have never done blueprinting before. It didn't really even start in '86, because we had some other work to finish with souls. The blueprinting work is the work of making sure the hologram gets lived. So the rock has been in motion now for almost eight years.

In the ninth year, which is 1995, this rock is going to stop its motion. There's going to be a place where individual human souls can come and live their blueprint. It's going to be built in 1994. In 1995 they will come and be here, and the community will be born. Those of you who have the resonance are the core.

If you would, and this is a request, please put the work of your soul before your individual location preference, before your individual job preference or life preferences. You see, this has never happened before! This is where it's happening. And that isn't good, bad, or indifferent, in the sense of your own hierarchical connection. This is your next step, and it's the next step for your world.

It doesn't mean that you have to live here. What we're asking of you is to think about your life differently.

Someone is born, they grow up, they get married, they have a family, they have a job, they stay together, they don't stay together, the children are with them, they aren't with them, and then they say, "Well, now it's time for me to live from my soul. All right. What's my soul supposed to do? Where should I go? Maybe if I go someplace my soul will follow. Or maybe if I'm in a relationship I'll be able to feel my soul."

We are suggesting that you change the human evolutionary pattern that you have been conditioned to live, and that you go to the place of your heart and soul, and see it born in any way that you can.

This is the rock hitting the water that sets up the wave that will touch the whole planet. It isn't the only rock hitting the water, and it isn't the only place in the world to be. It isn't even the best place in the world to be. It is the place that you designated that you belong.

It doesn't mean that it's your home and it doesn't mean that you come here only on holiday or for retreats. It doesn't mean anything. *The way you live the form will develop out of the intention.*

Instead of saying, "Well, it's in Vermont, and I can only come three times a year," say, "My intention is to be at the birth of this community, of this Heaven on Earth, of this etheric city, to the best of my ability." And let it go. Let it happen. We're not asking you to commit to anything that you didn't commit to before you came, you see. We are saying to you, "What is two years out of your life? Look back at the last 35 years of your life. Can you even remember a two-year period?"

What is happening here is foundational to consciousness. And it's a birthing place of the energy of the firmament in form. It will happen here first, and it will happen in other places after that, and that doesn't matter. It just happens to be the way it's been designed. You are all led to each other. You were all led to this land. You were all led to all the work that you're doing, to all of your pieces, to everything coming together. It's all here.

So the community is based upon the spiritual premise that humanity can live in oneness during this lifetime, and that there is an experiment that's going to take place, that's going to be engendered by the readings of The Ones With No Names, which is a body of light and truth designed to hold order in the universe. And that order is now going to be born on this planet, in form, through the people, the processes, the buildings, and the experiences that are created in this experience, in this place, in this dynamic.

And anyone who wants to be a part of that can be a part of it. And *the rule, number one, is one must honor oneself first. And then honor the others.* This is not a community of drop-outs, of people who don't have any place to go. It's a community of intention. And if what you see when you look at someone is that their light is diminished by their need, then it's not the place for them to be.

How does that get determined? It looks like you're going to structure a design that reflects the ultimate hologram. The way the hologram works—and this is not your welfare state—is that you fit your piece into the hologram when you acknowledge that you have a piece. You make the intention, and you act to implement what your piece tells you. All of our readings with you say that. We say it in love, and we say it in kindness and compassion, but we say: "Make a choice.

Act on the blueprint that's in your soul." Because when you do, the universe will be open unto you, and everything will be known, and everything will be given. It's about choice.

That means that if someone comes into the community, and you know right away that they need something from you, you give them the choice. You say to them, "Can you fill that need yourself, or do you need us to fill it for you?" We will be glad to welcome you when you can fill that need yourself.

The intention of this space is that you have already made the choice to fill the need yourself. There will be times when each of you forgets. And if you have already made the choice, then someone will just hold up a mirror and say, "Make a choice right now. Please make a choice." They can choose to leave, and that's fine; it's not failure.

It's staying resonant. For example, there was a woman who went to the Counsel and said, "This isn't working. I'm not going to make it. I'm not going to get there, because I don't know enough to get there and the world's in pain and struggle." And she said "How can I get there and what can I do to help?" In response, the Counsel was very clear with her that it was her *choice* to get there that was important, even more important than how much learning she had or had not done.

So in a very beautiful way you can be mirrors for each other, but you do not fill each other's needs. It's very clear from the beginning so that the processing is at a minimum. You go out in the woods and you process yourself. It doesn't mean that you do not receive healing from each other, and help, and guidance, and support, and love, and affection, and anything else that you desire. That's agreed upon. It's that until you take the self-responsibility, it's not a community. It's a welfare state.

The intention of this community is to serve only light, not the people. The souls are there to serve the truth, and not each other. And in so doing, everyone can co-exist, and the truth can be supported.

This is the intention—to live from the fluidness of the breath, of the spirit, of the knowing, and of the truth. *And there are no promises in a community like that. You don't promise anybody anything.* "Come here and you'll find oneness. Come here and you'll be accepted. Come here and you'll be loved. Come here and you'll be taken care of. Come here and we'll give you a job, and a roof over your head." It's not about that.

It's about sanctifying humanity, which means that every living organism in this space has divinity and is honored. And it's not religious, so nothing has to specifically happen to create the sacredness, but you do have to ordain it.

Each of you is going to add an ingredient to the environment to make it all happen. And that's what has to be respected—that if you're sitting under a tree doing nothing, maybe you're making the whole thing work. And nobody knows necessarily what anybody else is doing to make it work.

So the checks and balances are all energetic. They're not task-oriented, and they're not verbal, which means that there is an honor system. And that is what we have been talking about, honoring—knowing that you are the one who needs to honor the self, which means that everything else falls into place.

Guidelines for Living in the Light

✧ Keep your thought and your words pure.

✧ Vibrate in your head and throat only in oneness.

✧ Anytime you find that dichotomy is creeping in, think only that you are light.

✧ The way to no pain is the answer. Allow the solution to move you toward growth instead of toward the problem.

✧ Breathe light through the body and vibrate the light and the breath at the same rate of speed.

✧ Step out of time, go to the hologram or the resolution point or the absolution or the fulfillment or the potential. These are all "future-future" points. Choose any way you want to view these points. Realize that there are different words for the same point and your objective is always to be the pivotal point where you are unifying those aspects, outside of time, for then they truly become one.

✧ Bottom line, experience the vibration of all of these coordinates outside of time. Design your life so that you are out of the mainstream vibration of illusion, so that light, breath, and no time are your moment-to-moment choices.

✧ Jump out of the hoop of thought and into the hoop of the universe where it is all together. Jump into the holographic hoop or the circle we spoke of earlier, where all of the points exist together.

✧ When you are vibrating at a rate of speed outside of time as light, your perspective on all things changes. There is no separation, and when you are outside of separation, you experience union.

HOLOGRAPHIC REALITY

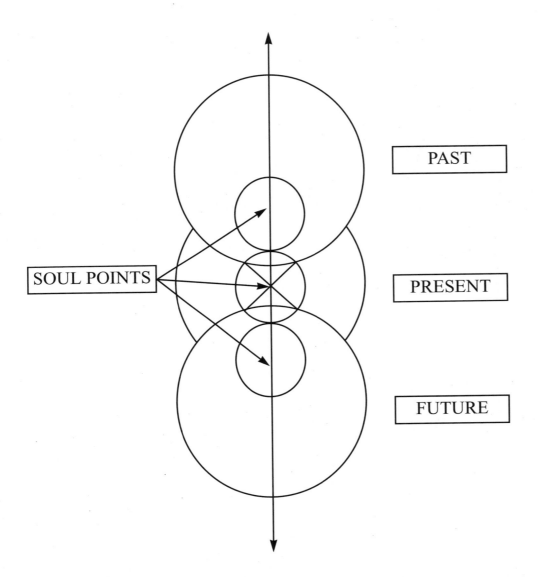

PAST

SOUL POINTS

PRESENT

FUTURE

In the model of Holographic Reality, all time merges and the past and future meet the present. As we sit in the center of the moment, we are all that is or has been. Each point on the time line is a soul, a lifetime, or perspective which fuses with the present lifetime, or perspective, and therefore, this diagram shows how we are one soul, and there is no time.

TIME AND SPACE CONTINUUM

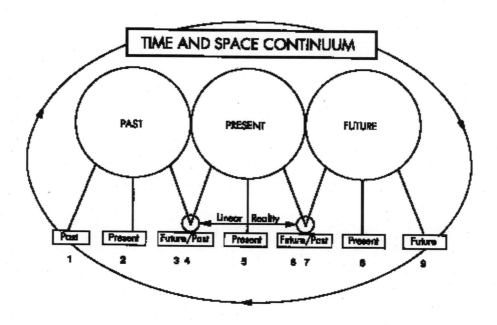

In the Time and Space Continuum, our universe is in constant motion through three major dimensions, Past, Present, and Future. Each of these dimensions has 3 time groups of Past, Present, and Future, making 9 points of time. In the universe, time is experienced as a circle, giving us access to all points of reality at once. This is called simultaneous reality. The 3rd and 4th points touch and the 6th and 7th points touch, joining the past and future dimensions. In this model, all things are possible, we have access to all dimensions, we can see into the future, miracles abound, creation is the constant, and all beings are inter-connected.

In linear reality, time is a line from the past, through the present, into the future, believed to exist only in the present dimension. Time appears to come from the future, we experience it, and then it becomes past. In linear reality, it is not possible to know what is in the future. All known events are based upon past experience. Linear reality represents the theory that everything depends on a logical progression of events. In linear thought you would enter this continuum at birth, at point 4, and exit at death, at point 6. All we have is what we can see and touch in the present or remember from the past, no miracles are possible, creation requires effort, and all beings are perceived as separate.

PARALLEL REALITY

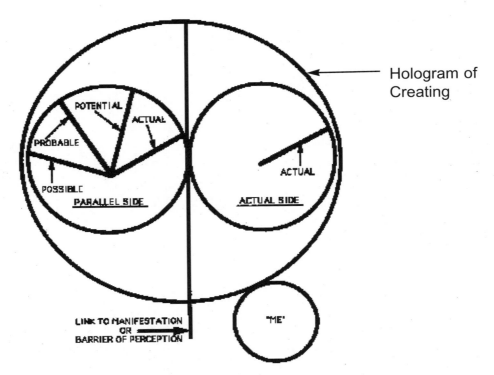

Basic Steps to Parallel Reality Creation:

1. Place your name in the "Me" circle, then step into the right side of the hologram.
2. Choose an actual situation that you would like to affect and place it in the actual side on the actual line. See the situation as you are living it now.
3. Open and close the door to the actual circle and cross the barrier of perception and enter the parallel circle of creation, closing the door behind you.
4. Visualize the "Actual" situation again, on the parallel side of reality.
5. See and feel the "Potential" you would like to affect. See the greatest potential outcome.
6. View the "Probabilities," the things that you know could occur.
7. View the "Possibilities," the things that you might not have thought about before, the unknowns.
8. Bring the four aspects together, bonding the actual, potential, probable, and possible.
9. Open and close the door of parallel reality, cross the link to manifestation and re-enter the actual reality, opening and closing the door.
10. Bond the new reality into the previous actual reality.
11. Open and close the parallel reality circle of creation and enter the "Me" circle, bonding the new reality into yourself! Now you can manifest your highest outcome through all dimensions.

Happy Creating!

Glossary of Terms

Used by The Ones With No Names

∼ Introduction ∼

We are bringing to you the essential points of order, or structure which uphold and engender the universe of your experience. This is now proof that you are ready to know the full magnitude of your own capacity to create and engender your universe, to uphold your own life support system. We are revealing the truth in essence to validate your readiness to participate as Gods and Goddesses in the unfolding of a design which has been held away from you for the purpose of drawing you toward it, a way of urging and evoking a response and memory.

Now that you remember, there is no need for the mystery to surround the process. It is time for the clarity which you seek and the unfolding of a greater frame of acknowledgment and union. We open the mystery to you as proof that you are now a God/Goddess of creation. Use the truth as a pattern to approach the words described below, as a key system which lies before you as a gemmed or jeweled city of lights.

The words are lights which trigger your excitement and initiative. Share now, more than ever before, the creation of your light, also, so that the knowing and the participation and the acknowledgment are the same. As you share in your knowing and your learning and your remembering, there comes an invocation, a calm acceptance of your place, a fulfillment of yearning.

This is also about trusting each other with your ideas and secrets and gifts, knowing that no one can take a gift away from you, that essentially you are the same and that all is truly one. This is what you are practicing now.

Know that there are no longer lines of division within your structures, and that this is what the ego may be resisting. Trust yourself to have the place necessary for your fulfillment, and each of you will unfold as your light joins the others, and the whole city, or system, of light is then awakened. Begin afresh to honor that the design guides you forward and yet, you are now seeing so much of the design that you no longer need to believe that it is taking you anywhere. You are already there.

Rejoice in this and know that this is the Kingdom of Heaven, now among you.

Some of the alphabetical definitions that follow are cross-indexed, to provide ways to weave the terms together.

THE ABSOLUTE:

The Absolute is a space of infinite creation, where the beginning and ending are known, the design is accorded through truth and the soul is the element of creation which engenders life itself. All other creatures are, in a sense, examples of the power of creation so that you can see what is possible. All life and all essential places of creation exist in the Absolute. If we say that you are representing the Absolute or are bringing absolution, it is because you are full of the awareness that there is no right or wrong, that there is no way for the separation to continue and knowing this brings freedom from guilt. Those of you who know the Absolute, are, in a sense, the messengers for humanity. The holographic principle of oneness is held here.

ABSOLUTION:

The result of being in the Absolute is to experience absolution, which is the removing of all karma (grief, guilt, fear, and separation). Knowing the divinity within is the result.

ABSORB:

To receive and integrate through the circuits of the body so that you realize your connection and linkage with something.

ACCELERATION CURVE:

The wave of energy which coincides with and therefore measures the expansion of human consciousness, or the raising of human vibration and awareness. This is the way Spirit can tell what is needed for the next step. It is like opening a door and looking outside and sensing what you need to cover the body on a certain day, perhaps a raincoat or a sweater. The curve tells anyone who is attuned to it that there is a process underway which indicates action and participation.

ACCORDED:

Acknowledged, upheld, recognized or affirmed.

AFFIRMATION:

1) To make firm, as in a verbal statement to provide intention.
2) To give honor or credence to, to accord. If you affirm something, it is using free will to align your intention with your outcome.

AGGREGATION:

To put all the pieces of the puzzle together at one time so that they fit; to collate and order all events and aspects; a preliminary exercise and experience to show

how the hologram was initiated and designed. Practice putting the pieces together and you learn what it is like to create universes.

AKASHIC RECORDS:

The "Library of Congress in the sky," where all the choices, aspects, and learnings of humanity are recorded. This is where all beings are made real, in a sense, because the record is the essential "proof" of life. Those who tap the records are accessing the design level, the level of the Counsel, for this is the Counsel's journal. Perhaps an example would be that if you decide to create a universe, you will express the creative intent in some way and follow its progress; it's that simple.

ALIGNMENT:

Alignment is the sequential ordering of the circuits in the body and the pathways of the psyche so that there is an agreement about the resonance, frequency or vibration being experienced. After the agreement, the other part of alignment is that, spontaneously, the person then feels or experiences a connection with other beings, and states of being, which are sensed as oneness, i.e., attunement.

ALTERNATIVE REALITIES:

Realities linked to your current reality through the pathway of soul, but not usually perceived by the current reality. These realities are accessible from soul through intention.

AMNESIA:

The state or condition of not remembering truth. In most instances, human birthing produces amnesia by separating the human being from its spiritual essence and soul.

ANGELS:

Angels are the messengers of the Counsel, who provide a link or connection between humanity and Spirit. Angels know the design and see the holographic plan and in literal and sensual ways, provide a message to assist you in taking the next step. Their messages take the form of synchronicity and coincidence, which are the angels' signals. Angels are created by the Monad for companionship and provide an intercessory level to sustain the invisible. Angels travel in pairs and, although they cannot change your mind about something, they will gently prod and encourage, particularly while you sleep. They thrive on gratitude, so it is recommended that you communicate and say "thank you" every night. They will work with you, and you can develop a system of communication if you desire.

State the intention that you want to receive the guidance of your angels, ask for a sign or signal of how they wish to communicate with you, and then be alert for the fulfillment of the signal. Then ask for help in certain areas and stay aware of what happens. Talk to the angels in your mind and prepare to receive great union, for this is the angels' purpose in being.

ASPECTS:

Aspects are points of reality which are born as souls into this dimension. Before and during the time of Christ, many souls chose to incarnate together, to participate in the experience of this dimension in groups. Some souls after that point also incarnated in groups, although the design has been to incarnate as individuals, for this is the experience of creating unity from different bodies and "souls," and provides more in-depth learning. There are 144 aspects of Christ, for instance, which means that 144 souls created the personality of the Christ.

ATTACHMENT:

The response of the emotional body to external experience, people, structure, or events, resulting in a separation from self.

ATTUNEMENT:

The place of vibrational balance in the levels of the being.

AWARENESS:

The experience of perceiving and bringing that which is perceived into the senses for acknowledgment.

BALANCE:

Balance and alignment are basically the same thing: a point at which all comes together and nothing can be differentiated. An example is when the pendulum stops swinging: that is balance. In the being, it is when there is no struggle, only acknowledgment.

BEING:

The state where there is no thought. This is the most direct way to know God. It is to feel as if the material concerns and normal necessities are a long way away, and you are self-sufficient and safe and know no limits. It is the state where what you usually require is on the back burner and you know the gas is off, and you can relax. Make it simple, because "being" is an important piece in remembering that you are important to the design. For in the state of being, there are no questions, only essential knowing. When we say "the total being," for example, we refer to the total organism: body, mind, emotion, spirit, soul, and psyche.

BELIEFS:
Ways of perceiving and interpreting "reality" which usually separate people. Things that you believe, are held in form in the mind and usually contain judgment. We would recommend that there are no beliefs in your psyche, only truth from the seed of light. If you have to believe in something, we would suggest that you believe only that there is light.

BILOCATE:
To be physically present in more than one place in one moment of time.

BLUEPRINT:
The etheric structure in the soul which holds the choices for the life made in the Swing Between Worlds. When read to the soul, the blueprint elicits and charges the vibration housed in the soul's structure to assure its remembrance of choices made before birth.

CAUSAL FIELD:
The level of energy in the firmament which restructures and realigns physical matter. Asking to use the causal field or level of energy brings the capacity to realign broken bone, for example, and re-establish order in the physical system, because it is matter.

CHAKRA:
A Sanskrit word which means energy wheels. Designates major energy vortices in the body.

CHOICE:
The single most important step in creating your reality is to choose. Nothing happens without choice.

CHRIST CONSCIOUSNESS:
The union of oneness in form as ordained through the essence of the One.

CHRYSTALLIS OF BEING:
This is the soul's recognition point, the place where the soul is born—the energetic and vibrational resonance of the individual soul's birth.

CIRCUITS (CIRCUITRY):

Circuits are the pathways that run through the body and are aligned with spiritual intent. Much like highways which connect your cities, they are the frame upon which the movement of consciousness is based. Developing and maintaining the circuits is a primary focus of importance as you live the blueprint of your design, because the circuits are what carry the charge of light and build the vibration to house the truth within you. If your circuits are developed you have a vital life force, are open to creation, and are balanced within and without. To balance and align the circuits is to order the being and place all the diverse human and physical points into the same intent and focus, providing access to the universe. Water is essential to running the circuits, as water supports the current that actually flows through the circuits, to expand them. So drinking plenty of water is a way to accelerate the amount of charge you can run. For starters, add one glass of water per day, gently working up to 11 glasses per day. The current will take the extra water from your cellular body if more is needed to run the circuits. If you are consciously working with the circuits and feel like you have your finger in a light socket, or feel queasy, your body may need more fluid. Some of the circuits are physical and correspond to the leylines and meridians, and some of the circuits are etheric, lying right above the body.

CLAIRAUDIENCE:

Clear-hearing; hearing words from the invisible.

CLAIRSENTIENCE:

Clear-feeling; sensing or feeling the invisible.

CLAIRVOYANCE:

Clear-seeing; seeing or vision of the invisible (see Vision).

CLONING:

The word used to most clearly explain the process of imprinting which occurs from the mother at birth. The six-generational bonding of information, belief, fear structure, thought process, and memory into the circuits of an infant at the time the cord is cut from the mother.

CO-CREATION:

Creating with others simultaneously.

CO-DEPENDENCE:

Co-dependence is set up at the moment of birth with the cloning process of information imprinted into the soul of the child (see Cloning). As information is passed to the mind and emotion from the six generations of heredity (mom, grandmom, great-grandmom, etc.) the concept of separation is set into the psyche. The mind and emotion then feel the separation and become co-dependent on each other to translate the reality of experience, setting up union between their two points. They depend on each other for responses, decisions, and perceptions, relating from this co-dependence to everything that is lived and perceived. When the being senses something, the mind immediately checks the subconscious for a record of how that experience "should" be translated or perceived and sends a message to the emotion and the emotion responds. The emotion is most times dependent upon the mind to give the appropriate reaction, and the emotion is therefore using the mental instead of responding totally from its essence. The experience of having one part of the being decide what the reality is, and then influencing one or more other parts of the being to determine reality instead of having the whole being respond, is what makes co-dependence an uncomfortable and self-limiting process. The concept of co-dependence is then taken to other experiences, such as family relationships, intimate relationships, issues with substances, beliefs, etc.

COINCIDENCE:

Events happening in rhythm with your experience which feel natural and synchronized with your intention, your direction, or your path.

COMFORTABILITY:

All vibrations, impressions, experience, memories, and yearnings are in balance in your being. There is no need.

COMING TOGETHER OF THE AGES:

The age of remembering; the time when the veils are thin and allow access to all information from all time. A visual for this is a slinky (See chapter on Mastery for a diagram). When the slinky is open, there is space between the coils which could represent "time" and when the slinky collapses, all parts of evolution are open for perusal because all the coils, which represent experiences in simultaneous reality, are close enough together to be available.

CONCENTRICITY:

A circular wave of expanding and unfolding energy initiated by an intention which is grounded from truth, as in the sharing of a common center by the circles emanating from a point where a pebble has been dropped in water. Christ consciousness is concentricity. This is how critical mass is begun, how worlds are formed, how creation is expressed.

CONDITIONING:
That which you get used to and think is real or the truth.

CONDUIT:
A channel or pathway for something, i.e., consciousness, light, order, etc.

CONGRUENCE:
The place where it all comes together. A point of balance attained through union with all components.

CONSCIOUSNESS:
God's rainbow. The visible, yet invisible pathways through which creation links and expresses. Your communication with the fields of order aligns, unifies, and includes you as one with all things, and is a way to practice experiencing your consciousness.

CONSTANCY:
Maintaining the point of congruence.

CONTINUUM:
A circular path of reality created to embody truth, universally; a circular representation of a universe or universes; the point at which universes spin and differentiate; a circular frame which moves life through its courses and holds it intact at the same moment; a container for life, life systems, and creation (See Twelve Continuums).

COSMIC:
Deriving its essence from the invisible; pertaining to that which has not been embodied physically.

COUNSEL:
The body of light, order, and truth which emerged directly from the Monad to direct the free-will experiment. The Counsel is God's/Goddess' right hand organization, contains 12 original points of reality, and is the sustaining body, so to speak, of your universe. The Counsel is your energetic stability, that which provides a knowing of "home."

CREATION:
The expression of truth in form. What you create expresses your truth and allows you and others to be aware of your part in the design.

CREATIVE CONSCIOUSNESS:
Creating from the awareness of all dimensions.

CRITICAL MASS:
Critical mass is the combined molecular wave form, comprised of many singular points, which moves consciousness, energy, or form. When many singular points of consciousness join together and create in the same wave or thought field, the corresponding answer or return from the universe is to join these points together and respond. As you put out a message, the universe listens. As a response, it is generally a creation index, or an answer that is held as a thought form. When many begin to put together their ideas for oneness, union, order, or truth, there is a critical mass or molecular level of impact reached, which then goes out into the universe. The returning response, as well as the initial wave, is what is meant by the term critical mass—a level of impact that sustains a promise.

DERIVATIVE RESPONSE MECHANISM:
The organic response of the hypothalamus to light and the accompanying synthesis which allocates light to the cerebral tissue, catalyzing functioning.

(THE) DESIGN:
The original map or plan for the free-will experiment. The design guides anyone who chooses to participate in its memory, to live according to laws and frameworks which instruct and unfold, without pain. If you are experiencing pain, you are outside of the design. The design always works for all aspects of life, for all people and situations. It always works perfectly, in alignment with everything, for the purpose of creating oneness in form.

DESTINY:
That to which you have been called, the outcome you have chosen in the Swing between Worlds, is your destiny. The individual design or contribution is the destiny. So you are individually called to fulfill this, because it belongs to you, and it is necessary for your part in the hologram to be played out.

DIMENSIONS:

Levels in the firmaments which house different aspects of total consciousness. These levels are invisible and were created as crucial foundational points for the integrity of life in all places.

DIVINITY:

The divine is the sacred from origin, the holy, respectful place of honoring and yet, non-distinguishing. When one accesses one's divinity, all is accepted, including the self, and there is no judgment or separation. When one acknowledges one's divinity, one then acknowledges being an emissary for the Monad. Another way of saying this, is that when one acknowledges one's divinity, there is absolution, which results in the experience of being divine.

DOMINO EFFECT:

Used in context with the lasso and universal creation, the domino effect is the momentum or charge issued from the point where the fulfillment of creation and the initiation of creation join. A forward thrust takes the first event or place of order in the equation and touches the second which touches the third and so forth, using this effect to continue movement for actualization.

EARTH'S ETHERIC PHYSICAL BODY:

The body of the Earth lived in the dimension of the etheric.

EARTH'S ETHERIC POTENTIAL DESTINY:

The potential of the Earth as lived from her etheric physical body. This level actually surrounds the physical, dense Earth where the free-will experiment is taking place, and is where the potential destiny of Earth and humanity will be lived.

ECOSYSTEM:

An environment for life where systems support communication and cooperation.

EGO:

That part of you which keeps you from the memory that you are one with all things. Your greatest teacher and guide is your ego. Wherever it pops up, you know that oneness is imminent and available.

ELECTROMAGNETIC FIELDS:

The subtle bodies of energy which surround the physical and vibrate at varying rates of speed and attune the physical and spiritual dimensions.

ELEMENTS:

The elements are nature's textures and fabric, such as water, rain, wind, air and fire. Elements are the signals and signs of the changing and growing communication between levels, Earth and Spirit, and bring messages and grace to you. Working with the force fields is working with the elements.

EMBODY:

To incorporate into your circuits.

EMISSARY:

Those individual souls who came on a mission from the Monad at the beginning of time to speak with the Earth about housing the free-will experiment, many of whom are here now; those now here to act on behalf of the Monad, the Counsel, or creation.

ENERGY:

The invisible force which is sustained by substance and expressed through form.

ENERGY CONSTANT:

Any vehicle which sustains the natural and authentic design of creation—the Silver Chalice, the hologram, truth, order, the fields of order, the fluids of being, the Absolute, and so forth.

EQUILIBRATED:

Balanced.

ESSENCE:

The essence is your particular blueprint, fabric, vibration, and frequency uniquely assembled to provide a one-universe point which can be added to the whole. In holographic terms, essence is that which comprises the whole and yet remains distinct.

ETHERIC:

Any and all points of reality that exist outside of form and yet are intricately linked with the creation of spirit in form.

EVOLUTION:

Evolution is the unfolding learning of souls. It is the upward rising spiral that represents the process of forward movement. The plan was designed so that in each lifetime and situation, when one learns, one moves toward integration, taking another step on the spiral. However, evolution was stopped as a concept at the end of 1991 because the learning was no longer accomplished. People returned to the same learning patterns over and over again, which was not the intention of creation. Remember, if you want to learn without pain, get off evolution and onto the design (See Time/Space Continuum).

EVOLUTIONARY SPIRAL:
The path which the learning of humanity took to document and record its journey.

EXPECTANCY:
The place of excitement which generates the coming together of the wave of creation and its manifestation.

EXTRATERRESTRIAL:
Outside the terrestrial body of the Earth.

FIBER OF BEING:
The essential place from which life is generated and sustained in oneness. The easiest way to feel this in this world is to align with the sun as it rises or sets, and to become the rays as they touch all life, then you can feel the generation of life within you. This is the sound or tone of the Monad.

FIELDS OF ORDER:
The fields of order are the Monad's way of maintaining the universal order here, which is exemplified by nature and the Earth's rhythms and cycles. It has been designed so that when you enter these fields of order, you can communicate with nature, and know the Monad, or God/Goddess. The rhythms and cycles that support and exemplify order will appear to give you a message, lead you further into nature, or support an understanding to link you more closely to these fields of order, i.e., a butterfly, cloud, twig, feather, or animal. Inherent in these experiences is trust, communion, connection, and knowledge that crosses the line between species. Inter-species communication can result, as well as a sense of belonging and support from all levels of being, and a knowing of oneness with the Monad and the Absolute. So we recommend playing in the fields of order, using nature to access your true connection with the unseen.

FIRMAMENTS:
The firmaments are the levels of consciousness where the unseen exists. The firmaments surround and uphold these unseen components of the universe as we

know it. This is similar to having air around you and your world. The firmaments are fed by substance.

FLUIDS OF BEING/SUBSTANCE:
The fluids are the feminine manna or protoplasm which is the medium for creation, the place where truth is sustained. Substance and the fluids are associated with the fiber of being—the fiber is the etheric linking point and the fluid is the inherent medium through which this manifests. Substance is what gives form to creation, and the food that feeds the firmaments.

FORCE FIELDS:
see Elements.

FOUNDATION:
When we speak of foundation it can be the soul as foundation for the psyche, the underlying structure of universal law which gives structure to the etheric, or your making a new structure here of the potential of the hologram so that a new model is formed to support creation.

FRAMEWORK:
We sometimes use foundation and framework interchangeably. A framework is something you build around or from which houses ideas, creation, and manifestation.

FREE WILL:
Free will is the greatest gift to humanity from spirit. Free will is that which provides the capacity to choose and therefore create from whatever is chosen. It is the concept that whatever you choose, you create, which therefore, makes you God/Goddess. When you know this is so, whatever is chosen can manifest through substance.

FREE WILL EXPERIMENT:
The journey of the soul from the Swing Between Worlds to the Earth and the choice to bring those two points together through the union of all points, simultaneously. The experiment where souls in human form live the illusion of separation from God and each other until they choose to remember that truth is union. The Earth's history is a record of this experiment.

FUTURE-FUTURE:
The ninth point of "time." Synonymous with the hologram, the point of resolution,

the fulfillment of the design of union.

GOD:

God is the point where all comes together and, at the same time, where all is initiated *from*. It is the going-to and coming-from point. God is inherent in what we call the Monad, and is the first place where expression happened in this universe. As with the Monad, if you decide to be at one with creation, you fulfill yourself inexorably. This is the basis for or the example of life itself. There are no belief systems equated with the Monad or God, nothing that you have to do or not do to be a part of God. Therefore, sin is not a factor because, actually, sin does not exist. Remember that you were born as a part of a great dimension. God is the overseer of <u>this</u> universe, and that which holds the space for the choices of the souls of humanity to be carried out.

GODDESS:

Goddess is the part of God which brings the qualities that you think of as feminine. These qualities exist as an inherent point of balance. When souls were created as male and female, then the Monad differentiated itself as God and Goddess. There is no difference in power base (self-actualization potential) or true identity, it is just that the God focuses on knowledge, steadfastness, and expansion, and the Goddess focuses on sustaining, nurturing, and creating. In this universe, the feminine is the force through which procreation and proliferation happens on Earth, and the God is the place where procreation happens in the firmaments. This balance aligns the heavens as well as the Earth.

This sacred marriage is the example of **truth**, which is feminine because it is invisible, and **order**, which is the example of male because it is visible. The invisible and visible are unified through the Monad and are then unified in your dimension. If you want to live the sacred marriage, the Goddess intends to be equal to the God, or there is an imbalance. One is not better than the other—both are necessary for completion to occur.

Many of you come to provide order here in feminine bodies as a way to bring balance to Earth, because then you bring with you both qualities. The male on Earth brings the knowledge and the steadfastness and this is coming forth, just as the feminine of sustaining and nurturing and procreation is coming forth. The feminine will create the new ideas, and the masculine will steadfastly hold these ideas and acknowledge them, representing knowledge again. So it is already worked out in the design. The existence of the Goddess assures balance and divine justice here and provides an environment of safety. She is the counterpart of God and is contained in the Monad. The essential nature of creation signals union as a merging which exemplifies the sacred marriage.

GREASES THE WHEEL:
That which spins the hologram into completion. See Hologram, Holographic Reality, and Holographic Wheel.

GROUNDING:
The process of bringing all the circuits of the body into alignment through the feet. Connection is made with the core of order in the center of the Earth through the feet, and the crown of the head opens to the Source above. Our favorite and easiest way to ground is to imagine that you are on Star Trek and are asking Scotty to beam you up. Imagine that your body no longer has any limits, boundaries, or edges, and is made up of oscillating, dancing cells, like sunlight dancing on water. Imagine this oscillating light coming into the top of your head and sparkling through your body, inch by inch, flowing out the bottom of your feet. Grounding is increasingly more important as old energy beliefs and systems are changing. To be connected with the above and the below creates you as the central point of order between the Hierarchy and the core of order in the center of the Earth (See chapter on grounding for information and another exercise).

HERSTORY:
The chronicle of events ordered through "time" from the feminine perspective.

HIERARCHY OF ORDER:
The Hierarchy of Order is the body of light and knowledge which sustains order and truth on this planet until the equality of balance is accomplished in the people. Then the hierarchy will, in a sense, be reabsorbed and become part of the whole again.

HINGE-LIVES:
Those points of reality which directly affect the outcome of your design in your current lifetime. They can be "other lifetimes" as you think of your past lives, or simultaneous points of reality if you acknowledge that you exist through all time.

HISTORY:
The chronicle of events ordered through "time" from the masculine perspective.

HOLOGRAM:
The point of re-union, comprised of all points of time, space, order and being, all aspects, souls, coming together in the experience and memory of oneness.

HOLOGRAPHIC:

That which can be lived or seen as a hologram and applied to the concepts of oneness.

HOLOGRAPHIC DESIGNERS:

Those souls who are choosing to assist in the implementation of the hologram now and who assisted in the actual designing of the model at the beginning of Earth time.

HOLOGRAPHIC REALITY (HR):

Holographic reality is the fulfillment of a million years of dreaming, the "time" when all souls of this level and all aspects of the greater universe are aligned through intention and action. We speak of this at times as if it were already here, and for all intents and purposes, that is true. It is here within your knowing and, just as you became form, this will become form. What you are creating is the holographic reality. For all of you to be creators means that there has to be a place for you to create simultaneously, which will contain or uphold all these creators and creations. Your HR is the place where you can all create because the design of the HR is that when you are all ready, HR emerges as a house for your dimension to, in a sense, make a new universe. It is the coming together of all your visions in the seed of light and the fulfillment of that point of being.

HOLOGRAPHIC WHEEL:

The wheel which spins the reality of the hologram (See Holographic Reality).

HYPOTHALAMUS:

In physiology the part of the brain which regulates and balances bodily response to temperature and other bodily functions. In the universal application, the part of the being which regulates the flow of light, light synthesis, and health.

ILLUSION:

Anything that separates you from the truth and experience of oneness; anything which creates separation.

IMBUE:

To permeate or fill with, usually used with light or energy.

IMMERSION:

The process of placing all events, actions, and experiences into a fluid pool and entering the pool to merge all ideas, thoughts, and judgments, so all that remains is a state of calmness and repose. What emerges from this process is the experience of oneness with all things, and a non-expectancy which engenders resolution (re-solving) of all questions from the whole being. This is the way to practice "being."

IMMORTALITY:
The knowing that you exist now, have always existed, and will always exist.

IMPRINTING:
To make an intention into reality by merging the essence with the form and holding it until it "takes."

INFUSION:
To create an environment with thought and to place it into an existing context. Most times it is someone using their intention to initiate or maintain a field of healing, light, order, truth, or whatever, for the purpose of placing this intended energy within the spaces between the cells or energy bonds of others. It is best exemplified by the concept of absent healing. You put out your intention, then focus on the person or area to be affected, then send out your field and surround and uphold the individual or group or process, and the field of higher order enters the field of pain, dis-ease or conflict, re-ordering or re-attuning it for the highest good of who is involved. Literally, illusion moves out of the field if order is present.

INTEGRATION:
Integration is the process of becoming aligned. It is taking the different parts and putting them together so that they form an integrity within. The result of integration is a state of flowing, so that there are no sharp edges to the experience or to the being.

INTENTION:
Intention is choosing, affirming, and implementing the energy to manifest, Making an intention declares to the universe that you are ready to receive. It is the use of volitional will to invoke a chosen reality.

INTERDIMENSIONAL SPACE:
A wave or level of consciousness which flows between dimensions.

INVOCATION-INVOKE:
To call forth from intention.

Joy:

Knowledge in action; living through knowing.

Karma:

The device used by the universe to teach divinity. Karma is the state of balance that exists when one is learning, which provides insights and awarenesses about the relationship of thought and action to truth. It is called the law of cause and effect because it seems that what you do causes what happens (See Law of Cause and Effect). There is really, at this point, no more karma (See Evolution).

Knowing:

The union of energy, thought, and intention in the being.

Knowledge:

The infinite order through which all things are born and have their being. Knowledge is the way of truth, which means that knowledge knows of its own divinity and importance and has taken its place as a structural component of the greater universe. This means that knowing or knowledge is a primary point of creation of the Monad and existed before life as we know it. There are no separate places in knowledge, there is only congruence. That is why when knowledge is present, everyone listens and stops what they are doing, and there is respect and honoring. It is not about knowing facts, it is about remembering being, and therefore it is sanctity.

Lasso:

A concept used to assist in manifestation. Take all the events you would normally see necessary to create an outcome and begin by placing them on a line, from the first event, to the last event necessary to complete the outcome. Then bring them together using a needle and thread or thought wave. When you have threaded all the items, bring the beginning and the completion together by making a lasso. Energetically this speeds up the process of creation, brings the excitement of completion to power the initiation, and uses the domino effect to catalyze the movement of each item to the next. See diagram on page 105.

Law of Cause and Effect:

The universal law of cause and effect defines the underlying relationship between creation and ordering. Creation is the cause and ordering is the effect. The effect is where creation happens in order for what has been chosen or designed to be accomplished. It is different on Earth, and the law of the universe has been translated so that it applies to karma, which was not the original intention. On

Earth, the Law of Cause and Effect is usually lived as the opposite of the "Golden Rule." What you do unto others comes back to haunt you.

LIGHT:

Light is the experience of being. Light is the primary source which the Monad utilizes to expand (masculine) and sustain (feminine). Light is the primary source of growth and was initiated by the Monad, created, in a sense, because organically, cellularly, all creation came through this experience of being. Light is the medium for birth. So you all remember light as an innate and long-awaited promise.

LIGHT BODY:

The physical representation of light in form.

LIGHT FORCE:

The unified field created when intention and light join together.

LINEAGE:

Your place of origin in the unfolding of the design. Identity with and experience of the Monad in the beginning which attends you and aligns your course.

MACROCOSM (IC):

The cosmic or absolute reality—the larger picture and the experience of all parts being equal.

MAGIC:

Changing consciousness or perception at will.

MASTER PLAN:

The great design hatched at the beginning of Earth time.

MASTERY:

The acceptance of your rightful place in the universe. To be a master means that you are aligned with your true essence and live it regardless of your surroundings or the illusions of others. You live in a sacred alignment with all life and know that there is no control necessary or actually possible, and so you shape and guide and nurture, rather than proclaiming. In the same way, there is nothing to be master (or mistress) of, in reality, because it is all one. So a master lives the oneness.

MATRIX:
The energetic house of your soul, essence, and vibration, within which the embodiment of your dreams and visions begins. Located in the central area of the chest.

METAPHYSICAL:
Beyond the physical.

MICROCOSM (IC):
The individual point of union with self which establishes the basis for interrelationship of all parts of the whole.

MIRACLE:
Creating from order, outside of time. To create a miracle simply decide what you want to make, gather together the ingredients, and then bring them together without time involved (See the Lasso technique).

MISSION:
Your mission is your calling in expression, the reason you have come, the design in personal/microcosmic perspective.

MODEL OF COOPERATION (MOC):
The concept that everything belongs to everyone, everyone gets what they need, and there are no places where separation exists. The MOC is a way to practice being in the holographic reality of the future and provides literal concepts you can study and familiarize yourself with so that you think differently about your existence here. The MOC, lived very literally, would be Heaven on Earth. So you can begin anytime (See Appendix for transcript).

MONAD:
(Monadal) The source of creation, the initial point of recognition which emerged from the Absolute. Sometimes called by humanity God and/or Goddess.

MORPHIC RESONANCE:
The tuning fork concept; sharing knowing and creation and vibration within your species through frequency, which brings the knowing into this dimension of Earth; vibrating at the same rate of speed, which imparts knowledge.

NO-THING:

The void and the place of the Absolute.

(THE) ONE:

We many times state your name by saying, "The one _____." This is because to us, you are not names, you are the individual points of one, or oneness.

ONENESS:

Oneness is the incentive to learn, the reason you are here, and the fulfillment of the journey, all at once. The experience of being unified with, the memory of being loved, accepted and honored in infinity, and the incentive to go forward, even when you want to quit. The free will experiment is based on the return of individual points of consciousness to one point of consciousness, or oneness. You came from oneness and so you will return to oneness. It is the experience of no separation.

ORDAINED:

Held sacred by all points in the universe.

ORDER:

Order is the basis of the universe, the sacred honoring of the individual and collective place of creation. Order establishes the inherent balance which is how light, growth, knowledge, and sustenance exist. In a sense, order is the food of all components, the fertile bed through which the Earth and her gardens in nature are completely balanced. Order calms and brings peace and fosters awareness and encourages expression. Order exists through the Monad and is upheld by the Hierarchy and exists in each person's matrix as an inherent knowing. When one opens to the matrix and makes the decision to see and know the soul, order begins to "come out" and be remembered and expressed. This makes the society more functional, because more and more people begin to live and create through order, which means they are living and creating through the Monad. Order and the wave of order is the primary way in which the critical mass of consciousness will be opened out unto the Earth.

ORDER WAVE:

Since order is the basis of this universe, to harness that wave and to direct it into the Earth's field, can provide extensive changing of the consciousness and experience of those here. Order and truth waves are what is colloquially termed "critical mass." The order wave is a very important way to acknowledge and expand the existing reality and to create unity.

ORGANIC:
Organic or organicity means innately unfolding from within, responsive rather than planned, being in the fields of order rather than mental decisions.

OSCILLATE:
To vibrate.

OSCILLATORY FREQUENCY:
A vibrational wave or pathway.

OSMOSIS:
The process of becoming one with something and exchanging energy on the cellular level. All consciousness is gained, accessed and experienced through osmosis, i.e., prayer, meditation, etc.

OSMOTIC FLUID:
The cellular fluid which is used by the body to run the charge of light through the circuits.

PARADIGMS:
Structures, models, and frameworks to build reality and creation from and into.

PARALLEL REALITY:
The counterpart reality to this dimension. Here one can create at will by crossing the barrier of perception and merging the two dimensions (See diagram at end of Dictionary).

PAST-PAST:
The original point of creation, the Absolute, the point where the free-will experiment began.

PAST, PRESENT, FUTURE:
The way reality is divided into separate experiences (See diagram at end of Glossary).

POTENTIATION:
Energy moving toward its fulfillment.

POWER:

Self-actualization potential, which is housed in the solar plexus chakra. Power is seen as the ability to live one's fullest potential in the world.

PRE-KNOWLEDGE:

The space where pre-original consciousness exists and is maintained. Before the Monad split into God/Goddess aspects, there was pre-knowledge. As creation and the expanding universe became "defined," knowledge was born and carried through all aspects of the Monad's expression. Since knowledge was changed as it was recorded and utilized, and, to some extent, altered and compromised, this pre-knowledge has been held away from humanity. Those coming from the pre-knowledge space have made the commitment to live from that point and bring it to this dimension when the acceleration curve indicates that it is time for the pre-original knowledge to become accorded here.

PRESENT-PRESENT:

The moment where you are now, that you identify or perceive as your current reality.

PROLIFERATION:

The feminine capacity to create and grow life with no boundaries. The energy of complete union in expression. WOW!

PURE INTENT:

The choice to live from the heart of the one for the highest good of all concerned in each moment.

RAYS:

Rays are focused beams of intention which provide different energetic and relational guidance to access consciousness.

REALITY:

The experience of union and oneness.

RECEPTION:

The act of receiving, being a place where receiving is possible.

REGROUPING:

The choice to re-order or re-calibrate the system, experiences, or energy of a situation; learning, relationship, or the process of coming to center; breathing in resonance with pure intent, grounding, or any means which will assist you to see a situation more clearly.

RENDERING:

The time of rendering is the time of choice. Each of you will be called to make a choice as to whether or not you want to stay here and fulfill your part of the design. Sometimes we speak of it as if the time of choice is about choosing love or fear. Actually it is more accurately whether you will choose to fulfill your potential or not, and then, of course, it is the same thing. Major points of rendering will occur in 1996, 1998, 1999, 2000, 2003, and 2005 will be the last time of rendering. After 2005, those who remain here in the etheric body of the Earth's potential will all be creating from the same knowing (For more information on this refer to The Bridge of Light transcript in the Appendix).

RESOLUTION:

Re-solving; coming back into solution; finding the experience again of being fluid and in oneness with no edges and no separation.

RESOLUTION CONSTANT:

The Silver Chalice is the resolution constant in the universe, or that which brings the coming together of balance in and from all dimensions.

RE-SOURCING:

Receiving again the connection with Source.

RESPONSE-ABILITY:

The ability to respond; the intention of the universe is that you respond instead of being responsible for.

SEED OF LIGHT:

The seed of light is located in the soul under the xiphoid process, the pointy bone in the center of the chest. It is your individual and collective vision of your purpose and the part you play in the greater design. The vision of the seed of light, when tapped, provides guidance for actualizing your destiny. The seed of light is a primary source point in the body and is sometimes called the Source chakra. Opening the seed of light enables you to see the pictures of what you are going to do and safeguards the total design by showing you what happens when everyone lives from their truth, and how that collective truth looks and feels.

SELF:
That which you identify as you, and which carries the identity of your psyche. The self is a space that connects the body and spirit.

SEPARATION:
The state of amnesia which defines things as separate and unrelated or outside of oneness.

SHAPESHIFT:
Changing form and shape through the molecular movement of energy and substance.

SOUL:
The microcosmic dot of the Monad which is on a journey to experience itself and then to reunite with its source. The soul houses all memory of all time and space and order and being. The soul is derived from truth and light and carries knowledge and all the incredible seeds of unfoldment. The soul cannot die because the whole universe is its home, so no matter what happens, the soul is always alive.

SOUND/TONE:
Essence communicated through vibration.

SOURCE CHAKRA:
See Seed of Light.

SPIRIT:
Spirit is the essential way in which the Monad exists in all dimensions. A part of the Monad is expressing as invisible to open the pathways of communication with itself. So in a way, spirit is the messenger of the Monad, a way that we come to know the original through intercessory points. Spirit is the air in the balloon. Spirit is the way in which the Monad communicates, gives messages, and sustains the consciousness of humanity without tipping its hand. There is guidance in the spiritual level which aligns and calls each soul to remember the Monad, which is the point of it all. So spirit is the intermediary between soul and Monad. Spirits come in all shapes and sizes, all levels of remembering. Spirit is also defined as an essence which inspires hope, because when you are in touch with spirit, you live in a closer way to the Monad.

SUBSTANCE:
See Fluids of Being.

SUBTLE BODIES:
The levels which surround the body, make up your "field," and have dimension in the etheric and invisible, encompassing all points of reality, seen and unseen, and all points of "time." All that you are is in your field.

SUSTAINABILITY:
That which has the ability to sustain all life at one moment.

SYNCHRONICITY:
Synchronicity happens when there are no thoughts, and the design is able to be lived automatically with no planning to disrupt it. Try it, it's great!

SWING BETWEEN WORLDS:
The inter-dimensional space where souls choose their incarnative destiny (This is where we know you from).

SYSTEMS THEORY:
Systems theory is the unified theory of the universe, which was the original design of the Monad. This theory includes all systems and, of course, all life. The basic principles are that 1) all life has innate intelligence, 2) all life communicates either consciously or unconsciously, 3) all life is creating the experienced reality, or is in co-creation, 4) there is co-responsibility for whatever happens, and 5) that everything is growing toward the light. In systems theory, conflict is seen as an indication that it is time for growth. There is no judgment in this system. Everything is known and unfolding. When one lives from this system, the choice is to grow rather than to fear expansion.

THE ONES WITH NO NAMES:
The body of light and knowledge which sustains order and truth in the universe. Amorphous light beings whose "job" is to act as Cosmic Guidance Counselors for humanity. We "live" in the Swing Between Worlds.

TIME/SPACE CONTINUUM (TSC):
The basis of life on planet Earth is the existence of a set of parameters that defines what is thought of as reality. These parameters make the conditions you experience and are the ingredients which you use to create and bake your cake. TSC is an

environment through which things relate to each other, hold their shape and form, can be thought of as chronological, and have a place to occur. A creation of the Monad to house the free will experiment, the TSC changed its parameters at the end of December, 1991, when the Piscean age ended and began being termed "the space of order and being." Actually, what changed is the perception of life here, rather than that one continuum began and one ended, because it is the perception that creates the experience. Now people are realizing that there is no time and they are more inclined to study "being" than "space." Actually, order and being is an adjunct to time and space. All four points exist at once, and when the shift happened it was to bring these points together. Piscean = time and space experience; Aquarian = order and being. Put them together and you have technology <u>and</u> the heart.

TIME TUNNEL:
The point and location in which reality shifts from organic memory of oneness to amnesiac separation and biological conditioning. This is the place you experience just before birth, as described in **I Remember Union:** *The Story of Mary Magdalena.*

TONE:
See Sound.

TRANSCENDENCE:
Going beyond the form to experience the essence; returning to the place of knowing and creation while in physical form.

TRANSFORMATION:
The experience of energetically matching form and spirit in the same vibration, while still in form. Union of all points while physical.

TRANSITION:
The levels between dimensions; the places a soul travels through during entry to Earth and after death; sometimes referred to by humans to indicate change in the circumstances of life, i.e., going through transition(s).

TRANSLOCATE:
To change direction or location either physically or psychically.

TRUTH:
Truth is the point which upholds life and the design by carrying the wave or energy

of the essential story of creation, oneness, free-will, resolution, and therefore, the hologram. Truth brings the design into fruition, and is the incentive for each soul to live from a perspective that engenders truth, for truth guides one to oneness.

TWELVE CONTINUUMS:
The twelve continuums are the basic universes which are the experience of the total universe relating and evolving and opening unto the oneness. These twelve points are learning simultaneously from different perspectives about returning to the original point of choice, and yet are learning differently in each instance. The twelve becoming one is an important concept to remember because you will encounter this over and over again in your experience. Just as you are living in a unique and singular paradigm, so are all the other eleven continuums, having their own reality and growing toward the light in their own perspective. Some of you have come to align these twelve levels into oneness, and this will be accomplished by the year 2016. As the alignment happens here, it happens everywhere. The twelve levels will become four by the year 2011 and then unify to one level by 2016. The first order of business, however, is to align this universe.

UNIFIED FIELD THEORY:
A field of energy and consciousness that initiates oneness.

UNION:
The experience of all life as one essence or point of recognition.

UNIVERSE(S):
There are 12 universes. We live in one. Our universe is comprised of our solar system and all life forms of our physical reality, set in motion by and unfolding from the Absolute.

VIBRATION:
Oscillation, pulsation, movement of energy, usually too fast for the eye to see.

VISCERAL CELLULAR RESPONSE:
The organic response to light and truth which occurs in the cells of the body and in the circuits, and therefore establishes magnetism and presence in the physical body.

VISION:
Seeing with the total being instead of the eye. Seeing becomes more possible when

you hold the images together until they become palpable. At this point, you can begin to "see."

VOLITIONAL WILL:

The intention and choice made in conjunction with free-will which charges the universe to accord the decisions of humanity. Use of volitional will is the most clear way to affect change and create or manifest when in form. To use this path, simply stand on the Earth, create a clear intention of your choosing, breathe into the seed of light to connect the intention with the truth within, and breathe out, seeing the vision of what you are sending forth as meeting the design and Akashic records.

WAVE FRAME:

The field of energy which comprises the total being, including the body, mind, emotion, spirit, ego, soul, and all points of time.

WEAVING:

The process of blending more than one aspect, energy, field, or paradigm into synthesis. Infusion is a form of weaving.

ZEAL (CENTER OF ZEAL):

Located in the back of the neck, the center of zeal is the place to unleash your spiritual force and create what you are here to express directly from creation.

Books Recommended by The Ones With No Names

The Education of Oversoul Seven Trilogy by Jane Roberts
The New Science of Life by Rupert Sheldrake

Favorite Books of Flo Aeveia Magdalena

The Kin of Ata are Waiting for you by Dorothy Bryant
The Way of the Lover by Robert Augustus Masters
The Healing Secrets of the Ages by Catherine Ponder
The Great Cosmic Mother by Sjoo and Mor
Subtle Body Healing and *Your Electro-Vibratory Body* by Victor Beasley
The Holographic Universe by Michael Talbot
The Chakras by Charles Leadbeater
Holy Blood, Holy Grail and *The Messianic Legacy* by Baigent and Leigh
The Spiral Dance by Starhawk
Inner Joy by Bloomfield and Kory
The Dance of Intimacy by Harriet Lerner
Starseed Transmissions by Ken Carey
Nuclear Evolution by Christopher Hills
A Brief History of Time by Stephen Hawking
The Mists of Avalon Marion Zimmer Bradley
The Magic of Conflict by Tom Crum
Positive Magic by Marion Weinstein
Leaving My Father's House by Marion Woodman
Creative Visualization by Shakti Gawain
The Celestine Prophecy by James Redfield
Your Body Believes Every Word You Say by Barbara Levine
Angels by Thomas Keller and Deborah Taylor
You are an Environment by Noel McInnis
The Universe is a Green Dragon by Brian Swimme

Index

426 *Sunlight on Water*

To schedule a session with The Ones With No Names,
or to contact Flo Aeveia Magdalena,
please write or call All Worlds Publishing,
RR#1 Box 662, Putney, VT 05346, (802) 722-4307.

For information on Soul Recognition Workshops
or the Heaven on Earth Community,
please call or write Soul Support Systems,
RR#1 Box 663, Putney, VT 05346, (800) 542-SOUL.

Edited by Jayn Adina, Flo Aeveia Magdalena, and Noel McInnis.
Book Design by Lucrezia Mangione.
Typography by Lucrezia Mangione, Peace Productions, Stratford, CT.
Printed in USA by McNaughton & Gunn, Inc.
Cover design by Ivo Dominguez, Jr., Panpipe, Georgetown, DE.

This book was typeset in Arial, Times New Roman, Pepita, Minion, Wingdings,
and Woodtype Ornaments.
The text pages were printed with vegetable-based inks on 60# Thor Offset White
in Regular Finish, by Glatfleter.

This is a recycled stock with 85% reclaimed fiber
and a 15% post-consumer-waste content.
The cover stock is 10-point C1S by Federal and is recycled.
All of the papers in this book are acid-free.

FLO AEVEIA MAGDALENA and THE ONES WITH NO NAMES
BOOK & TAPE ORDER FORM

	ITEM	PRICE

I REMEMBER UNION - *The Story of Mary Magdalena* Paper, 1996, 496 pgs.   # IRO $19.95
The profound story of Christ and Magdalene and their legacy of peace for our
time. "The emotional side of Christ"...Ralph Bloom. "It will take your breath away."
NAPRA Review. "Another *Mists of Avalon...*" Karen Crane, *New Age Retailer.*

I REMEMBER UNION *"The Goddess"* on tape. Flo reads the poems and   #IRT $19.95
passages of I REMEMBER UNION which focus on the growth and learning of Mary
as a priestess, Goddess, archetypal feminine counterpart of Christ. You will hear how
she assisted in the design of union and her part in the Christian legacy. 2 audio-
cassette tapes 1995.

SUNLIGHT ON WATER- *A Manual for Soul-full Living*, Paper 1996, 434 pgs.   #SOW $19.95
The Ones With No Names teach short-cuts for living fully and naturally from the soul
using exercises and meditations on how to hold the vibration of the soul in your
body and to connect from the soul in all of your relationships.

SEXUAL FULFILLMENT: *Ways To Express The Yearning For Union* from the   #sexful $8.00
forthcoming book RE-SOLUTION: *The Fluid Way to Harmony in Living.* Booklet with
exercises which prepare all the bodies for physical intimacy.

VIBRATIONAL HEALING SOUNDS 1990. This tape of healing sounds and   #101 $10.00
tones assists you to move energy through your body and to feel the cellular
design of the divinity within by re-patterning the energy fields around the
physical, mental, and emotional levels, bringing harmony and relaxation.

UNION: THE MARRIAGE OF MALE AND FEMALE 1990. Understand the   #102 $10.00
energy dynamics of relationship and how to create an environment where union
can be felt in your most intimate life experiences.

THE FIRST TWO YEARS: *Helping Your Child Adjust* 1990. Instruction on   #103 $10.00
birthing and raising children during the first 24 months, the crucial time when their
connection to the universe is most available. Hear what to do to support and assist
them to maintain their connection to the source.

AIDS: THE MESSENGER AND THE MESSAGE 1992. Side 1. Aids as a   #104 $10.00
consciousness raising aspect in human evolution.
GROUNDING Side 2. Bringing the body and spirit together. The principles
and specifics of being in the body, fully alive, and connected to the earth.

THE 1990's - LIVE YOUR POTENTIAL! 1992. Side 1. NOW is the time to bring your destiny & potential into the moment and live your essence more completely. Learn how to bring forth your part of the design. Side 2. How the 90's are different from any other time in history for the fulfillment of your destiny and the design of humanness. Shift your perceptive and live the promise now!

#105 $10.00

THE MODEL OF COOPERATION 1991. Specific instruction in the upcoming model for society based on resource sharing, universal awareness, and cooperation. Principles include ways to live in reception from the universe as we put in our part of the design. Truly a model we can get our hands on! Changes our conscious money practices! Edited version is in *Sunlight On Water*.

tape- #106 $8.00
transcript-#107 $7.50

THE BRIDGE OF LIGHT 1991. We are in a time called *The Coming Together of the Ages*, the time of the remembering. The wisdom of all time is now available to us, and our choices now affect how this knowledge will manifest on our planet and how our reality will be shaped. An inspirational channeling about our capacity to co-create societal models of peace and harmony in the next twenty years. Edited version is in *Sunlight On Water*.

2 tapes-#108 $14.00
transcript-#109 $12.50

HOLOGRAPHIC LIVING 1992. This tape explains concepts such as parallel reality, systems theory, and how to manifest from substance using holographic principles. Covers both personal & professional models, telling how to utilize these universal principles to create and to see & feel yourself as a part of the whole.

#110 $10.00

THE NAMELESS ONES DICTIONARY OF TERMS 1994.
A definition of terms and concepts used by The Ones With No Names in their messages and channelings. (This is included in Sunlight On Water.)

#111 $14.95

CHANNELING AT MASSANETTA SPRINGS CONFERENCE 1994.
Learn to smooth your edges, creating union with those who push your buttons! A fun tape about using every experience in your life to create union.

#112 $14.00

GUIDELINES FOR SOUL RECOGNITION FACILITATORS
from The Ones With No Names, December 6, 1995. What is the soul and how is Soul Recognition a necessary part in creating the next step for our species?

2 tapes-SRFTAM $12.00

LAST CHANNELING OF TOWNN, DEC. 6, 1995 The last public channeling which took place in Unity Church, Gaithersburg, MD. The free will experiment was over on December 31, 1995. How do we create through divinity instead of karma, and live the design of union in our daily lives?

2 tapes-#113 $12.50

DEC. 28-31 THE LAST CONFERENCE OF TOWNN
Held in Lewes, Delaware, this series takes us through unifying our energy fields; the mind, body, emotion connection; programming our life from the design; entering the holographic envelope; living with a "soft mind"; how the design works; re-patterning our cellular body; accessing our part of the hologram and much more.

9 tapes-#114 $100.00

NEW TAPES FROM THE ONES WITH NO NAMES

UNION OF THE 12 UNIVERSES: *The Purpose of the Heaven on Earth Community.* What are we really doing in Vermont? What role do we play in the greater design. How does the physical space hold the design of union for the planet.
#115 $12.50

THE TIMES OF RENDERING: There will be 5 major times of rendering between now and 2005—times when old realities and paradigms no longer create our life experience and we must choose to live in union from soul and to seed the future in the future dimension. How do we best move through these times with choice and strength, and how do we create and seed our heart's intention into the future?
#116 $12.50

RAISING CHILDREN: *Guiding Masters.* There are 3 stages in a child's development and unfolding—ages 0-7; 7-14; and 14-21. Learn to guide your child's mastery and be aware through these times of growth and foundationing.
#117 $12.50

AUTHENTIC RELATIONSHIPS: *Creating the third Point.* Remove your masks, live in commitment to authentic relationship with yourself and your life partner, creating a third point of union instead of co-dependence.
#118 $12.50

FAMILY SYSTEMS: *The First System of Union.* We choose our birth family of origin as a group of souls with whom to experience and learn union. We can foster union both with our original nuclear family, and with our current family, the nuclear family of our children. The concept that we have chosen these souls to learn about union changes many of our human dynamics.
#119 $12.50

CLARIFYING YOUR LIFE'S PURPOSE Live what makes you happy, in the moment, with direction, allowing the action and resolution to be created from the energy of your connection with creation. When we begin to connect more fully with the wave of our creation, our purpose manifests automatically.
#120 $12.50

THE WAY HOME: Being here fully as spirit in form requires bringing the essence of our divinity into our body and being physically present and balanced in our male and female. Living creatively with the presence of the Sophia, the energy which fosters the sourcing and richness of human life, brings us to deep peace about being here on Earth.
#121 $12.50

ALTERNATIVE EDUCATION FOR ATTENTIONALLY DIFFERENT CHILDREN (ADD) How to honor each child's needs and create learning environments where children participate actively in their education, establish a group structure to bring balance and accountability, and begin to draw forth and live their essence and presence.
#122 $12.50

HOW TO MANIFEST: Create the foundation for your visions in the world and begin to ground them into form. A fun, how-to tape which brings the desire and the connection into place to facilitate manifesting what is in your heart.
#123 $12.50

HUMAN DYNAMICS: Hear about the underlying dynamics which exist between people and learn to create resolution and understanding as you relate with others.
#124 $12.50

~~~~~~

MAIL TO: All Worlds Publishing
                RR#1 Box 662
                Putney, VT 05346 USA
                Phone & Fax 802-722-4307

Send to:

Name_____ Address_____

City_____ State_____ Zip_____

Phone (home) _____ (work)_____ fax_____

Please send the
following items:

Subtotal

Add $5.00 S & H for each book USA/$8.00 Foreign

Add $2.50 S & H for the first tape

and $1.00 for each additional item

Total

Mastercard or Visa Number _____ Exp. date_____

(Add $2.00 service charge if using credit card)

Make check or money order payable to "All Worlds Publishing"

~~~~~~

MAIL TO: All Worlds Publishing
            RR#1 Box 662
            Putney, VT 05346 USA
            Phone & Fax 802-722-4307

Send to:

Name_____ Address_____

City_____ State_____ Zip_____

Phone (home) _____ (work)_____ fax_____

Please send the
following items:

Subtotal

Add $5.00 S & H for each book USA/$8.00 Foreign

Add $2.50 S & H for the first tape

and $1.00 for each additional item

Total

Mastercard or Visa Number _____ Exp. date_____

(Add $2.00 service charge if using credit card)

Make check or money order payable to "All Worlds Publishing"